McGRAW-HILL MATHEMATICS

Math in my World

Douglas H. Clements

Kenneth W. Jones

Lois Gordon Moseley

Linda Schulman

McGraw-Hill School Division

New York   Farmington

PROGRAM AUTHORS

Dr. Douglas H. Clements

Kenneth W. Jones

Lois Gordon Moseley

Dr. Linda Schulman

CONTRIBUTING AUTHORS

Dr. Liana Forest

Christine A. Fernsler

Dr. Kathleen Kelly-Benjamin

Maria R. Marolda

Dr. Richard H. Moyer

Dr. Walter G. Secada

CONSULTANTS

Multicultural and Educational Consultants

Rim An

Sue Cantrell

Mordessa Corbin

Dr. Carlos Diaz

Carl Downing

Linda Ferreira

Judythe M. Hazel

Roger Larson

Josie Robles

Veronica Rogers

Telkia Rutherford

Sharon Searcy

Elizabeth Sinor

Michael Wallpe

Claudia Zaslavsky

COVER PHOTOGRAPHY Jade Albert for MMSD; i. MMSD.

PHOTOGRAPHY All photographs are by the McGraw-Hill School Division (MMSD), David Mager for MMSD, Ken Lax for MMSD and Scott Harvey for MMSD except as noted below.
Table of Contents • Bruce Plotkin/Liaison International: iii b. • Tony Arruzo/The Image Works: iv m. • Amanda Merullo/Stock Boston, Inc.: v m. • Charles Thatcher/Tony Stone Images: vi m. • Doug David: vi b. • Chris Luneski/Image Cascade: vii t. • HMS Images/The Image Bank: vii m. • Peter Beck/The Stock Market: viii b. • Terry Vine/Tony Stone Images: ix t. • Darryl Torckler/Tony Stone Images: ix m. • Henley & Savage/The Stock Market: ix b. • Richard Gross/The Stock Market: x m. • **Chapter 1** • Tom McCarthy/The Stock Market: 1 t. • Henley & Savage/The Stock Market: 1 b. • Brent Petersen/The Stock Market: 3 • Brent Petersen/The Stock Market: 17 • Doug David: 32 b. • Eric Wheater: 40 b.r. • **Chapter 2** • Tom McCarthy/The Stock Market: 43 • Lawrence Migdale/Stock Boston, Inc.: 44 • Brooklyn Museum of Art: 50 b.l. • Tony Arruza/The Image Works: 55 t. • Nancy Simmerman/Tony Stone Images: 66 • Bruce Plotkin/Liaison International: 73 t. • **Chapter 3** • John Stuart/The Image Bank: 77 • Tom Tracey/The Stock Market: 89 t.r. • Jeff Greenberg/Photo Researchers: 97 • **Chapter 4** • Porter Gifford/Gamma Liaison: 123 • George Kleiman/Photo Researchers: 138 t.r. • **Chapter 5** • Doug David for MMSD: 153 t.r.i. • Doug David for MMSD: 154 • Amanda Merullo/Stock Boston: 158 • John M. Roberts/The Stock Market: 159 • Stephanie Hollyman/Liaison International: 169 • Russkinne/Comstock: 178 • **Chapter 6** • Steve Niedorf/The Image Bank: 183 • Charles Thatcher/Tony Stone Images: 193 t. • Charlie Westerman/Liaison International: 193 b. • D. Young-Wolff/PhotoEdit: 200 • Maxwell Mackenzie/Uniphoto: 206 • **Chapter 7** • HMS Images/The Image Bank: 231 • Monica Stevenson for MMSD: 235 b.i. • Chris Luneski/Image Cascade: 243 t.r. • Don Smetzer/Tony Stone Images: 244 • Superstock, Inc.: 250 b.r. • **Chapter 8** • Vedros & Associates/Liaison International: 269 t.r. • Doug David for MMSD: 270 • Mark Segal/Tony Stone Images: 272 t.r. • Tom Tracy/The Stock Market: 274 • Doug David for MMSD: 280 b.i. • Doug David for MMSD: 294 b.r. • **Chapter 9** • Uniphoto: 297 • Index Stock: 301 t. • Frank Moscati/The Stock Market: 302 b.r. • Richard Hutchings/PhotoEdit: 302 t.l. • Steve Dunwell/The Image Bank: 302 t.r. • David Young-Wolff/Tony Stone Images: 302 b.l. • Comstock: 302 m.l. • Bob Daemmrich/Uniphoto: 302 m.r. • Tom McCarthy/PhotoEdit: 308 t.l. • Daemmrich/The Image Works: 308 t.r. • Myrleen Ferguson MR/PhotoEdit: 308 m.l. • Jim Pickerell/The Image Works: 308 m.r. • Tony Freeman/PhotoEdit: 308 b.l. • David Young Wolff/Tony Stone Images: 308 b.r. • Doug David: 310 b. • Vivian Holbrooke/The Stock Market: 321 b.r. • Brad Martin/The Image Bank: 322 t.r. • **Chapter 10** • Stephen Dalton/Photo Researchers: 333 • Peter Beck/The Stock Market: 334 t. • Lawrence Migdale: 334 b. • David Forbert/Superstock, Inc.: 341 • Kelvin Altken/Peter Arnold, Inc.: 345 • Darryl Torckler/Tony Stone Images: 357 t. • Kevin & Cat Sweeney/Tony Stone Images: 357 b. • Terry Vine/Tony Stone Images: 364 • Michael Lustbader/Photo Researchers: 372 m.r. • **Chapter 11** • Henley & Savage/The Stock Market: 375 • Michael L. Peck & Dolores R. Fernandez: 391 t. • Renee Lynn/Photo Researchers: 394 b.m.i. • **Chapter 12** • Robert E. Daemmrich/Tony Stone Images: 409 • Superstock, Inc.: 415 • Richard Gross/The Stock Market: 425 • Joe Sohm/Chromosohm/Photo Researchers: 426 • David Young-Wolff/PhotoEdit: 437

ILLUSTRATION Winky Adam; 213, 216, 248, 250 • Jo Lynn Alcorn: 383, 386 • Bill Basso; 85, 86, 119, 120 • Shirley Beckes; 23, 24 • Menny Borovski; 27, 36, 37, 89, 115, 117, 123, 124, 132, 234, 235, 236, 238, 239, 245, 246, 250, 252, 256, 257, 296, 298, 301, 302, 317, 318, 319, 320, 324, 325 • Ken Bowser; 83, 84, 302, 312, 337 • Lizi Boyd: 219, 277, 294, 388, 389, 402, 403 • Hal Brooks; 91, 92 • Roger Chandler: 345, 346, 353, 368 • Genevieve Claire: 356, 363, 364, 397, 398 • Margaret Cusack; 184, 188, 232 • Nancy Davis: 270, 276 • Betsy Day: 206, 214, 223 • Daniel Del Valle; 106, 109, 133, 134, 243, 314, 327 • Denise & Fernando: 180 • Eldon Doty: 178, 181 • Gloria Elliott: 142, 145, 146, 159, 160, 169 • Arthur Friedman: 326 • Doreen Gay-Kassel; 7, 9, 156, 165, 335, 336, 338, 341, 357, 376, 380, 382 • Michael Grejniec; 112, 113, 114, 137, 148, 157, 174, 175, 176, 177, 189, 190 • Shari Halpern: 149, 151, 162, 163, 194, 203, 204, 205, 221 • Tom Leonard: 358 • Franklin Hammond; 88 • Oki Han: 164 • Eileen Hine: 165 • Rita Lascaro: 144, 199, 228, 291, 292, 390, 396, 303, 304 • Jim Maltese: 47, 48, 53, 72 • Claude Martinot: 5, 6, 19, 20, 410, 422, 430, 433, 437, 439, 444 • Hatley Mason; 121, 135, 136, 138, 234, 241 • Bonnie Matthews; 242 • Daphne McCormack; v • Hima Pamoedjo; 33, 39, 54, 73, 79, 80, 93, 130 • Brenda Pepper; 87, 94, 101, 102, 103, 127, 128, 129, 139 • Lisa Pomerantz; 15, 35, 38, 350, 351, 354, 406 • Mary Power; 62, 64, 315, 316, 324, 325, 359, 365, 370, 371 • Ellen Rixford; 31, 32 • Audrey Schorr; 45, 46, 95 • Fred Schrier; 259 • Jackie Snider: 171, 172, 265, 267, 289 • Terri Starrett; 16 • Matt Straub; 21, 22, 39, 97, 98, 273, 274, 275, 281, 287, 288, 412, 414, 416, 418, 436, 445 • Peggy Tagel; 2, 3, 42, 43, 182, 183, 230, 231, 262, 263, 296, 297, 305, 306, 332, 333, 374, 375, 408, 409 • Mike Takagi; 13 • Don Tate; 44, 55, 67, 68, 70, 71, 107, 108, 239, 240, 241, 434 • Terry Taylor: 195, 196, 199, 200, 207, 209, 221, 222, 225, 228, 417, 423, 435 • George Ulrich; 299, 300, 311 • Sally Jo Vitsky; 4, 81, 122, 285, 286, 290, 419, 420, 424 • Matt Wawiorka; 11, 25, 41 • Nina Wallace: 404, 405.

McGraw-Hill School Division ✕

A Division of The McGraw-Hill Companies

Copyright © 1999 McGraw-Hill School Division,
a Division of the Educational and Professional Publishing Group of The McGraw-Hill Companies, Inc.

McGraw-Hill School Division
1221 Avenue of the Americas
New York, New York 10020

Printed in the United States of America
ISBN 0-02-110316-X/1
6 7 8 9 043/073 04 03 02 01 00

Contents

 These lessons develop, practice, or apply algebraic thinking through the study of patterns, relationships and functions, properties, equations, formulas, and inequalities.

3 Beginning to Add

THEME: Food for 10

4 Beginning to Subtract

THEME: Folktales and Rhymes

5 Adding and Subtracting to 10

THEME: Number Fun

 These lessons develop, practice, or apply algebraic thinking through the study of patterns, relationships and functions, properties, equations, formulas, and inequalities.

v

6 Numbers to 100 and Graphing

THEME: One Big Family

7 Geometry and Fractions

THEME: High-Flying Kites

8 Money

THEME: Our Store

 These lessons develop, practice, or apply algebraic thinking through the study of patterns, relationships and functions, properties, equations, formulas, and inequalities.

9 Time

THEME: Fun and Games

10 Adding and Subtracting to 18

THEME: Under the Water

11 Exploring Measurement

THEME: Dinosaurs and Me

 These lessons develop, practice, or apply algebraic thinking through the study of patterns, relationships and functions, properties, equations, formulas, and inequalities.

12 Exploring 2-Digit Addition and Subtraction

THEME: Music

Welcome to your new math book!

This year you will learn about many ways to use math in your world.

How many children in all?

How much does it cost?

How long is a foot?

Dear Family,

I am beginning the first chapter in my mathematics book. During the next few weeks I am going to learn about numbers and patterns and solving problems.

I will also learn about rhinos and other wild animals.

Learning about Rhinos

Let's talk about rhinos and tell things we know about them. We can make a drawing of a rhino.

My Math Words

I am going to use these math words in this chapter.

Please help me make word cards for these math words. I can use the word cards when I practice numbers.

more
count
number
fewer
problem
pattern
order
penny
cents, ¢
tally marks

Your child,

_____
Signature

At Home

Numbers to 10
Theme: Rhino Country

RHINO COUNTRY

READING • ARITHMETIC • WRITING

Make Predictions Look at the cover of *Rhino Country*. What do you think the book is about?

Listen to the story.

How do the pictures help tell the story?

What Do You Know?

Match.

How many 🦏 ?

How many 🐦 ?

Name _____

Working Together

You need  .

Make a group.

Put some here.

Draw your group.

Draw a group with **more**.

Practice!

Show the 🦏 group.

Draw a group with more.

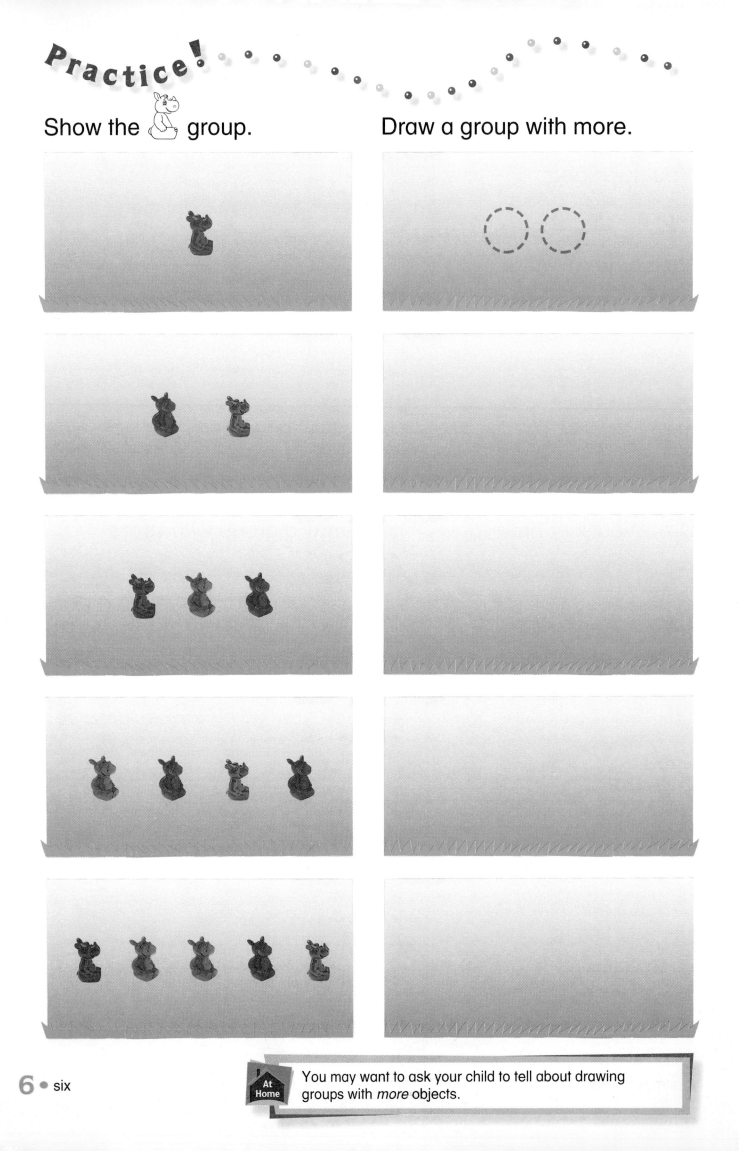

At Home You may want to ask your child to tell about drawing groups with *more* objects.

Name _____

Talk

Count the parts.

Talk about the **numbers**.

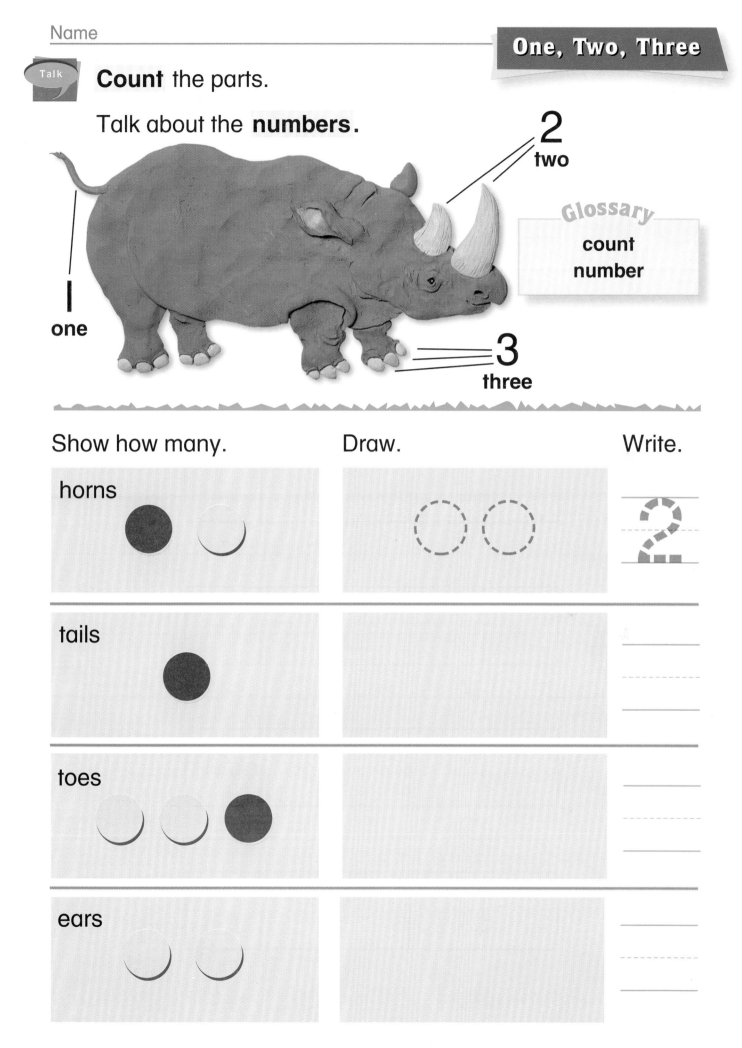

2
two

1
one

3
three

Glossary

count
number

Show how many.   Draw.   Write.

horns

2

tails

toes

ears

Practice!

Count.	Draw.	Write.

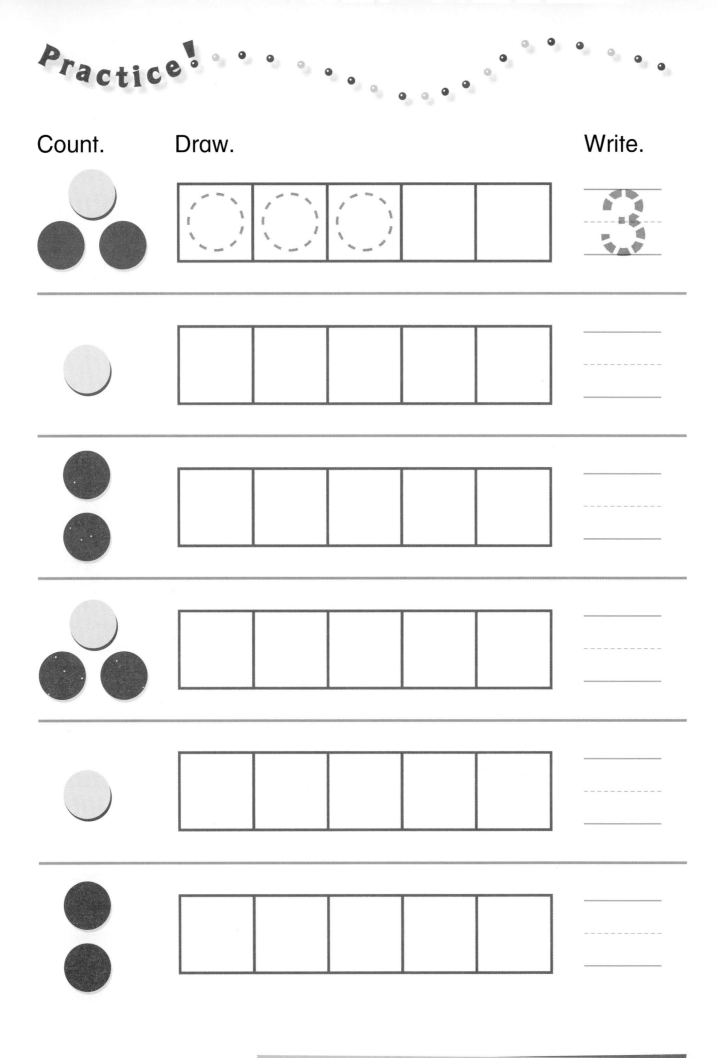

At Home — Ask your child to count things found at home.

Name _____

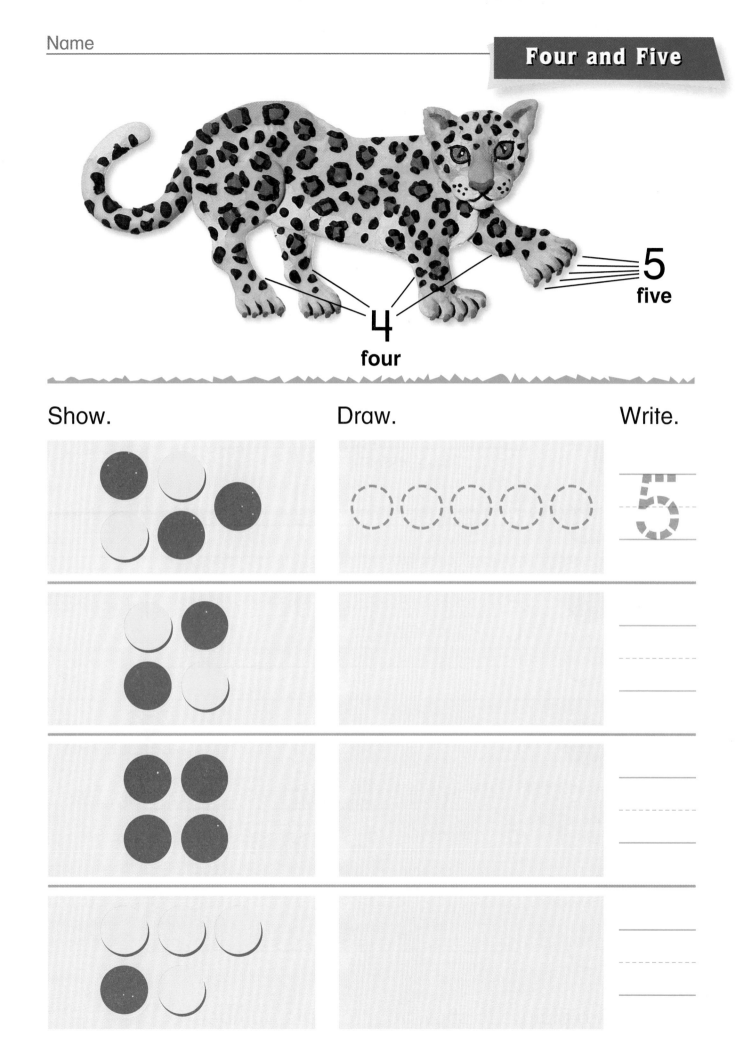

5
five

4
four

Show.

Draw.

Write.

Practice!

Count.	Draw.	Write.

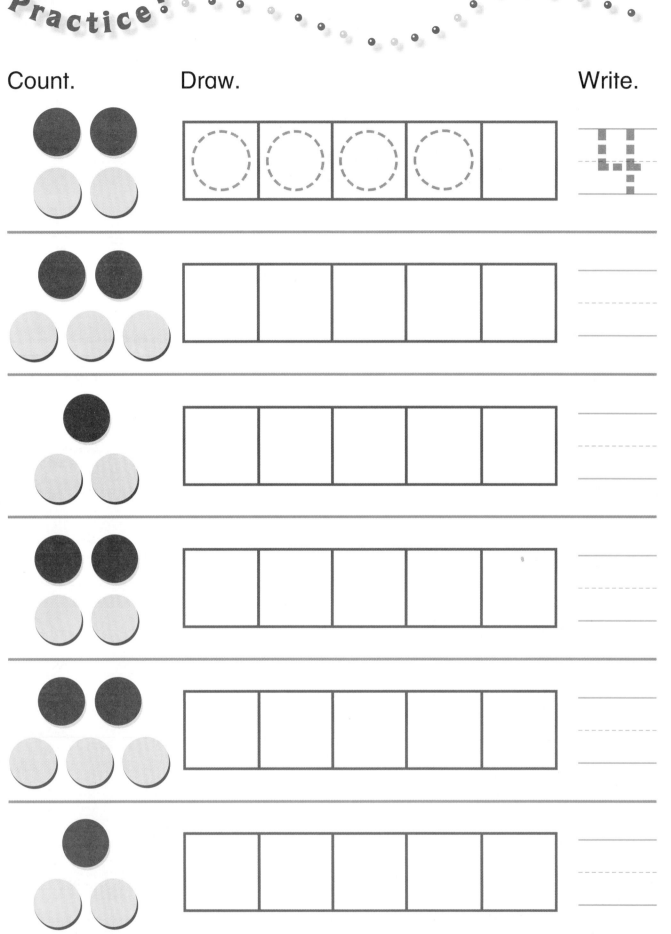

Draw a picture to show your favorite number.

At Home — Encourage your child to count objects and tell you how many.

Extra Practice
Activity !

Where's the Rhino?

Color.

one 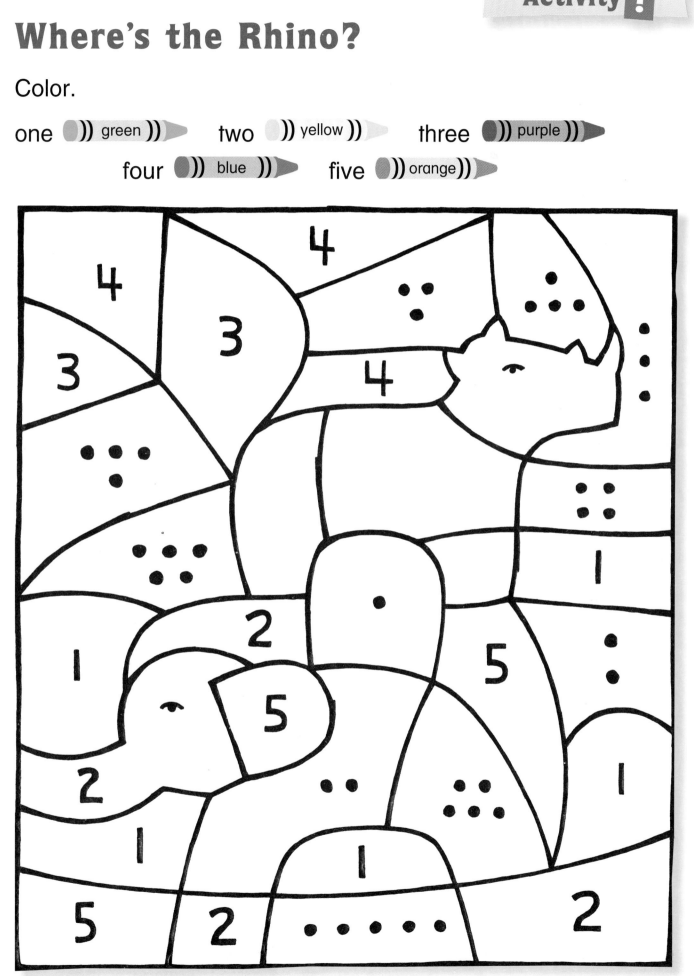 green   two yellow   three purple

four blue   five orange

McGraw-Hill School Division

Write the numbers.

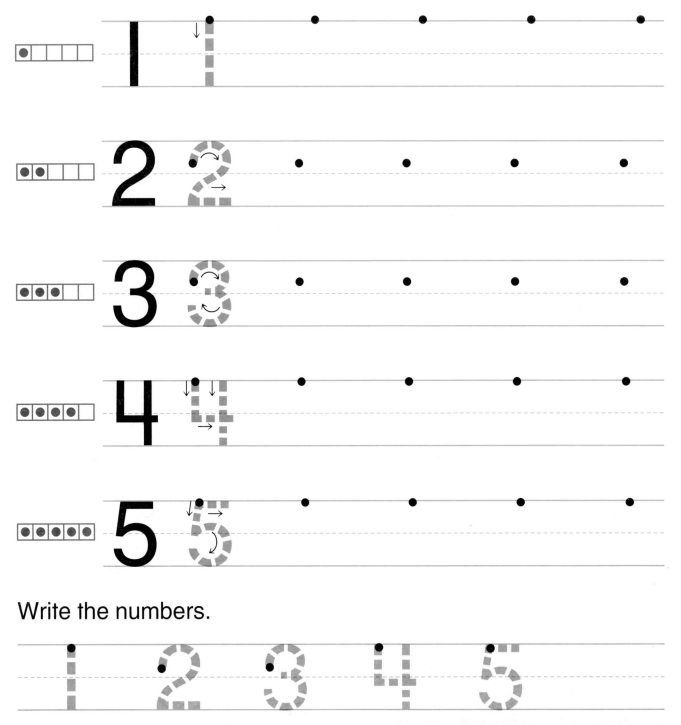

Write the numbers.

Name _____

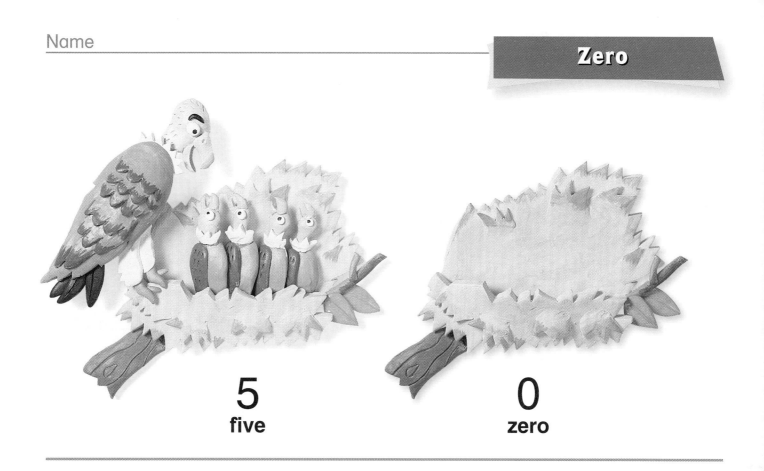

5
five

0
zero

Write how many.

Practice!

Count. Write how many.

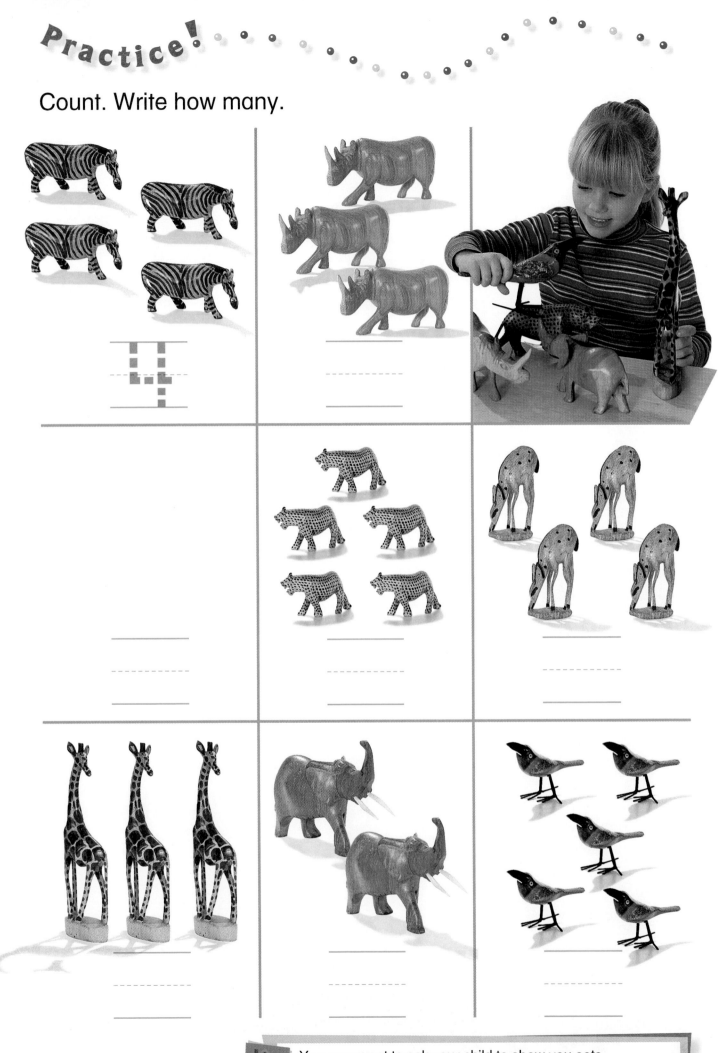

Midchapter Review

Draw.   Write.

2 | | | | |
_____

5 | | | | |
_____

3 | | | | |
_____

4 | | | | |
_____

Do your best!

Write how many.

_____   _____

_____   _____

 Show 5 in many different ways.

Animal Walk

You need a 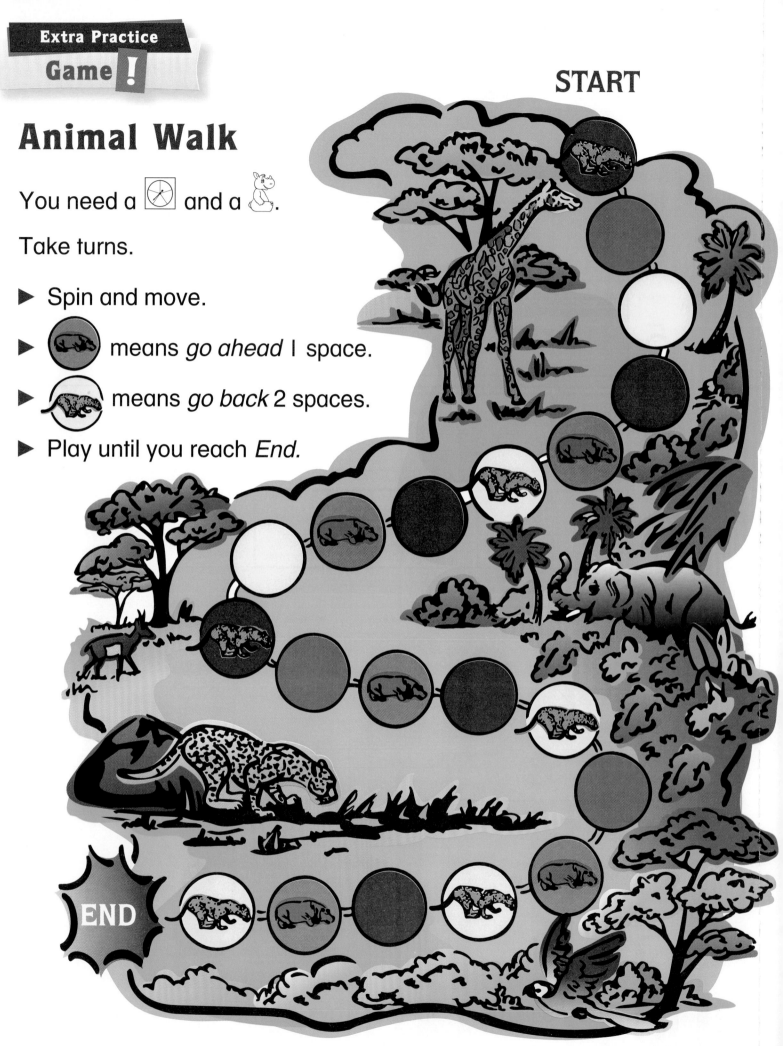 and a 🦛.

Take turns.

▶ Spin and move.

▶ 🦛 means *go ahead* 1 space.

▶ 🐆 means *go back* 2 spaces.

▶ Play until you reach *End.*

START

END

Name _____

Counting on Ourselves

 Talk Count the parts of a rhino.

Working Together

▶ Find things that show 0, 1, 2, 3, 4, 5 on your partner.

▶ Draw what you find.

▶ Write the numbers.

Decision Making

 Make a class picture for 0, 1, 2, 3, 4, 5. Decide how to show what each group counted.

 **Write a report.**

1 Tell about the class picture.

2 What can you tell about the numbers?

More to Investigate

PREDICT What else can you count in your classroom?

EXPLORE Find things that show other numbers.

FIND How would your class picture change?

Name _____

Working Together

You need .

Make a group.

Put some here.

Glossary
fewer

Draw your group.

Draw a group with **fewer**.

McGraw-Hill School Division

Count.

Draw a group with fewer.

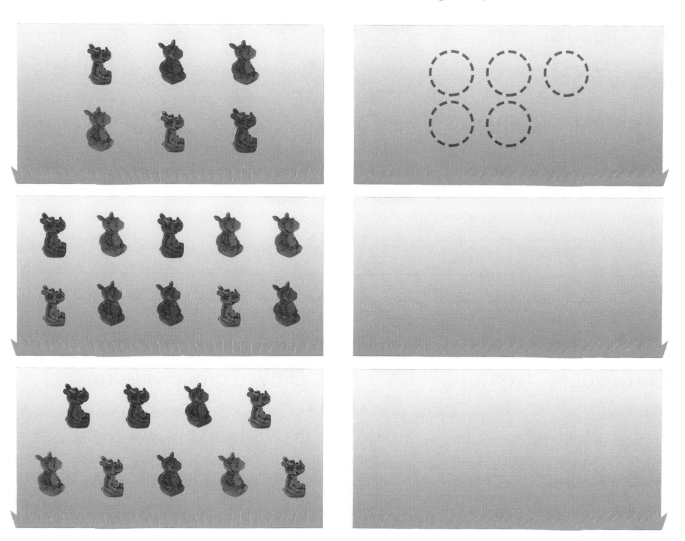

More to Explore   Estimation

Do <u>not</u> count.

Look.
Ring the group with fewer.

 At Home   You may want to ask your child to tell about drawing sets with *fewer* objects.

Name _____

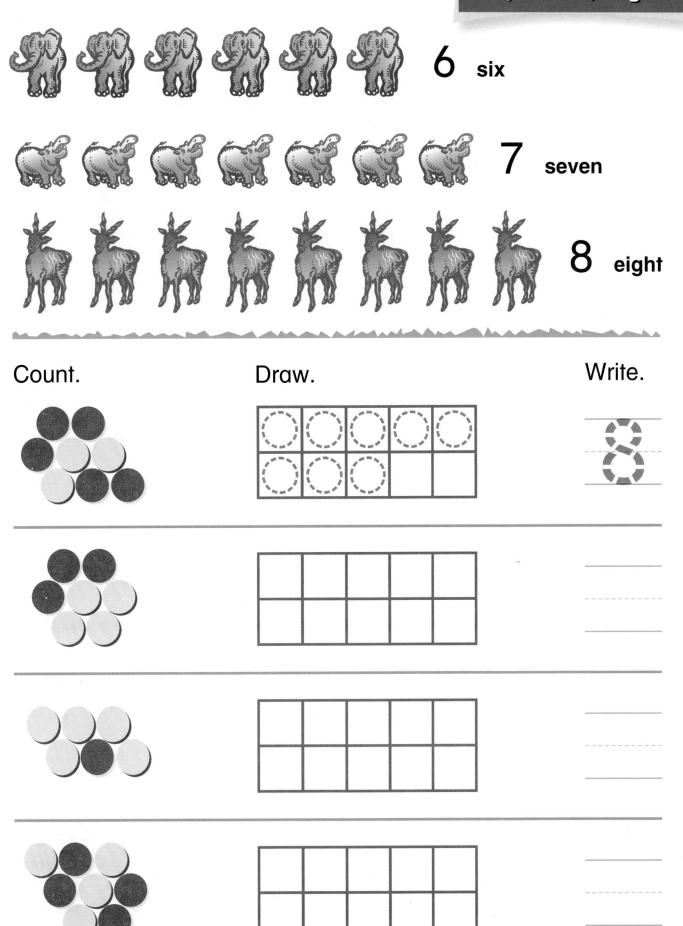

6 six

7 seven

8 eight

Count.   Draw.   Write.

McGraw-Hill School Division

Practice!

Write how many.

3

Make Predictions

READING ARITHMETIC WRITING

Talk What will happen when the sun goes down?

 At Home Encourage your child to tell you a story about the picture.

Name _____

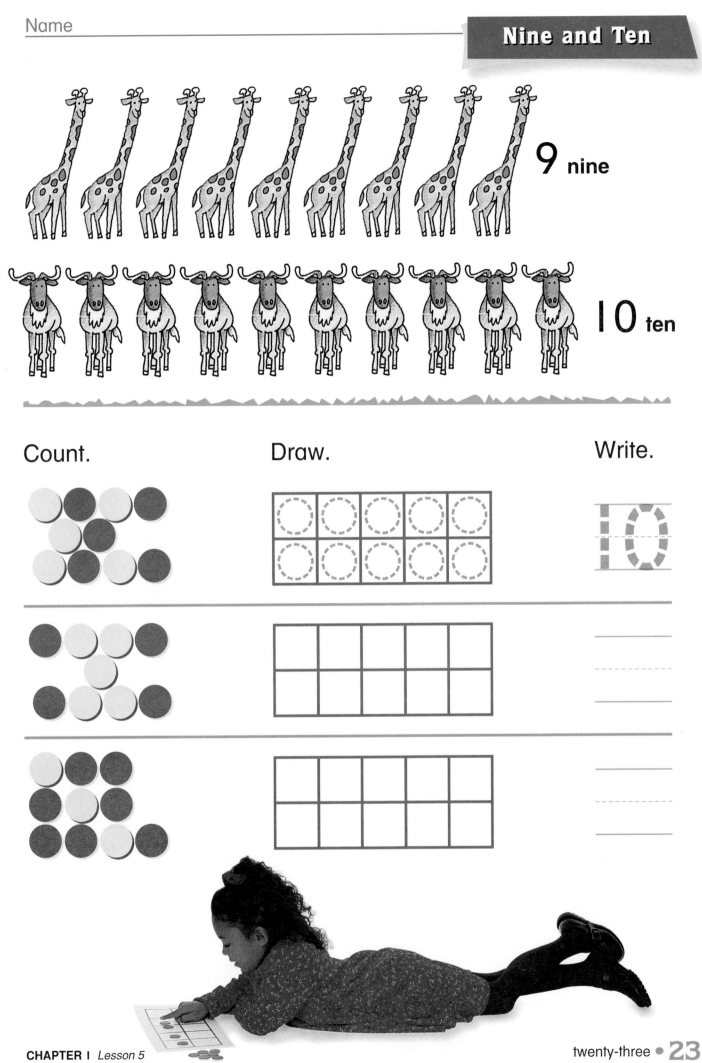

9 nine

10 ten

Count.   Draw.   Write.

CHAPTER 1 *Lesson 5*

Practice!

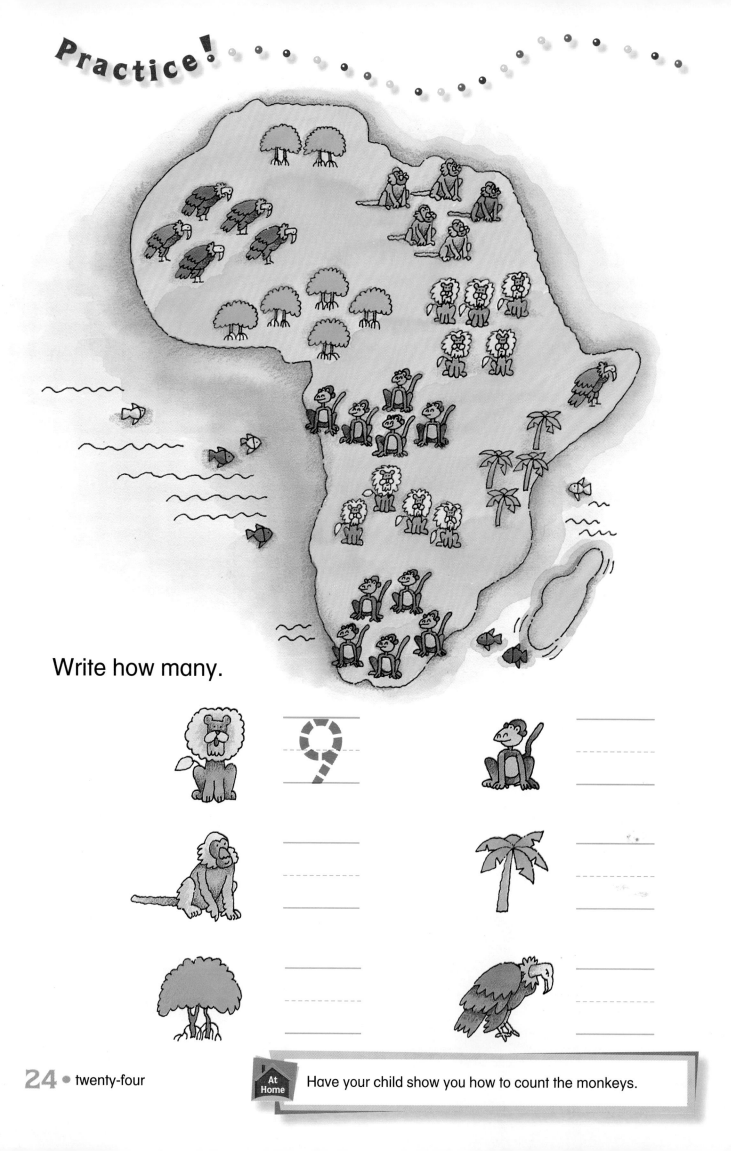

Write how many.

9

At Home Have your child show you how to count the monkeys.

Climb to the Top

You need 10  and a .

Take turns.

▶ Spin.

▶ Put a on the dots for the number.

▶ Play until you cover all the spaces.

Cultural Note
The girls are playing a game from Africa called *Mankala*.

Write.

0 0

6 6

7 7

8 8

9 9

10 10

Write the numbers.

0 1 2 3 4 5

6 7 8 9 10

Name _____

Use a Pattern

You need 10 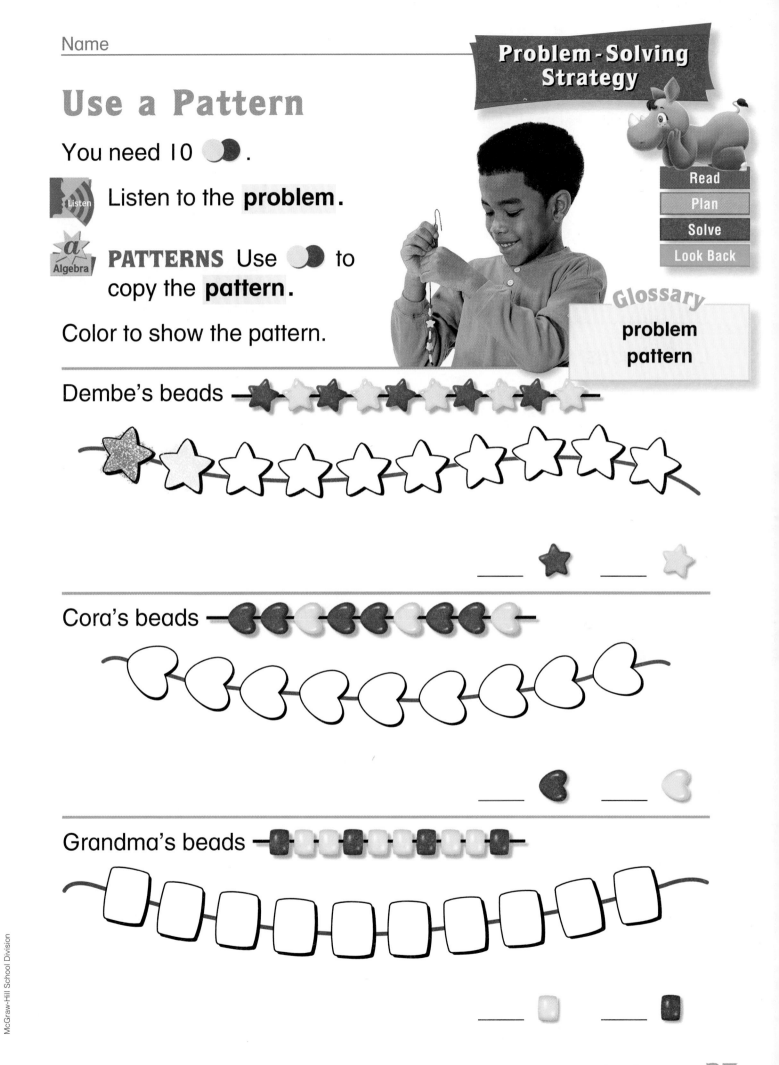.

Listen Listen to the **problem**.

Algebra **PATTERNS** Use ◐ to copy the **pattern**.

Color to show the pattern.

Glossary
problem
pattern

Dembe's beads —⭐⭐⭐⭐⭐⭐⭐⭐⭐⭐—

_____ ⭐ _____ ⭐

Cora's beads —❤❤❤❤❤❤❤❤❤❤—

_____ ❤ _____ ❤

Grandma's beads —▪▪▪▪▪▪▪▪▪▪—

_____ ▫ _____ ▪

McGraw-Hill School Division

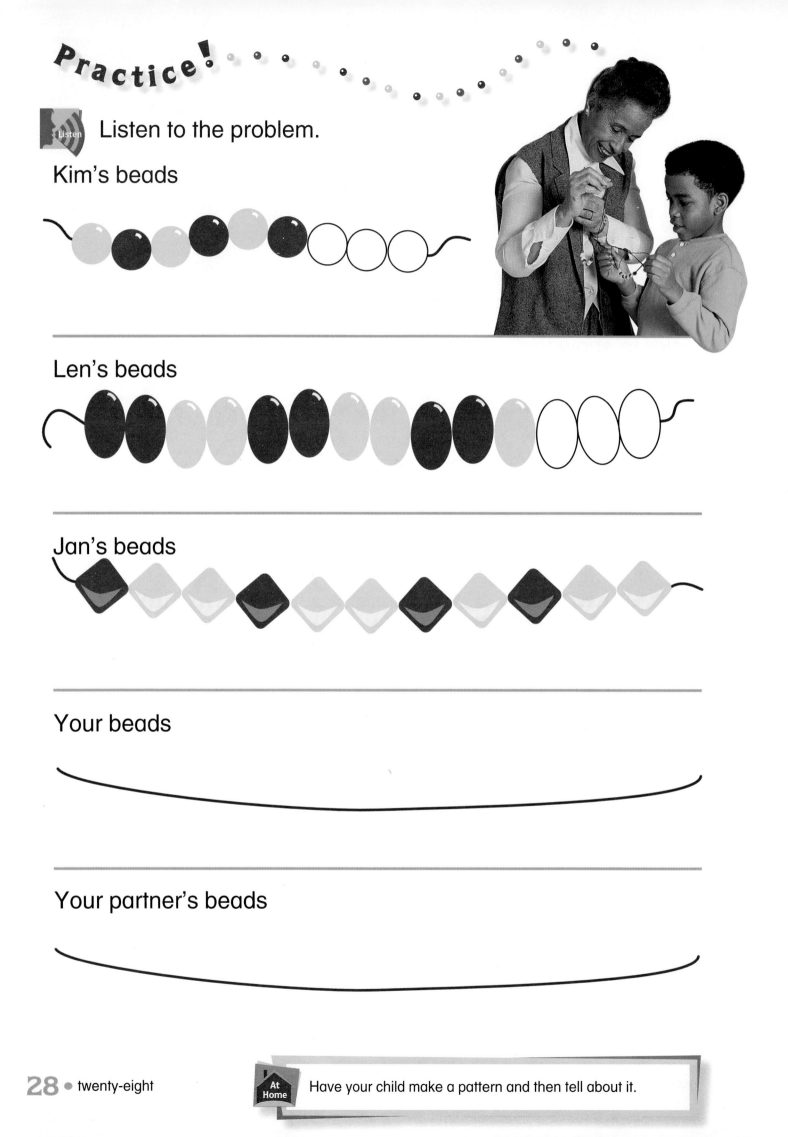

Listen to the problem.

Kim's beads

Len's beads

Jan's beads

Your beads

Your partner's beads

At Home Have your child make a pattern and then tell about it.

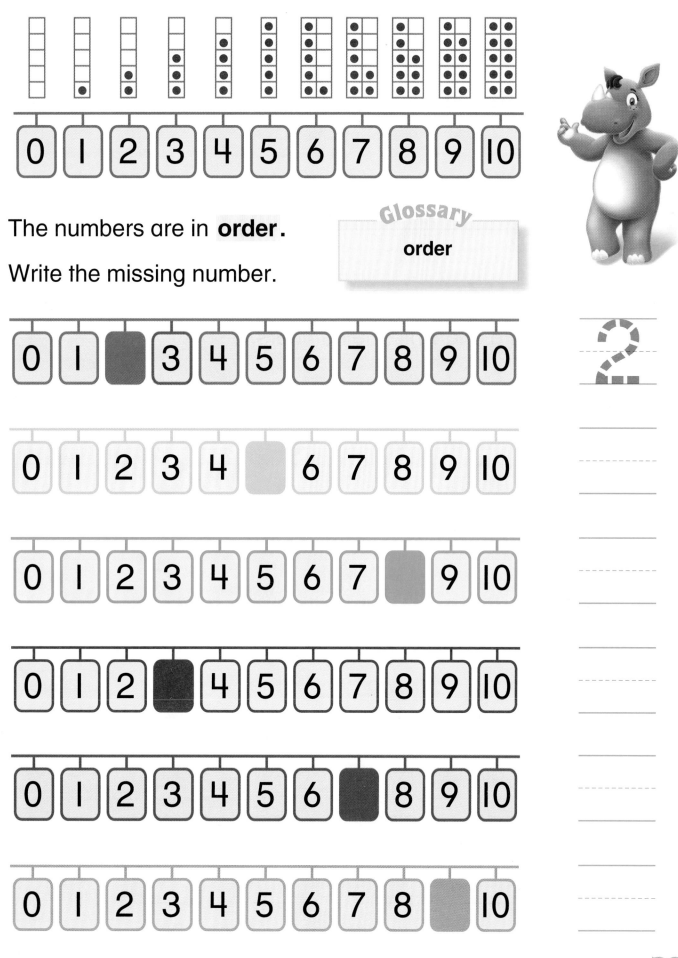

0 1 2 3 4 5 6 7 8 9 10

The numbers are in **order**.

Write the missing number.

Glossary
order

0 1 ▢ 3 4 5 6 7 8 9 10

0 1 2 3 4 ▢ 6 7 8 9 10

0 1 2 3 4 5 6 7 ▢ 9 10

0 1 2 ▢ 4 5 6 7 8 9 10

0 1 2 3 4 5 6 ▢ 8 9 10

0 1 2 3 4 5 6 7 8 ▢ 10

| 0 | 1 | 2 | 3 | 4 | 5 | 6 | 7 | 8 | 9 | 10 |

Write the numbers in order.

0   1   3

6   7   10

Count backward and write the numbers.

10   9   5

4   0

number words

Write the number.

| zero | one | two | three | four | five |

| six | seven | eight | nine | ten |

At Home   Encourage your child to count things at home, outside, and in pictures.

I **penny**

I ¢

I **cent**

2 pennies

2¢

2 cents

Glossary

penny

cent, ¢

Working Together

You need 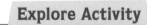.

► You show some .

► Your partner shows some .

► Draw all the .

► Write how many cents.

 _____ ¢

_____ ¢

_____ ¢

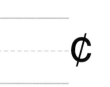 _____ ¢

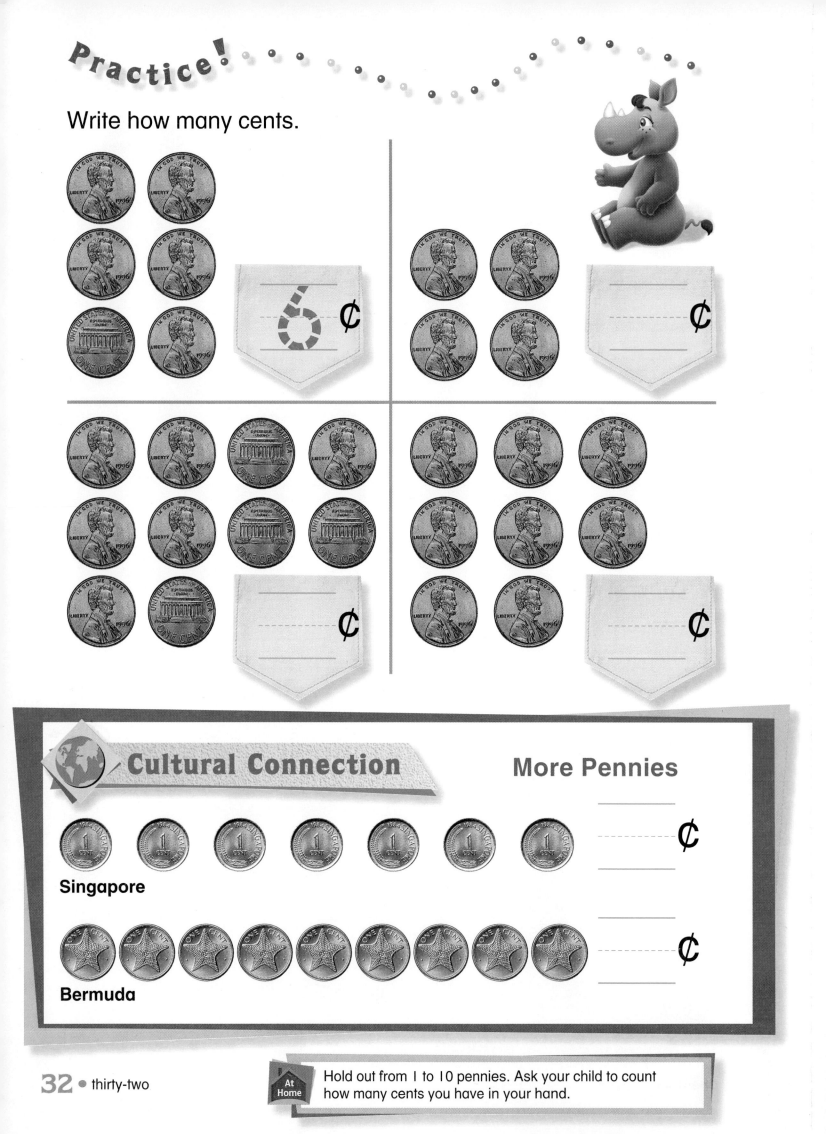

Practice!

Write how many cents.

6 ¢

_____ ¢

_____ ¢

_____ ¢

At Home Hold out from 1 to 10 pennies. Ask your child to count how many cents you have in your hand.

Name _____

Number Patterns

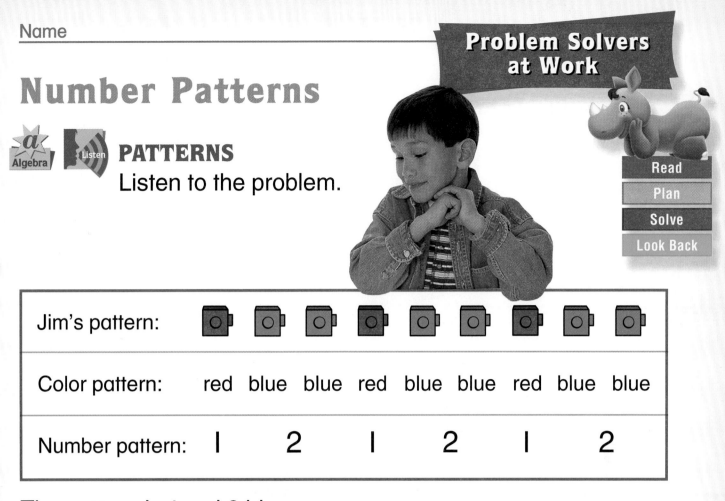

Algebra **Listen** **PATTERNS**
Listen to the problem.

Read
Plan
Solve
Look Back

Jim's pattern:									
Color pattern:	red	blue	blue	red	blue	blue	red	blue	blue
Number pattern:	1	2		1	2		1	2	

The pattern is 1 red 2 blue.

Use numbers to show the pattern.

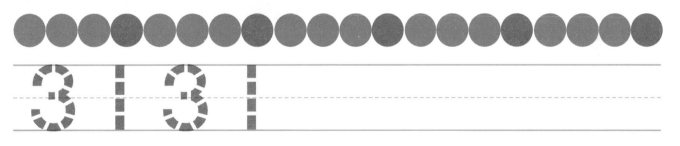

3 1 3 1

READING ARITHMETIC WRITING **Make Predictions** How many stripes will be on the next zebra?
Draw the stripes. Write the numbers.

_____

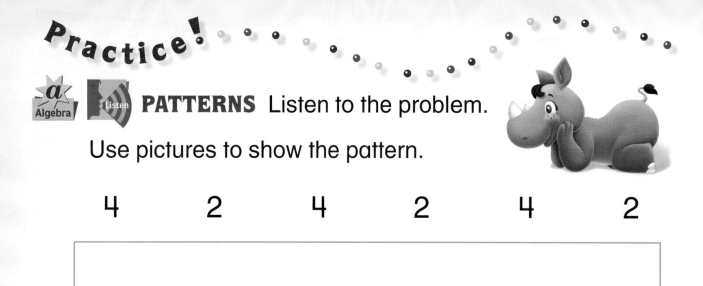

𝑎 Algebra 🔊 Listen **PATTERNS** Listen to the problem.

Use pictures to show the pattern.

| 4 | 2 | 4 | 2 | 4 | 2 |

Write and Share

Jessi drew this pattern.

Jessi Cox
Hawthorne School
Indianapolis,
Indiana

Use numbers to show
Jessi's pattern.

_____

_ _

Write ✎ Draw a pattern. Your partner writes the numbers.

Your partner's pattern:

_____

_ _

_____

 At Home Ask your child to show his or her pattern with numbers.

Chapter Review

Language and Mathematics

Choose the correct word to complete the sentence.

1 If you have 3¢ you have 3 _____.

2 You can _____ to show how many.

> count
> pattern
> pennies

Concepts and Skills

Write how many.

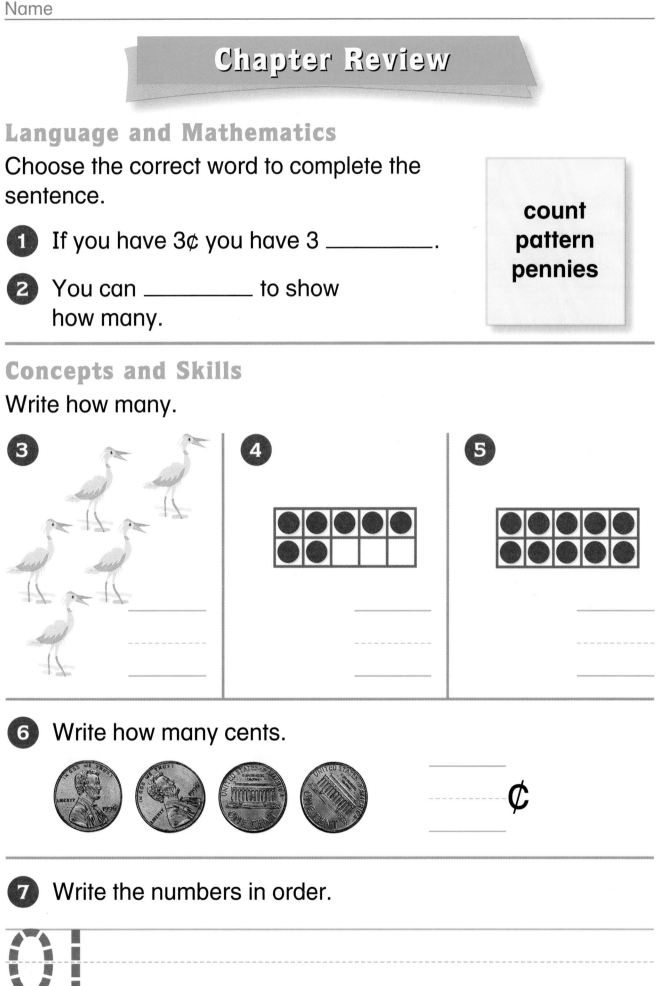

3

4

5

6 Write how many cents.

_____ ¢

7 Write the numbers in order.

01

Problem Solving

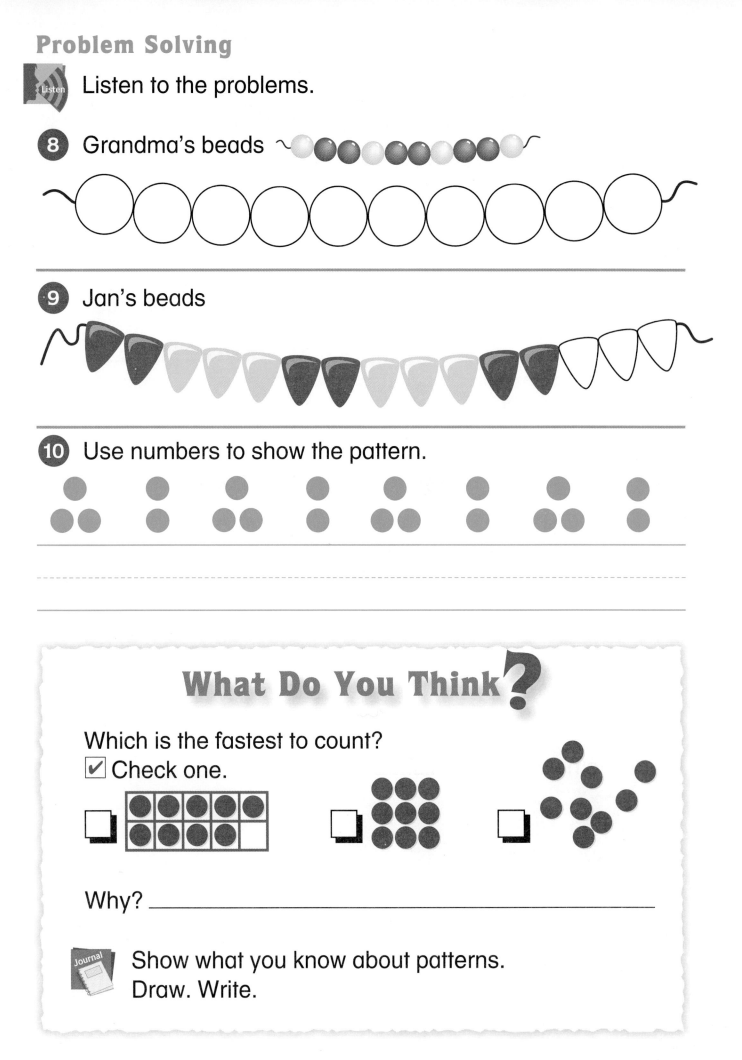

Listen to the problems.

8 Grandma's beads

9 Jan's beads

10 Use numbers to show the pattern.

What Do You Think?

Which is the fastest to count?
☑ Check one.

☐   ☐   ☐

Why? _____

Show what you know about patterns.
Draw. Write.

Chapter Test

Write how many.

1 ○ ○ ○
   ○ ○ ○
   _____

   _____

2 ● ● ● ● ●
    ● ● ● □ □
    _____

    _____

3 ● ● ● ● □
    □ □ □ □ □
    _____

    _____

Write how many cents.

4 _____ ¢

   _____

5 _____ ¢

   _____

6 _____ ¢

   _____

Write the numbers in order.

7 5 6 ___ ___ ___ ___ 10

8 0 ___ ___ 2 ___ ___ 5

Listen to the problem.

9 Jeff's beads

10 Vicky's beads

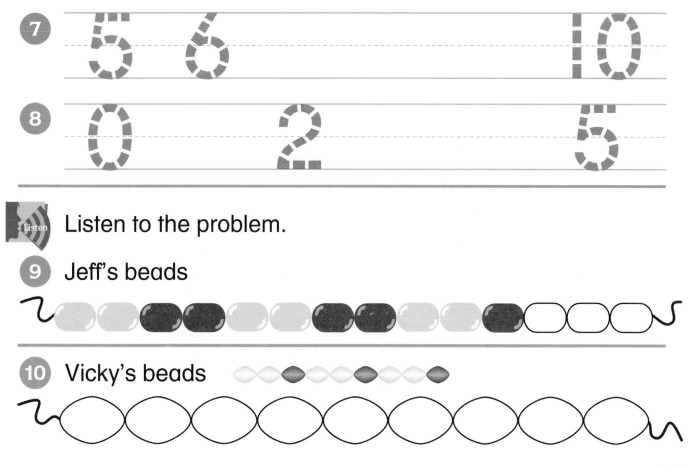

What Did You Learn?

Listen to the problem.

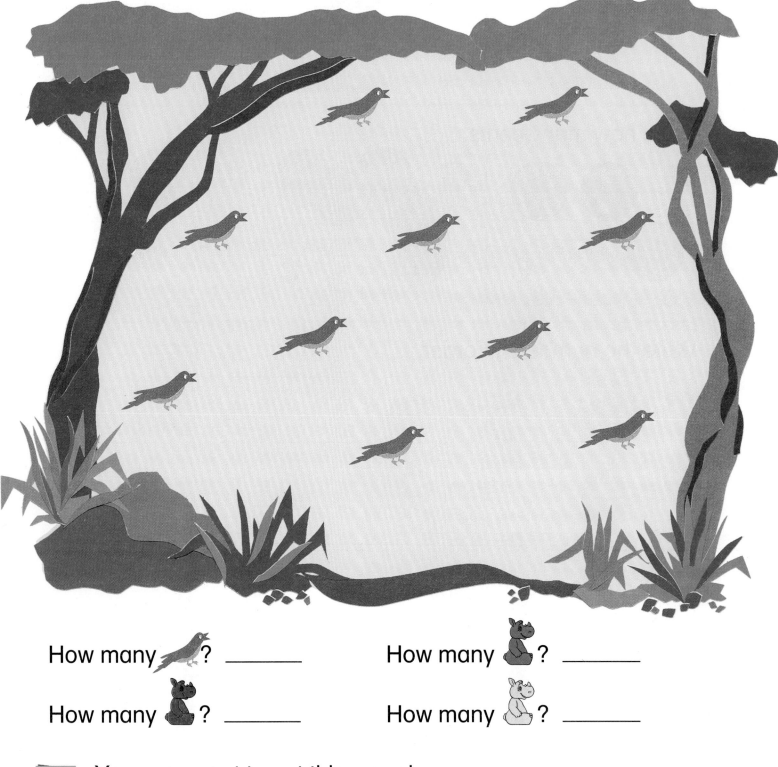

How many 🐦? _____   How many 🦏? _____

How many 🦏? _____   How many 🦏? _____

 You may want to put this page in your portfolio.

Math Connection
Statistics

Name

Tally Marks

Ask 10 friends.
Use **tally marks** to show how many.

| = 1 vote

卌 = 5 votes

Which animal do you like the best?	
🦛	
🦏	
🐅	

Write how many.

McGraw-Hill School Division

Kamba Counting

The Kamba people have a way to show numbers with their fingers.

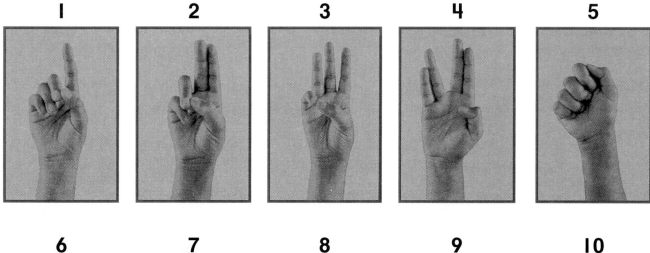

1	2	3	4	5

6	7	8	9	10

Talk

Show 6 with your fingers.
Show 6 the Kamba way.
Why do both ways use two hands?

▶ Think of a number.
  Make it the Kamba way.

▶ Show your friend.
  Let your friend say the number.

Name

The Dotted Giraffe!

PLAYERS 2

MATERIALS 10 pennies

DIRECTIONS Say a number from 1 to 10. Put a penny on the space that shows that number of dots. Play until you cover all the spaces.

 Play this game with your child to practice counting from 1 to 10.

At Home

Dear Family,

I am beginning a new chapter in my mathematics book. I will be learning about parts of numbers.

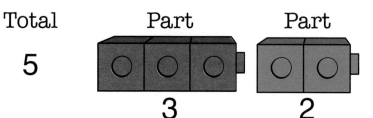

Total   Part   Part

5   3   2

Five can be 3 and 2, or 4 and 1, or just 5.

I will also learn about transportation and all the ways I can get around.

Learning about Transportation

Let's talk about different ways children can get to school. We can write a story about a bus ride.

My Math Words

I am going to use these math words in this chapter.

total
part
table

Please help me make word cards for these math words. I can use the word cards when I explore parts and totals.

Your child,

_____
Signature

Exploring
Part-Part-Whole

Theme: Getting Around

Draw Conclusions Words and pictures help tell a story.

Listen to the story *Bus Stops*.

Tell about the stops that the bus made.

Name

What Do You Know?

1

Talk

How many ? ____

How many ? ____

2

Talk

How many ? ____

How many ? ____

Portfolio

Draw some in a wagon.

Write how many .

Write how many .

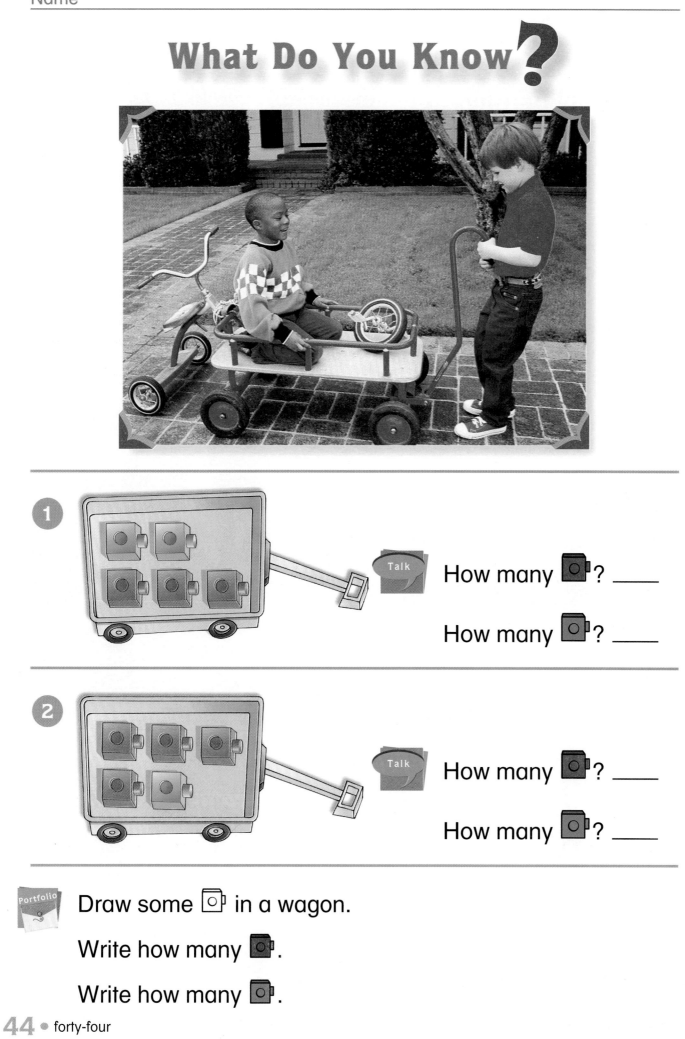

Name _____

Working Together

You need 10 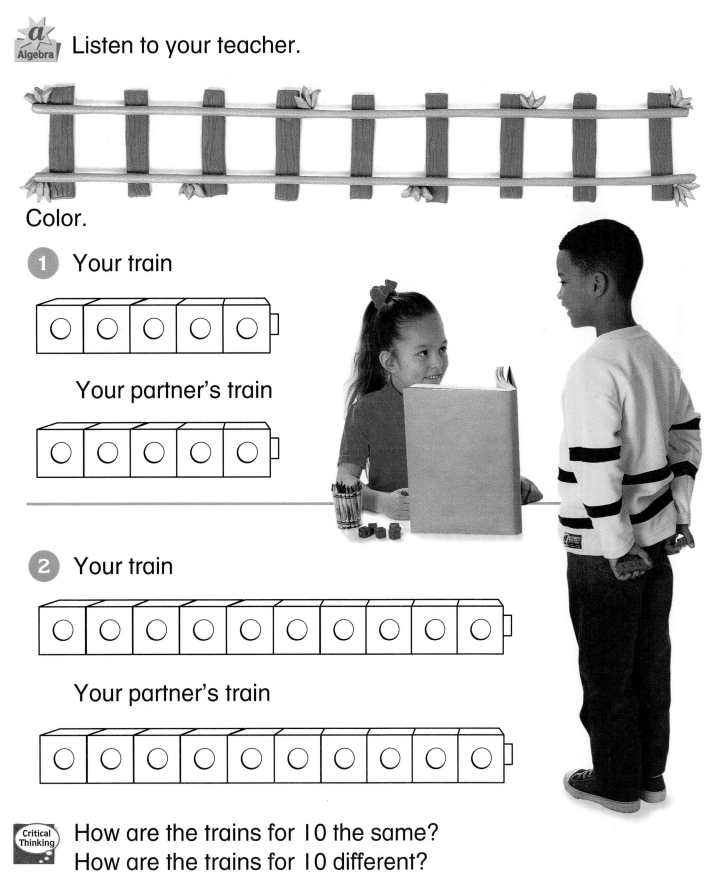, 10 , a))) red)))▶, and a))) blue)))▶.

a **Algebra** Listen to your teacher.

Color.

1 Your train

Your partner's train

2 Your train

Your partner's train

Critical Thinking How are the trains for 10 the same?
How are the trains for 10 different?

McGraw-Hill School Division

Practice!

Make trains with 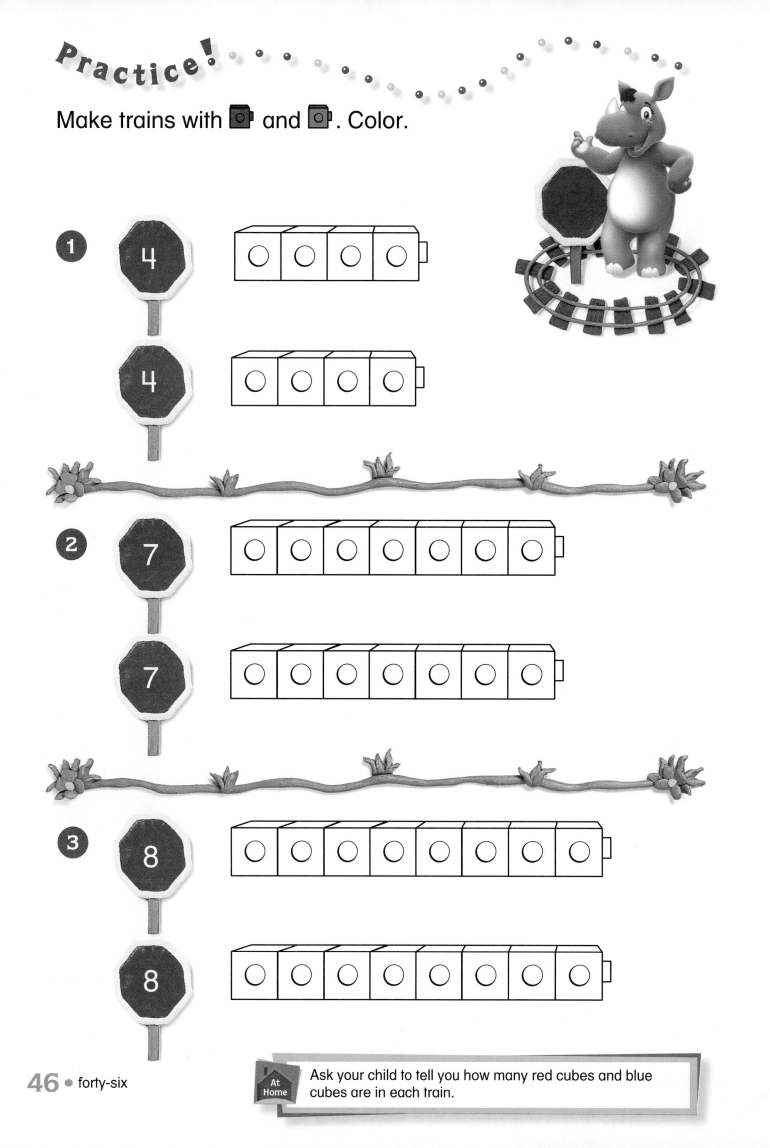 and . Color.

1 4

4

2 7

7

3 8

8

At Home

Ask your child to tell you how many red cubes and blue cubes are in each train.

Make Cube Trains

You need 10 🔳, 10 🔳, a)) red)) ,
and a)) blue)) .

a Algebra **PATTERNS** Make a train for the **total**.
Use 🔳 and 🔳 to show the **parts**.

Glossary
parts
total

Draw. Write how many 🔳 and 🔳.

Total   Parts

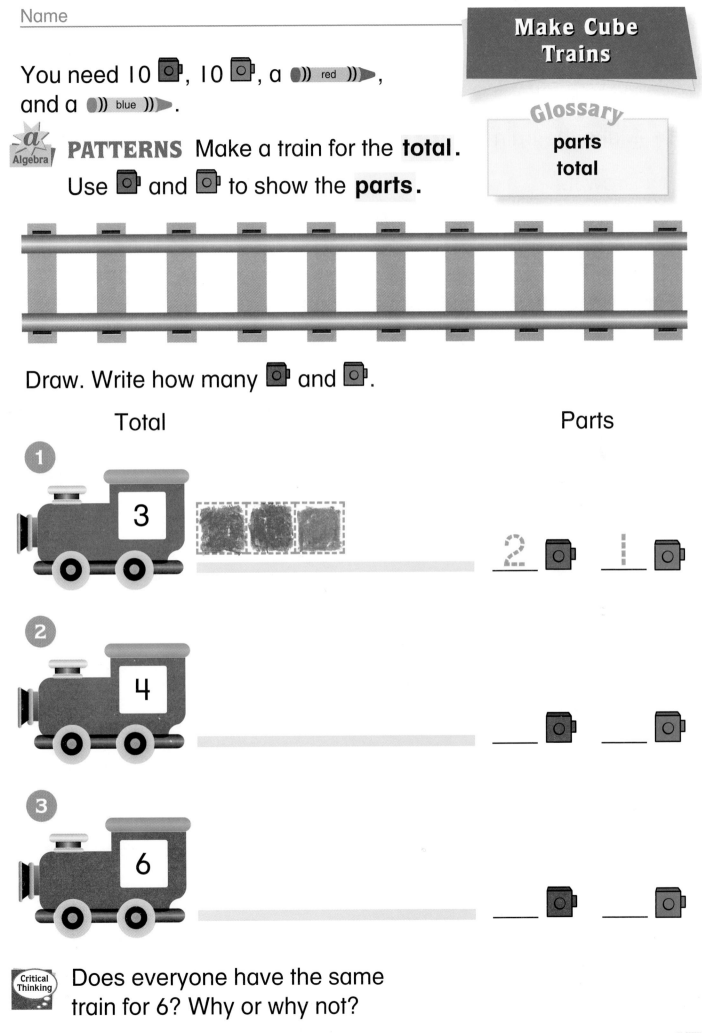

1 3   2 🔳   1 🔳

2 4   🔳   🔳

3 6   🔳   🔳

Critical Thinking Does everyone have the same train for 6? Why or why not?

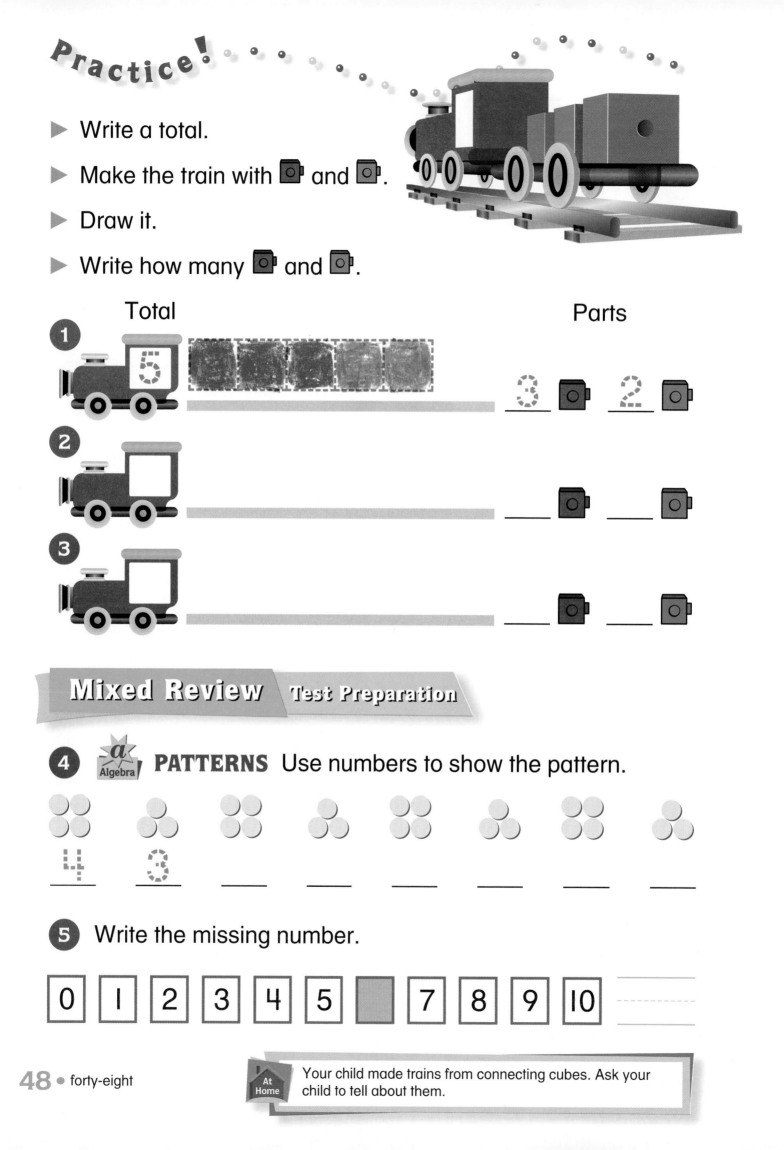

Practice!

▶ Write a total.

▶ Make the train with 🔲 and 🔲.

▶ Draw it.

▶ Write how many 🔲 and 🔲.

Total		Parts
1	5	3 🔲 2 🔲
2		___ 🔲 ___ 🔲
3		___ 🔲 ___ 🔲

Mixed Review Test Preparation

4 ⭐ *a* Algebra **PATTERNS** Use numbers to show the pattern.

4 3 ___ ___ ___ ___ ___ ___

5 Write the missing number.

| 0 | 1 | 2 | 3 | 4 | 5 | | 7 | 8 | 9 | 10 |

At Home Your child made trains from connecting cubes. Ask your child to tell about them.

Name _____

You need 10 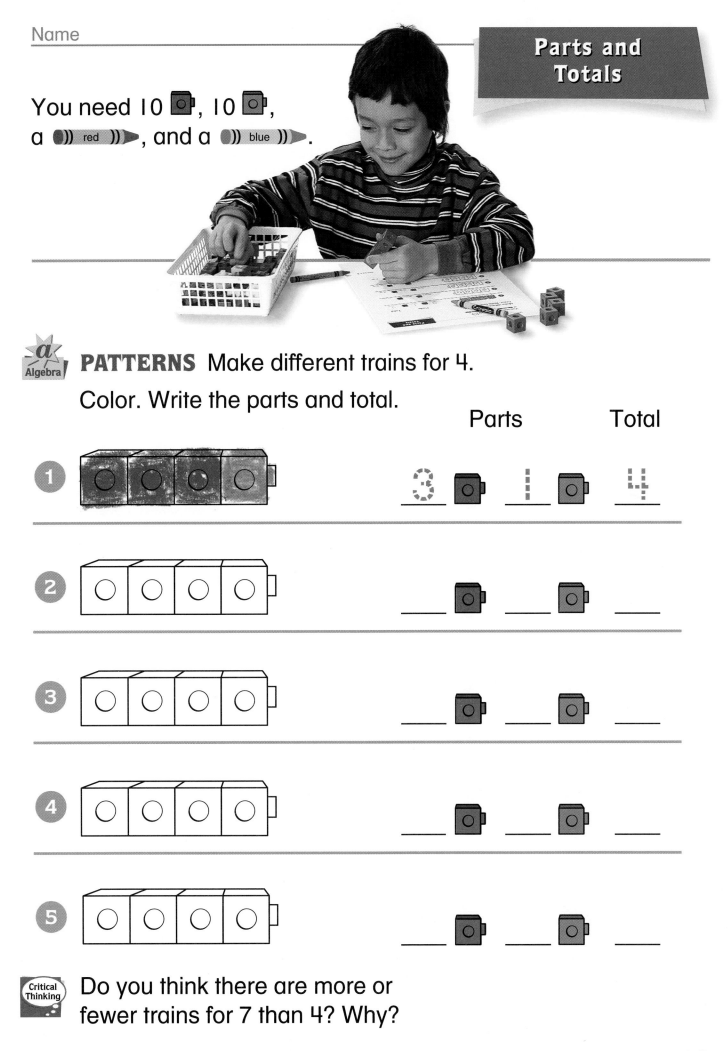, 10 ◻, a ◖ red ◗, and a ◖ blue ◗.

★ **Algebra**

PATTERNS Make different trains for 4.

Color. Write the parts and total.

Parts   Total

1.   3 ◻   1 ◻   4

2.   ___ ◻   ___ ◻   ___

3.   ___ ◻   ___ ◻   ___

4.   ___ ◻   ___ ◻   ___

5.   ___ ◻   ___ ◻   ___

Critical Thinking Do you think there are more or fewer trains for 7 than 4? Why?

Make different trains for 3 with 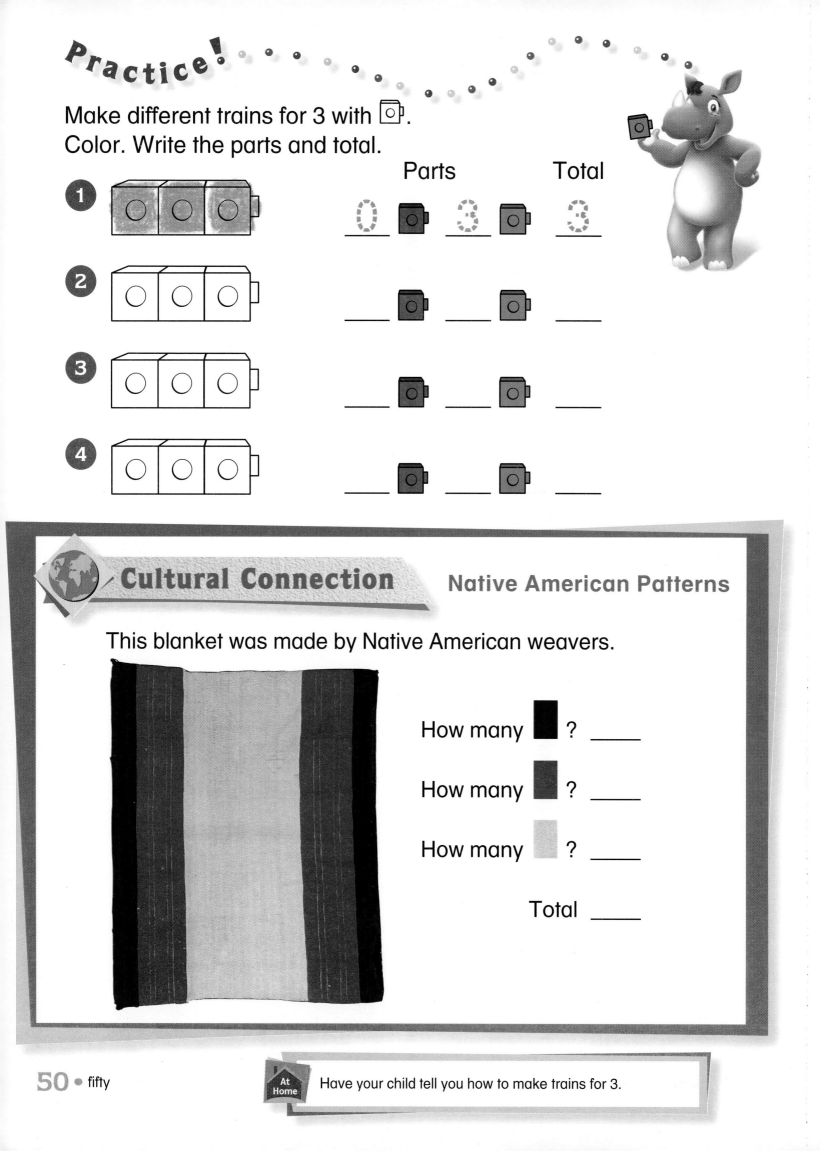.
Color. Write the parts and total.

		Parts		Total

1. _0_ ▨ _3_ ▨ _3_

2. ___ ▨ ___ ▨ ___

3. ___ ▨ ___ ▨ ___

4. ___ ▨ ___ ▨ ___

Cultural Connection Native American Patterns

This blanket was made by Native American weavers.

How many ■ ? ____

How many ▨ ? ____

How many ▢ ? ____

Total ____

At Home Have your child tell you how to make trains for 3.

Name _____

Act It Out

Algebra | **Listen** Listen to the problem.

1

_3_ girls   _2_ boys   _5_ children

2 At the [BUS STOP]

_____ children   _____ sitting   _____ standing

3 At the [TRAIN STATION]

_____ blue trains   _____ red trains   _____ trains

Critical Thinking How can you solve problem 1 using cubes?

Practice!

1 At the 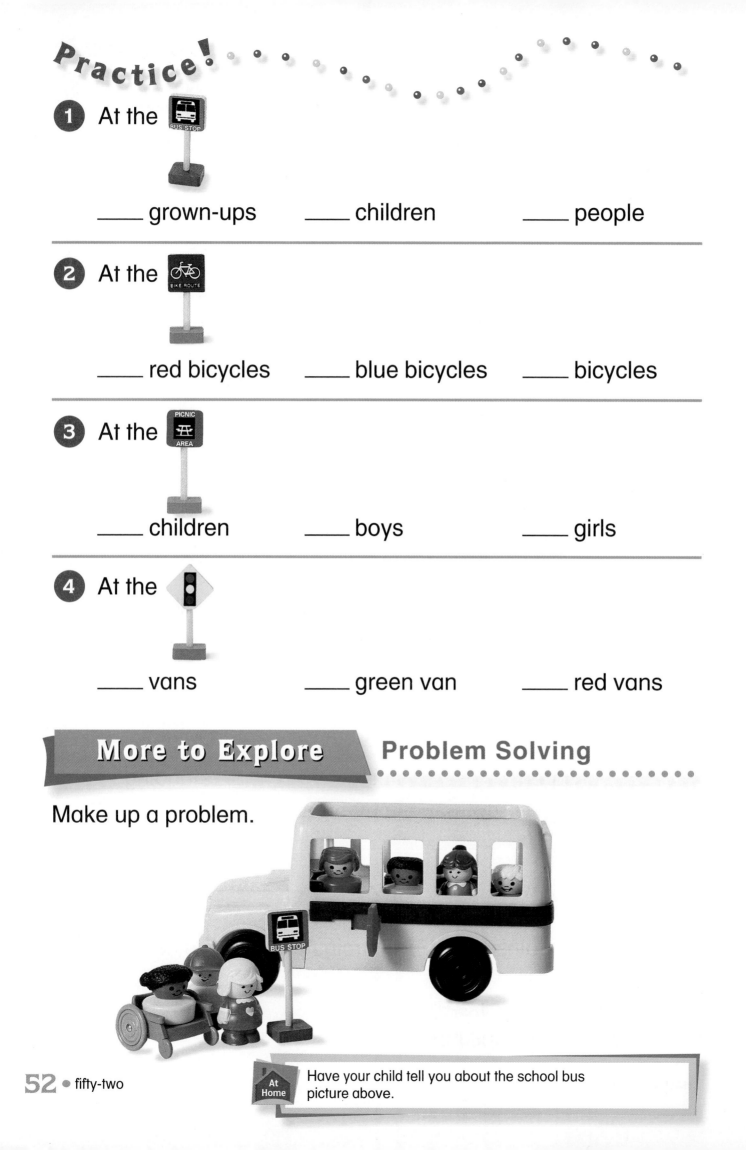 🚌 BUS STOP

_____ grown-ups   _____ children   _____ people

2 At the 🚲 BIKE ROUTE

_____ red bicycles   _____ blue bicycles   _____ bicycles

3 At the 🏕 PICNIC AREA

_____ children   _____ boys   _____ girls

4 At the 🚦

_____ vans   _____ green van   _____ red vans

More to Explore   Problem Solving

Make up a problem.

At Home Have your child tell you about the school bus picture above.

Midchapter Review

Draw a train.
Write how many 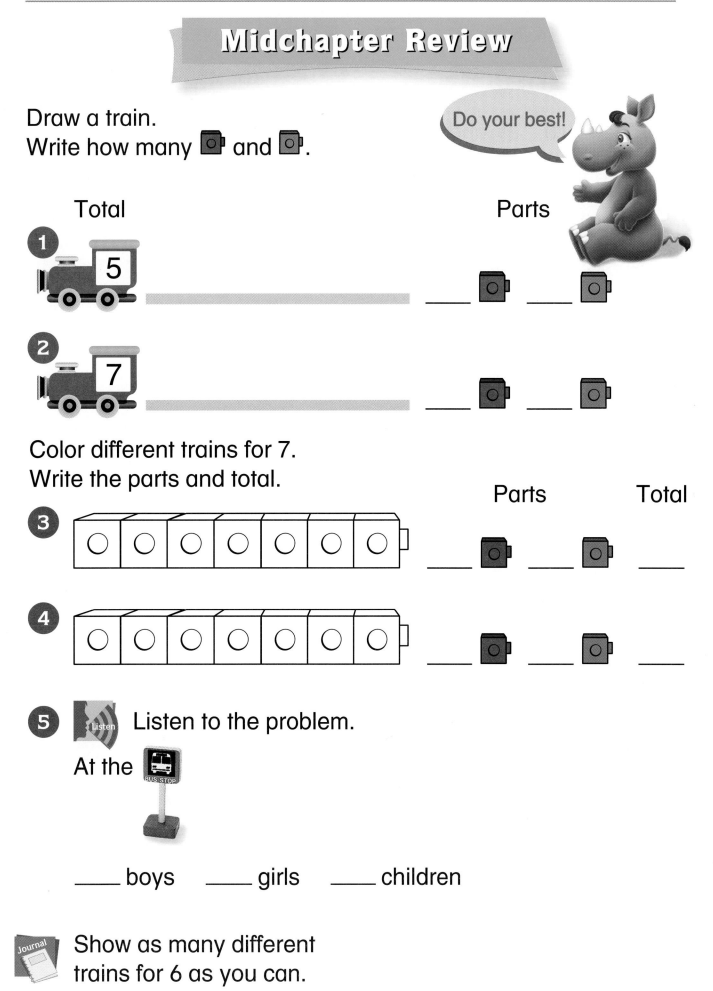 and ▢.

Do your best!

Total   Parts

1 5 _____   ___ ▢   ___ ▢

2 7 _____   ___ ▢   ___ ▢

Color different trains for 7.
Write the parts and total.

Parts   Total

3 ○ ○ ○ ○ ○ ○ ○   ___ ▢   ___ ▢   ___

4 ○ ○ ○ ○ ○ ○ ○   ___ ▢   ___ ▢

5 Listen   Listen to the problem.

At the 🚌 BUS STOP

____ boys   ____ girls   ____ children

Journal Show as many different
trains for 6 as you can.

Shake and Spill

You need 10  and a .

▶ Take turns.

▶ Put 10 counters in the .

▶ Shake and spill.

▶ Cross out the row that shows your parts.

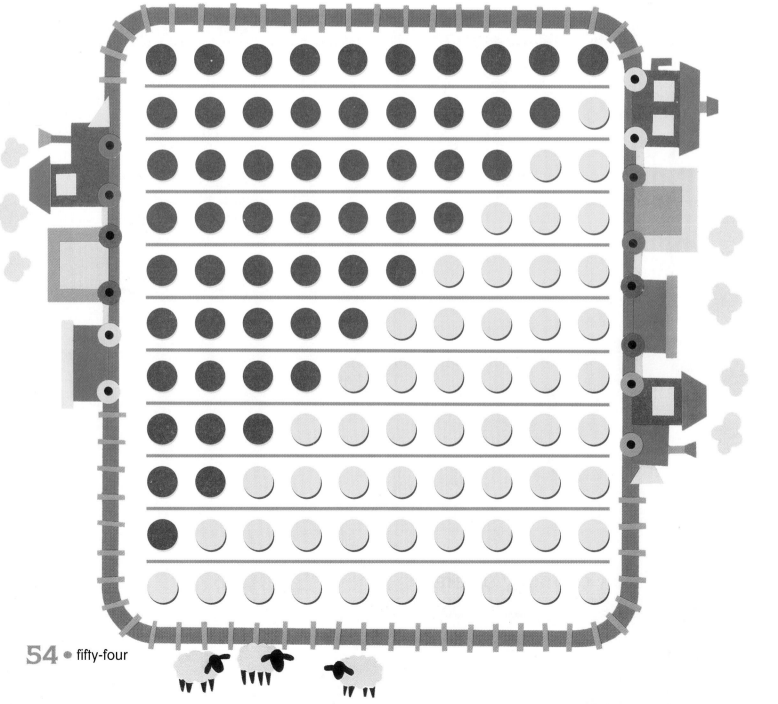

Name _____

Neighborhood Traffic

Talk What is traffic? Does it go by your school?

Working Together

Take a survey.

Decide what to count.

Cultural Note
One way people get around in Haiti is on buses called *tap-taps.*

Show how many your group counted.

Decision Making

Talk

Decide how to show what you learned about traffic. You could make a class display.

Portfolio

Write a report.

1. Show how you counted and recorded.

2. Tell what the class learned.

More to Investigate

PREDICT   What if you counted at a different time. What would the numbers show?

EXPLORE   Choose a different time. Take a survey. Make a new class display.

FIND   How are the displays the same? How are the displays different?

Name _____

You need 10 ⚪⚫

and a ▦.

a Algebra ▶ Show the parts.

▶ Write the total.

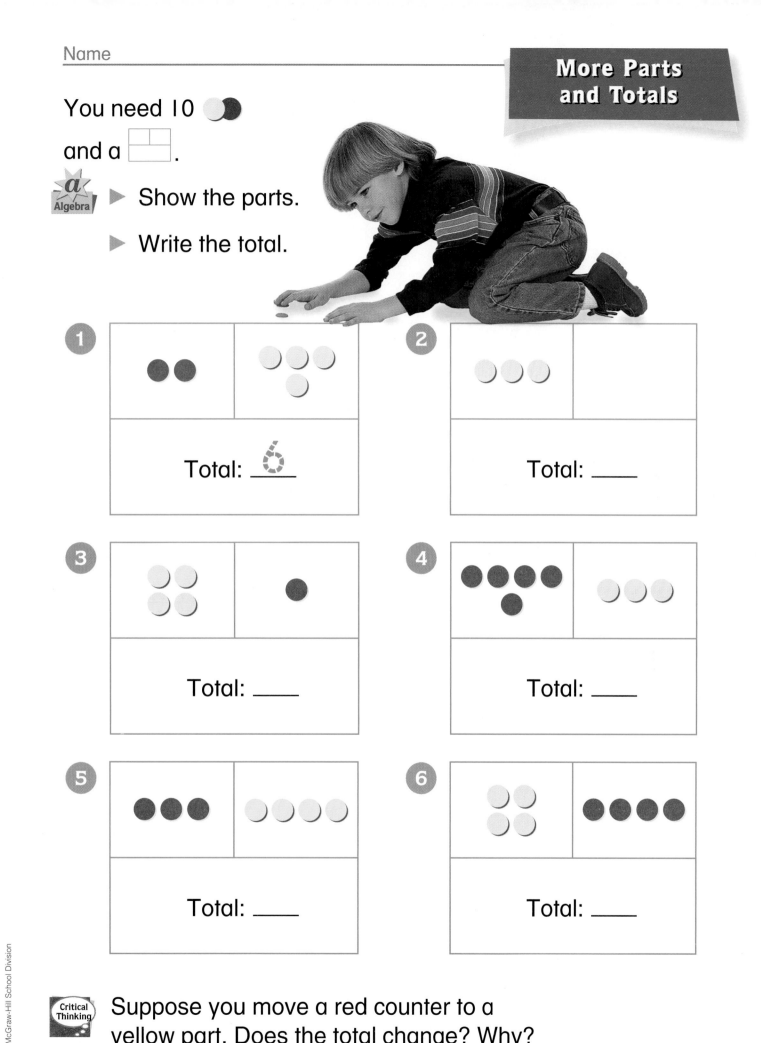

1

Total: 6

2

Total: ___

3

Total: ___

4

Total: ___

5

Total: ___

6

Total: ___

Critical Thinking Suppose you move a red counter to a yellow part. Does the total change? Why?

Use counters
if you want to.

How many cars in all?
Find the total.

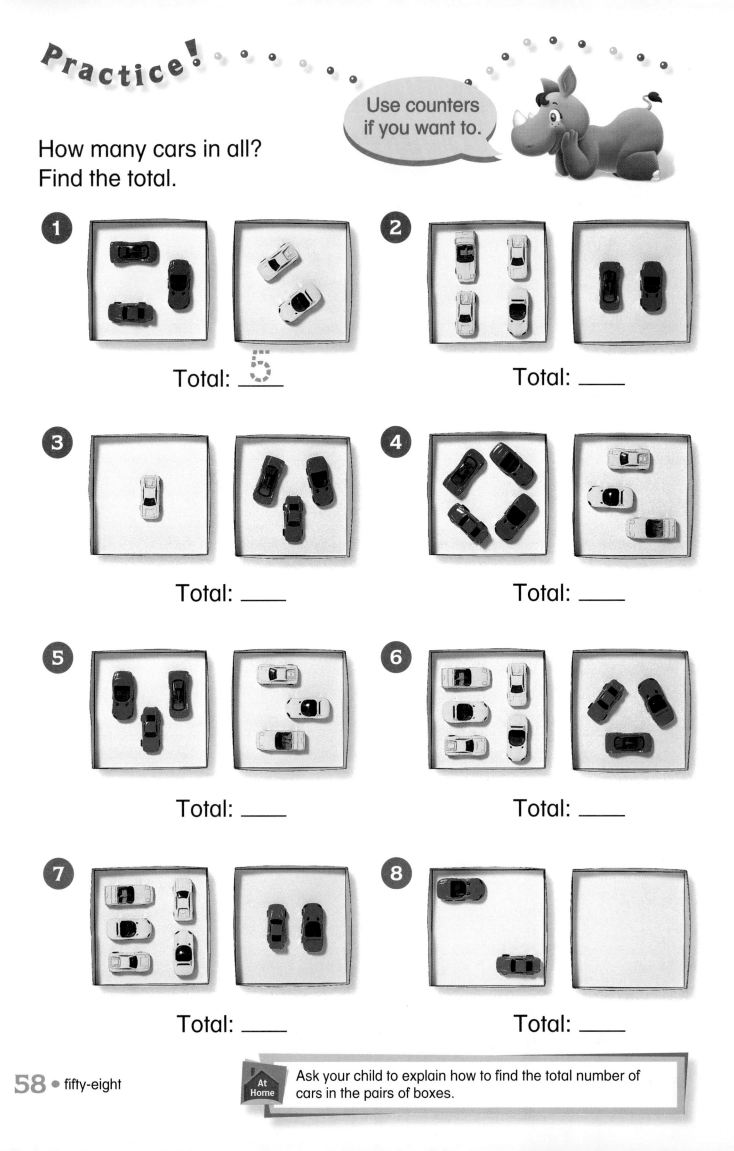

1 Total: 5

2 Total: ____

3 Total: ____

4 Total: ____

5 Total: ____

6 Total: ____

7 Total: ____

8 Total: ____

At Home — Ask your child to explain how to find the total number of cars in the pairs of boxes.

You need 10 ⚫⚪ and a ▭.

Find the total.

1
2	5
7	

2
1	4

3
2	2

4
6	4

5
2	4

6
3	1

7
0	1

8
5	3

9
7	1

Critical Thinking How can you show 8 another way?

Practice!

Use counters if you want to.

Find the total.

1

2	2
4	

2

0	2

3

1	4

4

2	1

5

5	2

6

4	5

Mixed Review   Test Preparation

Write how many.

7 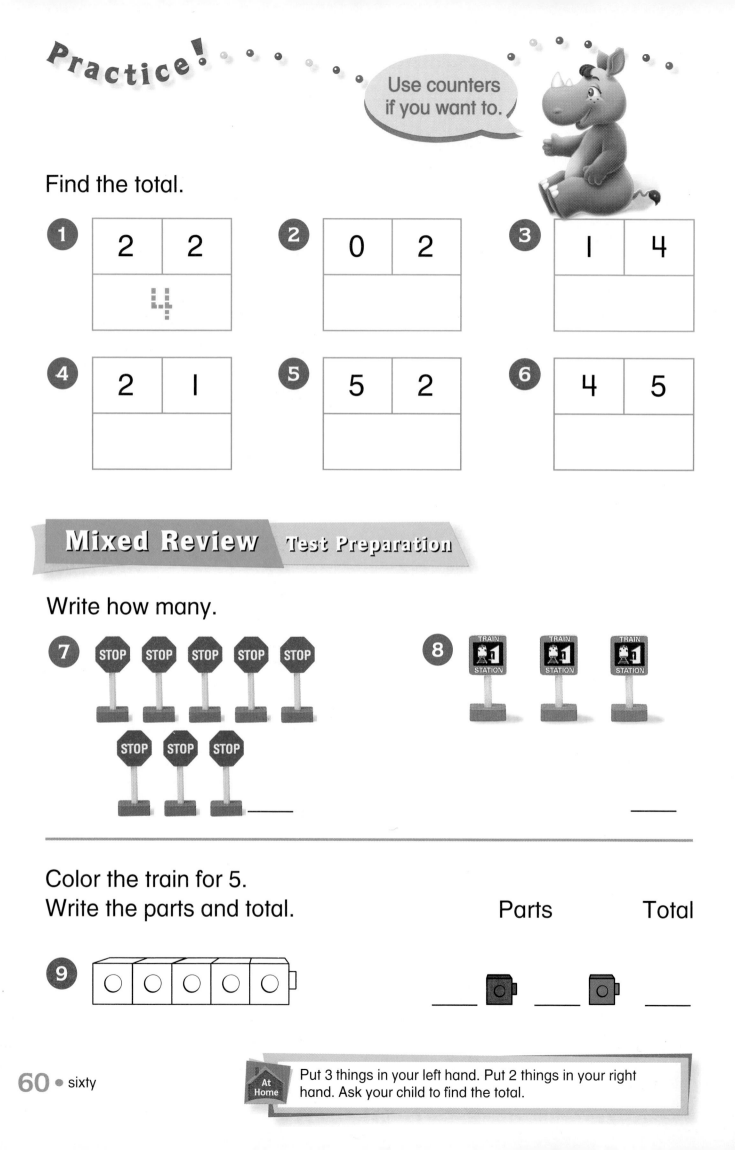 STOP STOP STOP STOP STOP STOP STOP STOP _____

8 TRAIN STATION TRAIN STATION TRAIN STATION _____

Color the train for 5.
Write the parts and total.

Parts   Total

9

_____ _____ _____

At Home — Put 3 things in your left hand. Put 2 things in your right hand. Ask your child to find the total.

Name _____

Algebra

Working Together

You need 10 ⬤◐ .

▶ Take turns.

▶ You show one part.

▶ Your partner shows the missing part.

▶ Write.

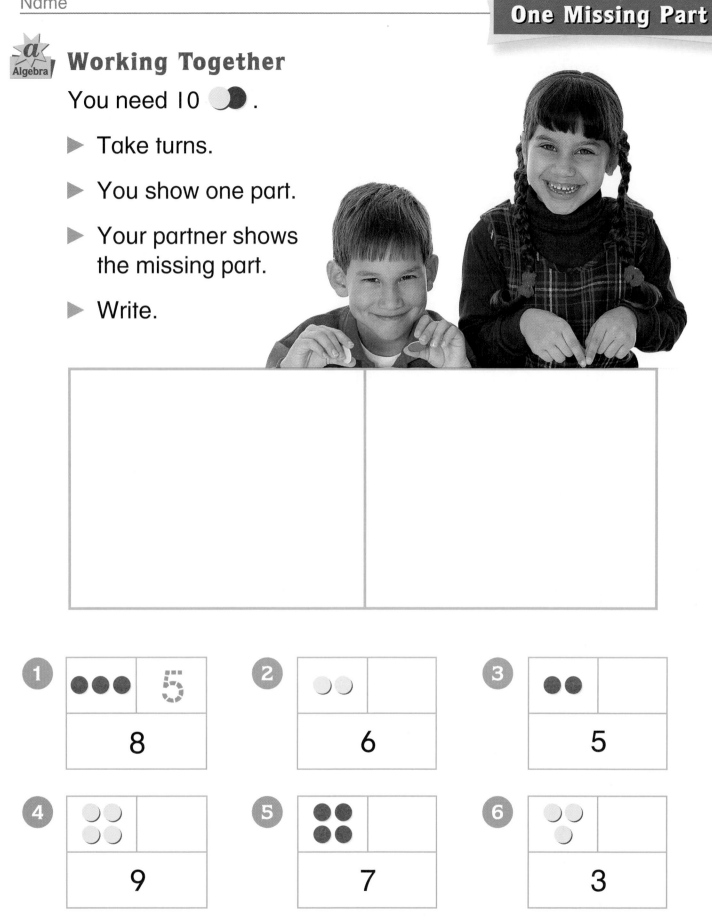

1. ●●● 5 | 8

2. ○○ | 6

3. ●● | 5

4. ○○ ○○ | 9

5. ●● ●● | 7

6. ○○ ○ | 3

Critical Thinking When can two parts be the same number?

> Use counters if you want to.

How many trucks are in the box?

1 Total: 7 trucks

2 Total: 4 trucks

3 Total: 8 trucks

4 Total: 6 trucks

5 Total: 5 trucks

6 Total: 9 trucks

READING • ARITHMETIC • WRITING

Draw Conclusions

Listen to *Bus Stops* one more time.

Use the pictures.

How many people got off the bus?

Choose a picture.

Ask a question for a partner to answer.

 At Home Show your child 8 pennies. Hide some with your hand. Ask your child how many are hidden.

Find the Missing Part

You need 10 ⬤ and a ▭.

a Algebra

▶ Show the total.

▶ Show the part.

▶ Find the missing part.

▶ Write.

1

2	4
6	

2

5	
10	

3

1	
7	

4

6	
8	

5

4	
5	

6

0	
4	

7

5	
9	

8

2	
7	

9

1	
3	

Critical Thinking When is a missing part zero?

Practice!

Use counters if you want to.

Find the missing part.

1
2	2
4	

2
3	
10	

3
	4
6	

4
2	
2	

5
	6
9	

6
	4
8	

More to Explore Logical Reasoning

Ring the correct box.

The box has 2 🚗.

It has more 🚚 than 🚗.

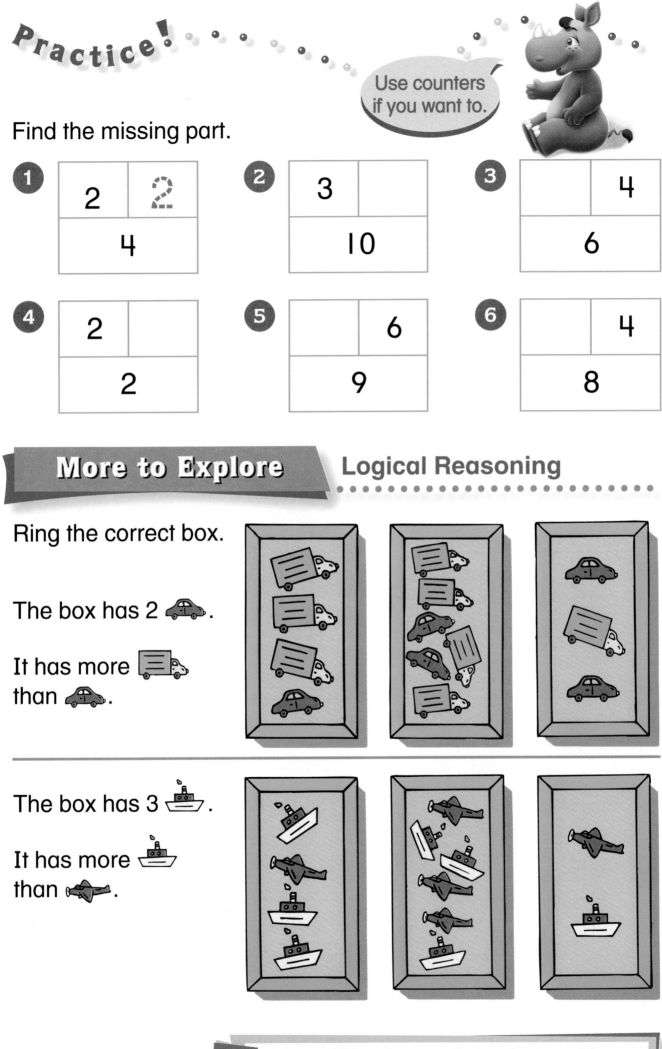

The box has 3 🚢.

It has more 🚢 than ✈.

 At Home — Ask your child to tell you a math story about one of the transportation pictures.

Name

Guess and Count

You need paper and 10 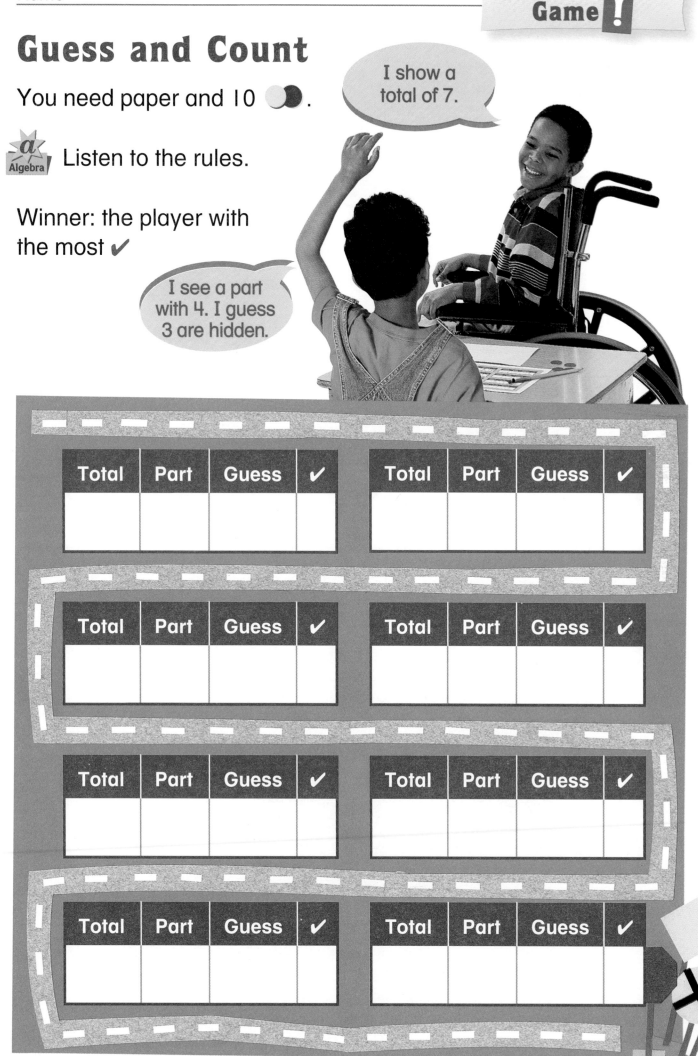.

Algebra Listen to the rules.

Winner: the player with the most ✔

> I show a total of 7.

> I see a part with 4. I guess 3 are hidden.

Total	Part	Guess	✔

Total	Part	Guess	✔

Total	Part	Guess	✔

Total	Part	Guess	✔

Total	Part	Guess	✔

Total	Part	Guess	✔

Total	Part	Guess	✔

Total	Part	Guess	✔

Algebra Find the total.

1

1	6
7	

2

8	0

3

3	2

4

4	5

5

5	5

6

2	1

Find the missing part.

7

3	4
7	

8

5	
8	

9

0	
4	

10

2	
9	

11

	3
10	

12

3	
6	

Cultural Note

In winter some Inuit get around on snowmobiles.

Name _____

What Is the Question?

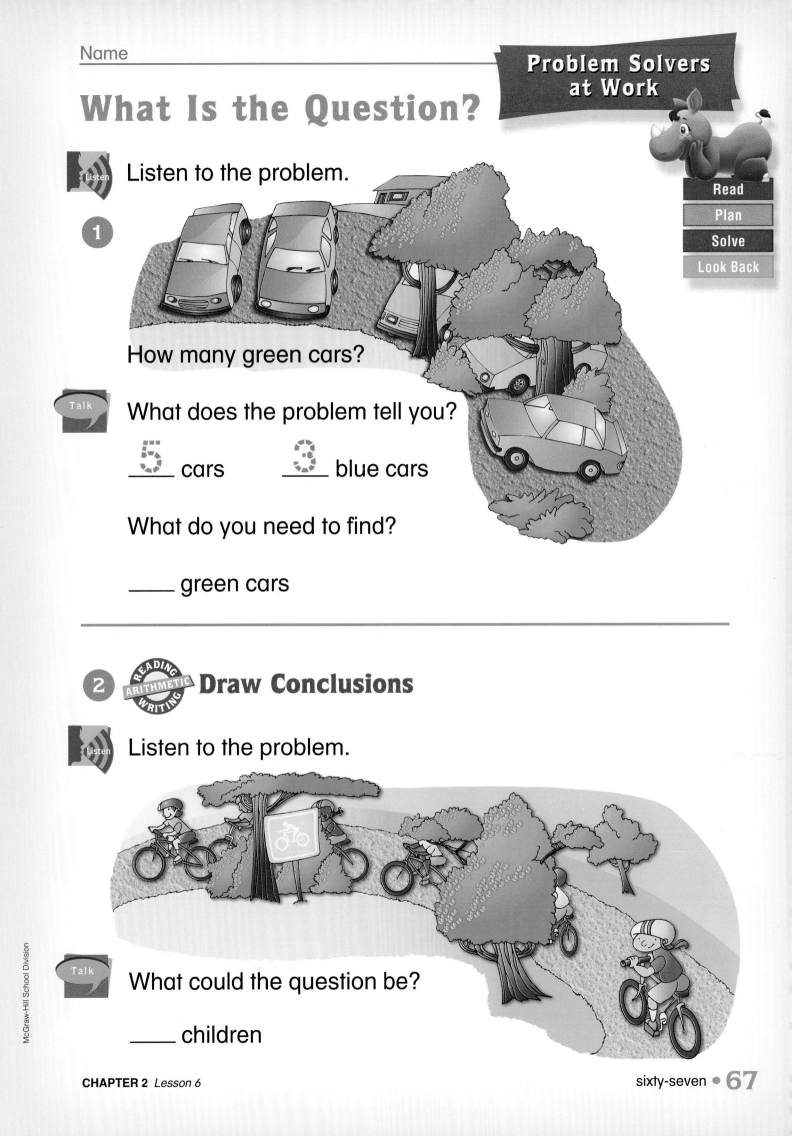

Listen Listen to the problem.

1

How many green cars?

Talk What does the problem tell you?

__5__ cars   __3__ blue cars

What do you need to find?

____ green cars

2 **READING ARITHMETIC WRITING** **Draw Conclusions**

Listen Listen to the problem.

Talk What could the question be?

____ children

Practice!

Listen Listen to the problem.

1 How many blue trucks?

_____ trucks   _____ red trucks   _____ blue trucks

Talk Kara said there were 7 blue trucks.
What did she do wrong?

Write and Share

Gerica wrote this problem.

How many hearts do you see?

Gerica Goodman
Elephant's Fork School
Suffolk, Virginia

STUDENT TO STUDENT

2 Solve Gerica's problem.   _____ hearts

3 Write   Draw a picture. Write a question.

Your partner's answer to your question: _____

Your answer to your question: _____

 At Home   We are learning to solve oral problems. Have your child make up problems for the pictures and questions on this page.

Chapter Review

Language and Mathematics

Choose the correct word to complete the sentence.

1 Two trains for 6 can show different _____.

2 You can use cubes as parts to show a _____.

parts
total

Concepts and Skills

Color different trains for 6.
Write the parts and total.

Parts   Total

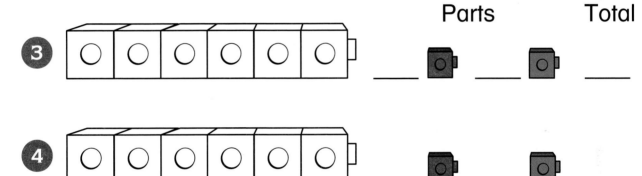

Find the total.

5	2	5

6	8	I

Find the missing part.

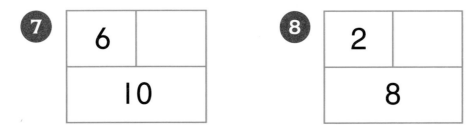

7	6	
	10	

8	2	
	8	

Problem Solving

Listen Listen to the problem.

9

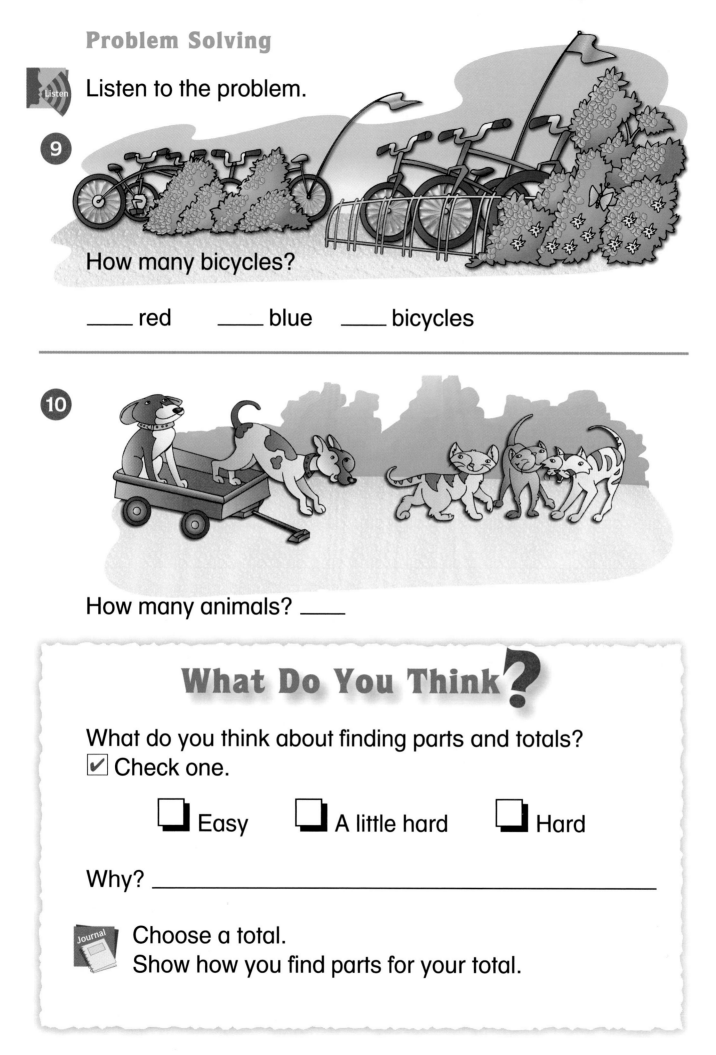

How many bicycles?

_____ red   _____ blue   _____ bicycles

10

How many animals? _____

What Do You Think?

What do you think about finding parts and totals?
☑ Check one.

☐ Easy   ☐ A little hard   ☐ Hard

Why? _____

Journal Choose a total.
Show how you find parts for your total.

Chapter Test

Color different trains for 5.
Write the parts and total.

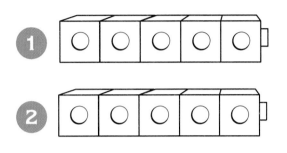

Parts   Total

1 ⬚ ⬚ ⬚ ⬚ ⬚

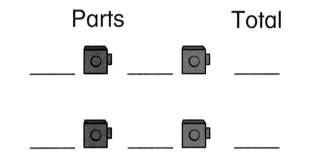

___ 🔲 ___ 🔲 ___

2 ⬚ ⬚ ⬚ ⬚ ⬚

___ 🔲 ___ 🔲 ___

Find the total or missing part.

3 | 1 | 6 |
   | | |

4 | 6 | 2 |
   | | |

5 | 2 | 2 |
   | | |

6 | 5 | |
   | 8 |

7 | | 7 |
   | 9 |

8 | 4 | |
   | 7 |

Listen Listen to the problems.

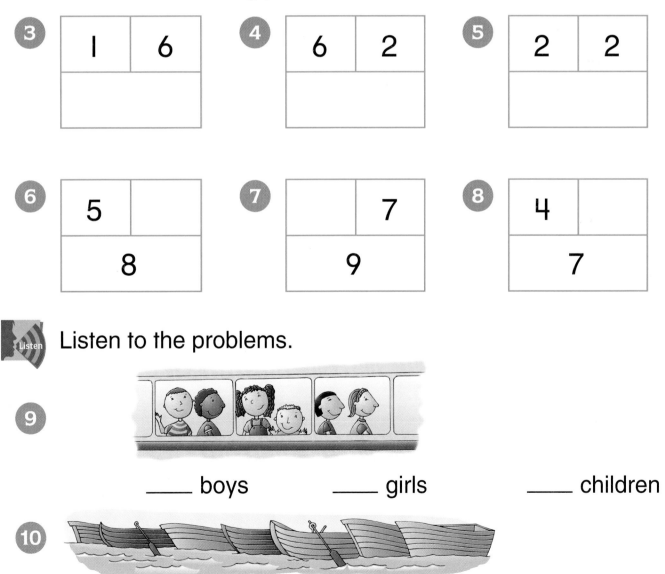

9 _____ boys   _____ girls   _____ children

10 _____ red boats   _____ blue boats   _____ boats

Performance Assessment

What Did You Learn?

 Listen to the problem.

Show trains for 7.
Write how many in each part.

Name _____

Complete a Table

PATTERNS Draw.

Complete the **table**.

Write how many.

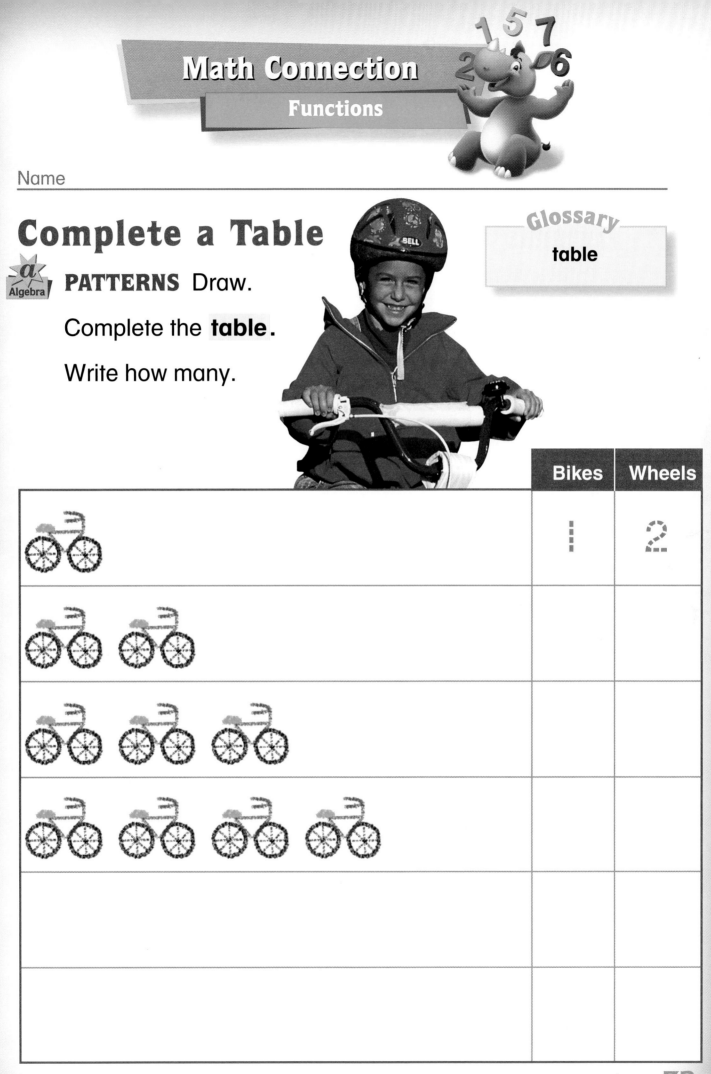

	Bikes	Wheels
	1	2

Make a Pattern

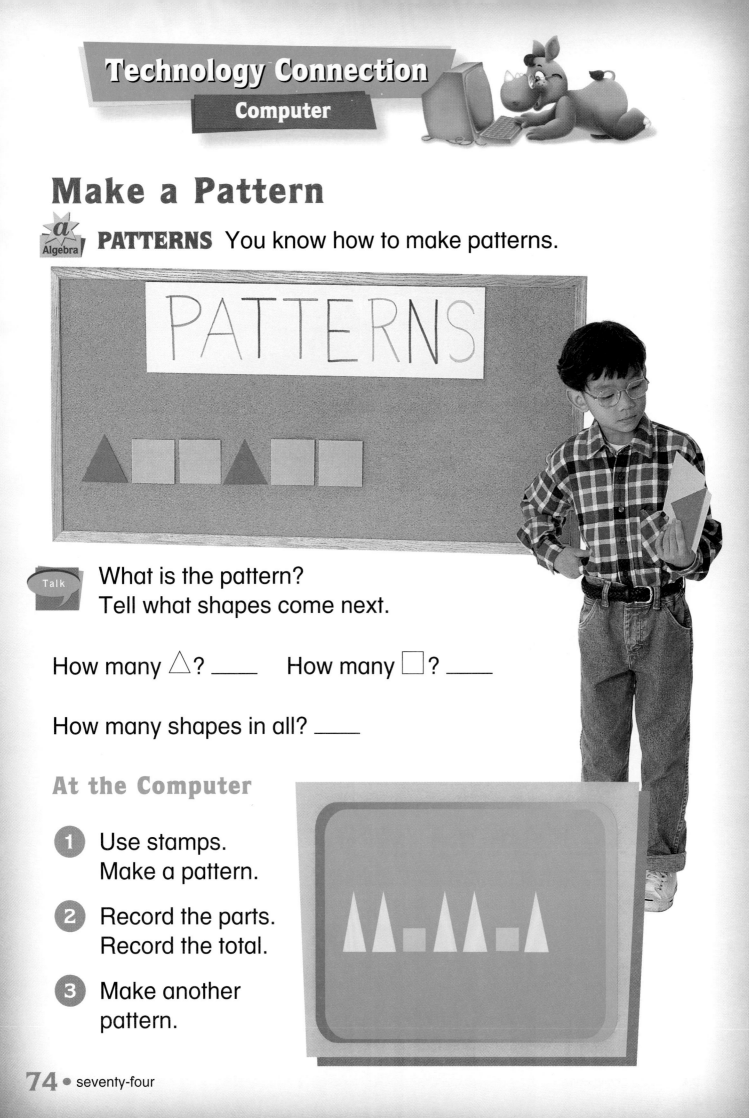

a Algebra **PATTERNS** You know how to make patterns.

Talk What is the pattern?
Tell what shapes come next.

How many △? ____   How many ☐? ____

How many shapes in all? ____

At the Computer

1 Use stamps.
Make a pattern.

2 Record the parts.
Record the total.

3 Make another
pattern.

Name _____

Wheel Count

Where we counted: _____

Number of wheels: _____

Number of vehicles: _____

We counted more _____ than _____.

Take your child to a spot where there are bicycles or cars.
Have your child count the number of vehicles and wheels.
Ask whether there are more wheels or vehicles.

At
Home

Dear Family,

I am starting a new chapter in my mathematics book. I am going to learn about adding numbers. This is like parts and totals, but I will use pictures and numbers to show addition.

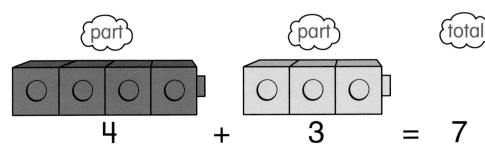

part   part   total

4   +   3   =   7

I will also learn about favorite foods and shopping for groceries.

Learning about Food and Groceries

Let's talk about our favorite foods. We can make a list of places to buy food.

My Math Words

I am going to use these math words in this chapter.

Please help me make word cards for these math words. I can use the word cards when I practice addition.

add
plus
equals
addition sentence
sum
count on

Your child,

_____
Signature

Beginning to Add
Theme: Food for 10

READING ARITHMETIC WRITING

CATHRYN FALWELL

FEAST FOR 10

Set a Purpose As your teacher reads *Feast for 10,* listen for ways to use numbers.

Listen to the story.

What did you find out about using numbers?

What Do You Know?

You need 10 .

Show parts here.

Write the total.

1

3	2

5	1

4	6

2

7	2

3	4

3	5

Show parts for your favorite number.

Name _____

Working Together

You need 10 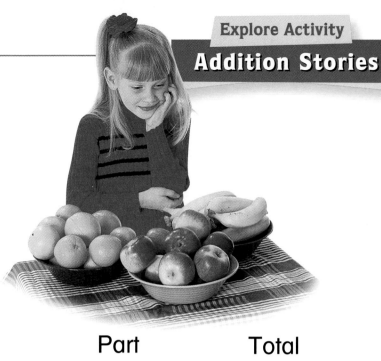.

Listen to the story.

Show the parts. Draw.

Write the total.

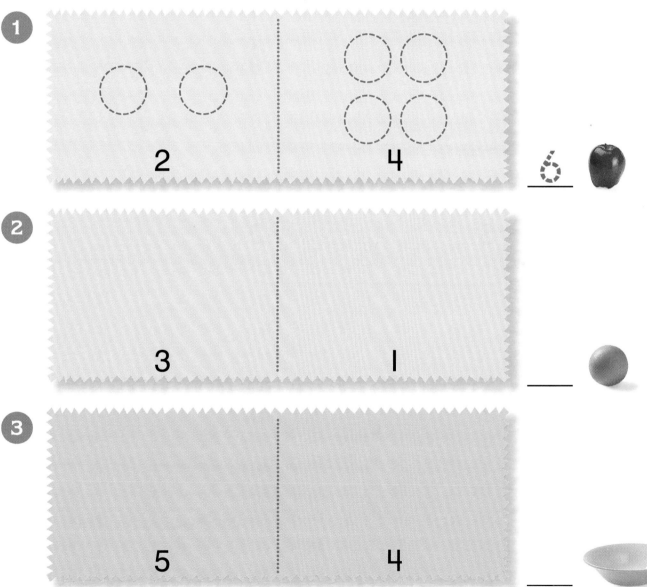

Part	Part	Total
1 2	4	6
2 3	1	___
3 5	4	___

 Why do you get the same totals
as your partner?

McGraw-Hill School Division

Practice!

Take turns.

You tell a story about parts. Your partner draws the parts and writes the total.

Part	Part	Total

1

○ | ○ ○ ○

1 | 3 | 4

2

3 | 2 | ___

3

2 | 5 | ___

4

5 | 5 | ___

 Draw and write to show parts and a total.

At Home   Ask your child to tell you a story about exercise 1 above.

Name _____

You need 10 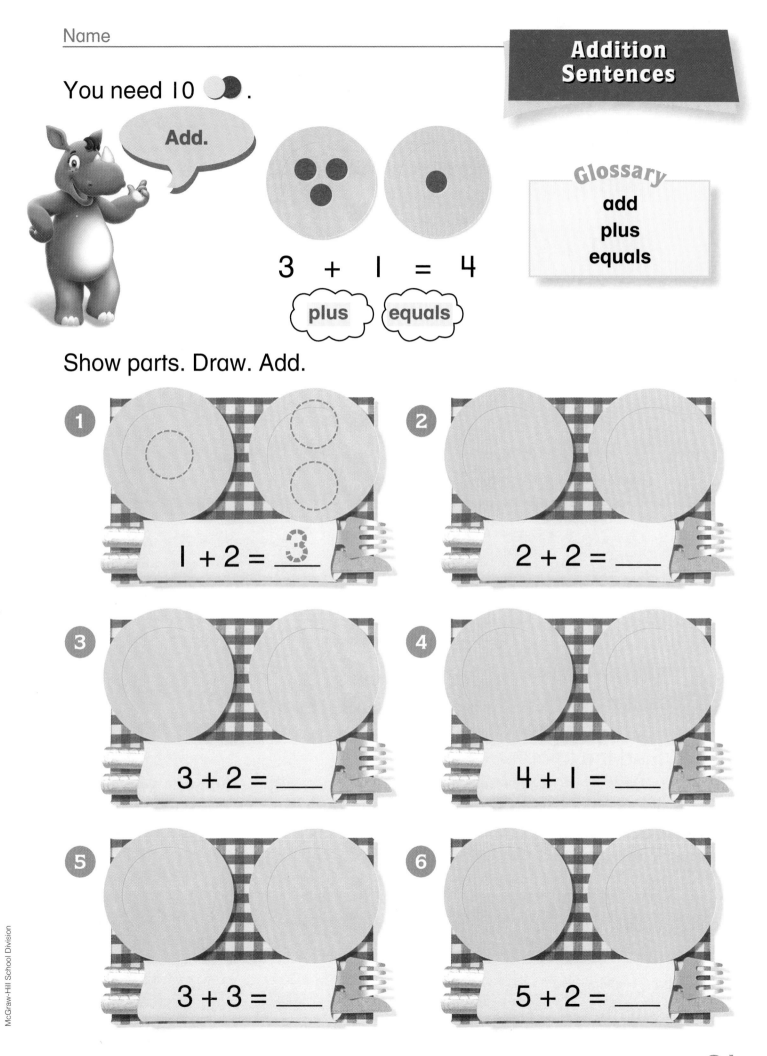.

Add.

3 + 1 = 4

plus equals

Glossary
add
plus
equals

Show parts. Draw. Add.

1   1 + 2 = 3

2   2 + 2 = ___

3   3 + 2 = ___

4   4 + 1 = ___

5   3 + 3 = ___

6   5 + 2 = ___

McGraw-Hill School Division

Practice!

Add.

1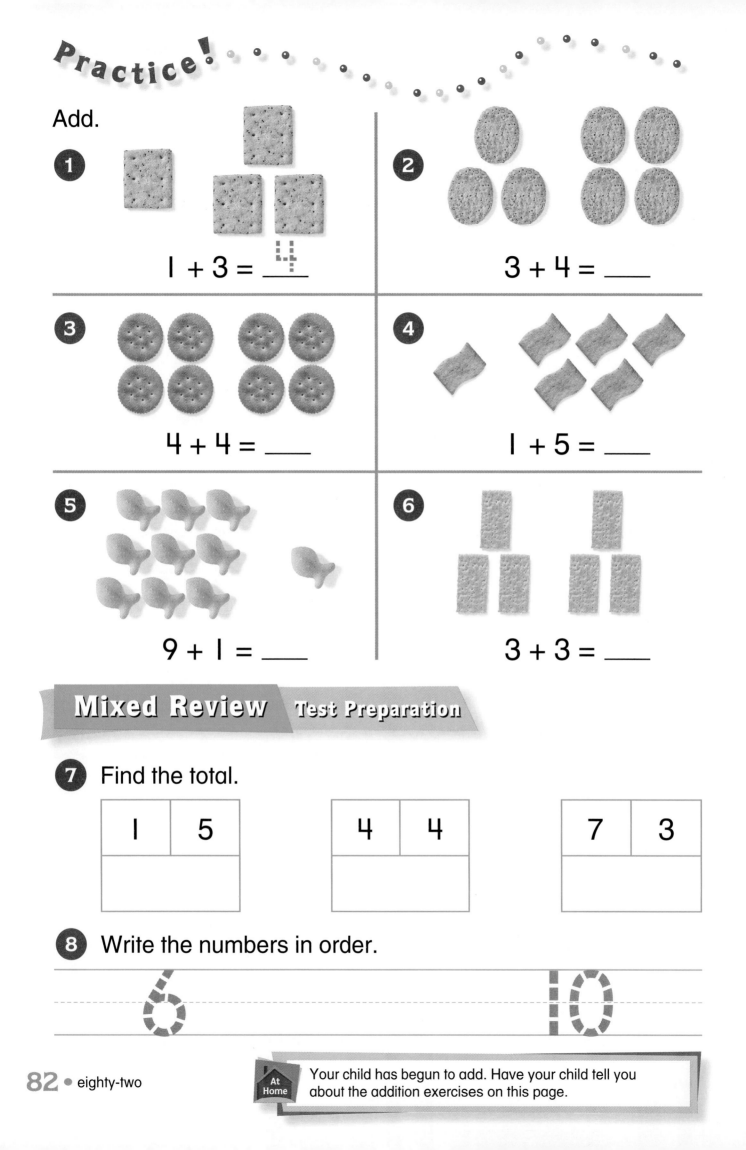

1 + 3 = __4__

2

3 + 4 = ___

3

4 + 4 = ___

4

1 + 5 = ___

5

9 + 1 = ___

6

3 + 3 = ___

Mixed Review · Test Preparation

7 Find the total.

1	5

4	4

7	3

8 Write the numbers in order.

6 ___ ___ ___ 10

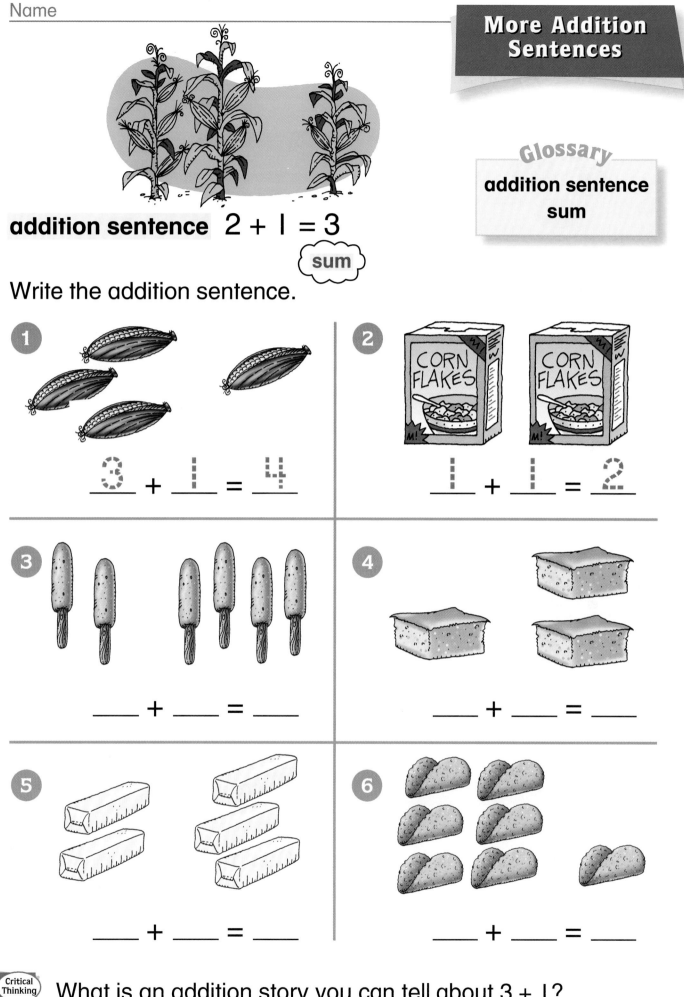

Glossary

addition sentence
sum

addition sentence 2 + 1 = 3

sum

Write the addition sentence.

1   $\underline{3} + \underline{1} = \underline{4}$

2   $\underline{1} + \underline{1} = \underline{2}$

3   ___ + ___ = ___

4   ___ + ___ = ___

5   ___ + ___ = ___

6   ___ + ___ = ___

Critical Thinking What is an addition story you can tell about 3 + 1?

Practice!

Write the addition sentence.

1
__4__ + __5__ = __9__

2
___ + ___ = ___

3
___ + ___ = ___

4
___ + ___ = ___

5
___ + ___ = ___

6
___ + ___ = ___

More to Explore   Patterns

PATTERNS Look for a pattern. Complete.

0 + 0 = ___   1 + 0 = ___   2 + 0 = ___

3 + 0 = ___   4 + 0 = ___   5 + 0 = ___

At Home: We are learning to write addition sentences. Have your child tell you about the exercises on this page.

Write an Addition Sentence

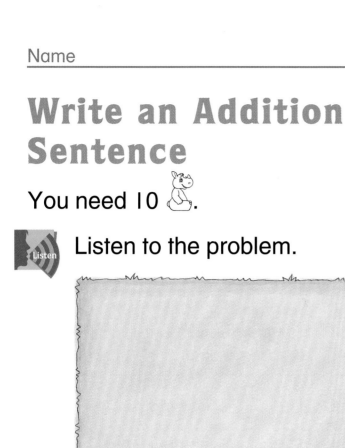

You need 10 .

Listen Listen to the problem.

Find how many in all.

1 At the store ____ 5 in all

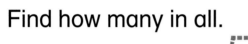

Talk Tell how you found the answer.

2 At the party ____ in all

___ + ___ = ___

3 At school ____ in all

___ + ___ = ___

Make up a problem for the picture.
Find how many in all.

1

_____ in all

_____ + _____ = _____

2

_____ in all

_____ + _____ = _____

3

_____ in all

_____ + _____ = _____

More to Explore   Spatial Sense

Find how many 🔲 in all.

_____ in all

_____ + _____ = _____

At Home — Ask your child to tell you a story about one of these pictures.

Name _____

Midchapter Review

Listen **Find how many in all.**

1) At the party _____ in all

___ + ___ = ___

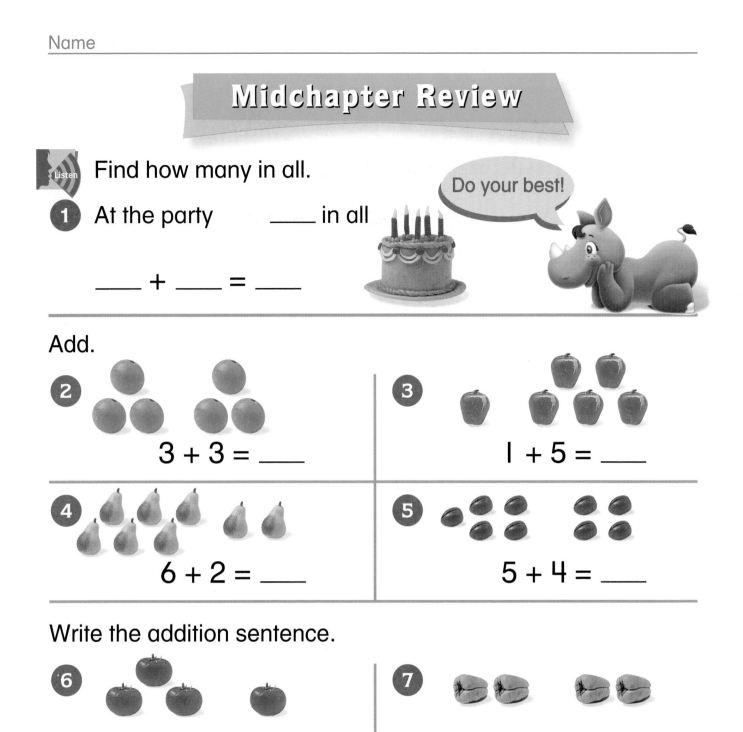

Do your best!

Add.

2) 3 + 3 = ___

3) 1 + 5 = ___

4) 6 + 2 = ___

5) 5 + 4 = ___

Write the addition sentence.

6) ___ + ___ = ___

7) ___ + ___ = ___

8) ___ + ___ = ___

9) ___ + ___ = ___

10) What does 2 + 1 = 3 mean?

_____

Journal **Draw a picture that shows addition.**

I Show, You Find

You need 2  and 10 ⌑.

Listen to the rules.

Take turns.

► You put 🐴 on 2 numbers.

► Your partner adds.

► Score 1 point if the sum is correct.

Play until you get 10 points.

1	4	2	5
6	3	4	1
2	5	3	6

Use ⵚⵚ to keep score.

| | |
| | |

Name

Ice Cream Time

Make an ice cream cone.

Working Together

You need I ●, I ●, I ●, and ✏.

▶ Find different ways to stack the ●, ●, and ●.

▶ Color to show each way.

How many ways to stack? _____

McGraw-Hill School Division

Decision Making

1 Choose your own 3 colors.
Find different ways to stack the ice cream.

Write a report.

2 Tell how many ways
you found to stack
each time.

3 How do you know you
found all the ways
to stack?

More to Investigate

PREDICT What if you have a 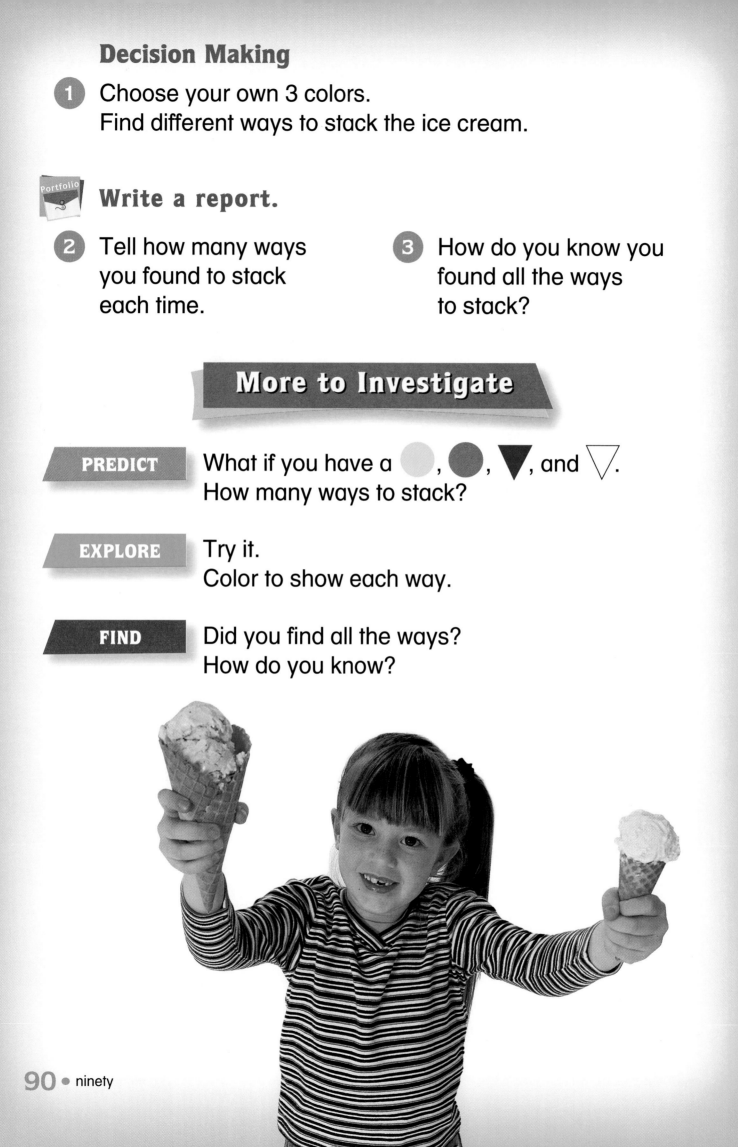, ● , ▼ , and ▽.
How many ways to stack?

EXPLORE Try it.
Color to show each way.

FIND Did you find all the ways?
How do you know?

Name _____

You need 10 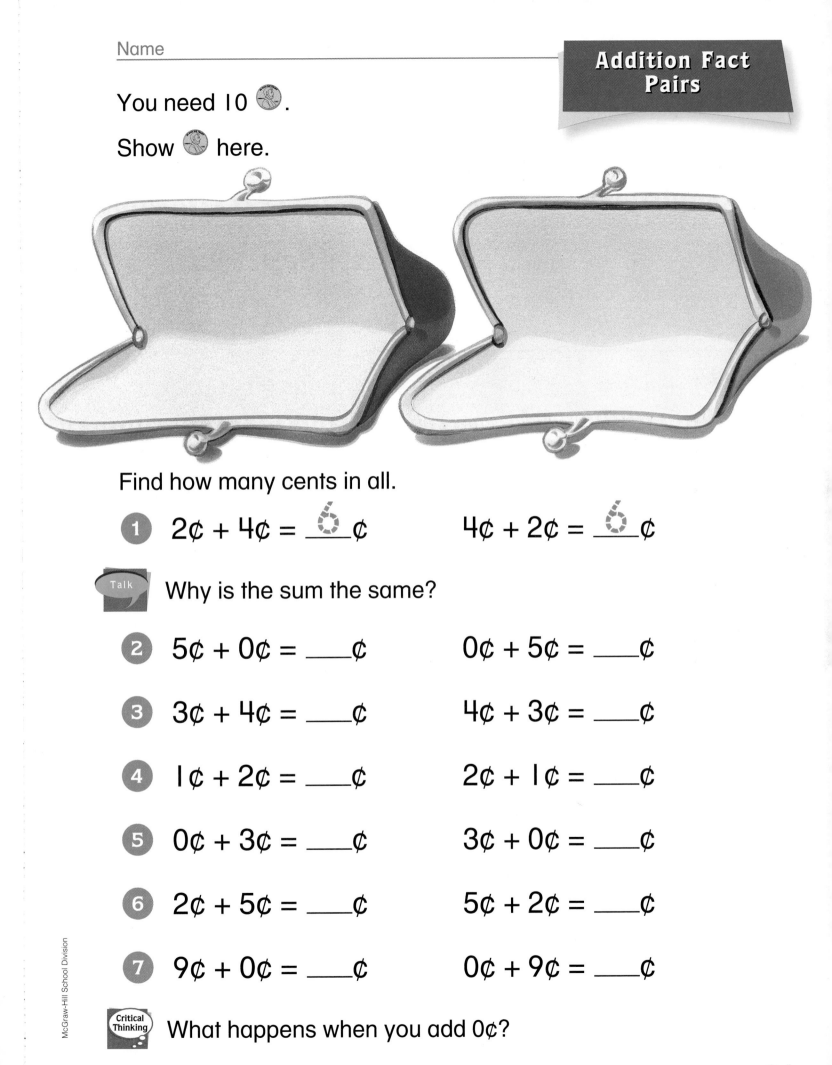.

Show here.

Find how many cents in all.

1 2¢ + 4¢ = __6__ ¢   4¢ + 2¢ = __6__ ¢

Talk Why is the sum the same?

2 5¢ + 0¢ = ___ ¢   0¢ + 5¢ = ___ ¢

3 3¢ + 4¢ = ___ ¢   4¢ + 3¢ = ___ ¢

4 1¢ + 2¢ = ___ ¢   2¢ + 1¢ = ___ ¢

5 0¢ + 3¢ = ___ ¢   3¢ + 0¢ = ___ ¢

6 2¢ + 5¢ = ___ ¢   5¢ + 2¢ = ___ ¢

7 9¢ + 0¢ = ___ ¢   0¢ + 9¢ = ___ ¢

Critical Thinking What happens when you add 0¢?

Practice!

Add.

1 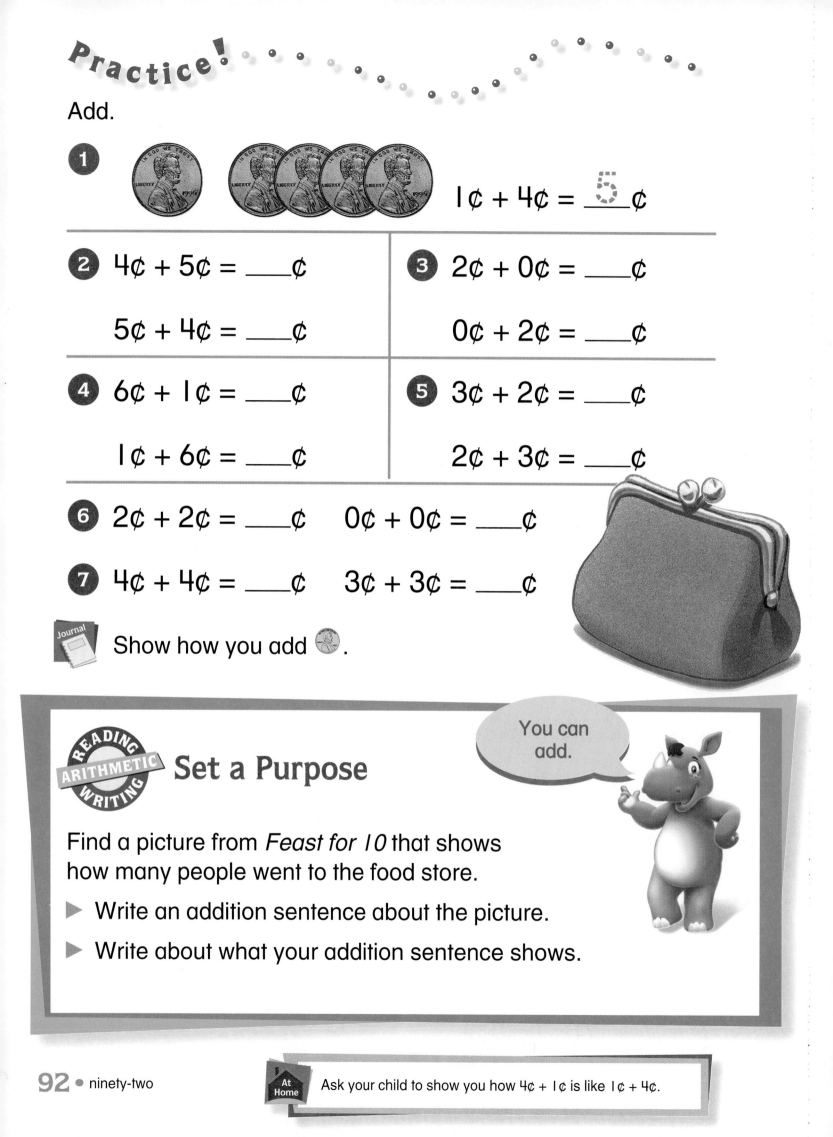   1¢ + 4¢ = __5__ ¢

2   4¢ + 5¢ = ___¢   **3**   2¢ + 0¢ = ___¢

     5¢ + 4¢ = ___¢   0¢ + 2¢ = ___¢

4   6¢ + 1¢ = ___¢   **5**   3¢ + 2¢ = ___¢

     1¢ + 6¢ = ___¢   2¢ + 3¢ = ___¢

6   2¢ + 2¢ = ___¢   0¢ + 0¢ = ___¢

7   4¢ + 4¢ = ___¢   3¢ + 3¢ = ___¢

Journal   Show how you add 🪙 .

READING · ARITHMETIC · WRITING   Set a Purpose

You can add.

Find a picture from *Feast for 10* that shows how many people went to the food store.

▶ Write an addition sentence about the picture.

▶ Write about what your addition sentence shows.

At Home   Ask your child to show you how 4¢ + 1¢ is like 1¢ + 4¢.

You can **count on** to add.
Start at 4. Count on 2.

Glossary

count on

4   5 6

4

$$4 + 2 = 6$$

Talk Do you have to count
the 4 eggs first? Why?

Count on to add.

3   4

1

3

$$3 + 1 = \underline{4}$$

2

6

$$6 + 2 = \underline{}$$

3

5

$$5 + 3 = \underline{}$$

4

8

$$8 + 1 = \underline{}$$

5

5

$$5 + 1 = \underline{}$$

6

3

$$3 + 3 = \underline{}$$

Critical Thinking Why can you count on to add?

Practice!

Count on to add.

1 ⟨6⟩ ⟨7⟩

6 + 1 = **7**

2 ⟨4⟩ ⟨5⟩ ⟨6⟩ ⟨7⟩

4 + 3 = ___

3 5 + 2 = ___   3 + 1 = ___   2 + 3 = ___

4 6 + 3 = ___   2 + 2 = ___   7 + 1 = ___

5 8 + 2 = ___   9 + 1 = ___   4 + 2 = ___

6 3 + 3 = ___   5 + 3 = ___   2 + 0 = ___

7 8 + 1 = ___   6 + 2 = ___   7 + 3 = ___

Mixed Review Test Preparation

8 Write parts for the total.

3	3
6	

10	

7	

9 Write how many cents.

___ ¢   ___ ¢

At Home Ask your child to tell you about counting on to add.

More Counting On

Here is another way to count on to add.

Start at 6. Count on 3.

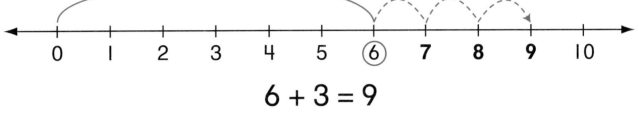

$$6 + 3 = 9$$

Count on to add.

1

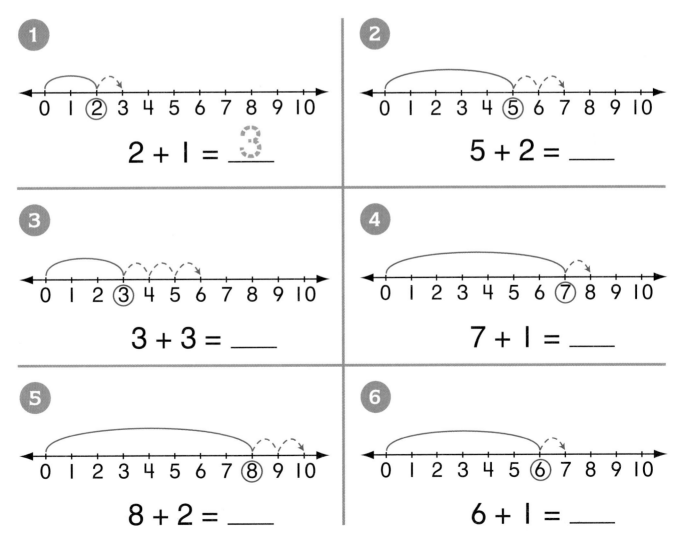

$$2 + 1 = \underline{3}$$

2

$$5 + 2 = \underline{}$$

3

$$3 + 3 = \underline{}$$

4

$$7 + 1 = \underline{}$$

5

$$8 + 2 = \underline{}$$

6

$$6 + 1 = \underline{}$$

Add.

$$0 \quad 1 \quad 2 \quad 3 \quad 4 \quad 5 \quad 6 \quad 7 \quad 8 \quad 9 \quad 10$$

1 $7 + 1 = \underline{8}$ $5 + 2 = \underline{}$ $4 + 1 = \underline{}$

2 $6 + 2 = \underline{}$ $4 + 3 = \underline{}$ $1 + 1 = \underline{}$

3 $2 + 1 = \underline{}$ $8 + 1 = \underline{}$ $7 + 2 = \underline{}$

4 $3 + 2 = \underline{}$ $7 + 3 = \underline{}$ $4 + 0 = \underline{}$

5 $5 + 3 = \underline{}$ $9 + 1 = \underline{}$ $6 + 1 = \underline{}$

Cultural Connection

The Ancient Inca

This is an old way to count.

$$0 \quad 1 \quad 2 \quad 3 \quad 4 \quad 5 \quad 6 \quad 7 \quad 8 \quad 9 \quad 10$$

Add on the rope.

$3 + 2 = \underline{}$ $5 + 1 = \underline{}$ $6 + 3 = \underline{}$

$5 + 2 = \underline{}$ $7 + 2 = \underline{}$ $8 + 1 = \underline{}$

$3 + 0 = \underline{}$ $3 + 1 = \underline{}$ $8 + 2 = \underline{}$

 At Home   Ask your child to show you how to count on to add on the number line.

Supermarket Race

You need 2 🐀 and a 🎲.

Take turns.

▶ Roll the 🎲.

▶ Move that many spaces.

▶ Next turn. Add.

▶ Move that many spaces.

Winner: first player to get to *Checkout*

Start

3 + 2	
6 + 2	

5 + 1	3 + 1	7 + 2	2 + 2

1 + 1

1 + 0	4 + 2	5 + 0	3 + 3	4 + 1	1 + 2	4 + 3
7 + 1						
2 + 3	5 + 3	2 + 1	5 + 2	2 + 0	6 + 3	6 + 1

Checkout

Add.

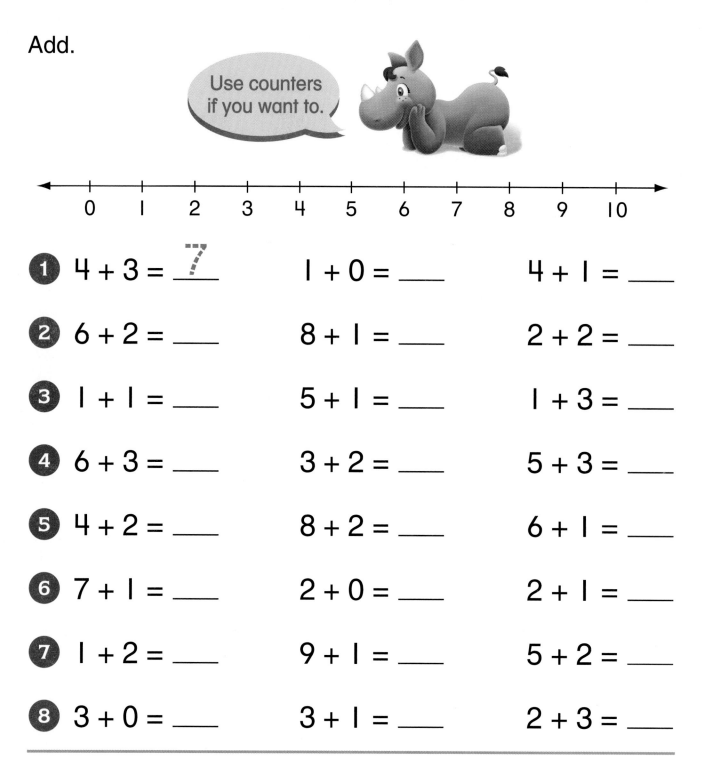

Use counters if you want to.

1. $4 + 3 = \underline{7}$ $1 + 0 = \underline{}$ $4 + 1 = \underline{}$

2. $6 + 2 = \underline{}$ $8 + 1 = \underline{}$ $2 + 2 = \underline{}$

3. $1 + 1 = \underline{}$ $5 + 1 = \underline{}$ $1 + 3 = \underline{}$

4. $6 + 3 = \underline{}$ $3 + 2 = \underline{}$ $5 + 3 = \underline{}$

5. $4 + 2 = \underline{}$ $8 + 2 = \underline{}$ $6 + 1 = \underline{}$

6. $7 + 1 = \underline{}$ $2 + 0 = \underline{}$ $2 + 1 = \underline{}$

7. $1 + 2 = \underline{}$ $9 + 1 = \underline{}$ $5 + 2 = \underline{}$

8. $3 + 0 = \underline{}$ $3 + 1 = \underline{}$ $2 + 3 = \underline{}$

Find how many in all.

9. _____ in all

___ + ___ = ___

10. _____ in all

___ + ___ = ___

Can You Add to Solve?

Listen Listen to the problem.

Talk What do you need to find?
Can you add to find the answer?

Read
Plan
Solve
Look Back

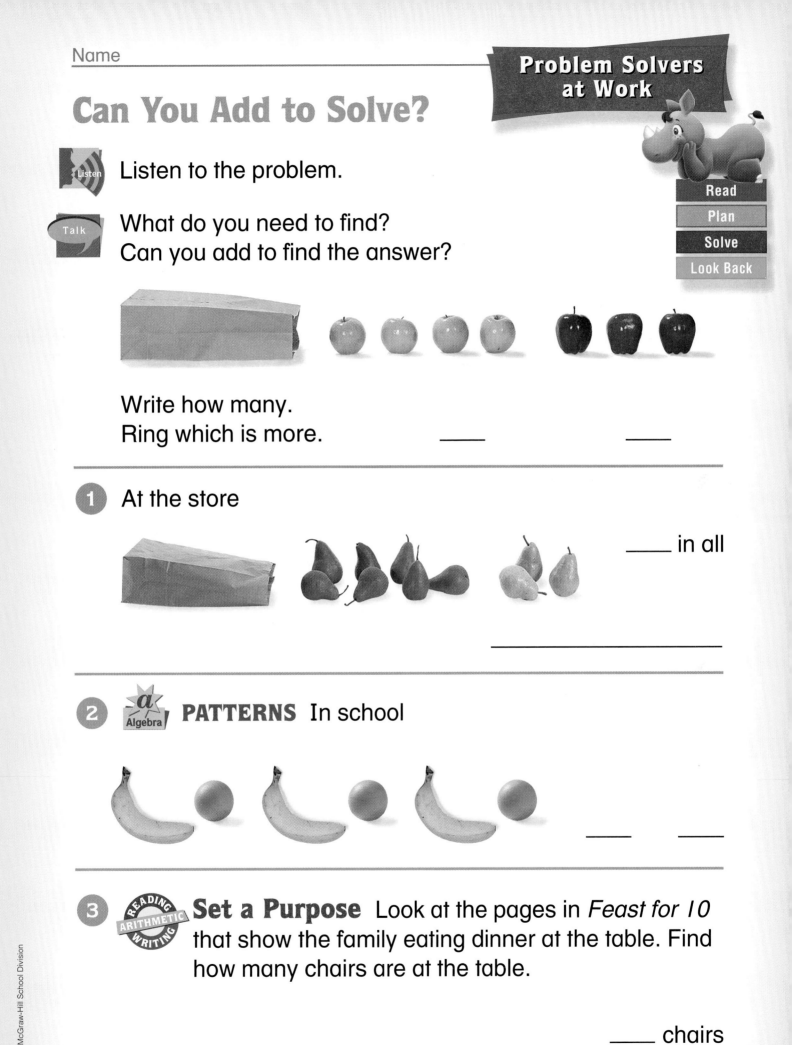

Write how many.
Ring which is more.   ____   ____

---

1 At the store

____ in all

_____

---

2 🌟 *a* Algebra **PATTERNS** In school

____   ____

---

3 READING ARITHMETIC WRITING **Set a Purpose** Look at the pages in *Feast for 10* that show the family eating dinner at the table. Find how many chairs are at the table.

____ chairs

1 How many in all?

_____ in all

_____

2 ⭐ **Algebra** **PATTERNS** Show what comes next.

_____ _____ _____

Write and Share

Diane wrote this problem.

How many birds and bears?

Diane Liu
P.S. 144
Forest Hills,
New York

3 Solve Diane's problem. _____

Talk How did you solve Diane's problem?

4 **Write** Write a problem.
Have a partner solve it.

Your partner's answer: _____

 At Home Ask your child to tell you about the problem he or she wrote.

Chapter Review

Language and Mathematics

Choose the correct word to complete the sentence.

addition sentence
count on
plus
sum

1 6 + 1 = 7 is an _____.

2 5 _____ 3 equals 8.

Concepts and Skills

Write the addition sentence.

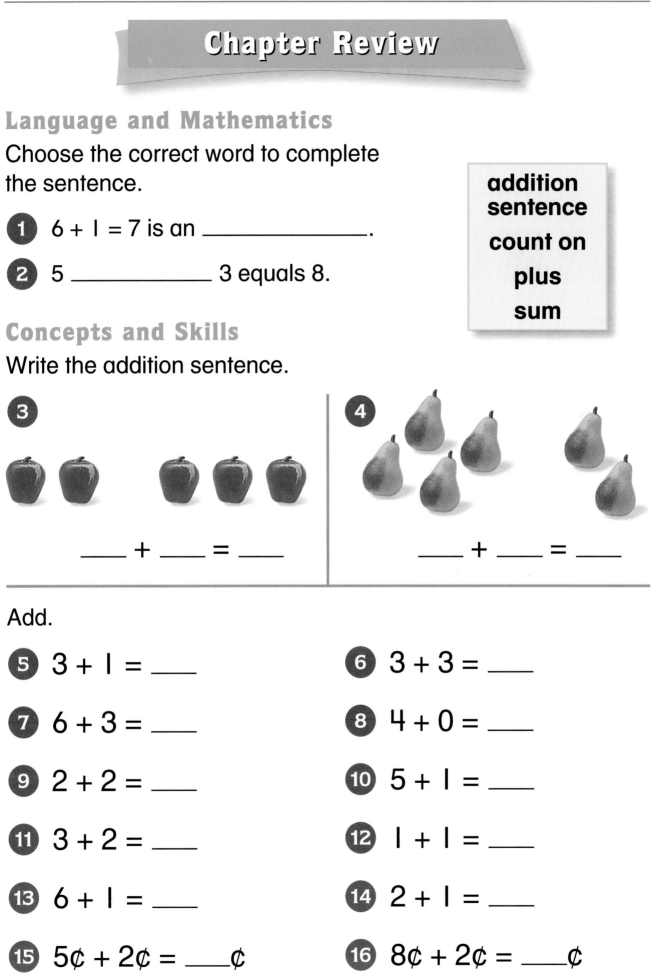

3

___ + ___ = ___

4

___ + ___ = ___

Add.

5 3 + 1 = ___

6 3 + 3 = ___

7 6 + 3 = ___

8 4 + 0 = ___

9 2 + 2 = ___

10 5 + 1 = ___

11 3 + 2 = ___

12 1 + 1 = ___

13 6 + 1 = ___

14 2 + 1 = ___

15 5¢ + 2¢ = ___¢

16 8¢ + 2¢ = ___¢

Problem Solving

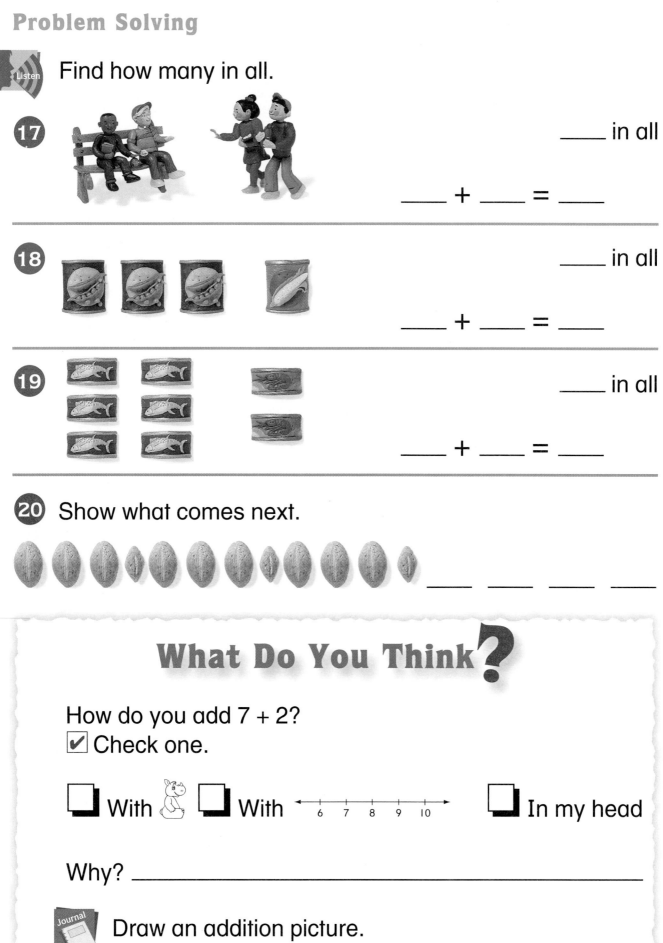

Find how many in all.

17 ___ in all

___ + ___ = ___

18 ___ in all

___ + ___ = ___

19 ___ in all

___ + ___ = ___

20 Show what comes next.

___ ___ ___ ___

What Do You Think?

How do you add 7 + 2?
☑ Check one.

☐ With 🐶   ☐ With 6 7 8 9 10   ☐ In my head

Why? _____

Draw an addition picture.
Write the addition sentence.

Name _____

Chapter Test

Write the addition sentence.

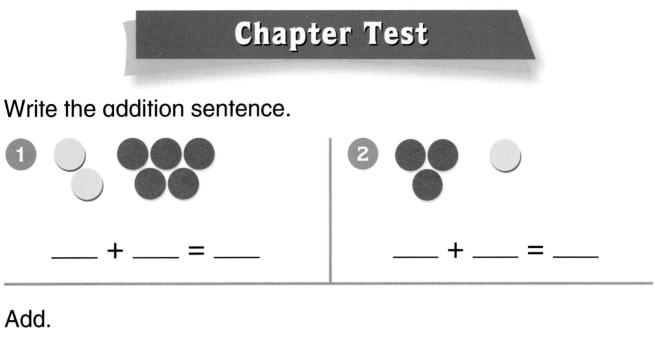

1 ___ + ___ = ___

2 ___ + ___ = ___

Add.

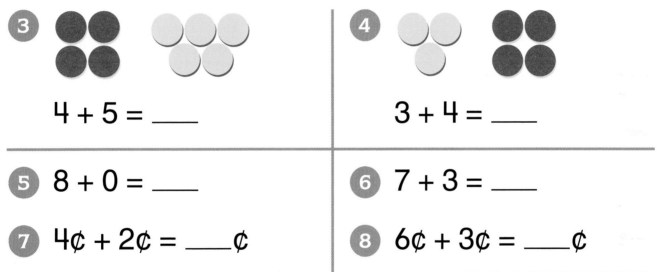

3 $4 + 5 =$ ___

4 $3 + 4 =$ ___

5 $8 + 0 =$ ___

6 $7 + 3 =$ ___

7 $4¢ + 2¢ =$ ___ ¢

8 $6¢ + 3¢ =$ ___ ¢

Listen Find how many in all.

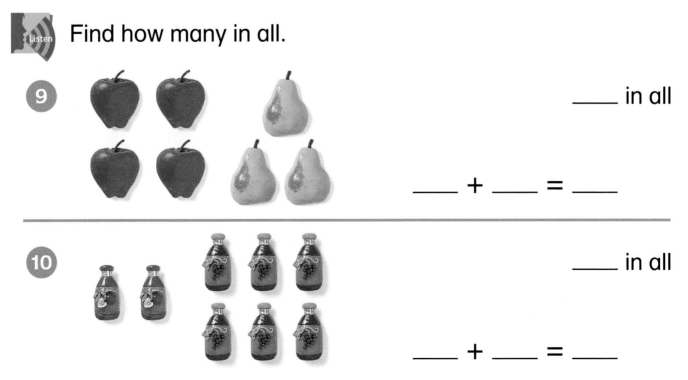

9 ___ in all

___ + ___ = ___

10 ___ in all

___ + ___ = ___

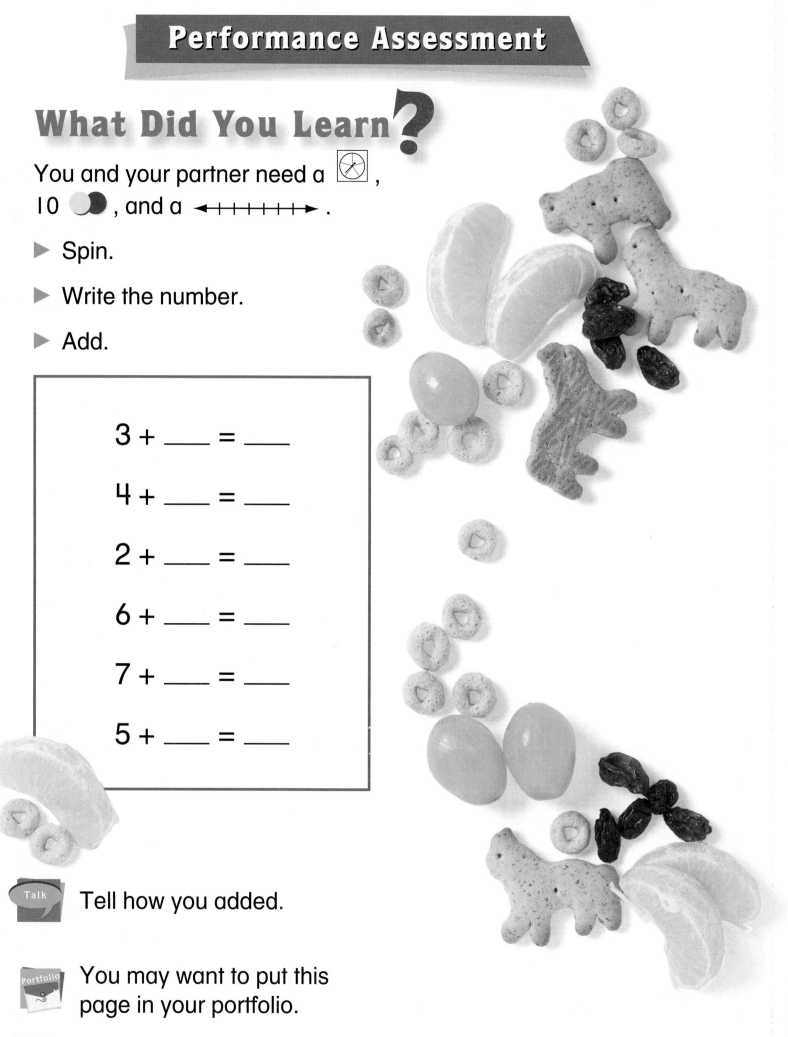

What Did You Learn?

You and your partner need a ⊗ ,
10 ◖◗ , and a ←++++++→ .

▶ Spin.

▶ Write the number.

▶ Add.

3 + ___ = ___

4 + ___ = ___

2 + ___ = ___

6 + ___ = ___

7 + ___ = ___

5 + ___ = ___

Talk Tell how you added.

Portfolio You may want to put this
page in your portfolio.

Math Connection

Patterns and Functions

Name _____

Addition Tables

a Algebra Complete the table. Use counting.

+	0	1	2	3	4	5	6	7	8	9
0	0	1	2	3		5	6	7	8	9
1	1	2	3	4	5		7	8	9	10
2	2	3	4	5	6	7		9	10	
3	3		5	6	7	8	9	10		
4	4	5	6	7	8	9	10			
5	5		7	8	9	10				
6	6	7	8		10					
7		8	9	10						
8	8		10							
9	9									

Use the table to add.

1   4 + 2 = _6_   5 + 3 = ___   2 + 2 = ___

2   7 + 3 = ___   6 + 2 = ___   4 + 3 = ___

Dot Stories

Talk What number stories can you tell about the pictures below?

You need 10 dots.

▶ Draw a picture using some dots.

▶ Tell a number story about your dot picture.

▶ Trade pictures with a partner.

▶ Tell another number story.

Cumulative Review

Mark your answer.

1 Ann has 5 crayons. How many crayons are in the box?

Total: 5 crayons

⬭ 2
⬭ 3
⬭ 4
⬭ 5

2 The numbers are in order. What is the missing number?

5, 6, ☐, 8, 9, 10

⬭ 5
⬭ 6
⬭ 7
⬭ 8

3 What is the word for the number?

3

⬭ two
⬭ three
⬭ four
⬭ five

4 Add.

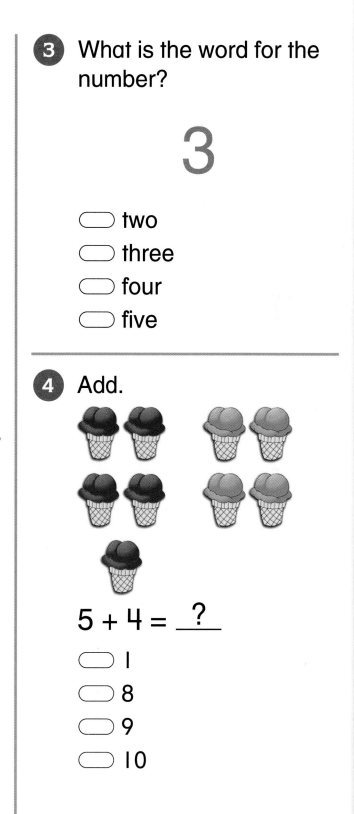

5 + 4 = ___?___

⬭ 1
⬭ 8
⬭ 9
⬭ 10

5 David's family is eating chicken drumsticks for dinner. There are seven drumsticks. Which number tells how many?

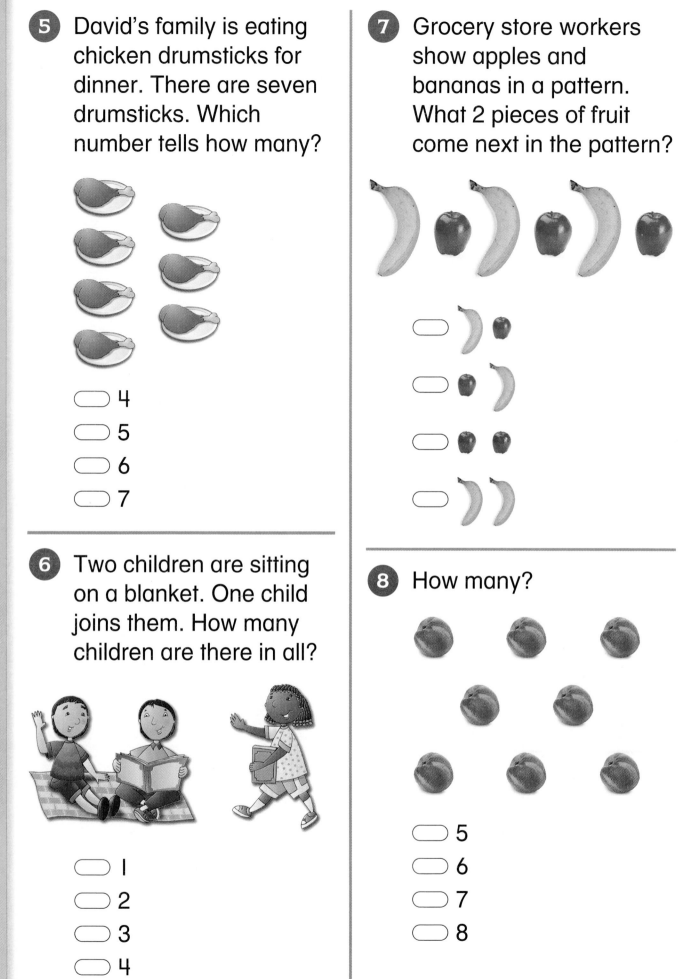

◯ 4
◯ 5
◯ 6
◯ 7

6 Two children are sitting on a blanket. One child joins them. How many children are there in all?

◯ 1
◯ 2
◯ 3
◯ 4

7 Grocery store workers show apples and bananas in a pattern. What 2 pieces of fruit come next in the pattern?

◯ 🍌 🍎
◯ 🍎 🍌
◯ 🍎 🍎
◯ 🍌 🍌

8 How many?

◯ 5
◯ 6
◯ 7
◯ 8

Name _____

Food Totals

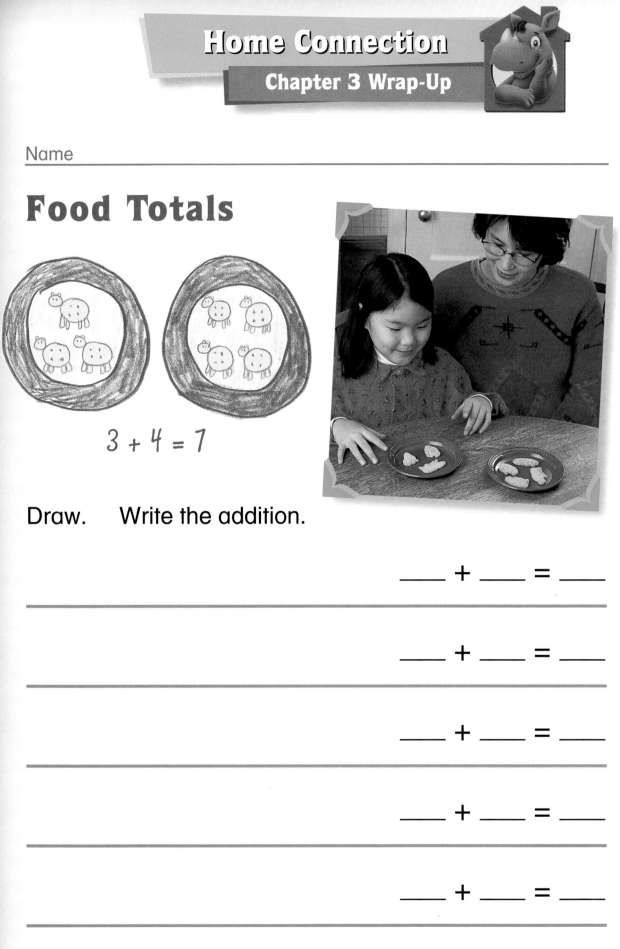

$3 + 4 = 7$

Draw.   Write the addition.

___ + ___ = ___

___ + ___ = ___

___ + ___ = ___

___ + ___ = ___

___ + ___ = ___

At Home Choose food items such as crackers, raisins, or dried macaroni to help your child practice addition. Use 2 plates to show 2 groups of a food item for a total of no more than 10. Your child draws to show the 2 groups, adds, and then writes the addition sentence.

At
Home

Dear Family,

I am starting a new chapter in my mathematics book. I am going to learn to subtract. I will use pictures and numbers to show subtraction.

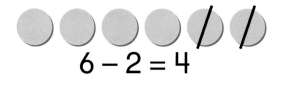

6 – 2 = 4

I will also learn about folktales and favorite stories.

Learning about Folktales

Let's talk about stories we like. We can draw a picture to show our favorite story.

My Math Words

I am going to use these math words in this chapter.

Please help me make word cards for these math words. I can use the word cards when I practice subtraction.

subtract
minus
equals
subtraction
   sentence
difference
count back

Your child,

_____
Signature

Beginning to Subtract
Theme: Folktales and Rhymes

THE GREAT BALL GAME
A MUSKOGEE STORY
RETOLD BY JOSEPH BRUCHAC
ILLUSTRATED BY SUSAN L. ROTH

READING ARITHMETIC WRITING

Ask Questions You may have questions as you listen to the first part of *The Great Ball Game*. The answers may be in the next part of the story.

What questions can you ask? Listen to the rest of the story. Tell about rhyme answers.

111

Name _____

What Do You Know?

You need 10 .

Show the total here.

Find the missing part.

1.

5	
7	

4	
5	

4	
8	

2.

	6
10	

	2
6	

	1
4	

Show how you find the missing part.

Name _____

Working Together

You need 10 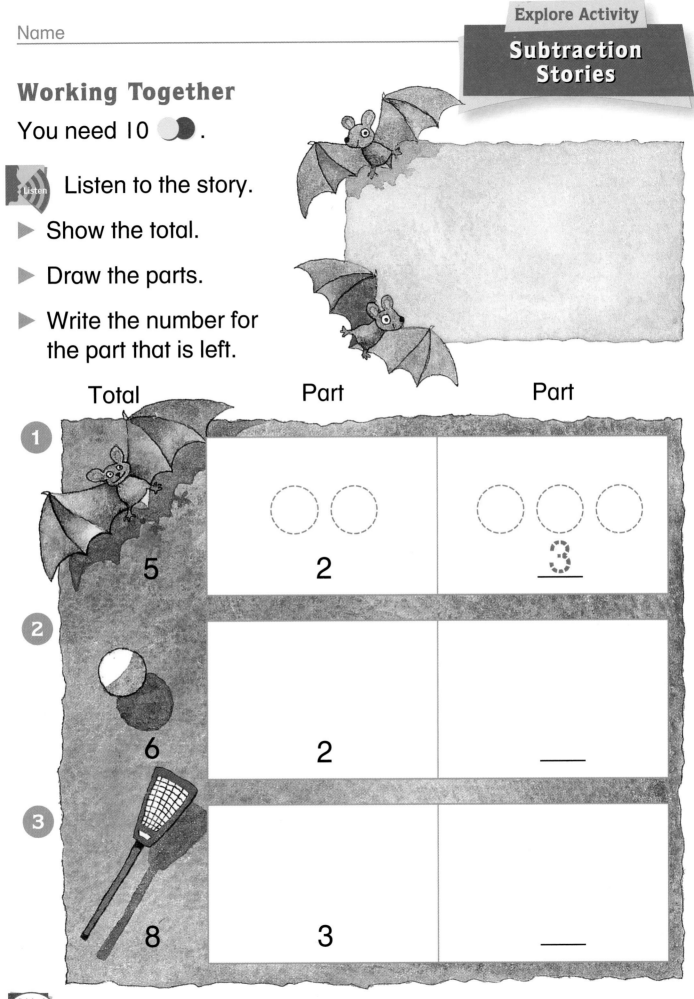.

Listen Listen to the story.

▶ Show the total.

▶ Draw the parts.

▶ Write the number for the part that is left.

	Total	Part	Part
1	5	○ ○ 2	○ ○ ○ 3
2	6	2	___
3	8	3	___

 Critical Thinking How can you check that the part you write is correct?

McGraw-Hill School Division

Practice!

Take turns.

▶ You show the total.

▶ Your partner takes part away and draws it.

▶ You draw and write the part that is left.

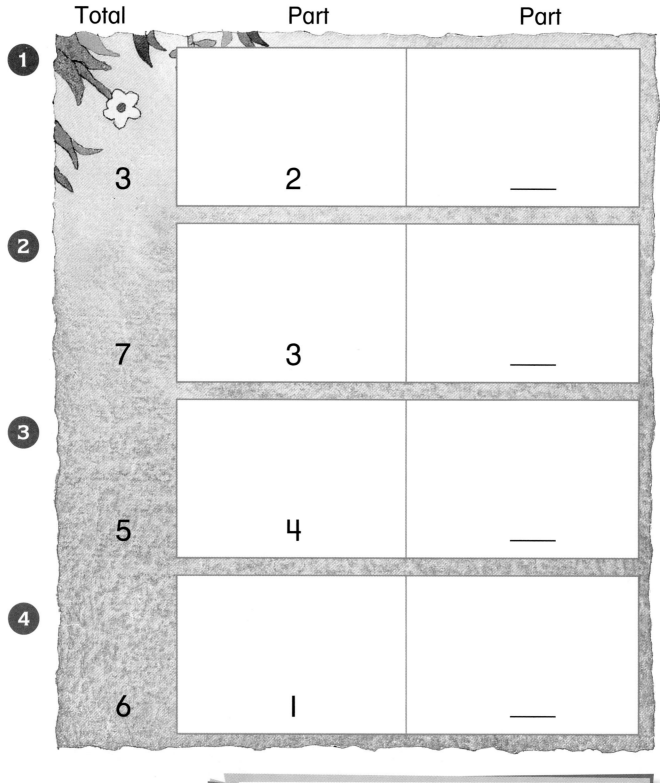

	Total	Part	Part
1	3	2	___
2	7	3	___
3	5	4	___
4	6	1	___

 At Home Have your child tell you a story about exercise 1 above.

You need 10 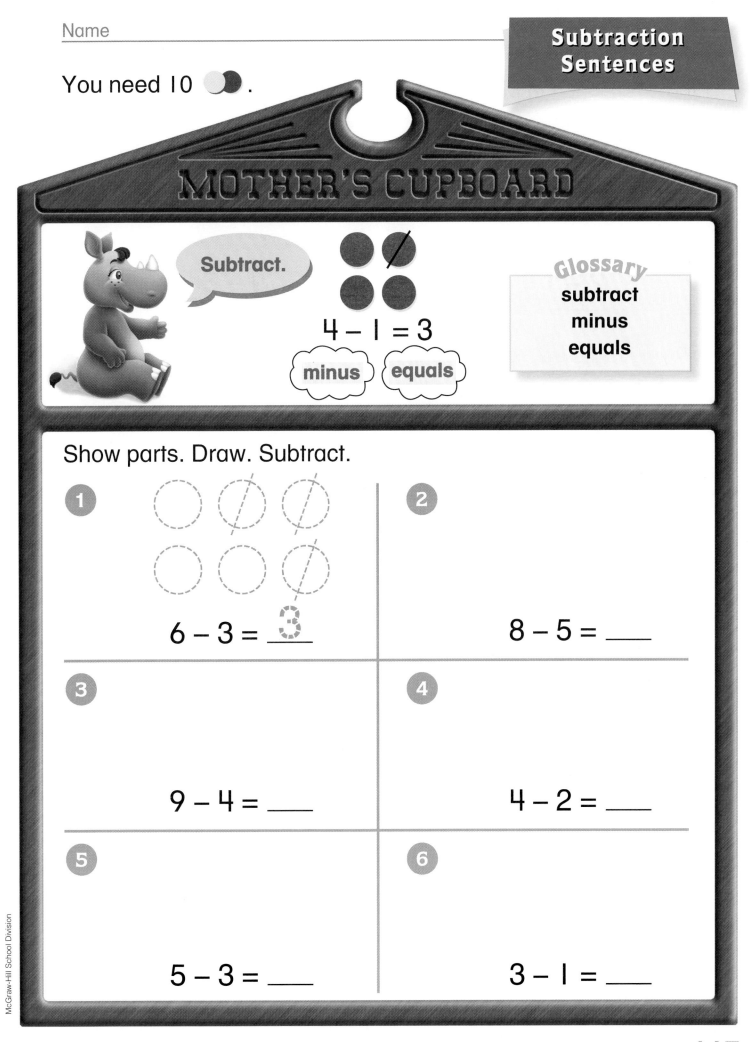.

MOTHER'S CUPBOARD

Subtract.

$4 - 1 = 3$

minus   equals

Glossary
subtract
minus
equals

Show parts. Draw. Subtract.

1   $6 - 3 = 3$

2   $8 - 5 = \underline{}$

3   $9 - 4 = \underline{}$

4   $4 - 2 = \underline{}$

5   $5 - 3 = \underline{}$

6   $3 - 1 = \underline{}$

McGraw-Hill School Division

Practice!

Find what is left in Mother Hubbard's cupboard.

1.

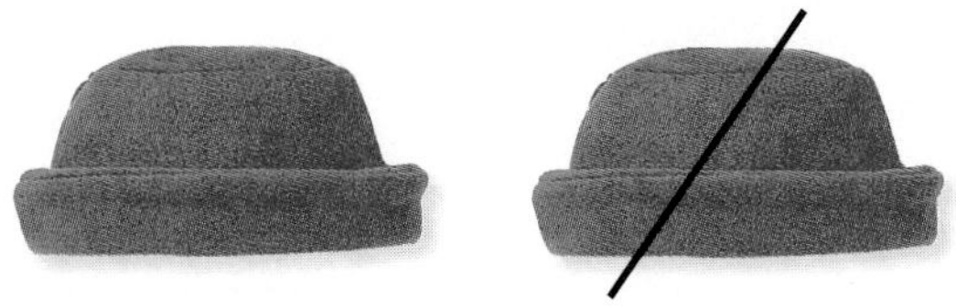

$2 - 1 =$ 1

2.

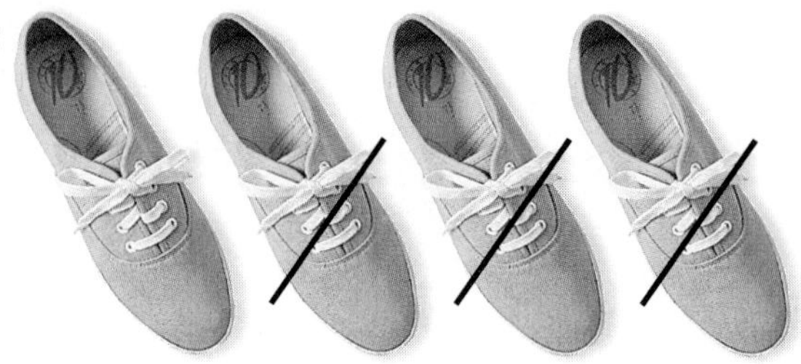

$4 - 3 =$ ____

3.

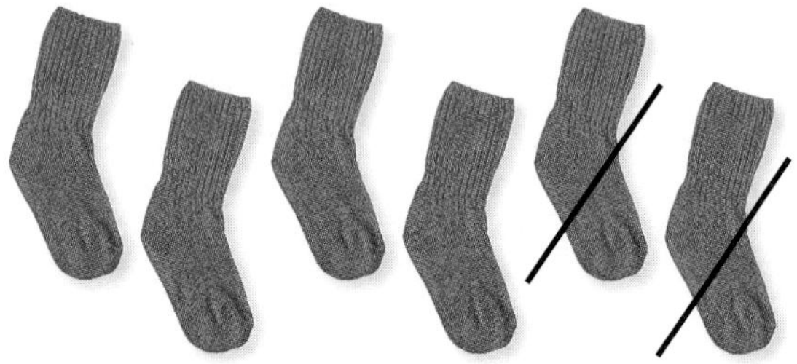

$6 - 2 =$ ____

4.

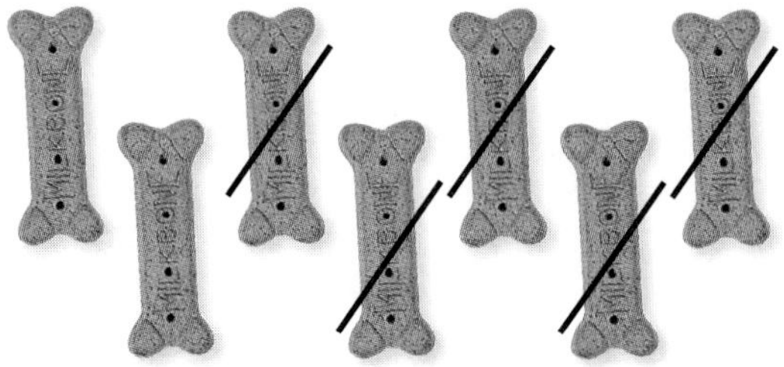

$7 - 5 =$ ____

5.

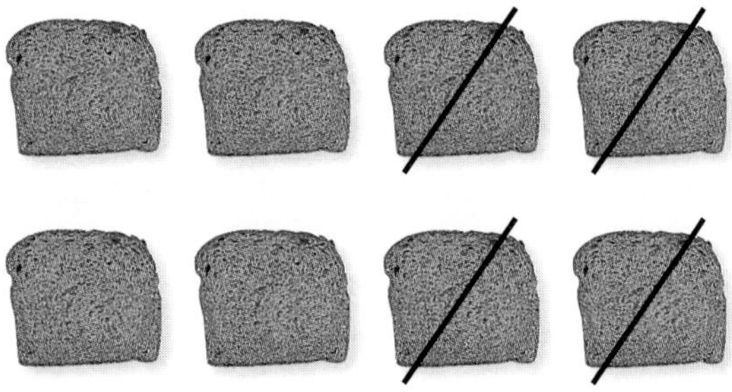

$8 - 4 =$ ____

6.

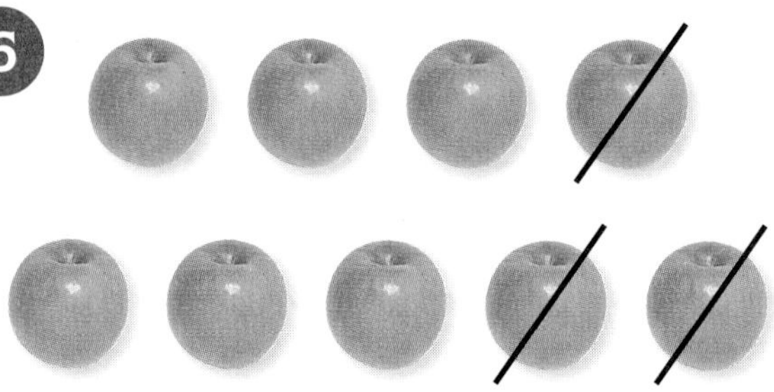

$9 - 3 =$ ____

Mixed Review Test Preparation

7. $5 + 1 =$ ____ $7 + 3 =$ ____ $6 + 2 =$ ____

8. Find the missing part.

5	
5	

2	
3	

1	
8	

At Home: Your child has begun to subtract. Have your child tell you about the subtraction exercises on this page.

Name _____

MOTHER'S CUPBOARD

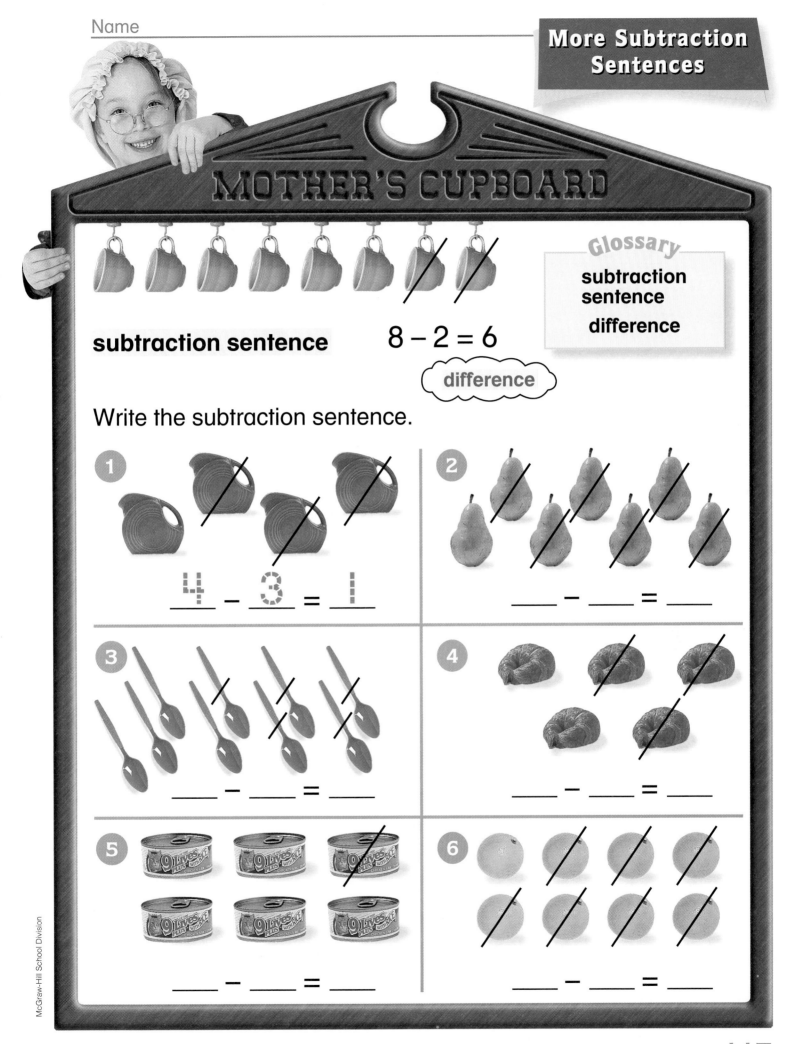

Glossary

subtraction sentence

difference

subtraction sentence $8 - 2 = 6$

difference

Write the subtraction sentence.

1 $4 - 3 = 1$

2   ___ − ___ = ___

3   ___ − ___ = ___

4   ___ − ___ = ___

5   ___ − ___ = ___

6   ___ − ___ = ___

CHAPTER 4 *Lesson 2*

Practice!

Write the subtraction sentence.

1

$$3 - 1 = 2$$

2

$$\underline{} - \underline{} = \underline{}$$

3

$$\underline{} - \underline{} = \underline{}$$

4

$$\underline{} - \underline{} = \underline{}$$

READING ARITHMETIC WRITING

Ask Questions

Tell a subtraction story for each picture.

▶ Ask a question.

▶ Write a subtraction sentence.

$$\underline{} - \underline{} = \underline{}$$

$$\underline{} - \underline{} = \underline{}$$

Name _____

Write a Subtraction Sentence

You need 10 .

Listen Listen to the problem.

Read
Plan
Solve
Look Back

1 At the river ___6___ are left.

__9__ – __3__ = __6__

Talk Tell how you found the answer.

2 At the waterfall ____ are left.

____ – ____ = ____

3 At the game ____ are left.

____ – ____ = ____

Talk Make up a different problem about 10 rhinos.

Practice!

Make up a problem for the picture.
Find how many are left.

1 _2_ are left.

_4_ – _2_ = _2_

2 ____ are left.

____ – ____ = ____

3 ____ are left.

____ – ____ = ____

More to Explore   **Number Sense**

There are 5 🐑 .
How many are hiding? ____

There are 10 🐐 .
How many are hiding? ____

 At Home
Ask your child to tell you a subtraction story about the ballplayers in problem 3.

Name _____

Do your best!

Find how many are left.

1 At the game ____ are left.

____ – ____ = ____

Subtract.

2 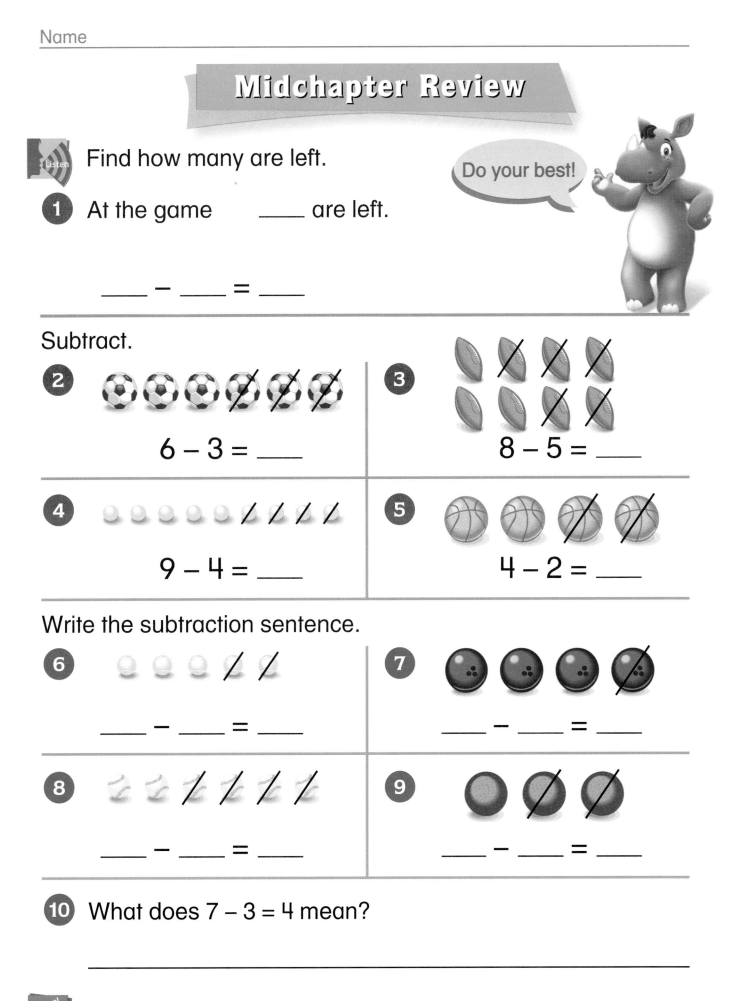 6 – 3 = ____

3 8 – 5 = ____

4 9 – 4 = ____

5 4 – 2 = ____

Write the subtraction sentence.

6 ____ – ____ = ____

7 ____ – ____ = ____

8 ____ – ____ = ____

9 ____ – ____ = ____

10 What does 7 – 3 = 4 mean?

_____

Journal

Draw a picture that shows subtraction.

Collect Them All

You need a .

Take turns.

▶ Roll the 🎲.

▶ Write the number you roll to show a difference.

▶ Fill the page.

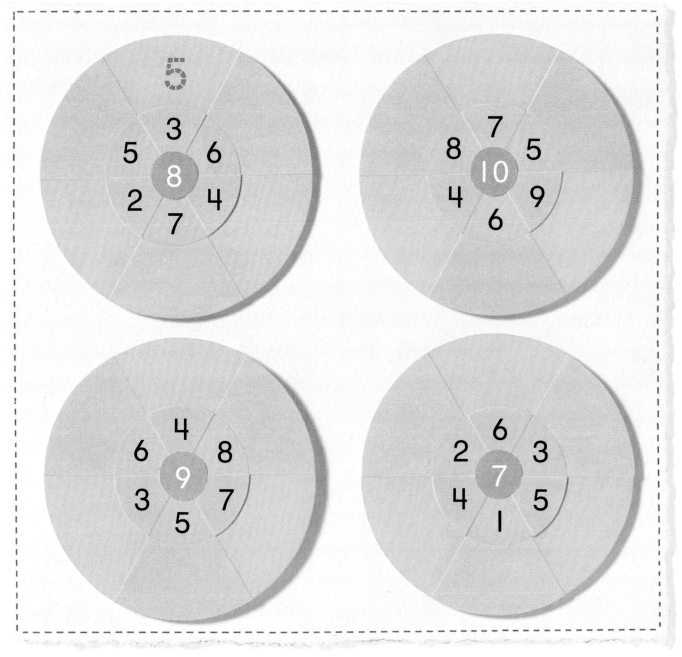

5

3
5   6
8
2   4
7

7
8   5
10
4   9
6

4
6   8
9
3   7
5

6
2   3
7
4   5
1

Collect Them All

Name

Books and More Books

Listen to
The Great Ball Game.

Talk

What kind of book is
The Great Ball Game?
What kinds of books do you
have in your classroom library?

Cultural Note

Ball games have
been played by
Native Americans
for centuries.

Working Together

▶ Sort some books from the
classroom library.

▶ Decide how you want to
sort the books.

How many different
kinds of books do you have?

_____

_____

Show how you sorted.

McGraw-Hill School Division

Decision Making

 Choose another way to sort the books.

Show how you sorted.

1 How many kinds of books do you have now?

_____

2 Do you have more or fewer kinds of books?

_____

Write a report.

3 Show what you found.

4 Tell how you sorted the books each time.

More to Investigate

PREDICT What kinds of books do your classmates like best?

EXPLORE Take a survey.

FIND What kind of book is the most popular book on your survey?

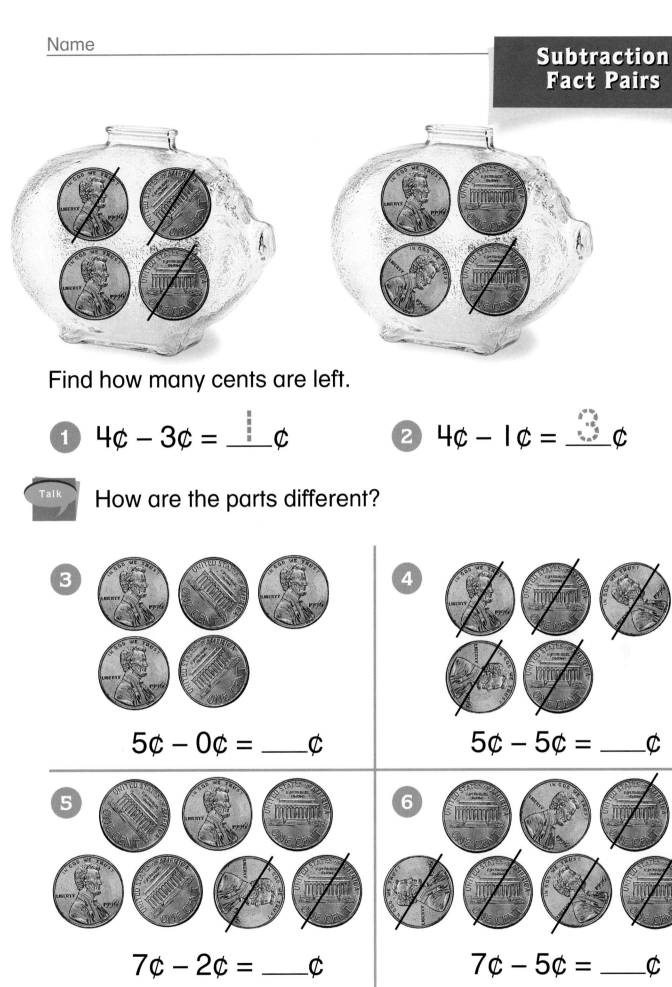

Find how many cents are left.

1 4¢ – 3¢ = __1__ ¢

2 4¢ – 1¢ = __3__ ¢

Talk How are the parts different?

3 5¢ – 0¢ = ___ ¢

4 5¢ – 5¢ = ___ ¢

5 7¢ – 2¢ = ___ ¢

6 7¢ – 5¢ = ___ ¢

Critical Thinking What happens when you subtract 0¢?

Practice!

Subtract. Use pennies if you want to.

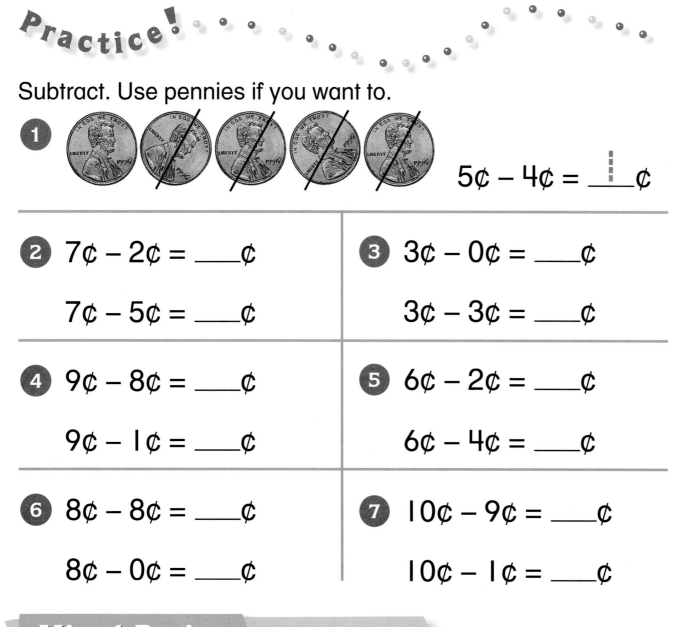

1. $5¢ - 4¢ = \underline{}¢$

2. $7¢ - 2¢ = \underline{}¢$

   $7¢ - 5¢ = \underline{}¢$

3. $3¢ - 0¢ = \underline{}¢$

   $3¢ - 3¢ = \underline{}¢$

4. $9¢ - 8¢ = \underline{}¢$

   $9¢ - 1¢ = \underline{}¢$

5. $6¢ - 2¢ = \underline{}¢$

   $6¢ - 4¢ = \underline{}¢$

6. $8¢ - 8¢ = \underline{}¢$

   $8¢ - 0¢ = \underline{}¢$

7. $10¢ - 9¢ = \underline{}¢$

   $10¢ - 1¢ = \underline{}¢$

Mixed Review Test Preparation

Count backward.

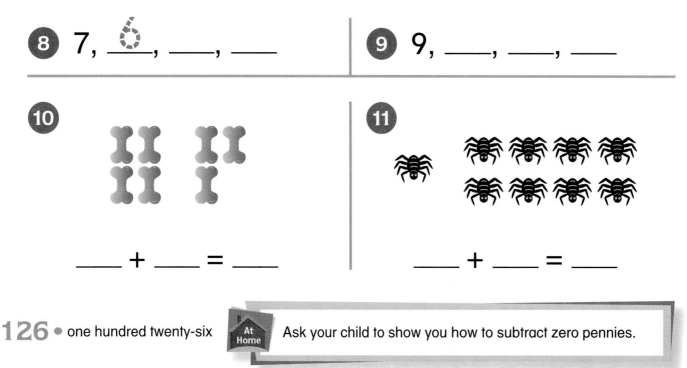

8. 7, 6, ____, ____

9. 9, ____, ____, ____

10. ____ + ____ = ____

11. ____ + ____ = ____

At Home Ask your child to show you how to subtract zero pennies.

Counting Back

You can **count back** to subtract.
Start at 7. Count back 2.

7   6   5

7

7 − 2 = 5

Talk How do you know how many beans are left in the bag?

Count back to subtract.

1

3   2

3

3 − 1 = 2

2

5

5 − 2 = ___

3

4

4 − 3 = ___

4

9

9 − 1 = ___

5

8

8 − 3 = ___

6

6

6 − 2 = ___

Critical Thinking How does counting back help you subtract?

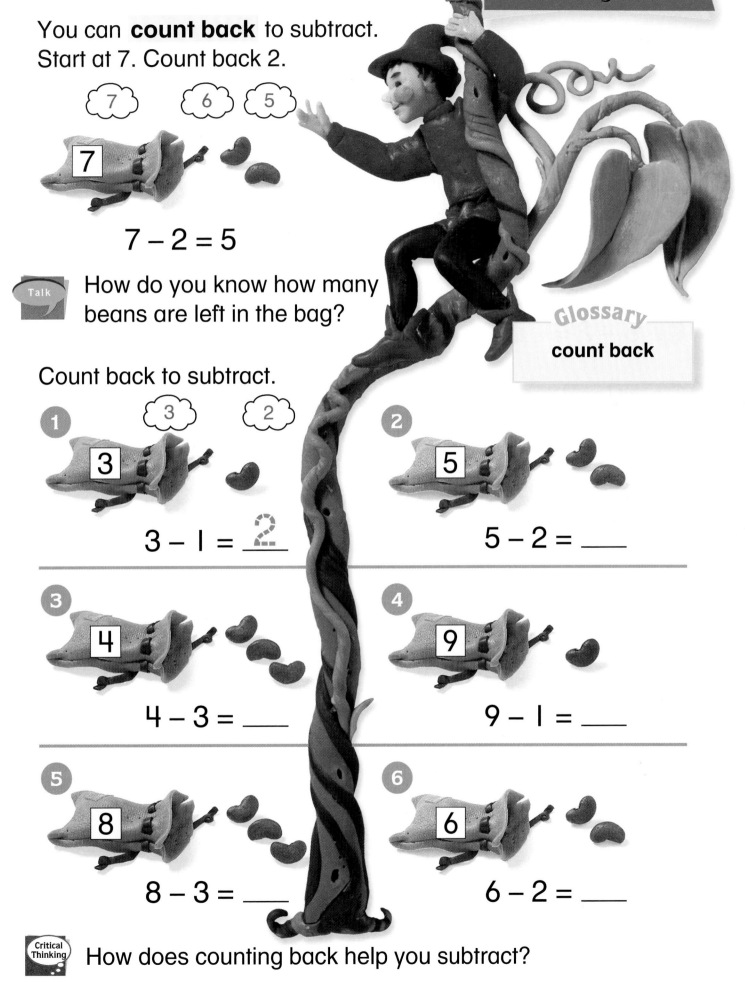

Practice!

Count back to subtract.

1   2   1

2

$2 - 1 = \underline{1}$

2   5   4   3   2

5

$5 - 3 = \underline{}$

3 $6 - 1 = \underline{}$ $7 - 2 = \underline{}$ $10 - 2 = \underline{}$

4 $8 - 2 = \underline{}$ $4 - 1 = \underline{}$ $9 - 2 = \underline{}$

5 $10 - 3 = \underline{}$ $3 - 2 = \underline{}$ $5 - 1 = \underline{}$

6 $9 - 1 = \underline{}$ $7 - 3 = \underline{}$ $8 - 3 = \underline{}$

7 $5 - 2 = \underline{}$ $10 - 2 = \underline{}$ $6 - 3 = \underline{}$

More to Explore   Patterns

a Algebra   **PATTERNS** Look for a pattern. Complete.

$9 - 1 = \underline{}$ $5 - 1 = \underline{}$

$8 - 1 = \underline{}$ $4 - 1 = \underline{}$

$7 - 1 = \underline{}$ $3 - 1 = \underline{}$

$6 - 1 = \underline{}$ $2 - 1 = \underline{}$

At Home   Ask your child to tell you about counting back to subtract.

More Counting Back

Here is another way to count back to subtract.

Start at 9. Count back 3.

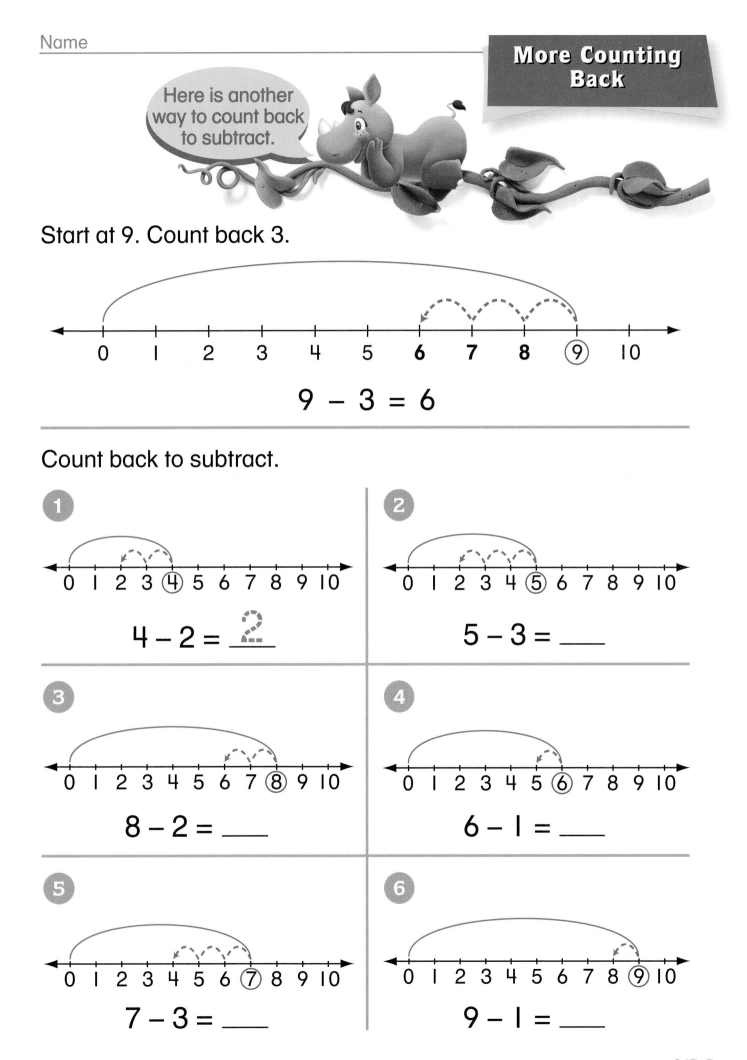

$9 - 3 = 6$

Count back to subtract.

1

$4 - 2 = 2$

2

$5 - 3 = $ ___

3

$8 - 2 = $ ___

4

$6 - 1 = $ ___

5

$7 - 3 = $ ___

6

$9 - 1 = $ ___

Practice!

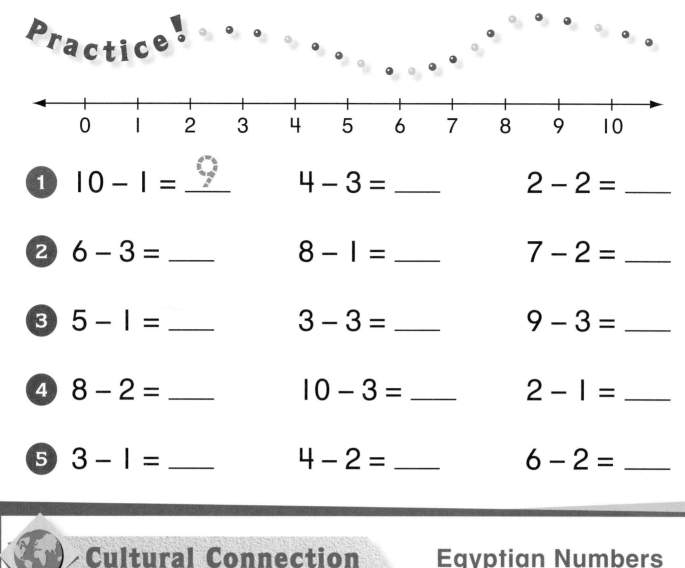

0 1 2 3 4 5 6 7 8 9 10

1 10 – 1 = __9__   4 – 3 = ____   2 – 2 = ____

2 6 – 3 = ____   8 – 1 = ____   7 – 2 = ____

3 5 – 1 = ____   3 – 3 = ____   9 – 3 = ____

4 8 – 2 = ____   10 – 3 = ____   2 – 1 = ____

5 3 – 1 = ____   4 – 2 = ____   6 – 2 = ____

Cultural Connection   Egyptian Numbers

These numbers were used a long time ago.

| = 1   ∩ = 10

You can subtract with Egyptian numbers.

| (10) | (1) | (9) | (6) | (2) | (4) |

∩ – | = ||||||||| _____ ||||| – || = _____

||||| – |||| = _____   ∩ – |||| = _____

 At Home Ask your child to show you how to count back to subtract on a number line.

Flying South

You need 2 🐾 and a ⊗.

▶ Put your 🐾 on 10.

▶ Take turns. Spin.

▶ Subtract. Move your 🐾 to the difference.

The first player to get to *South* wins.

10 9 8 7 6 5 4 3 2 1

SOUTH

Subtract.

Number line: 0 1 2 3 4 5 6 7 8 9 10

1 8 − 2 = 6   2 − 1 = ___   5 − 0 = ___

2 9 − 3 = ___   7 − 2 = ___   6 − 2 = ___

3 10 − 2 = ___   1 − 1 = ___   3 − 2 = ___

4 4 − 2 = ___   10 − 3 = ___   9 − 0 = ___

5 8 − 1 = ___   7 − 1 = ___   5 − 2 = ___

6 6 − 3 = ___   2 − 0 = ___   8 − 3 = ___

7 4 − 1 = ___   9 − 2 = ___   8 − 0 = ___

8 7 − 3 = ___   10 − 1 = ___   9 − 1 = ___

Find out how many are left.

9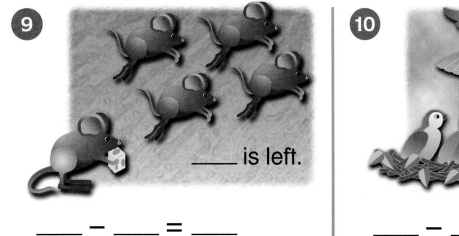
_____ is left.

___ − ___ = ___

10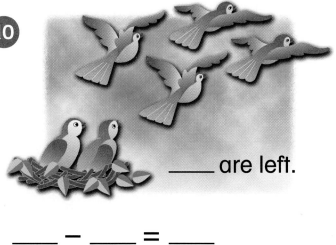
_____ are left.

___ − ___ = ___

Name _____

Can You Subtract to Solve?

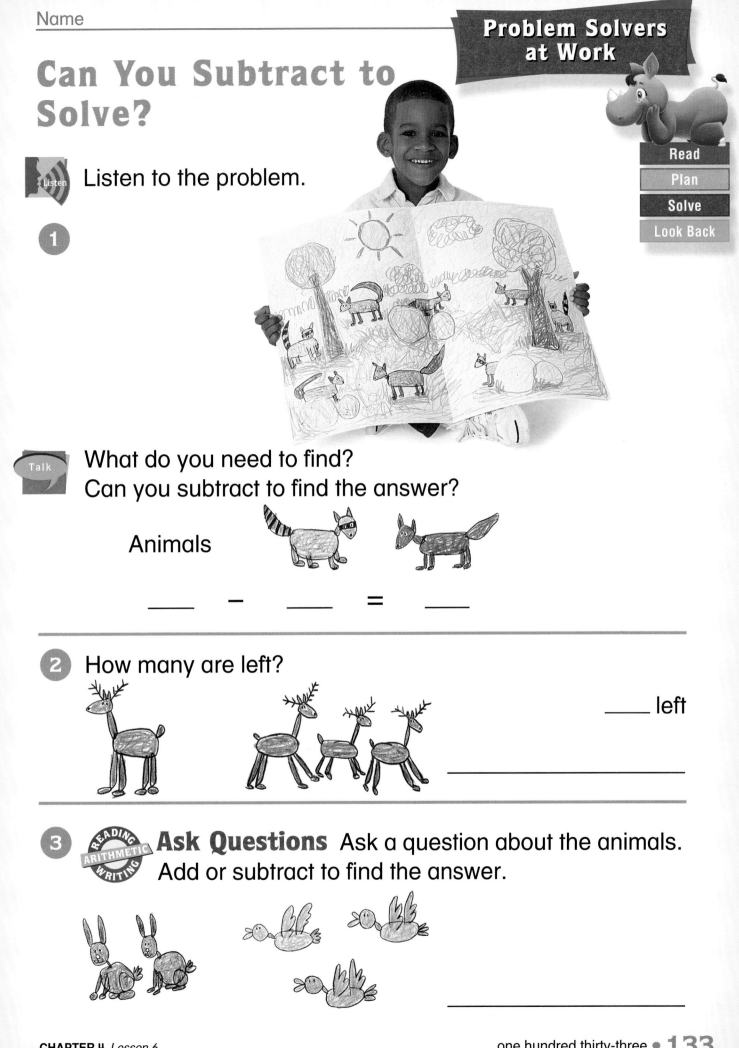

🔊 Listen to the problem.

1

💬 What do you need to find?
Can you subtract to find the answer?

Animals

____ **–** ____ **=** ____

2 How many are left?

____ left

_____

3 **Ask Questions** Ask a question about the animals.
Add or subtract to find the answer.

_____

McGraw-Hill School Division

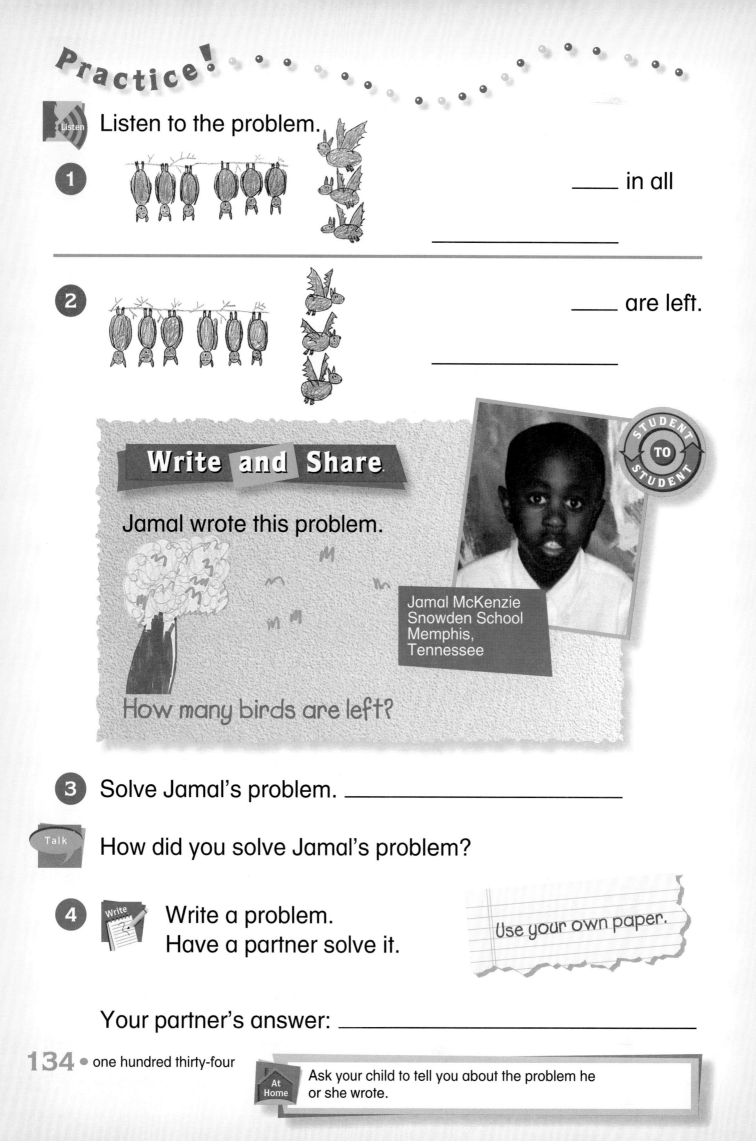

🔊 **Listen** Listen to the problem.

1 _____ in all

_____

2 _____ are left.

_____

Write and Share

Jamal wrote this problem.

Jamal McKenzie
Snowden School
Memphis,
Tennessee

How many birds are left?

3 Solve Jamal's problem. _____

💬 **Talk** How did you solve Jamal's problem?

4 ✏️ **Write** Write a problem.
Have a partner solve it.

Use your own paper.

Your partner's answer: _____

At Home Ask your child to tell you about the problem he or she wrote.

Chapter Review

Language and Mathematics

Choose the correct word to complete the sentence.

1 When you _____ you find the difference.

2 5 – 2 = 3 is a _____.

subtract
minus
subtraction
sentence
difference

Concepts and Skills

Write the subtraction sentence.

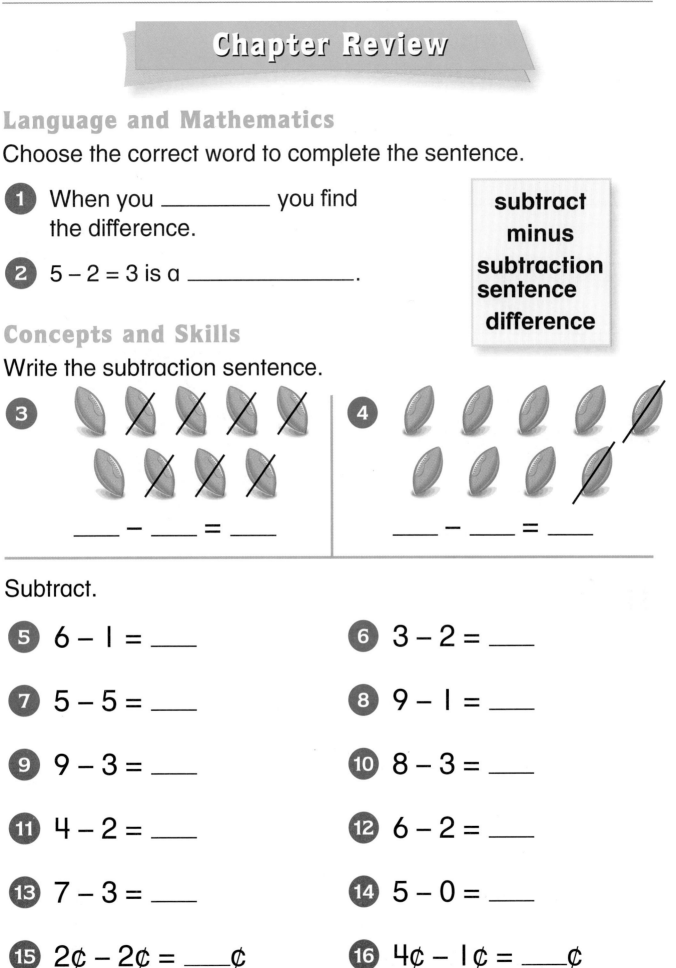

3 ___ – ___ = ___

4 ___ – ___ = ___

Subtract.

5 6 – 1 = ___

6 3 – 2 = ___

7 5 – 5 = ___

8 9 – 1 = ___

9 9 – 3 = ___

10 8 – 3 = ___

11 4 – 2 = ___

12 6 – 2 = ___

13 7 – 3 = ___

14 5 – 0 = ___

15 2¢ – 2¢ = ___¢

16 4¢ – 1¢ = ___¢

Problem Solving

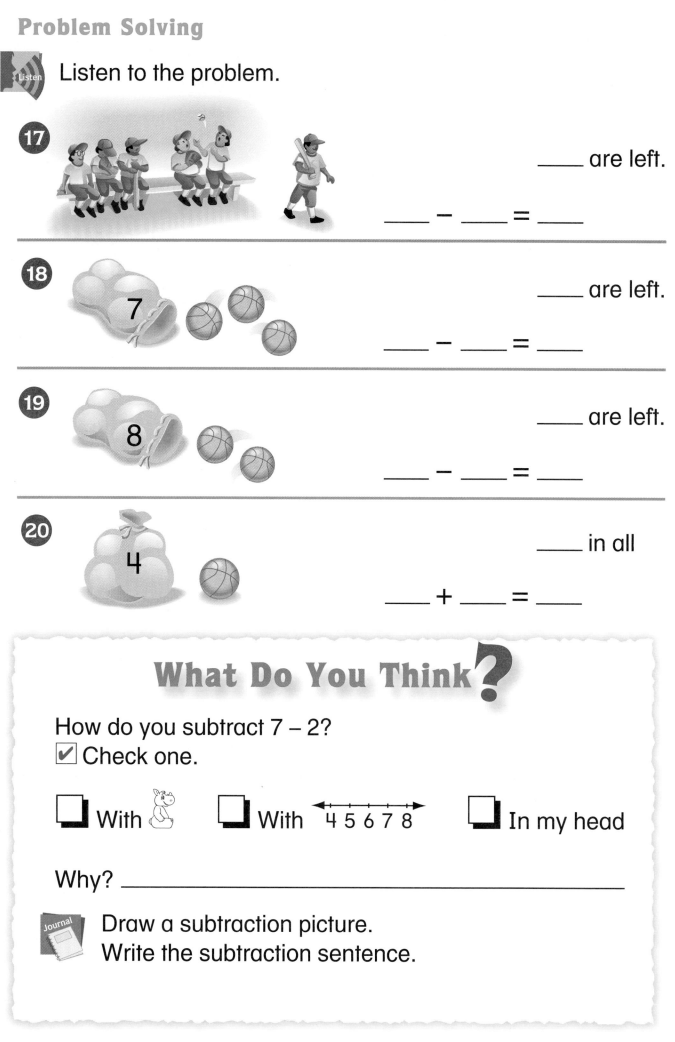

Listen Listen to the problem.

17 ____ are left.

____ − ____ = ____

18 ____ are left.

7

____ − ____ = ____

19 ____ are left.

8

____ − ____ = ____

20 ____ in all

4

____ + ____ = ____

What Do You Think?

How do you subtract 7 − 2?
☑ Check one.

☐ With 🐇   ☐ With ◄—4 5 6 7 8—►   ☐ In my head

Why? _____

Journal Draw a subtraction picture.
Write the subtraction sentence.

Chapter Test

Write the subtraction sentence.

1 ___ − ___ = ___

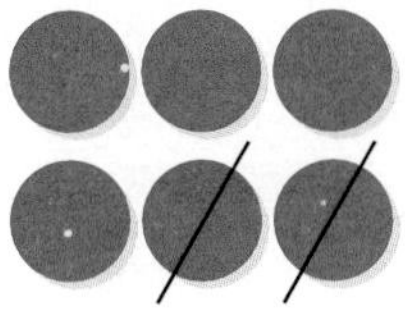

2 ___ − ___ = ___

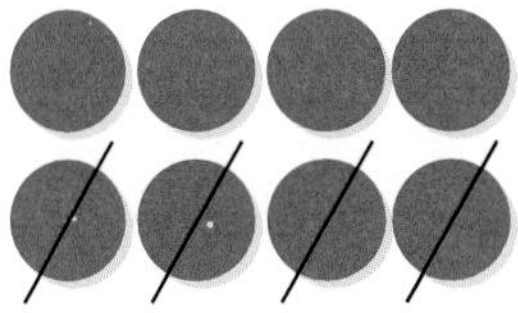

Subtract.

3 7 − 3 = ___

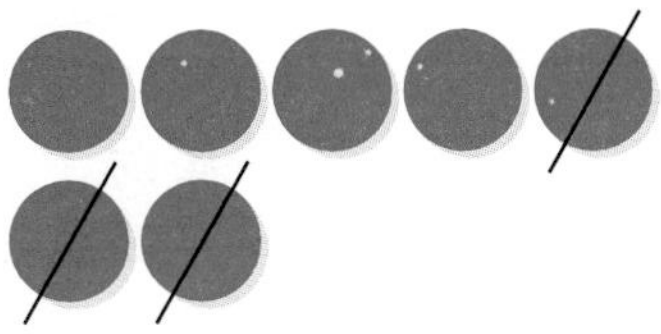

4 9 − 5 = ___

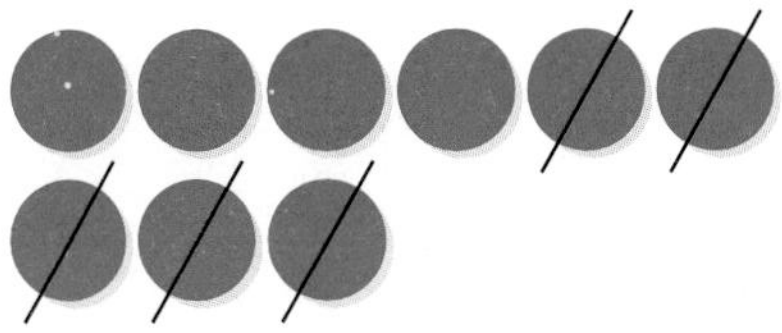

5 5 − 0 = ___

6 8 − 3 = ___

7 5¢ − 5¢ = ___¢

8 6¢ − 1¢ = ___¢

Find how many are left.

9 ___ are left.

___ − ___ = ___

10 ___ are left.

___ − ___ = ___

Performance Assessment

What Did You Learn?

You need 10 .

Make up a subtraction problem for each picture.

Write a subtraction sentence for each problem.

1

_____

2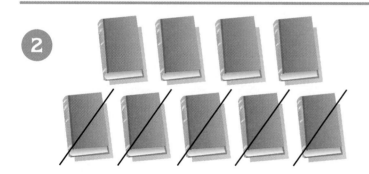

_____

3

_____

 You may want to put this page in your portfolio.

Name _____

Missing Addend

Algebra Find how many 🫘 are hidden.

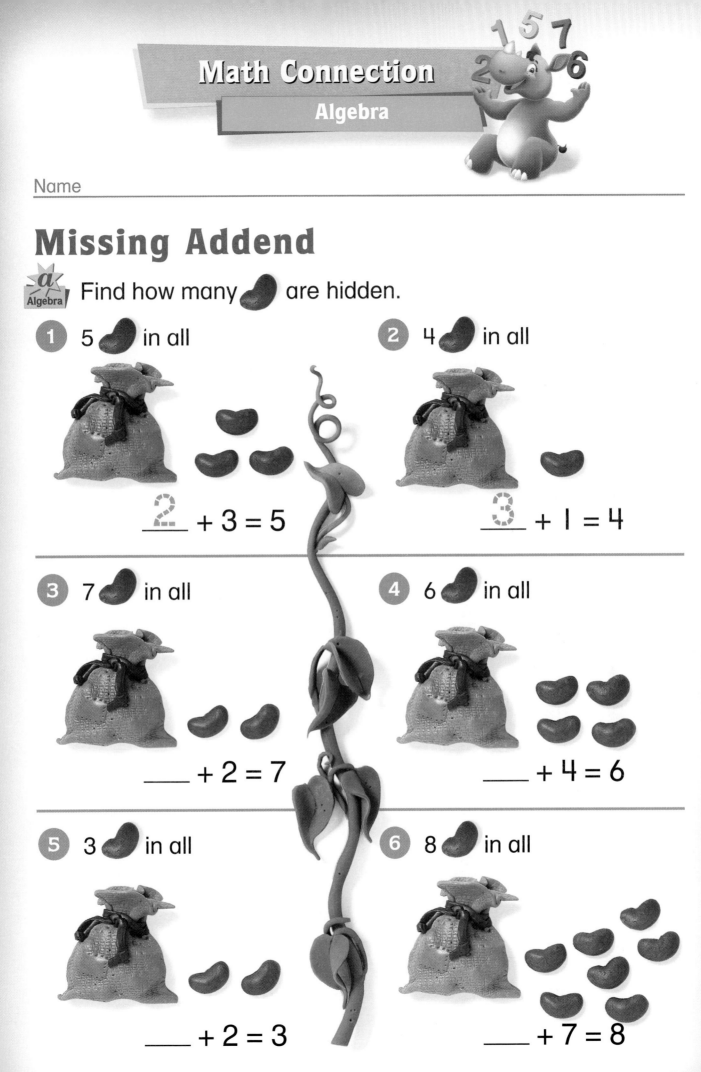

1 5 🫘 in all

___2___ + 3 = 5

2 4 🫘 in all

___3___ + 1 = 4

3 7 🫘 in all

_____ + 2 = 7

4 6 🫘 in all

_____ + 4 = 6

5 3 🫘 in all

_____ + 2 = 3

6 8 🫘 in all

_____ + 7 = 8

Technology Connection
Computer

Subtract Pennies

 Talk How does using counters help you subtract?

You have 8 pennies.
You spend 5 pennies.
How many pennies
are left?

_____ pennies

8 − 5 = 3

At the Computer

Use penny models to solve.

1 You have 6 pennies
You spend 2 pennies.
How many pennies are left?   _____ pennies

2 You spend 3 pennies.
You have 5 pennies left.
How many pennies did you start with?   _____ pennies

3 **Write** Write a problem.
Show how to solve it with penny models.

Name

Penny Subtraction

PLAYERS 2

MATERIALS 10 pennies, 2 colors of crayons

DIRECTIONS One player shows some of the pennies and tells an amount to subtract. The other player subtracts and colors to show how many cents are left.

Play until all the boxes are colored.

4¢	9¢	5¢
1¢	8¢	6¢
3¢	2¢	7¢

At Home Play this game with your child. Your child can count the pennies before you say the amount to subtract. Vary the starting amount. Your child uses the pennies to subtract.

McGraw-Hill School Division

At
Home

Dear Family,

I am beginning a new chapter in mathematics. I will be learning more about addition and subtraction.

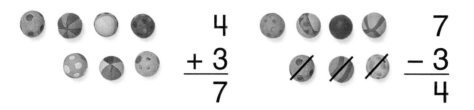

$$\begin{array}{r} 4 \\ +\ 3 \\ \hline 7 \end{array} \qquad \begin{array}{r} 7 \\ -\ 3 \\ \hline 4 \end{array}$$

I will also learn about the circus and ways to have fun with numbers.

Learning about the Circus

Let's talk about what we can see at a circus. We can draw a picture of our favorite circus act.

My Math Words

I am going to use these math words in this chapter.

Please help me make word cards for these math words. I can use the word cards when I practice addition and subtraction.

fact
related facts
graph

Your child,

_____
Signature

Adding and Subtracting to 10

Theme: Number Fun

Illustrations You can use pictures to answer questions in a story.

Listen to *Number One Number Fun.*

How do the pictures tell about the numbers?

What Do You Know?

5¢

6¢

2¢

4¢

3¢

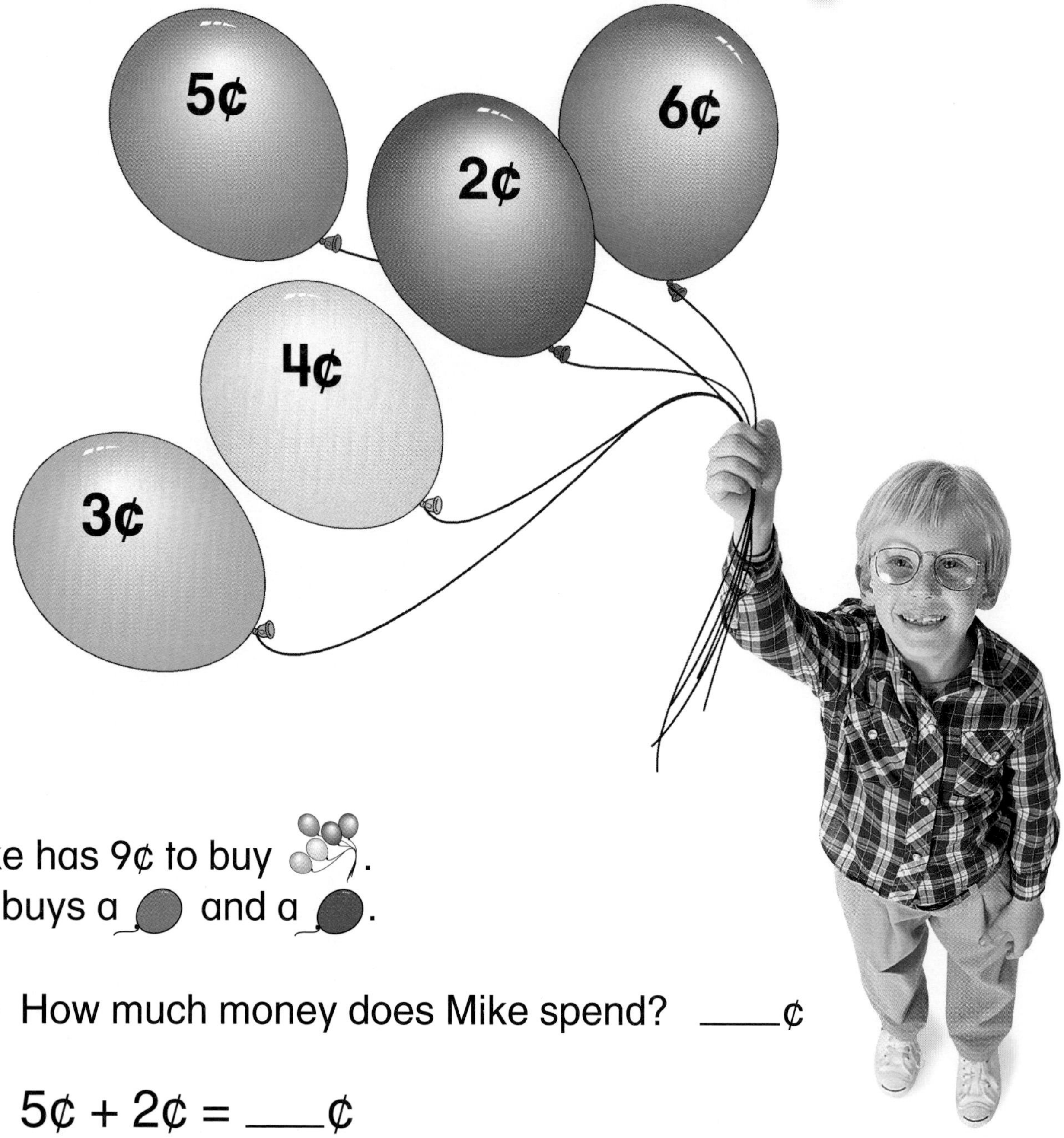

Mike has 9¢ to buy 🎈.
He buys a 🎈 and a 🎈.

1 How much money does Mike spend? ____¢

5¢ + 2¢ = ____¢

2 How much money does Mike have left? ____¢

Write the subtraction sentence. _____

Portfolio You have 9¢.
Show which ◯ you would buy.
Write the addition sentence.

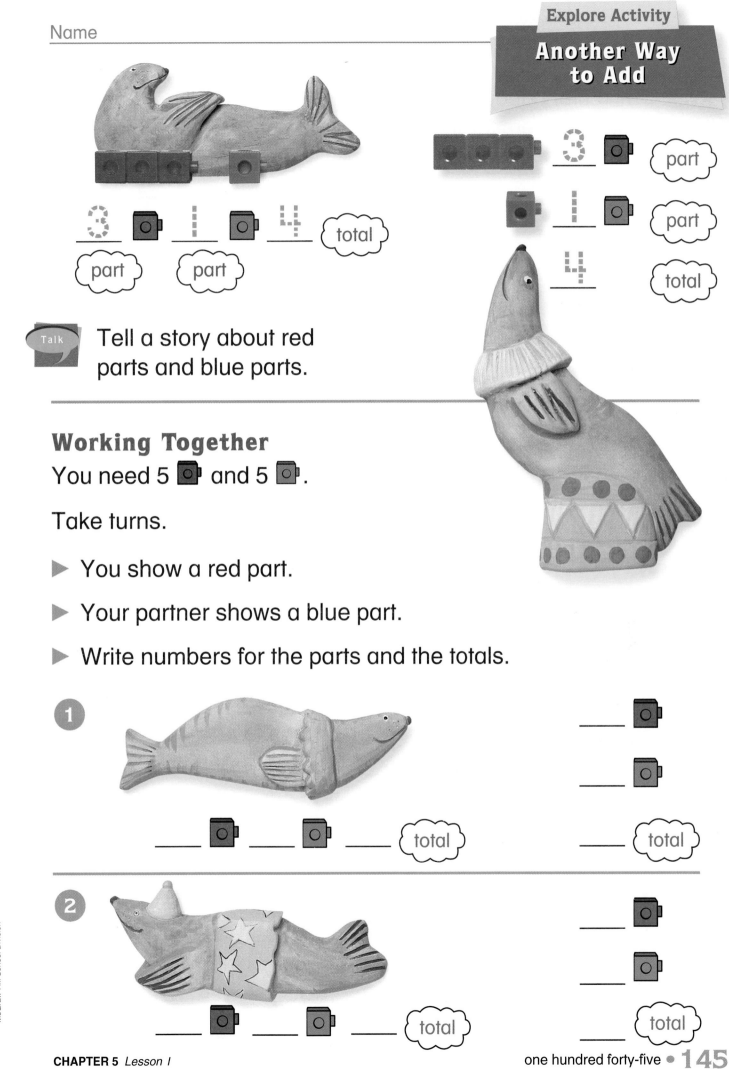

_____ 3 _____ 1 _____ 4 (total)

(part) (part)

_____ 3 (part)

_____ 1 (part)

_____ 4 (total)

Talk Tell a story about red parts and blue parts.

Working Together

You need 5 🔲 and 5 🔲.

Take turns.

▶ You show a red part.

▶ Your partner shows a blue part.

▶ Write numbers for the parts and the totals.

1

_____ 🔲 _____ 🔲 _____ (total)

_____ 🔲

_____ 🔲

_____ (total)

2

_____ 🔲 _____ 🔲 _____ (total)

_____ 🔲

_____ 🔲

_____ (total)

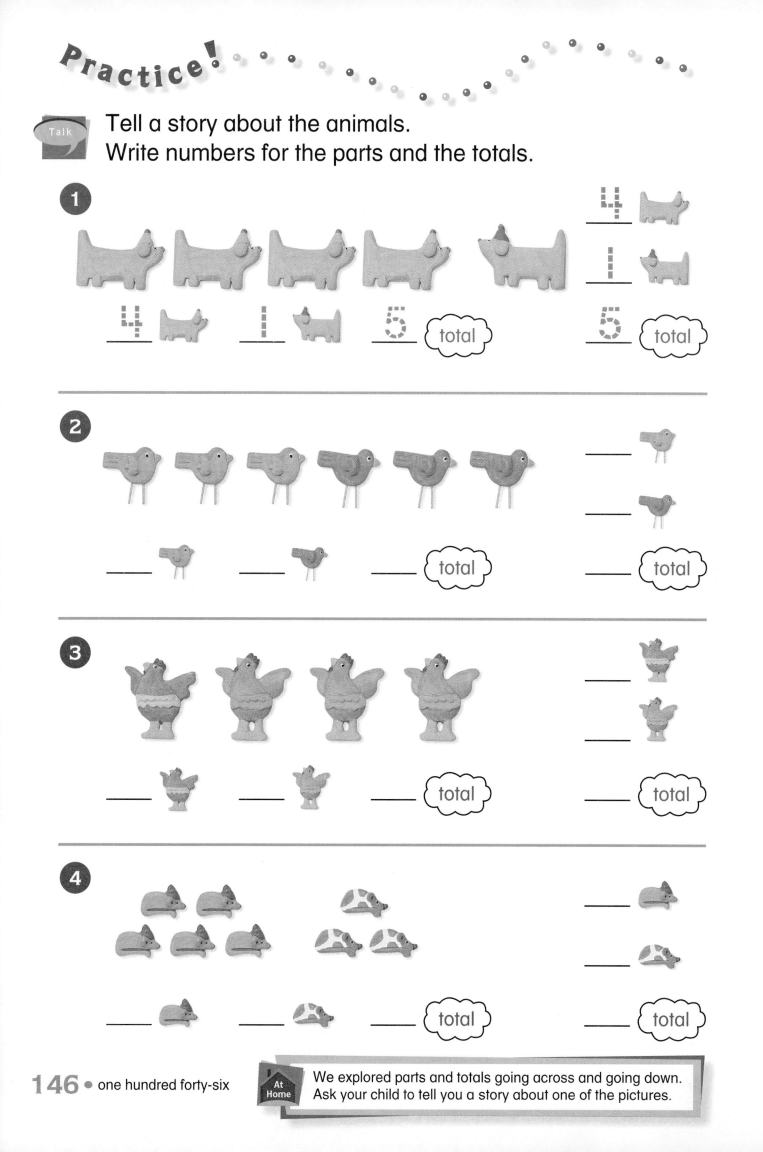

Practice!

Tell a story about the animals.
Write numbers for the parts and the totals.

1

_4_
_1_
___ 4 ___ 1 ___ 5 total
___ 5 total

2

___
___
___ ___ ___ total
___ total

3

___
___
___ ___ ___ total
___ total

4

___
___
___ ___ ___ total
___ total

At Home We explored parts and totals going across and going down.
Ask your child to tell you a story about one of the pictures.

Name _____

$4 + 2 = 6$

sum

$$\begin{array}{r} 4 \\ +\ 2 \\ \hline 6 \end{array}$$

sum

two ways to write addition

You need 9 ▦ and 9 ▦.

▶ Show parts with ▦.

▶ Color to show the parts.

▶ Find the sum.

1
$$\begin{array}{r} 3 \\ +\ 0 \\ \hline 3 \end{array}$$

2
$$\begin{array}{r} 1 \\ +\ 4 \\ \hline \end{array}$$

3
$$\begin{array}{r} 2 \\ +\ 2 \\ \hline \end{array}$$

4
$$\begin{array}{r} 5 \\ +\ 2 \\ \hline \end{array}$$

5
$$\begin{array}{r} 3 \\ +\ 1 \\ \hline \end{array}$$

6
$$\begin{array}{r} 3 \\ +\ 4 \\ \hline \end{array}$$

Critical Thinking: How could you use 🐴 to show addition?

Add.

1 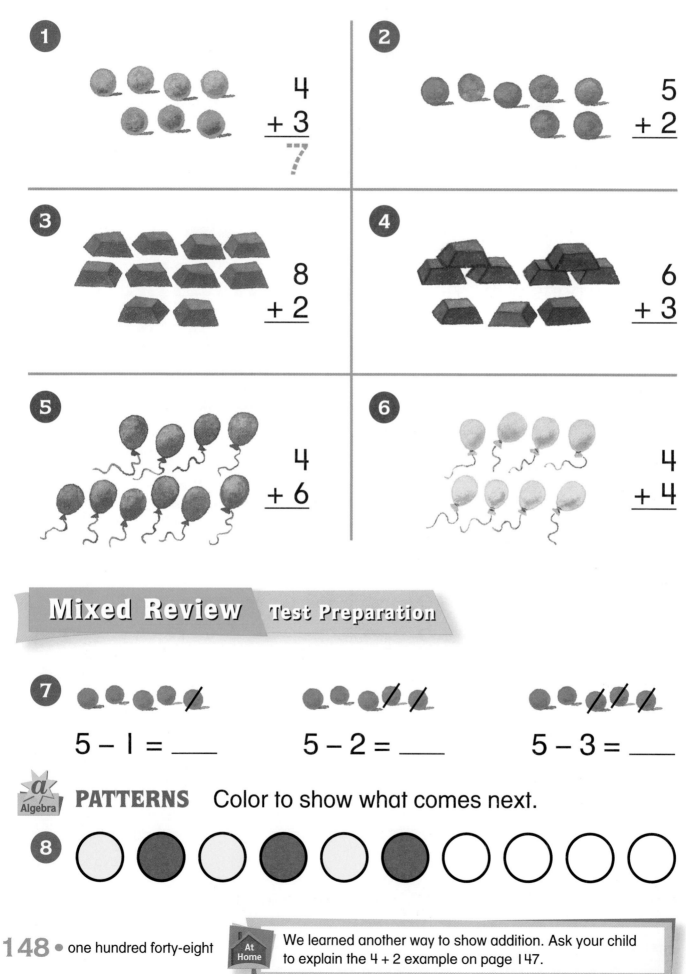   4
       + 3
       7

2   5
       + 2

3   8
       + 2

4   6
       + 3

5   4
       + 6

6   4
       + 4

Mixed Review   Test Preparation

7   5 – 1 = ____   5 – 2 = ____   5 – 3 = ____

α
Algebra   **PATTERNS**   Color to show what comes next.

8

At Home   We learned another way to show addition. Ask your child to explain the 4 + 2 example on page 147.

Name _____

Talk How are these **facts** the same?

related facts

Glossary
facts
related facts

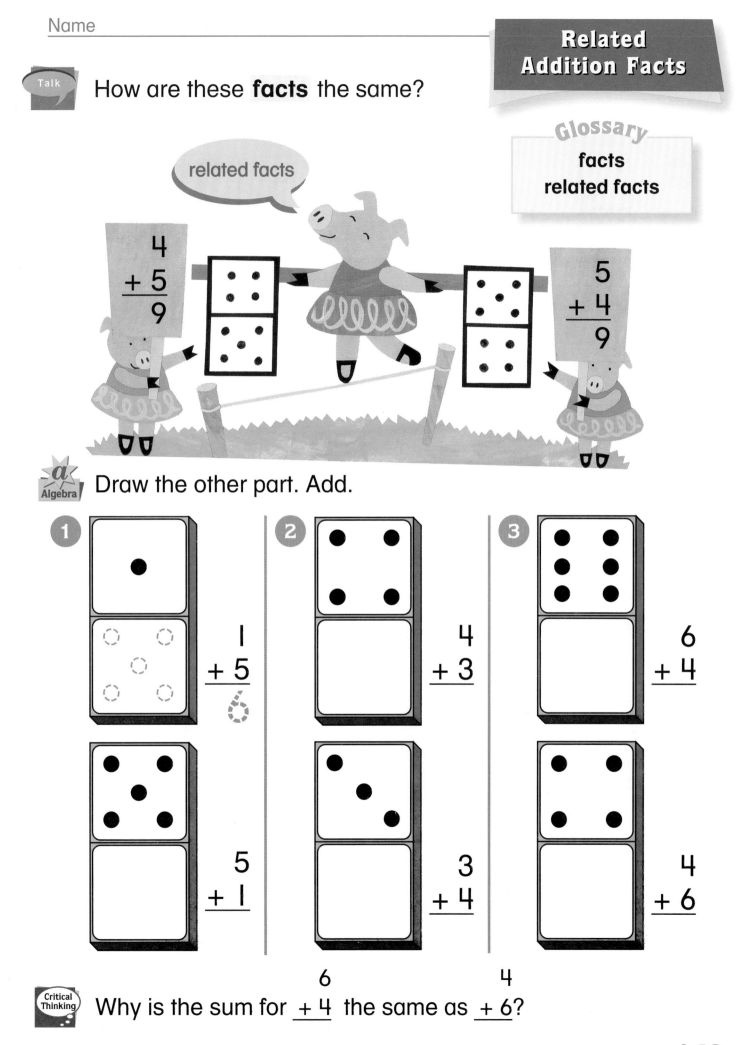

Algebra Draw the other part. Add.

1

$\begin{array}{r} 1 \\ +\ 5 \\ \hline 6 \end{array}$

$\begin{array}{r} 5 \\ +\ 1 \\ \hline \end{array}$

2

$\begin{array}{r} 4 \\ +\ 3 \\ \hline \end{array}$

$\begin{array}{r} 3 \\ +\ 4 \\ \hline \end{array}$

6

3

$\begin{array}{r} 6 \\ +\ 4 \\ \hline \end{array}$

$\begin{array}{r} 4 \\ +\ 6 \\ \hline \end{array}$

4

Critical Thinking Why is the sum for $\begin{array}{r}6\\+\ 4\\\hline\end{array}$ the same as $\begin{array}{r}4\\+\ 6\\\hline\end{array}$?

McGraw-Hill School Division

Use counters if you want to.

Add.

1

3
+ 3
___
6

2

4
+ 4
___

3

5
+ 5
___

4

7
+ 2
___

2
+ 7
___

1
+ 6
___

6
+ 1
___

9
+ 0
___

0
+ 9
___

5

5
+ 3
___

3
+ 5
___

4
+ 2
___

2
+ 4
___

3
+ 7
___

7
+ 3
___

6

2
+ 8
___

8
+ 2
___

6
+ 3
___

3
+ 6
___

8
+ 1
___

1
+ 8
___

Talk Tell about each pair of sums.

More to Explore   Algebra Sense

a **Algebra** Find the missing number.

5
+ 2
___
7

2
+ ☐
___
7

1
+ ☐
___
8

7
+ ☐
___
8

2
+ ☐
___
4

At Home   We learned about related addition facts. Ask your child to tell you how the pairs of exercises are the same.

Rhino Riddle

Add.

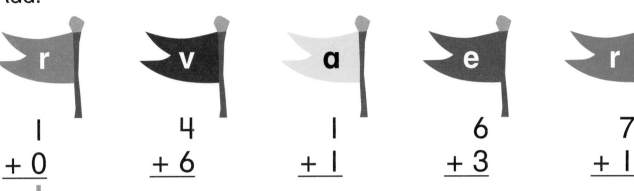

r	v	a	e	r
1 + 0	4 + 6	1 + 1	6 + 3	7 + 1

i	g	b	y	c
3 + 2	3 + 1	2 + 4	4 + 3	1 + 2

Match sums to answer the riddle.

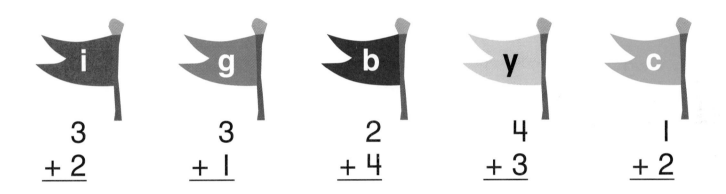

How does a rhino
go to the circus?

In a ___ ___ ___ ___
     10 9 8 7

___ ___ ___   ___ ___ r !
6 5 4   3 2 1

Add.

Use counters if you want to.

1

$$\begin{array}{r} 4 \\ + 6 \\ \hline 10 \end{array}$$

$$\begin{array}{r} 5 \\ + 2 \\ \hline \end{array}$$

$$\begin{array}{r} 3 \\ + 3 \\ \hline \end{array}$$

$$\begin{array}{r} 7 \\ + 2 \\ \hline \end{array}$$

$$\begin{array}{r} 4 \\ + 4 \\ \hline \end{array}$$

$$\begin{array}{r} 9 \\ + 1 \\ \hline \end{array}$$

2

$$\begin{array}{r} 3 \\ + 7 \\ \hline \end{array}$$

$$\begin{array}{r} 5 \\ + 4 \\ \hline \end{array}$$

$$\begin{array}{r} 2 \\ + 2 \\ \hline \end{array}$$

$$\begin{array}{r} 4 \\ + 1 \\ \hline \end{array}$$

$$\begin{array}{r} 9 \\ + 0 \\ \hline \end{array}$$

$$\begin{array}{r} 1 \\ + 6 \\ \hline \end{array}$$

3

$$\begin{array}{r} 5 \\ + 3 \\ \hline \end{array}$$

$$\begin{array}{r} 3 \\ + 1 \\ \hline \end{array}$$

$$\begin{array}{r} 7 \\ + 0 \\ \hline \end{array}$$

$$\begin{array}{r} 6 \\ + 4 \\ \hline \end{array}$$

$$\begin{array}{r} 5 \\ + 5 \\ \hline \end{array}$$

$$\begin{array}{r} 6 \\ + 0 \\ \hline \end{array}$$

4

$$\begin{array}{r} 8 \\ + 1 \\ \hline \end{array}$$

$$\begin{array}{r} 6 \\ + 2 \\ \hline \end{array}$$

$$\begin{array}{r} 0 \\ + 8 \\ \hline \end{array}$$

$$\begin{array}{r} 5 \\ + 1 \\ \hline \end{array}$$

$$\begin{array}{r} 0 \\ + 5 \\ \hline \end{array}$$

$$\begin{array}{r} 4 \\ + 5 \\ \hline \end{array}$$

Draw lines to match.

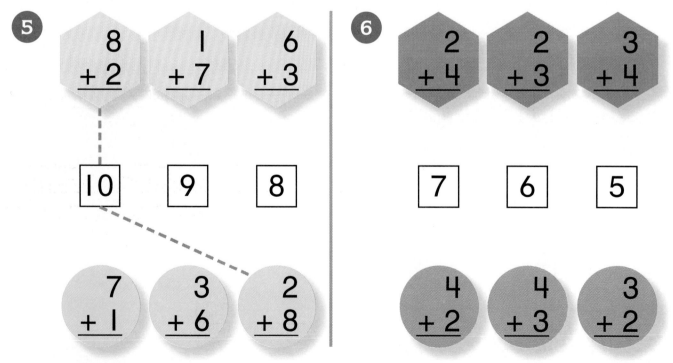

5

$$\begin{array}{r} 8 \\ + 2 \\ \hline \end{array}$$

$$\begin{array}{r} 1 \\ + 7 \\ \hline \end{array}$$

$$\begin{array}{r} 6 \\ + 3 \\ \hline \end{array}$$

| 10 | 9 | 8 |

$$\begin{array}{r} 7 \\ + 1 \\ \hline \end{array}$$

$$\begin{array}{r} 3 \\ + 6 \\ \hline \end{array}$$

$$\begin{array}{r} 2 \\ + 8 \\ \hline \end{array}$$

6

$$\begin{array}{r} 2 \\ + 4 \\ \hline \end{array}$$

$$\begin{array}{r} 2 \\ + 3 \\ \hline \end{array}$$

$$\begin{array}{r} 3 \\ + 4 \\ \hline \end{array}$$

| 7 | 6 | 5 |

$$\begin{array}{r} 4 \\ + 2 \\ \hline \end{array}$$

$$\begin{array}{r} 4 \\ + 3 \\ \hline \end{array}$$

$$\begin{array}{r} 3 \\ + 2 \\ \hline \end{array}$$

Name _____

Find how much money
Kim needs.

$$\begin{array}{r} 3\cent \\ + 5\cent \\ \hline 8\cent \end{array}$$

You need 10 🪙.
Add to find how much money.

1 6¢ 1¢
$$\begin{array}{r} 6\cent \\ + 1\cent \\ \hline \cent \end{array}$$

2 3¢ 4¢
$$\begin{array}{r} 3\cent \\ + 4\cent \\ \hline \cent \end{array}$$

3 8¢ 2¢
$$\begin{array}{r} 8\cent \\ + 2\cent \\ \hline \cent \end{array}$$

4 5¢ 4¢
$$\begin{array}{r} 5\cent \\ + 4\cent \\ \hline \cent \end{array}$$

5 7¢ 3¢
$$\begin{array}{r} 7\cent \\ + 3\cent \\ \hline \cent \end{array}$$

6 4¢ 6¢
$$\begin{array}{r} 4\cent \\ + 6\cent \\ \hline \cent \end{array}$$

Critical Thinking Which of the toys could you buy for 6¢?

Practice!

Use pennies if you want to.

Add.

1 2¢
    4¢

2¢
+ 4¢
6¢

2 5¢
    1¢

5¢
+ 1¢
___¢

3 9¢
    1¢

9¢
+ 1¢
___¢

4 3¢
    6¢

3¢
+ 6¢
___¢

5
1¢	7¢	2¢	4¢	1¢	3¢
+ 3¢	+ 2¢	+ 5¢	+ 4¢	+ 8¢	+ 3¢
___¢	___¢	___¢	___¢	___¢	___¢

6
5¢	4¢	3¢	9¢	6¢	8¢
+ 4¢	+ 3¢	+ 5¢	+ 1¢	+ 2¢	+ 2¢
___¢	___¢	___¢	___¢	___¢	___¢

7
3¢	5¢	4¢	8¢	4¢	5¢
+ 7¢	+ 5¢	+ 4¢	+ 1¢	+ 6¢	+ 3¢
___¢	___¢	___¢	___¢	___¢	___¢

Journal Draw and write about adding money.

 At Home — Show your child 2 pennies in one hand and 4 pennies in the other. Ask how much money you have in both hands.

Midchapter Review

Do your best!

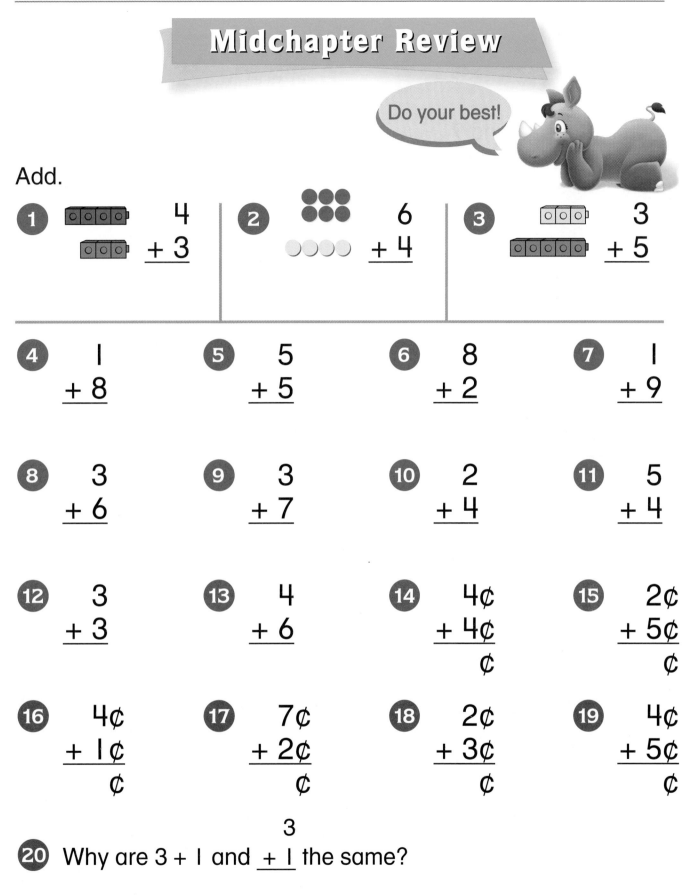

Add.

1 $\begin{array}{r} 4 \\ + 3 \\ \hline \end{array}$

2 $\begin{array}{r} 6 \\ + 4 \\ \hline \end{array}$

3 $\begin{array}{r} 3 \\ + 5 \\ \hline \end{array}$

4 $\begin{array}{r} 1 \\ + 8 \\ \hline \end{array}$

5 $\begin{array}{r} 5 \\ + 5 \\ \hline \end{array}$

6 $\begin{array}{r} 8 \\ + 2 \\ \hline \end{array}$

7 $\begin{array}{r} 1 \\ + 9 \\ \hline \end{array}$

8 $\begin{array}{r} 3 \\ + 6 \\ \hline \end{array}$

9 $\begin{array}{r} 3 \\ + 7 \\ \hline \end{array}$

10 $\begin{array}{r} 2 \\ + 4 \\ \hline \end{array}$

11 $\begin{array}{r} 5 \\ + 4 \\ \hline \end{array}$

12 $\begin{array}{r} 3 \\ + 3 \\ \hline \end{array}$

13 $\begin{array}{r} 4 \\ + 6 \\ \hline \end{array}$

14 $\begin{array}{r} 4¢ \\ + 4¢ \\ \hline ¢ \end{array}$

15 $\begin{array}{r} 2¢ \\ + 5¢ \\ \hline ¢ \end{array}$

16 $\begin{array}{r} 4¢ \\ + 1¢ \\ \hline ¢ \end{array}$

17 $\begin{array}{r} 7¢ \\ + 2¢ \\ \hline ¢ \end{array}$

18 $\begin{array}{r} 2¢ \\ + 3¢ \\ \hline ¢ \end{array}$

19 $\begin{array}{r} 4¢ \\ + 5¢ \\ \hline ¢ \end{array}$

20 Why are 3 + 1 and $\begin{array}{r} 3 \\ + 1 \\ \hline \end{array}$ the same?

_____

Journal Write or draw about ways to add.

Cover the Circus Wagon

You need 2  and 9 🐴.

Take turns.

▶ Roll the 2 🎲.

▶ Add. Put a 🐴 on the sum.

▶ Get 3 🐴 in a row.

3	6	9
7	5	2
10	4	8

Name _____

Circus Fun

Listen to *Number One Number Fun*.

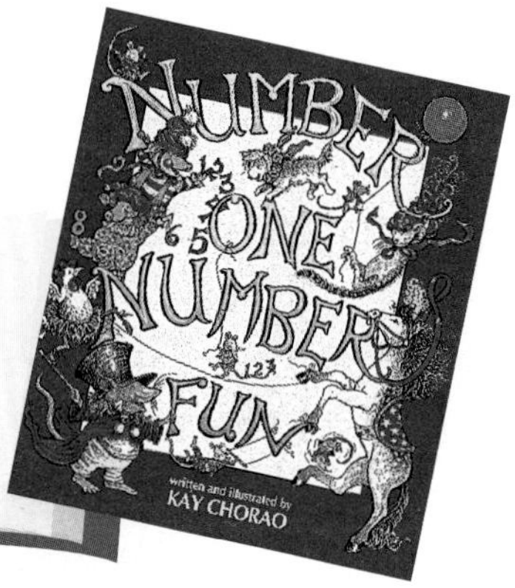

Take a survey. Ask this question:

"Would you be brave enough to swing on a trapeze?"

Make a class **graph**.

1. How many children said *yes*? _____

2. How many children said *no*? _____

3. Did more children say *yes* or *no*? _____

   How many more? _____

Decision Making

1 Write a question to ask.
Take another survey.

_____

_____

2 Make a class graph.

Write a report.

3 Tell what you
found out.

4 Use numbers to
show what you
learned.

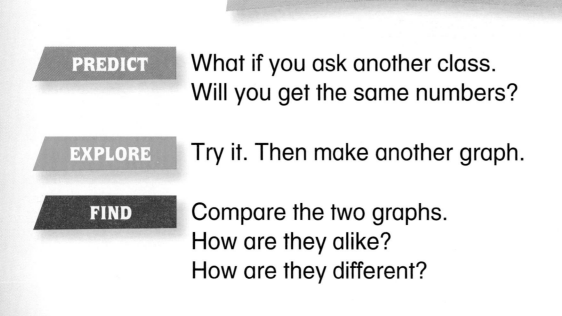

Cultural Note
In Russia, the Moscow
Circus School teaches
children math and
trains them to perform.

More to Investigate

PREDICT What if you ask another class.
Will you get the same numbers?

EXPLORE Try it. Then make another graph.

FIND Compare the two graphs.
How are they alike?
How are they different?

Name _____

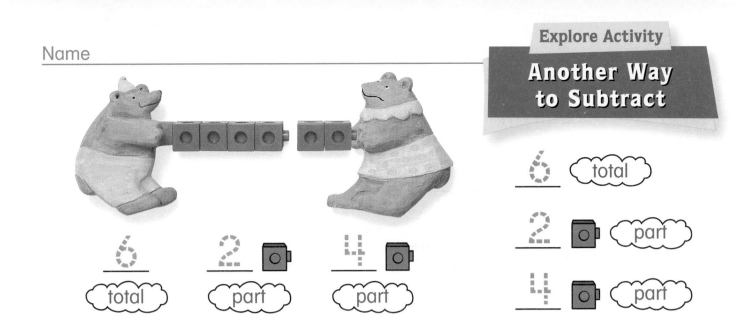

6 (total)

2  (part)

4  (part)

6 — (total) 2 □ (part) 4 □ (part)

 Talk Tell a story about taking away 2 cubes.

Working Together

You need 10 □.

Take turns.

▶ You make a train.

▶ Your partner snaps off a part.

▶ Write numbers for the totals and parts.

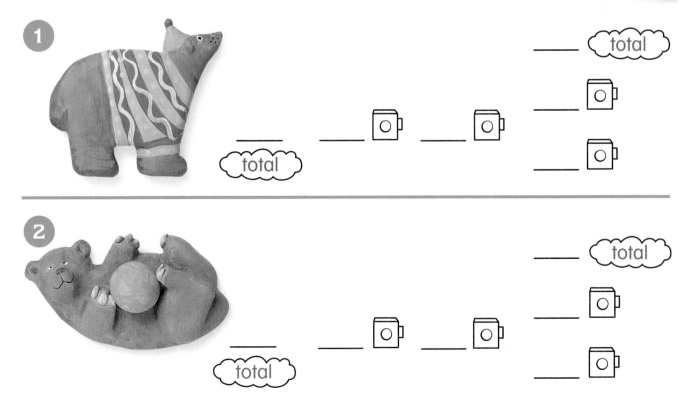

1 ___ (total)

___ (total)   ___ □   ___ □   ___ □

2 ___ (total)

___ (total)   ___ □   ___ □   ___ □

McGraw-Hill School Division

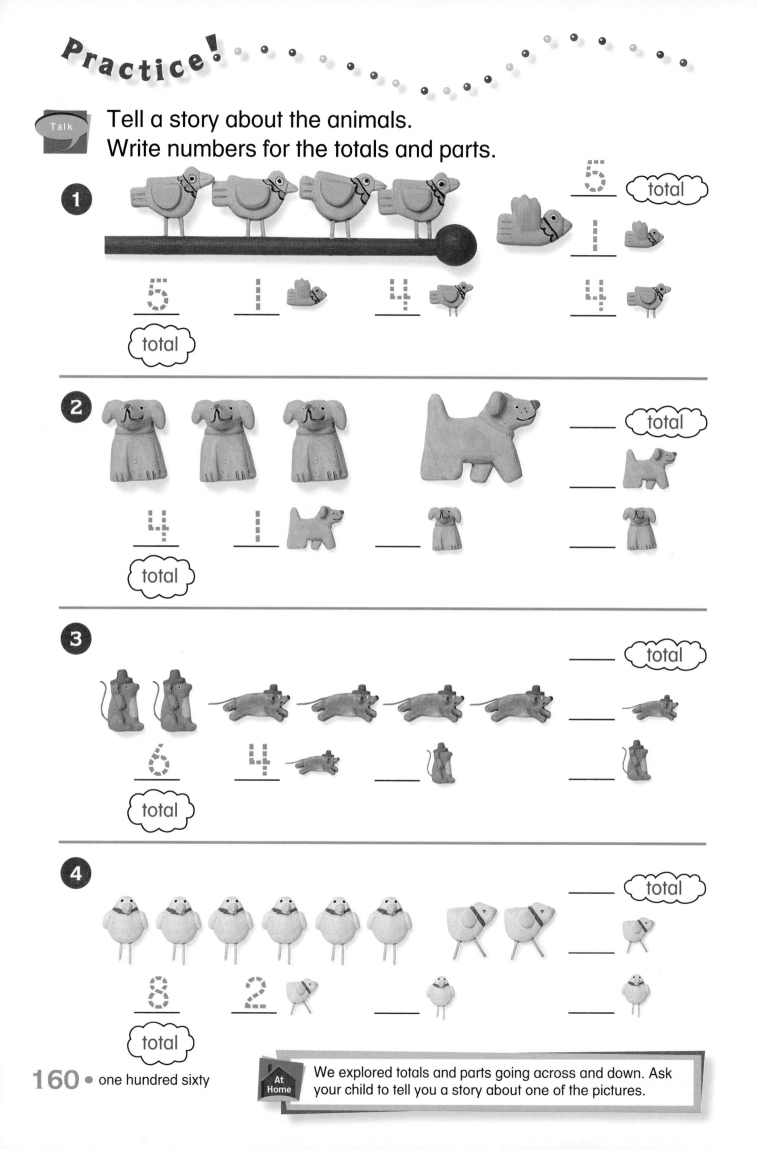

Practice!

Talk Tell a story about the animals.
Write numbers for the totals and parts.

1

5 _total_

1

4

5 _total_   1   4

2

___ _total_

___

4 _total_   1   ___   ___

3

___ _total_

___

6 _total_   4   ___   ___

4

___ _total_

___

8 _total_   2   ___   ___

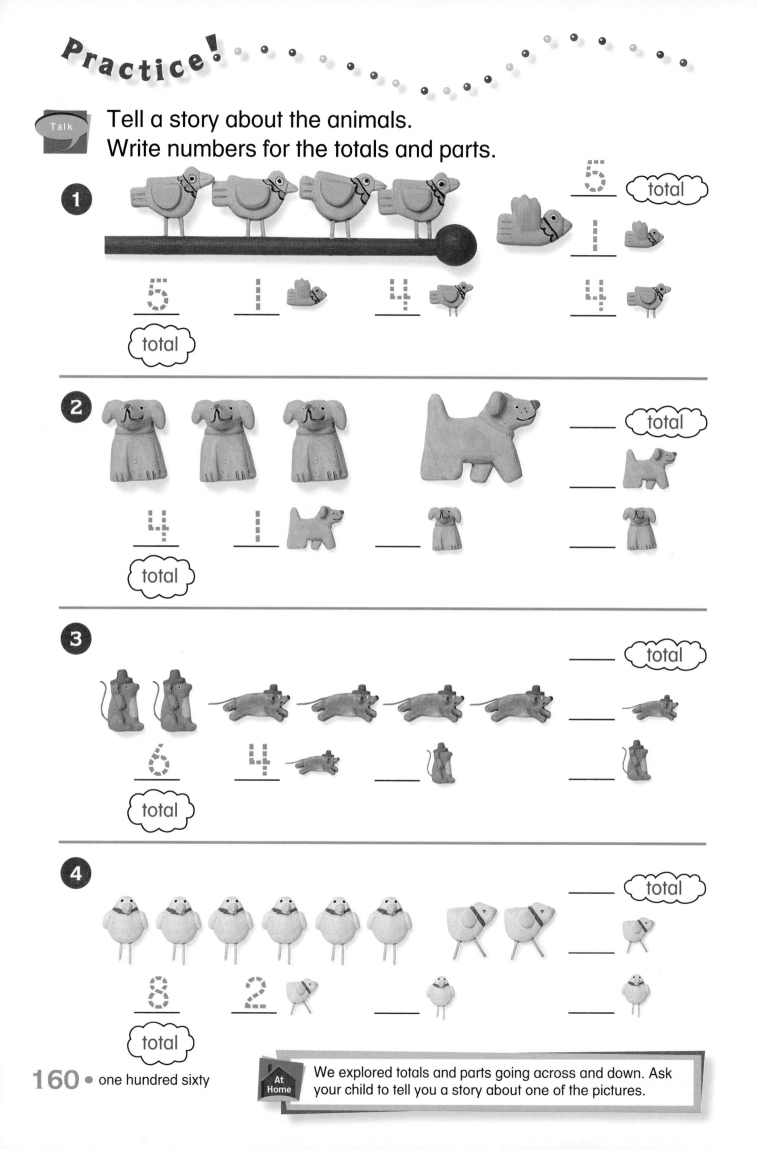

160 • one hundred sixty

At Home We explored totals and parts going across and down. Ask your child to tell you a story about one of the pictures.

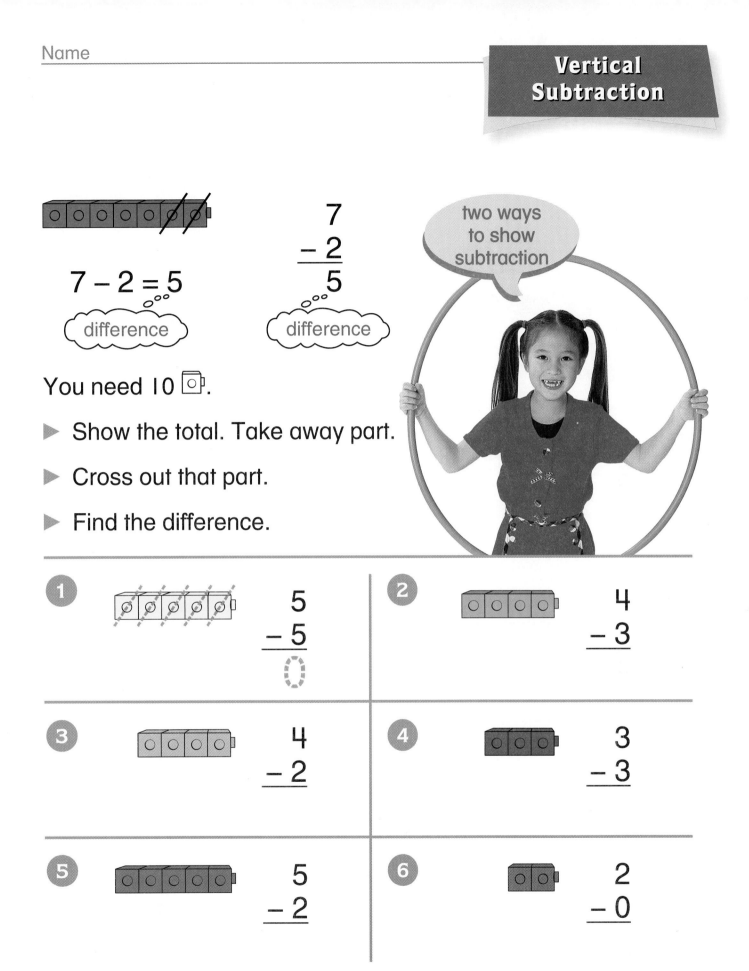

$7 - 2 = 5$

difference

$$\begin{array}{r} 7 \\ -\ 2 \\ \hline 5 \end{array}$$

difference

two ways to show subtraction

You need 10 ▢.

▶ Show the total. Take away part.

▶ Cross out that part.

▶ Find the difference.

1
$$\begin{array}{r} 5 \\ -\ 5 \\ \hline 0 \end{array}$$

2
$$\begin{array}{r} 4 \\ -\ 3 \\ \hline \end{array}$$

3
$$\begin{array}{r} 4 \\ -\ 2 \\ \hline \end{array}$$

4
$$\begin{array}{r} 3 \\ -\ 3 \\ \hline \end{array}$$

5
$$\begin{array}{r} 5 \\ -\ 2 \\ \hline \end{array}$$

6
$$\begin{array}{r} 2 \\ -\ 0 \\ \hline \end{array}$$

Critical Thinking What if there are 6 red and 2 blue cubes. What subtraction could you show?

Practice!

Subtract.

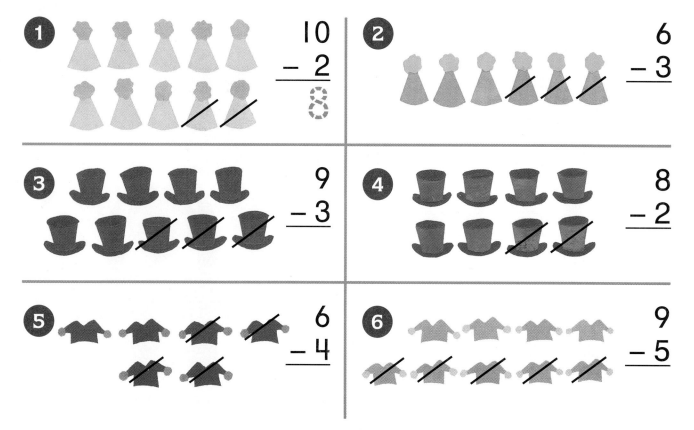

1 $\begin{array}{r} 10 \\ -\ 2 \\ \hline 8 \end{array}$

2 $\begin{array}{r} 6 \\ -\ 3 \\ \hline \end{array}$

3 $\begin{array}{r} 9 \\ -\ 3 \\ \hline \end{array}$

4 $\begin{array}{r} 8 \\ -\ 2 \\ \hline \end{array}$

5 $\begin{array}{r} 6 \\ -\ 4 \\ \hline \end{array}$

6 $\begin{array}{r} 9 \\ -\ 5 \\ \hline \end{array}$

Mixed Review   Test Preparation

Complete.

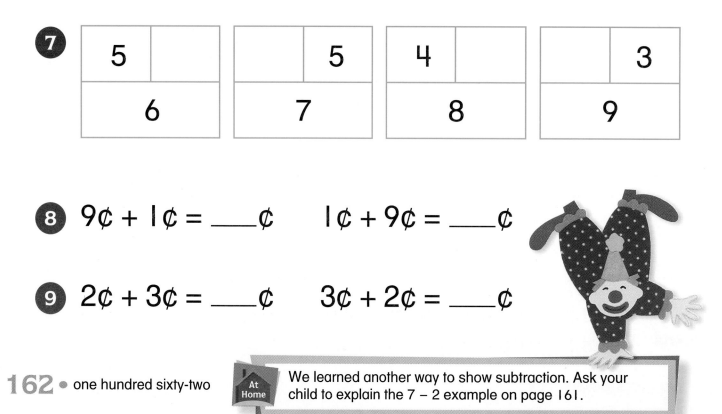

7

5	
6	

	5
7	

4	
8	

	3
9	

8 9¢ + 1¢ = ____¢   1¢ + 9¢ = ____¢

9 2¢ + 3¢ = ____¢   3¢ + 2¢ = ____¢

At Home — We learned another way to show subtraction. Ask your child to explain the 7 – 2 example on page 161.

Name _____

Talk How are these
facts different?

related facts

$$\begin{array}{r} 9 \\ -3 \\ \hline 6 \end{array}$$

$$\begin{array}{r} 9 \\ -6 \\ \hline 3 \end{array}$$

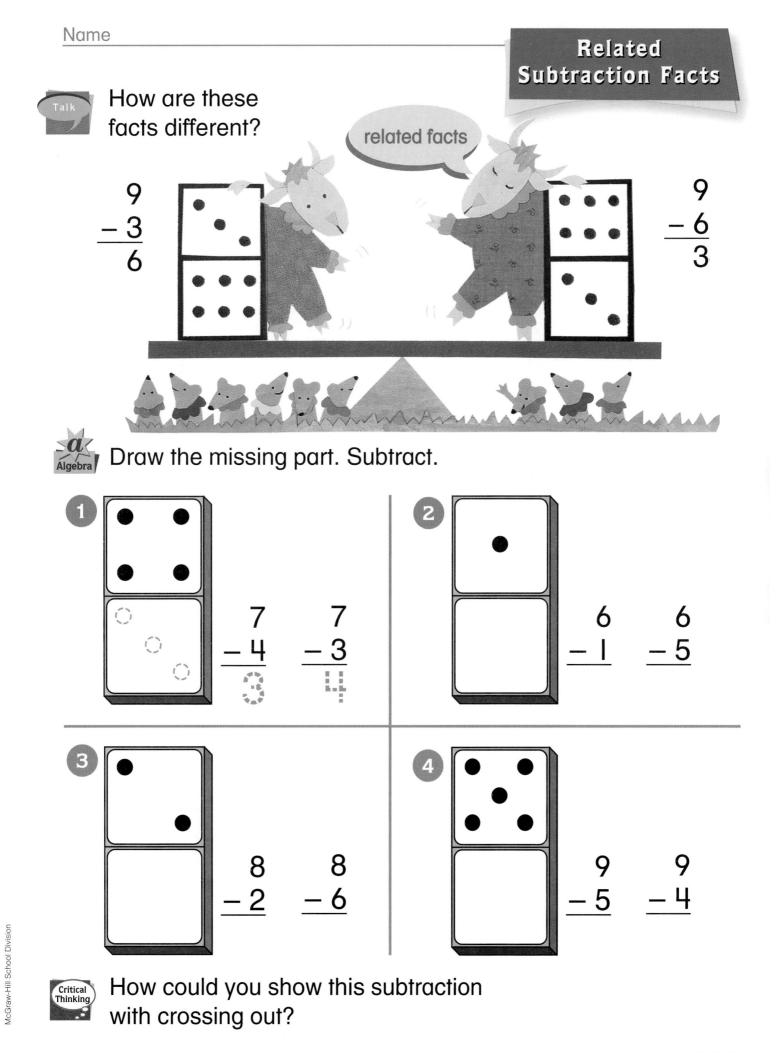

Algebra Draw the missing part. Subtract.

1

$$\begin{array}{r} 7 \\ -4 \\ \hline 3 \end{array}\qquad\begin{array}{r} 7 \\ -3 \\ \hline 4 \end{array}$$

2

$$\begin{array}{r} 6 \\ -1 \\ \hline \end{array}\qquad\begin{array}{r} 6 \\ -5 \\ \hline \end{array}$$

3

$$\begin{array}{r} 8 \\ -2 \\ \hline \end{array}\qquad\begin{array}{r} 8 \\ -6 \\ \hline \end{array}$$

4

$$\begin{array}{r} 9 \\ -5 \\ \hline \end{array}\qquad\begin{array}{r} 9 \\ -4 \\ \hline \end{array}$$

Critical Thinking How could you show this subtraction
with crossing out?

Use counters if you want to.

Subtract.

1
$$\begin{array}{r} 6 \\ -3 \\ \hline 3 \end{array}$$

2
$$\begin{array}{r} 8 \\ -4 \\ \hline \end{array}$$

3
$$\begin{array}{r} 10 \\ -5 \\ \hline \end{array}$$

4
$$\begin{array}{r} 7 \\ -2 \\ \hline \end{array}$$
$$\begin{array}{r} 7 \\ -5 \\ \hline \end{array}$$
$$\begin{array}{r} 9 \\ -2 \\ \hline \end{array}$$
$$\begin{array}{r} 9 \\ -7 \\ \hline \end{array}$$
$$\begin{array}{r} 8 \\ -5 \\ \hline \end{array}$$
$$\begin{array}{r} 8 \\ -3 \\ \hline \end{array}$$

5
$$\begin{array}{r} 6 \\ -4 \\ \hline \end{array}$$
$$\begin{array}{r} 6 \\ -2 \\ \hline \end{array}$$
$$\begin{array}{r} 10 \\ -7 \\ \hline \end{array}$$
$$\begin{array}{r} 10 \\ -3 \\ \hline \end{array}$$
$$\begin{array}{r} 7 \\ -1 \\ \hline \end{array}$$
$$\begin{array}{r} 7 \\ -6 \\ \hline \end{array}$$

6
$$\begin{array}{r} 9 \\ -9 \\ \hline \end{array}$$
$$\begin{array}{r} 9 \\ -0 \\ \hline \end{array}$$
$$\begin{array}{r} 10 \\ -2 \\ \hline \end{array}$$
$$\begin{array}{r} 10 \\ -8 \\ \hline \end{array}$$
$$\begin{array}{r} 9 \\ -1 \\ \hline \end{array}$$
$$\begin{array}{r} 9 \\ -8 \\ \hline \end{array}$$

Cultural Connection

Chinese Numbers

Chinese numbers are like pictures.

一	二	三	四	五
1	2	3	4	5

Write the Chinese number that is 1 less.

___ 二 ___ 五 ___ 二

 At Home

We learned about related subtraction facts. Ask your child to tell you how the pairs of facts are alike.

Number Fun House

Subtract. Color to match differences.

1 or 2))) blue)))

3 or 4)) green))

5)) purple))

6)) orange))

7)) yellow))

8)) red))

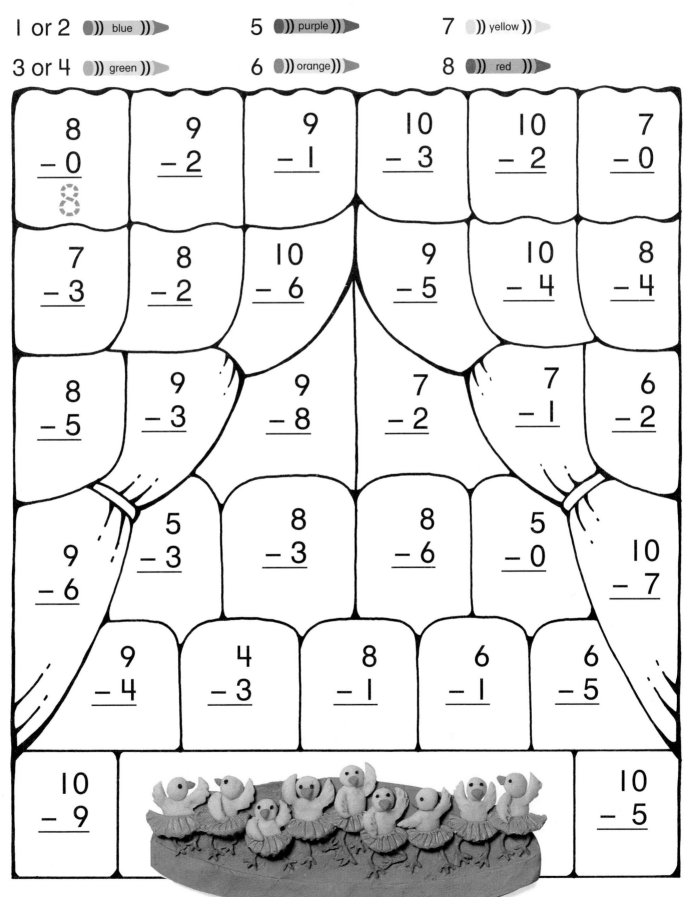

$$8 - 0 = 8$$

$$9 - 2$$

$$9 - 1$$

$$10 - 3$$

$$10 - 2$$

$$7 - 0$$

$$7 - 3$$

$$8 - 2$$

$$10 - 6$$

$$9 - 5$$

$$10 - 4$$

$$8 - 4$$

$$8 - 5$$

$$9 - 3$$

$$9 - 8$$

$$7 - 2$$

$$7 - 1$$

$$6 - 2$$

$$9 - 6$$

$$5 - 3$$

$$8 - 3$$

$$8 - 6$$

$$5 - 0$$

$$10 - 7$$

$$9 - 4$$

$$4 - 3$$

$$8 - 1$$

$$6 - 1$$

$$6 - 5$$

$$10 - 9$$

$$10 - 5$$

Subtract. Use counters if you want to.

1

10	6	9	7	9	8
− 9	− 6	− 8	− 6	− 0	− 3

2

8	10	6	8	5	9
− 8	− 5	− 1	− 6	− 5	− 2

 Algebra Match related facts. Subtract.

3

9	10	10
− 3	− 4	− 1
6		

10	9	10
− 9	− 6	− 6
	3	

4

9	9	10
− 5	− 2	− 7

9	10	9
− 7	− 3	− 4

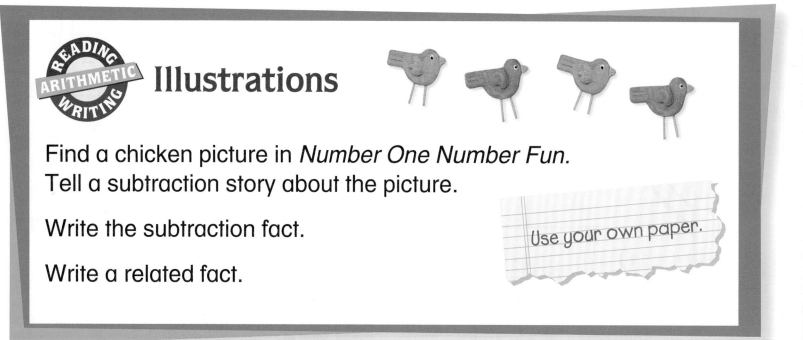

READING ARITHMETIC WRITING Illustrations

Find a chicken picture in *Number One Number Fun.*
Tell a subtraction story about the picture.

Write the subtraction fact.

Write a related fact.

Use your own paper.

Name _____

Find how much money Josh has left.

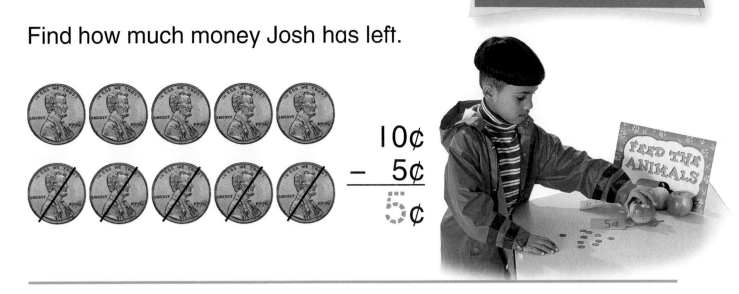

$$\begin{array}{r} 10¢ \\ - 5¢ \\ \hline 5¢ \end{array}$$

You need 10 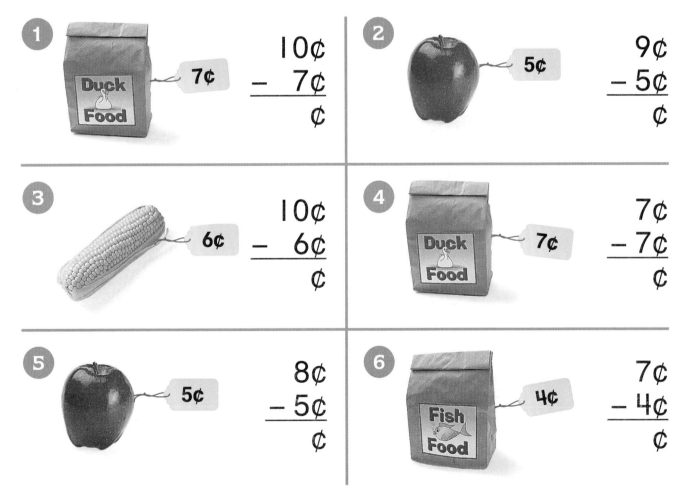.
Subtract to find how much money is left.

1 Duck Food 7¢
$$\begin{array}{r} 10¢ \\ - 7¢ \\ \hline ¢ \end{array}$$

2 5¢
$$\begin{array}{r} 9¢ \\ - 5¢ \\ \hline ¢ \end{array}$$

3 6¢
$$\begin{array}{r} 10¢ \\ - 6¢ \\ \hline ¢ \end{array}$$

4 Duck Food 7¢
$$\begin{array}{r} 7¢ \\ - 7¢ \\ \hline ¢ \end{array}$$

5 5¢
$$\begin{array}{r} 8¢ \\ - 5¢ \\ \hline ¢ \end{array}$$

6 Fish Food 4¢
$$\begin{array}{r} 7¢ \\ - 4¢ \\ \hline ¢ \end{array}$$

Critical Thinking You have 5¢. How much more money do you need to buy duck food?

McGraw-Hill School Division

Practice!

Use pennies if you want to.

Subtract.

1 6¢

$$\begin{array}{r} 9¢ \\ -\ 6¢ \\ \hline 3¢ \end{array}$$

2 1¢

$$\begin{array}{r} 7¢ \\ -\ 1¢ \\ \hline ¢ \end{array}$$

3 Fish Food 4¢

$$\begin{array}{r} 10¢ \\ -\ 4¢ \\ \hline ¢ \end{array}$$

4 3¢

$$\begin{array}{r} 8¢ \\ -\ 3¢ \\ \hline ¢ \end{array}$$

5
$$\begin{array}{r} 10¢ \\ -\ 7¢ \\ \hline ¢ \end{array}$$
$$\begin{array}{r} 9¢ \\ -\ 5¢ \\ \hline ¢ \end{array}$$
$$\begin{array}{r} 7¢ \\ -\ 3¢ \\ \hline ¢ \end{array}$$
$$\begin{array}{r} 8¢ \\ -\ 6¢ \\ \hline ¢ \end{array}$$
$$\begin{array}{r} 9¢ \\ -\ 2¢ \\ \hline ¢ \end{array}$$
$$\begin{array}{r} 6¢ \\ -\ 5¢ \\ \hline ¢ \end{array}$$

6
$$\begin{array}{r} 8¢ \\ -\ 2¢ \\ \hline ¢ \end{array}$$
$$\begin{array}{r} 10¢ \\ -\ 5¢ \\ \hline ¢ \end{array}$$
$$\begin{array}{r} 4¢ \\ -\ 1¢ \\ \hline ¢ \end{array}$$
$$\begin{array}{r} 9¢ \\ -\ 9¢ \\ \hline ¢ \end{array}$$
$$\begin{array}{r} 5¢ \\ -\ 2¢ \\ \hline ¢ \end{array}$$
$$\begin{array}{r} 7¢ \\ -\ 6¢ \\ \hline ¢ \end{array}$$

7
$$\begin{array}{r} 4¢ \\ -\ 4¢ \\ \hline ¢ \end{array}$$
$$\begin{array}{r} 10¢ \\ -\ 8¢ \\ \hline ¢ \end{array}$$
$$\begin{array}{r} 5¢ \\ -\ 1¢ \\ \hline ¢ \end{array}$$
$$\begin{array}{r} 9¢ \\ -\ 8¢ \\ \hline ¢ \end{array}$$
$$\begin{array}{r} 6¢ \\ -\ 3¢ \\ \hline ¢ \end{array}$$
$$\begin{array}{r} 8¢ \\ -\ 5¢ \\ \hline ¢ \end{array}$$

More to Explore   Patterns

a Algebra **PATTERNS** Complete.

$$\begin{array}{r} 9 \\ -\ 3 \\ \hline 6 \end{array}$$
$$\begin{array}{r} 8 \\ -\ 3 \\ \hline \end{array}$$
$$\begin{array}{r} 7 \\ -\ 3 \\ \hline \end{array}$$
$$\begin{array}{r} 6 \\ -\ 3 \\ \hline \end{array}$$
$$\begin{array}{r} \boxed{} \\ -\ 3 \\ \hline \end{array}$$
$$\begin{array}{r} \boxed{} \\ -\ 3 \\ \hline \end{array}$$
$$\begin{array}{r} \boxed{} \\ -\ 3 \\ \hline \end{array}$$

 At Home

Show your child 10 pennies. Ask how many you would have left if you spent 6¢.

Name _____

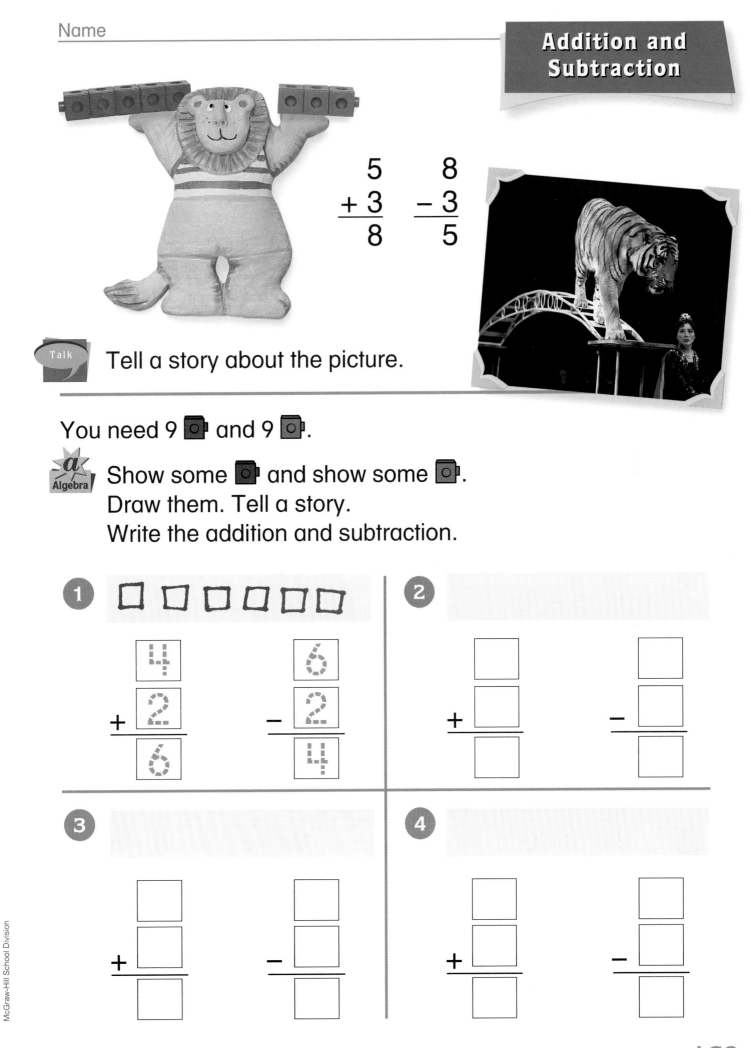

$$
\begin{array}{r} 5 \\ + 3 \\ \hline 8 \end{array}
\qquad
\begin{array}{r} 8 \\ - 3 \\ \hline 5 \end{array}
$$

Talk Tell a story about the picture.

You need 9 🎥 and 9 🎥.

Algebra Show some 🎥 and show some 🎥.
Draw them. Tell a story.
Write the addition and subtraction.

1 □ □ □ □ □ □

$$
\begin{array}{r} 4 \\ + 2 \\ \hline 6 \end{array}
\qquad
\begin{array}{r} 6 \\ - 2 \\ \hline 4 \end{array}
$$

2

$$
\begin{array}{r} \square \\ + \square \\ \hline \square \end{array}
\qquad
\begin{array}{r} \square \\ - \square \\ \hline \square \end{array}
$$

3

$$
\begin{array}{r} \square \\ + \square \\ \hline \square \end{array}
\qquad
\begin{array}{r} \square \\ - \square \\ \hline \square \end{array}
$$

4

$$
\begin{array}{r} \square \\ + \square \\ \hline \square \end{array}
\qquad
\begin{array}{r} \square \\ - \square \\ \hline \square \end{array}
$$

Practice!

> Use cubes if you want to.

Add or subtract.

1

$$\begin{array}{r} 2 \\ + 5 \\ \hline 7 \end{array}$$

$$\begin{array}{r} 7 \\ - 5 \\ \hline 2 \end{array}$$

2

$$\begin{array}{r} 6 \\ + 0 \\ \hline \end{array}$$

$$\begin{array}{r} 6 \\ - 6 \\ \hline \end{array}$$

3

$$\begin{array}{r} 8 \\ + 2 \\ \hline \end{array}$$

$$\begin{array}{r} 10 \\ - 2 \\ \hline \end{array}$$

$$\begin{array}{r} 3 \\ + 4 \\ \hline \end{array}$$

$$\begin{array}{r} 7 \\ - 4 \\ \hline \end{array}$$

$$\begin{array}{r} 1 \\ + 3 \\ \hline \end{array}$$

$$\begin{array}{r} 4 \\ - 3 \\ \hline \end{array}$$

4

$$\begin{array}{r} 5 \\ + 1 \\ \hline \end{array}$$

$$\begin{array}{r} 6 \\ - 1 \\ \hline \end{array}$$

$$\begin{array}{r} 7 \\ + 2 \\ \hline \end{array}$$

$$\begin{array}{r} 9 \\ - 2 \\ \hline \end{array}$$

$$\begin{array}{r} 6 \\ + 2 \\ \hline \end{array}$$

$$\begin{array}{r} 8 \\ - 2 \\ \hline \end{array}$$

5

$$\begin{array}{r} 0 \\ + 5 \\ \hline \end{array}$$

$$\begin{array}{r} 5 \\ - 5 \\ \hline \end{array}$$

$$\begin{array}{r} 4 \\ + 3 \\ \hline \end{array}$$

$$\begin{array}{r} 7 \\ - 3 \\ \hline \end{array}$$

$$\begin{array}{r} 3 \\ + 3 \\ \hline \end{array}$$

$$\begin{array}{r} 6 \\ - 3 \\ \hline \end{array}$$

6

$$\begin{array}{r} 3 \\ + 7 \\ \hline \end{array}$$

$$\begin{array}{r} 10 \\ - 7 \\ \hline \end{array}$$

$$\begin{array}{r} 8 \\ + 1 \\ \hline \end{array}$$

$$\begin{array}{r} 9 \\ - 1 \\ \hline \end{array}$$

$$\begin{array}{r} 5 \\ + 5 \\ \hline \end{array}$$

$$\begin{array}{r} 10 \\ - 5 \\ \hline \end{array}$$

 Journal Draw a picture that shows addition and subtraction. Write the facts.

 At Home We learned how addition and subtraction can be related. Ask your child about the exercises on page 169.

Choose the Operation

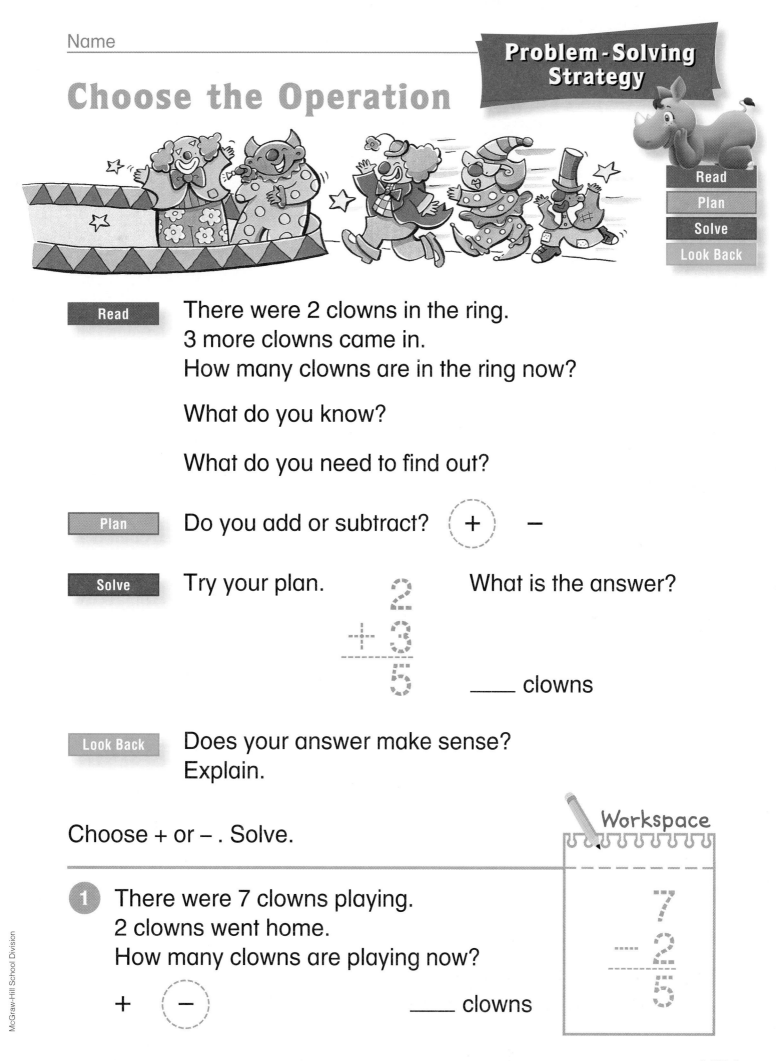

Read   There were 2 clowns in the ring.
3 more clowns came in.
How many clowns are in the ring now?

What do you know?

What do you need to find out?

Plan   Do you add or subtract? $+$ $-$

Solve   Try your plan.   What is the answer?

$$\begin{array}{r} 2 \\ +\,3 \\ \hline 5 \end{array}$$

____ clowns

Look Back   Does your answer make sense?
Explain.

Choose $+$ or $-$. Solve.

Workspace

1   There were 7 clowns playing.
2 clowns went home.
How many clowns are playing now?

$+$ $-$ ____ clowns

$$\begin{array}{r} 7 \\ -\,2 \\ \hline 5 \end{array}$$

Practice!

Choose + or –. Solve.

1 There are 3 dogs in one car.
There are 5 dogs in another car.
How many dogs are in the two cars?

+ – _____ dogs

$$\begin{array}{r} 3 \\ +5 \\ \hline 8 \end{array}$$

2 9 cats wear hats.
6 of the cats take off their hats.
How many cats still wear hats?

+ – _____ cats

3 There were 9 pigs in a pen.
2 pigs get away.
How many pigs are left?

+ – _____ pigs

4 8 goats dance in a circle.
I more goat joins them.
How many goats are there now?

+ – _____ goats

172 ● one hundred seventy-two

 At Home

We are learning how to read and solve problems. You may want to review those problems with your child.

Name _____

Use a Picture

The picture shows what is for sale at a backyard circus.

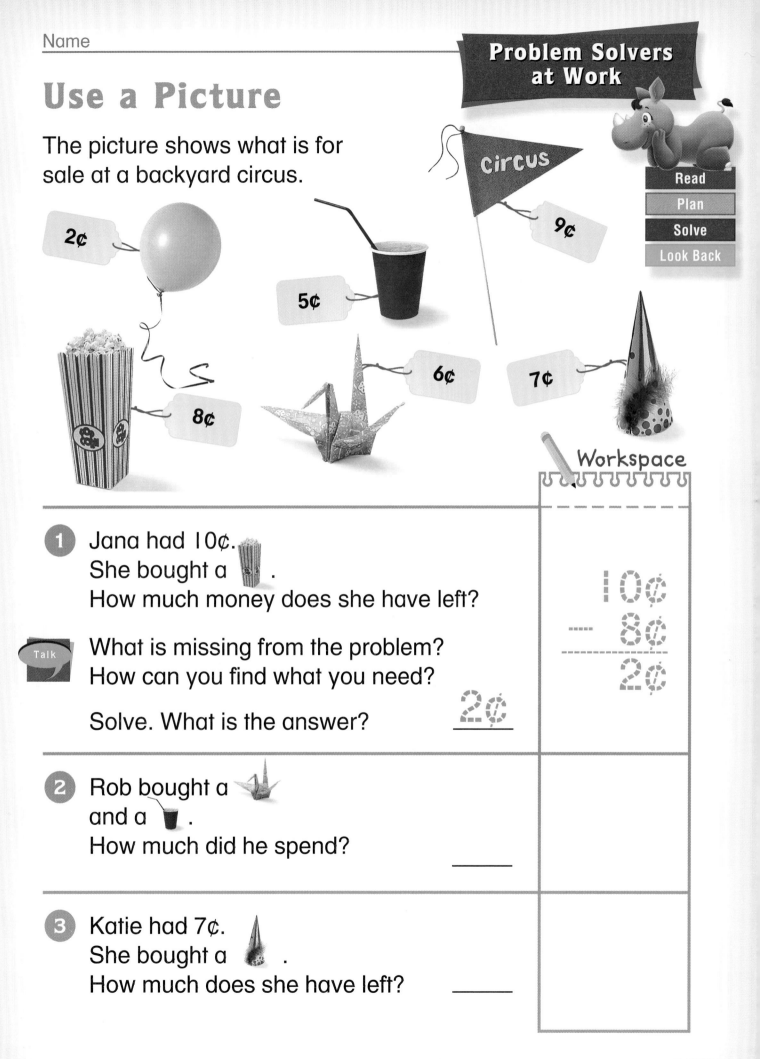

circus

2¢

9¢

5¢

6¢

7¢

8¢

Workspace

1   Jana had 10¢.
    She bought a 🍿 .
    How much money does she have left?

Talk What is missing from the problem?
    How can you find what you need?

    Solve. What is the answer? __2¢__

$$
\begin{array}{r}
10¢ \\
- 8¢ \\
\hline
2¢
\end{array}
$$

2   Rob bought a 🐦
    and a 🥤 .
    How much did he spend? _____

3   Katie had 7¢.
    She bought a 🎉 .
    How much does she have left? _____

6¢ 5¢ 3¢ 4¢

Workspace

Solve.

1 READING ARITHMETIC WRITING **Illustrations** Look at the picture of things to buy. Luis has 8¢. He buys a 😊. How much money does he have left? ____

2 Then Luis finds 2 more pennies. How much money does he have now? ____

Talk How did you solve problem 2?

Write and Share

Neil wrote this problem.

Jennifer had 10¢. She bought a 🎈 for 2¢. How much does she have left?

STUDENT TO STUDENT

Neil Perrette
O'Rourke School
Mobile, Alabama

3 Solve Neil's problem. ____

Talk How did you solve Neil's problem?

Use your own paper.

4 Write Write a problem. Have a partner solve it.

At Home Ask your child about the problem he or she wrote.

Chapter Review

Language and Mathematics

Choose the correct word to complete the sentence.

1. _____ show the same numbers.

2. 7 – 1 = 6 is a subtraction _____.

> fact
> related
> facts
> graph

Concepts and Skills

Add or subtract.

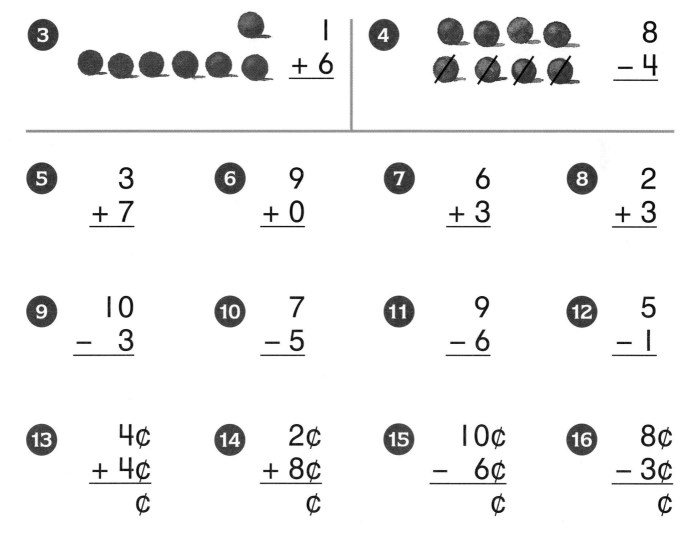

3.
$$\begin{array}{r} 1 \\ + 6 \\ \hline \end{array}$$

4.
$$\begin{array}{r} 8 \\ - 4 \\ \hline \end{array}$$

5.
$$\begin{array}{r} 3 \\ + 7 \\ \hline \end{array}$$

6.
$$\begin{array}{r} 9 \\ + 0 \\ \hline \end{array}$$

7.
$$\begin{array}{r} 6 \\ + 3 \\ \hline \end{array}$$

8.
$$\begin{array}{r} 2 \\ + 3 \\ \hline \end{array}$$

9.
$$\begin{array}{r} 10 \\ - 3 \\ \hline \end{array}$$

10.
$$\begin{array}{r} 7 \\ - 5 \\ \hline \end{array}$$

11.
$$\begin{array}{r} 9 \\ - 6 \\ \hline \end{array}$$

12.
$$\begin{array}{r} 5 \\ - 1 \\ \hline \end{array}$$

13.
$$\begin{array}{r} 4¢ \\ + 4¢ \\ \hline ¢ \end{array}$$

14.
$$\begin{array}{r} 2¢ \\ + 8¢ \\ \hline ¢ \end{array}$$

15.
$$\begin{array}{r} 10¢ \\ - 6¢ \\ \hline ¢ \end{array}$$

16.
$$\begin{array}{r} 8¢ \\ - 3¢ \\ \hline ¢ \end{array}$$

Problem Solving

Choose + or −. Solve.

17 There are 6 cats playing.
3 more cats come to play.
How many cats are
playing now?

+ − _____ cats

18 There are 8 dogs playing.
5 dogs run home.
How many dogs are
playing now?

+ − _____ dogs

Solve.

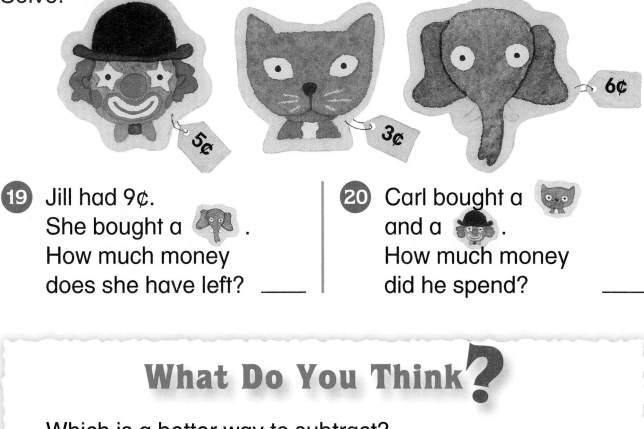

19 Jill had 9¢.
She bought a 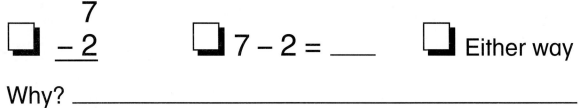.
How much money
does she have left? _____

20 Carl bought a
and a .
How much money
did he spend? _____

What Do You Think?

Which is a better way to subtract?
☑ Check one.

☐ $\begin{array}{r} 7 \\ -2 \\ \hline \end{array}$ ☐ $7 - 2 =$ _____   ☐ Either way

Why? _____

Journal Show how you add and subtract money.

Chapter Test

Add.

1 2
+ 3

2 3
+ 5

3 9   8
+ 1   + 0

4 1¢   4¢
+ 5¢   + 3¢

Subtract.

5 8
− 3

6 10
− 4

7 7   8
− 2   − 0

8 6¢   9¢
− 3¢   − 5¢

Choose + or −. Solve.

9 There are 6 clowns on a slide.
There are 4 clowns on a swing.
How many clowns is that in all?

+   −   _____ clowns

Solve.

10 Rhonda has 8¢.
She spends 6¢.
How much money does she have left?   _____

Performance Assessment

What Did You Learn?

You need 10 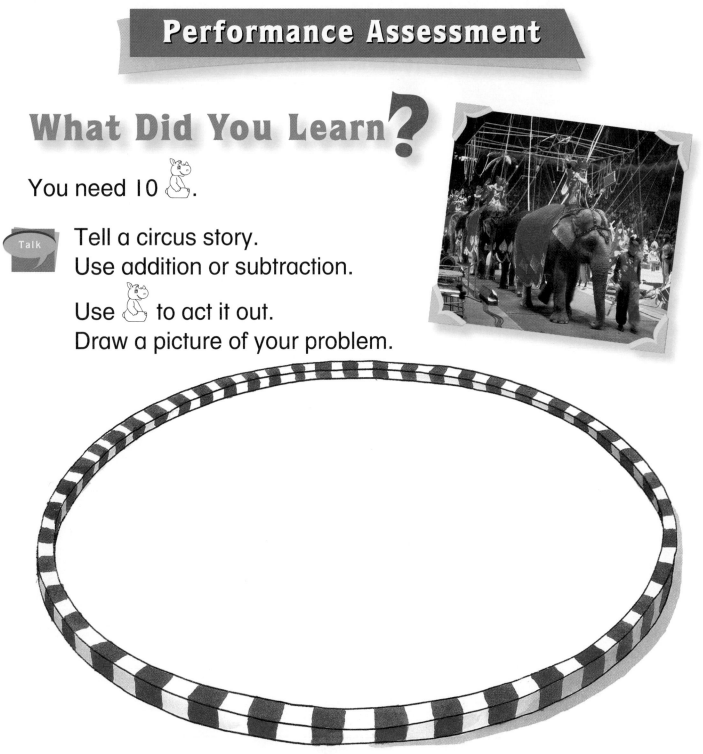.

Talk Tell a circus story.
Use addition or subtraction.

Use to act it out.
Draw a picture of your problem.

Show how you solve your problem.

Portfolio You may want to put this page
in your portfolio.

Name

Addition and Subtraction

Algebra **Talk** **PATTERNS** What patterns do you see?

Add 2.	
4	6
5	7
6	8

$4 + 2$
$5 + 2$
$6 + 2$

Complete the table.

Add 5.	
2	7
3	
4	

Subtract 3.	
5	
6	
7	

Add 0.	
7	
8	
9	

Make your own tables.

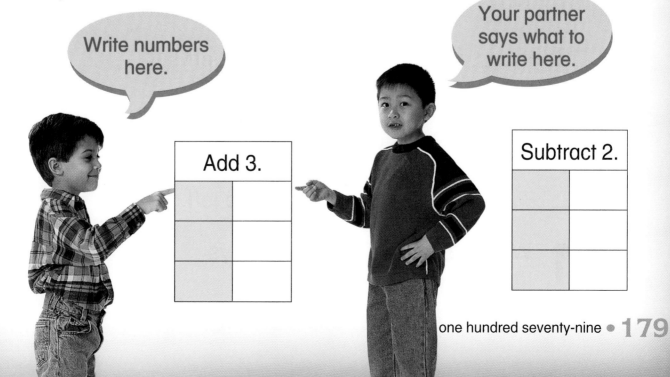

Write numbers here.

Your partner says what to write here.

Add 3.	

Subtract 2.	

Subtraction Song

Ten Little Monkeys

Ten lit - tle mon - keys jump - ing on the bed, One fell off and bumped his____ head. Ma - ma called the Doc - tor and the Doc - tor__ said, "No more mon - key bus - iness, jump - ing on the bed!"

Sing the song.

1 How many monkeys are left on the bed?

$\underline{10} - \underline{1} = \underline{9}$ $\underline{9}$ are left.

2 What if 2 monkeys fell off the bed.
How many monkeys are left on the bed?

____ – ____ = ____   ____ are left.

3 Write a problem about monkeys jumping off the bed.

Use your own paper.

Name _____

Circus Sums!

PLAYERS	2
MATERIALS	2 coins
DIRECTIONS	Drop 2 coins on the balloons. Add the 2 numbers. Find the sum below. Write the addition.

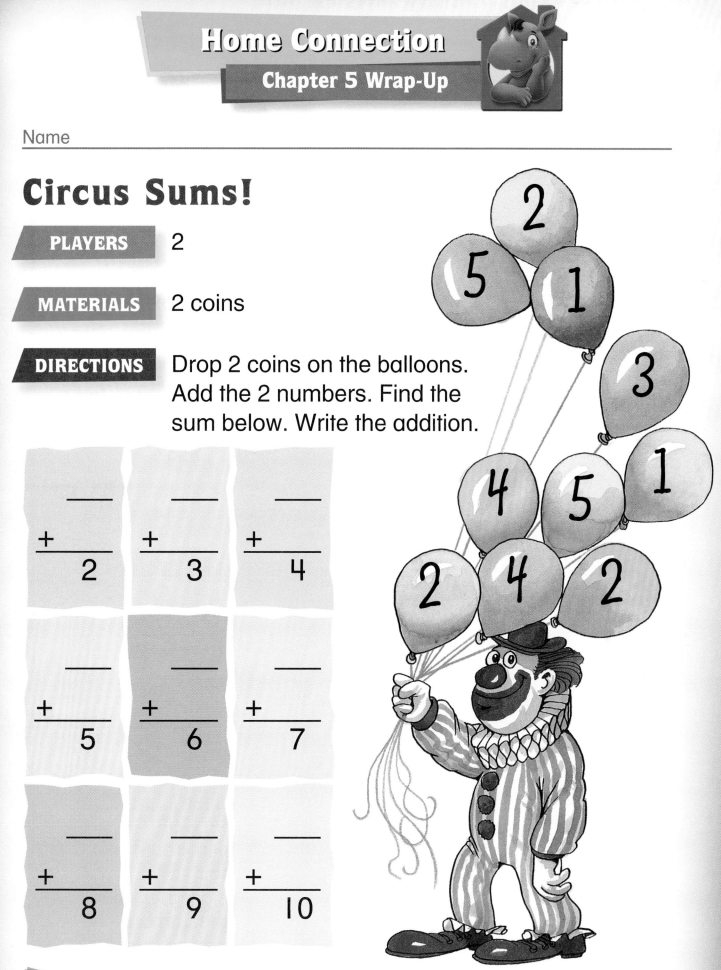

$$\frac{\underline{}}{+}\;2$$ $$\frac{\underline{}}{+}\;3$$ $$\frac{\underline{}}{+}\;4$$

$$\frac{\underline{}}{+}\;5$$ $$\frac{\underline{}}{+}\;6$$ $$\frac{\underline{}}{+}\;7$$

$$\frac{\underline{}}{+}\;8$$ $$\frac{\underline{}}{+}\;9$$ $$\frac{\underline{}}{+}\;10$$

 Play the game with your child to practice addition facts.

Dear Family,

My new chapter in mathematics will be about numbers. I will explore different ways to count and to show numbers. I will also make graphs.

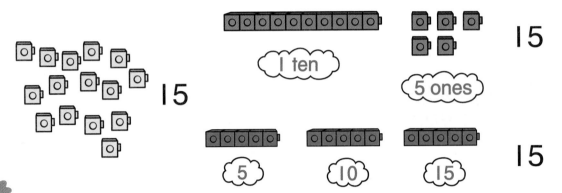

Learning about Families

Let's talk about the people that make up our family. We can draw a picture of a family celebration.

My Math Words

I am going to use these math words in this chapter.

Please help me make word cards for these math words. I can use the word cards when I practice using numbers to 100 and graphing.

Your child,

_____
Signature

tens
ones
estimate
order
before
after
between
skip-count
pair
is greater than
is less than
picture graph
bar graph

Numbers to 100 and Graphing

Theme: One Big Family

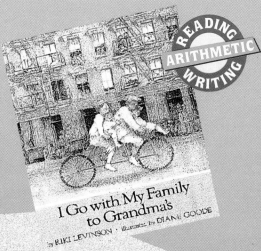

READING · ARITHMETIC · WRITING

Use a Graph Listen to the story *I Go with My Family to Grandma's*.

How many families meet at Grandma's?

How can you use counters on a graph to show the number of people in each family?

What Do You Know?

 Listen to the problem.

How many?

Guess _____ Count _____

Guess _____ Count _____

Guess _____ Count _____

Write about the shapes.
Which color has the most shapes?
Which color has the fewest shapes?

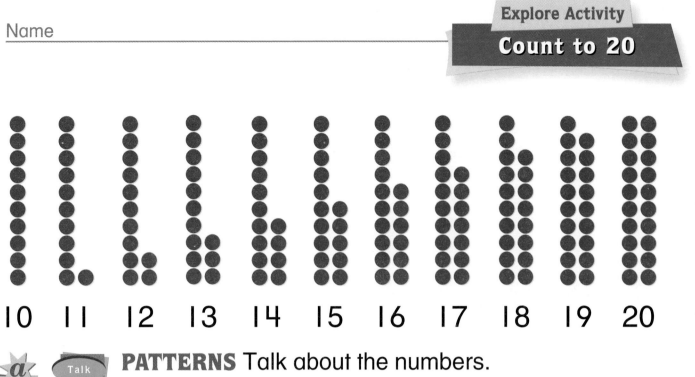

Name _____

10 11 12 13 14 15 16 17 18 19 20

a Algebra   Talk   **PATTERNS** Talk about the numbers.
Tell what pattern you see.

Working Together

You need 20 ⬤.

Take turns.

▶ You show some ⬤.

▶ Your partner counts.

▶ Draw and write to show
the number.

1 ▢

2 ▢

3 ▢

Count. Draw 1 more.   Write the number.

1
‌‌

⟳

_11_

2

_____

3

_____

4

_____

10   11   12   13   14   15   16   17   18   19   20

Write the missing numbers.

5 10, 11, ____, 13, ____, 15, ____, 17, 18, ____, 20

6 10, ____, 12, ____, 14, ____, ____, ____, ____, 19, 20

At Home   Practice counting to 20 with your child.

Working Together

You need 20 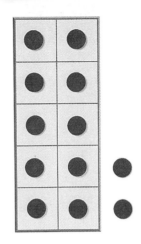 and a ⬚⬚⬚⬚⬚.

Take turns.

▶ Show 10 ◗◖.

▶ Your partner adds more ◖◗.

▶ Draw and write to show the numbers.

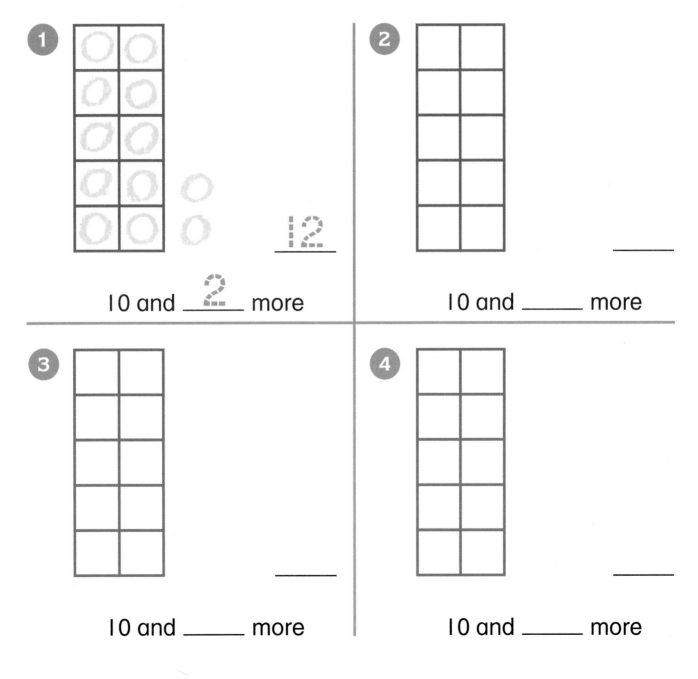

1

10 and __2__ more

2

_____

10 and _____ more

3

_____

10 and _____ more

4

_____

10 and _____ more

Practice!

Show the number with 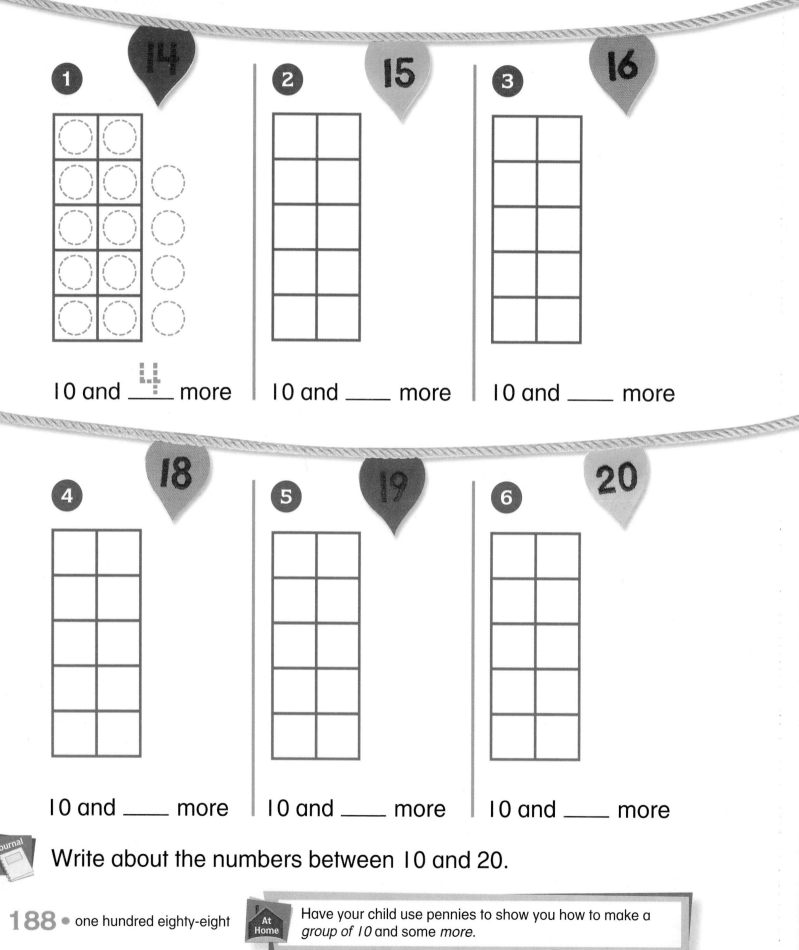 .
Draw and write how many. Say the numbers in order.

14 **1**

10 and **4** more

15 **2**

10 and ____ more

16 **3**

10 and ____ more

18 **4**

10 and ____ more

19 **5**

10 and ____ more

20 **6**

10 and ____ more

Journal Write about the numbers between 10 and 20.

At Home Have your child use pennies to show you how to make a *group of 10* and some *more*.

Name _____

1	2	3	4	5	6	7	8	9	10
11	12	13	14	15	16	17	18	19	20
21	22	23	24	25	26	27	28	29	30
31	32	33	34	35	36	37	38	39	40
41	42	43	44	45	46	47	48	49	50

50 apples

 **PATTERNS** Tell what patterns you see.

Working Together

You need 50 counters.

Take turns.

▶ Show some counters.

▶ Your partner counts.

▶ Draw and write the number.

1 _____

2 _____

Critical Thinking How many groups of 10 in 25?

Practice!

Count. Write the number.

1

$\underline{23}$

2

$\underline{\hphantom{00}}$

3

$\underline{\hphantom{00}}$

4

$\underline{\hphantom{00}}$

Mixed Review — Test Preparation

5 $4 + 1 = \underline{\hphantom{0}}$ $\qquad$ $5 + 3 = \underline{\hphantom{0}}$ $\qquad$ $3 + 2 = \underline{\hphantom{0}}$

6 Write how many.

$\underline{\hphantom{0}}$ $\qquad$ $\underline{\hphantom{0}}$ $\qquad$ $\underline{\hphantom{0}}$

At Home Practice counting to 50 with your child.

Name _____

Working Together

Your group needs 50 .

▶ You each take a handful of ▯.

▶ Count how many in all.

▶ Make groups of ten.

▶ Count again.

▶ Write how many **tens** and **ones**.

35

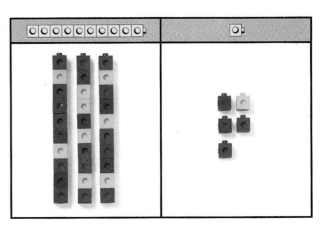

3 tens 5 ones

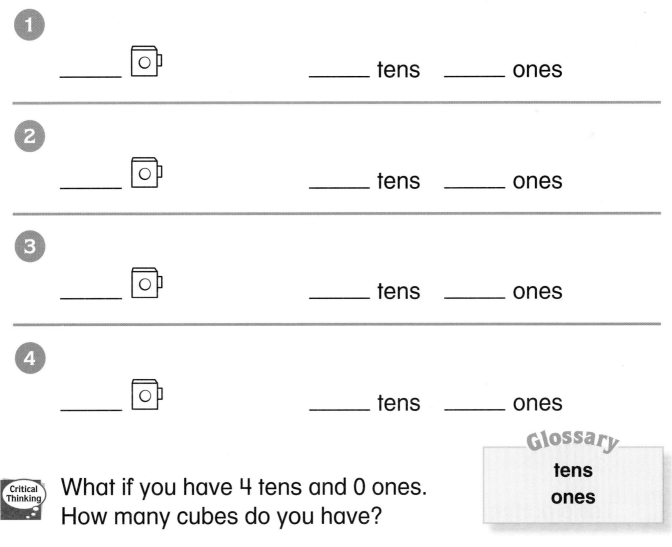

1 _____ ▯   _____ tens _____ ones

2 _____ ▯   _____ tens _____ ones

3 _____ ▯   _____ tens _____ ones

4 _____ ▯   _____ tens _____ ones

Critical Thinking What if you have 4 tens and 0 ones. How many cubes do you have?

Glossary

tens

ones

Count tens and ones.
Write the number.

Use cubes if you want to.

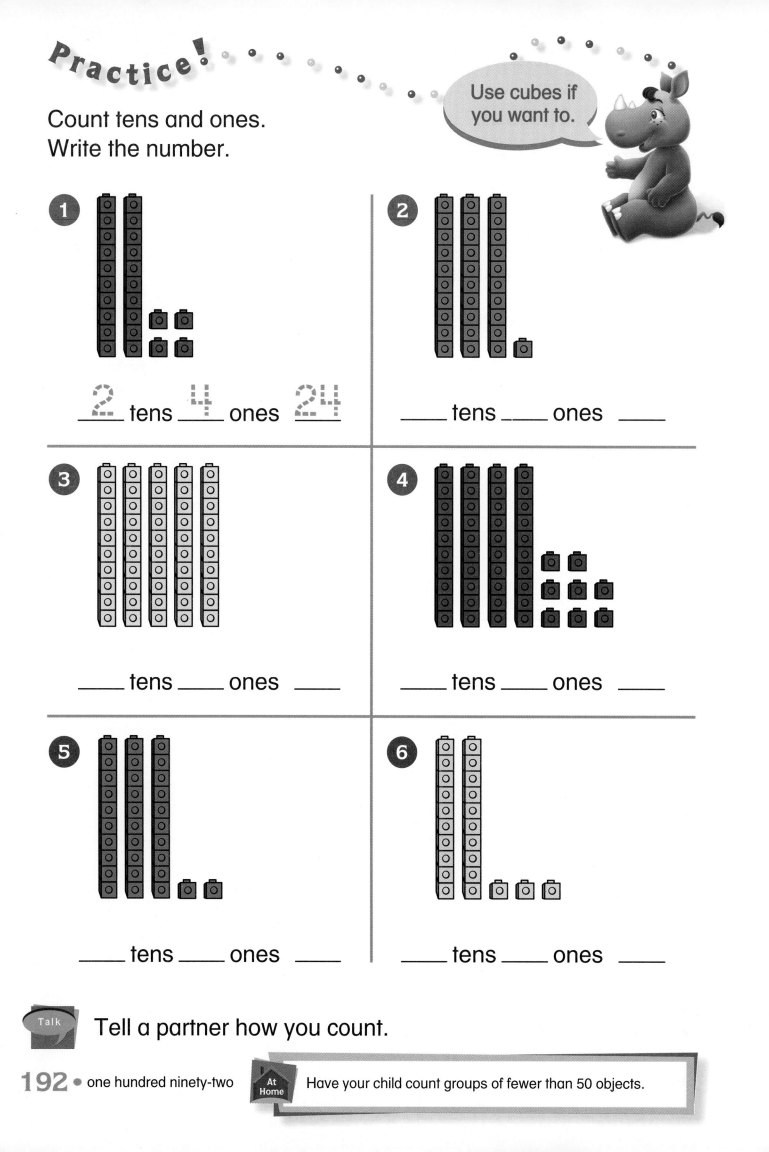

1 ___2___ tens ___4___ ones ___24___

2 _____ tens _____ ones _____

3 _____ tens _____ ones _____

4 _____ tens _____ ones _____

5 _____ tens _____ ones _____

6 _____ tens _____ ones _____

Talk

Tell a partner how you count.

At Home   Have your child count groups of fewer than 50 objects.

Problem-Solving Strategy

Use Estimation

Read | About how many children are in the picture?

Read
Plan
Solve
Look Back

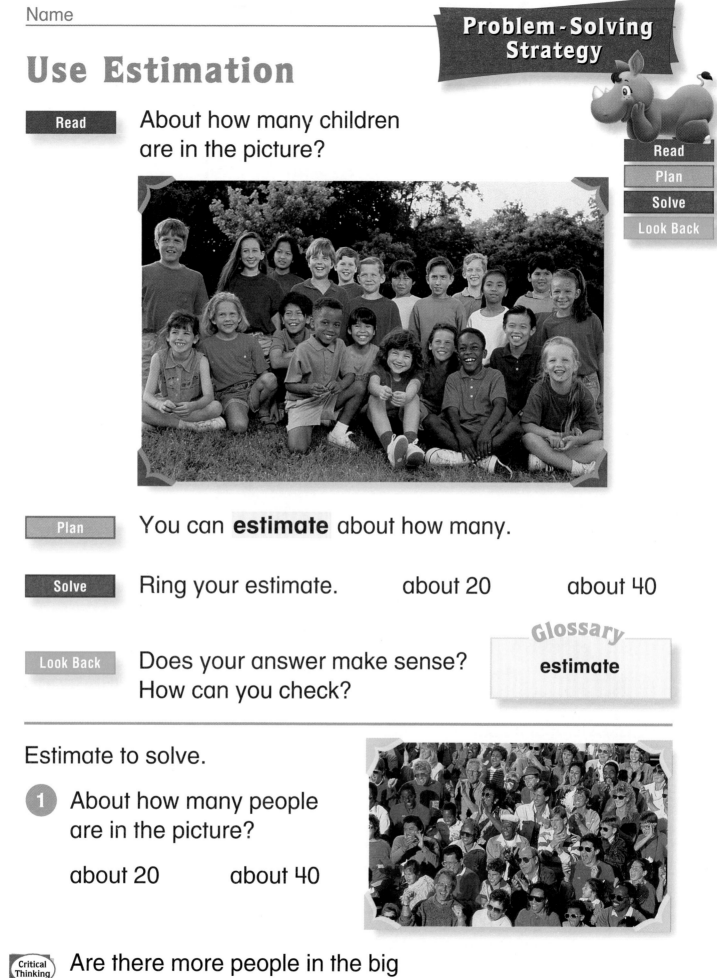

Plan | You can **estimate** about how many.

Solve | Ring your estimate.   about 20   about 40

Look Back | Does your answer make sense? How can you check?

Glossary

estimate

Estimate to solve.

1   About how many people are in the picture?

about 20   about 40

Critical Thinking Are there more people in the big picture or the little picture?

Practice!

Estimate to solve.

1 About how many people?

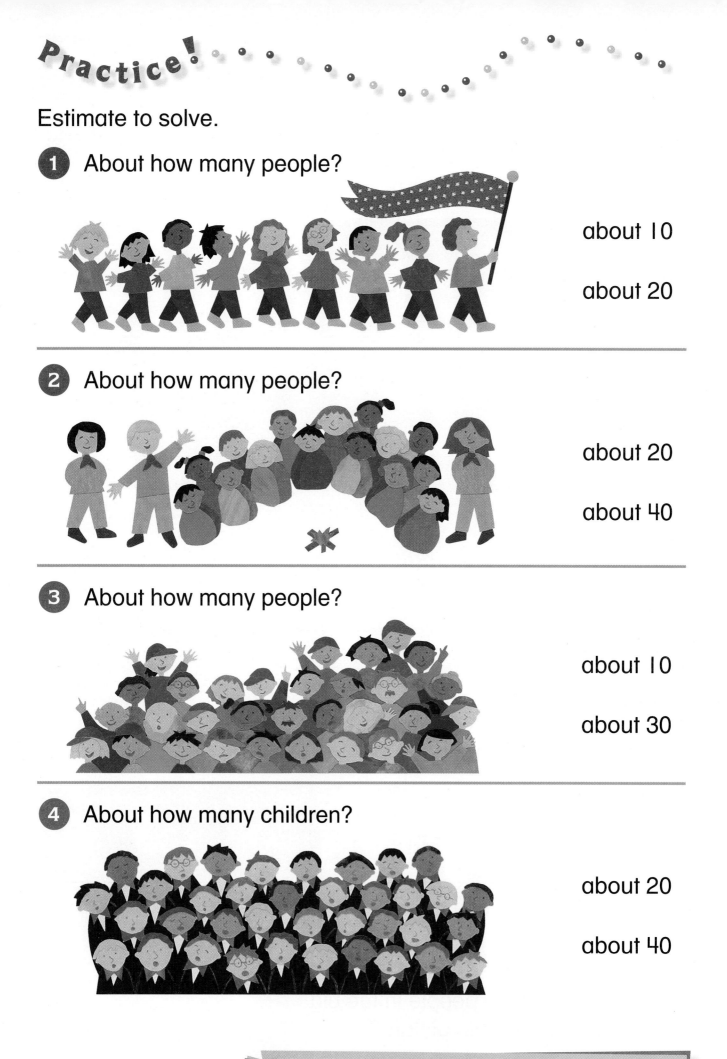

about 10

about 20

2 About how many people?

about 20

about 40

3 About how many people?

about 10

about 30

4 About how many children?

about 20

about 40

 At Home Show your child a handful of small objects. Ask about how many objects you have. Then count.

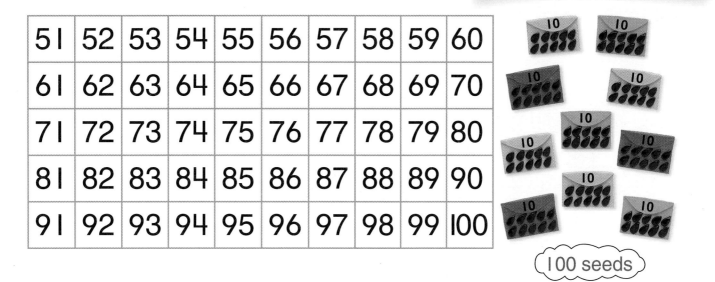

51	52	53	54	55	56	57	58	59	60
61	62	63	64	65	66	67	68	69	70
71	72	73	74	75	76	77	78	79	80
81	82	83	84	85	86	87	88	89	90
91	92	93	94	95	96	97	98	99	100

100 seeds

 PATTERNS Tell what patterns you see.

Working Together

Your group needs 100 counters.

▶ Each of you take a big handful of counters.

▶ Count how many in all.

▶ Draw and write the number.

1 _____

2 _____

Practice!

Count. Write the number.

1 61

2 _____

3 _____

4 _____

5 _____

Talk · **Tell a partner how you counted.**

At Home · Practice counting to 100 with your child.

Name _____

Working Together

Your group needs 100 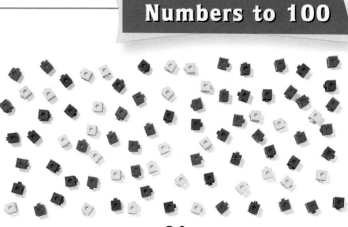.

▶ Each of you take a big handful of ⬜.

▶ Count how many in all.

▶ Make groups of ten.

▶ Count again.

▶ Write how many.

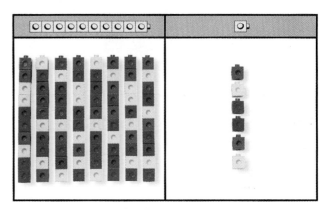

86

8 tens 6 ones

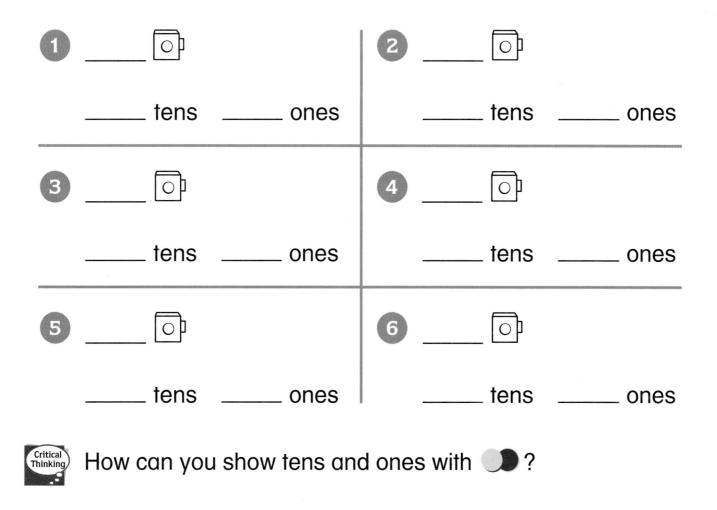

1 _____ ⬜

_____ tens _____ ones

2 _____ ⬜

_____ tens _____ ones

3 _____ ⬜

_____ tens _____ ones

4 _____ ⬜

_____ tens _____ ones

5 _____ ⬜

_____ tens _____ ones

6 _____ ⬜

_____ tens _____ ones

Critical Thinking How can you show tens and ones with ◐ ?

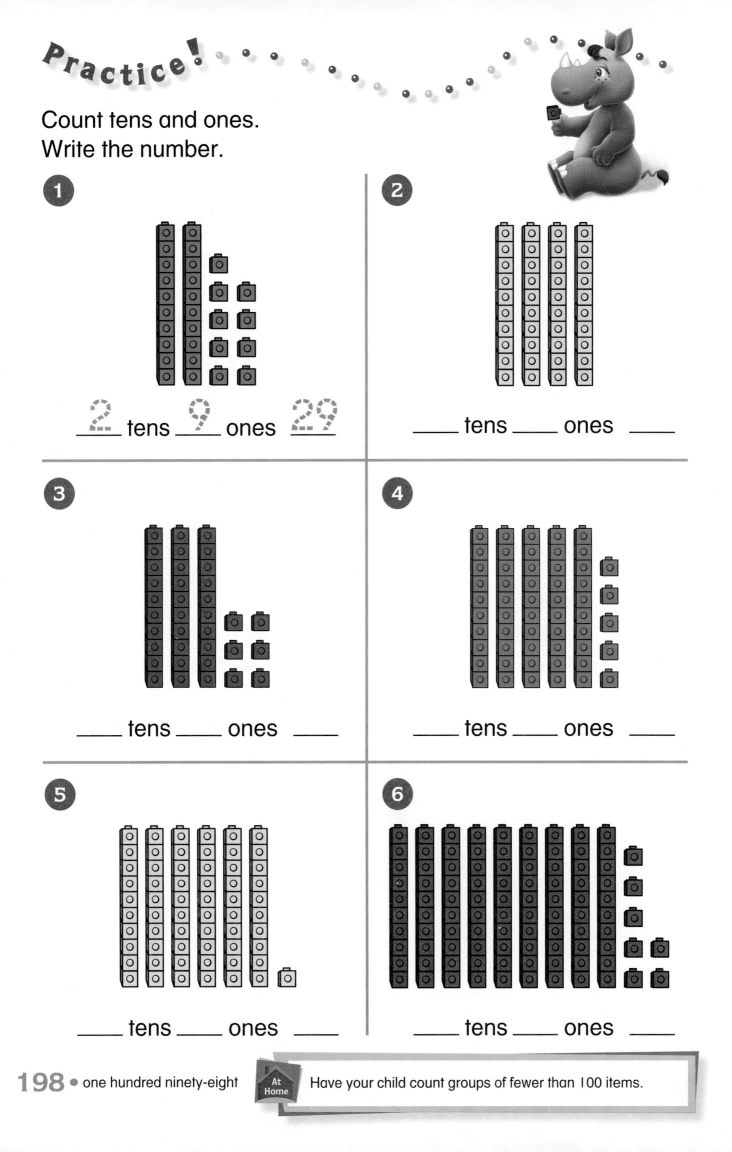

Practice!

Count tens and ones.
Write the number.

1

___2___ tens ___9___ ones ___29___

2

_____ tens _____ ones _____

3

_____ tens _____ ones _____

4

_____ tens _____ ones _____

5

_____ tens _____ ones _____

6

_____ tens _____ ones _____

At Home   Have your child count groups of fewer than 100 items.

Name _____

Do your best!

Write the number.

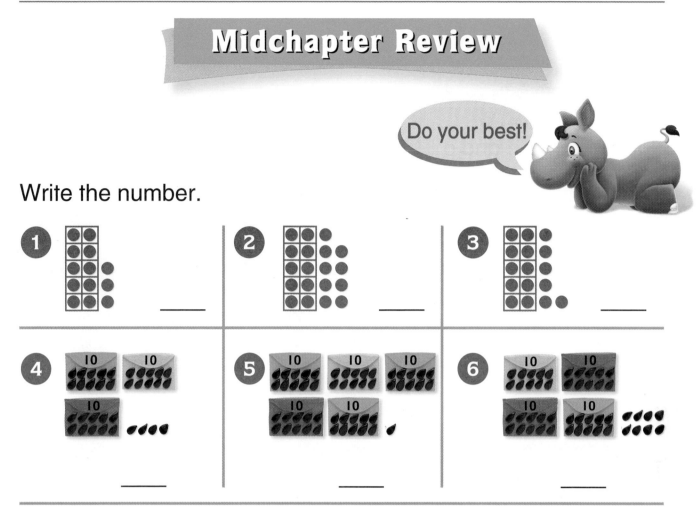

1 _____

2 _____

3 _____

4 _____

5 _____

6 _____

Count tens and ones. Write the number.

7 _____ tens _____ ones _____

8 _____ tens _____ ones _____

9 Estimate to solve. About how many?

about 10   about 20

10 How did you count to answer exercise 8?

_____

_____

Journal

Tell how you estimate about how many.

Around the Neighborhood

You need a ⊗ and a ✏.

Take turns.

► Spin.

► Find the number.

► Color the tens and ones.

► Play until you color all the spaces.

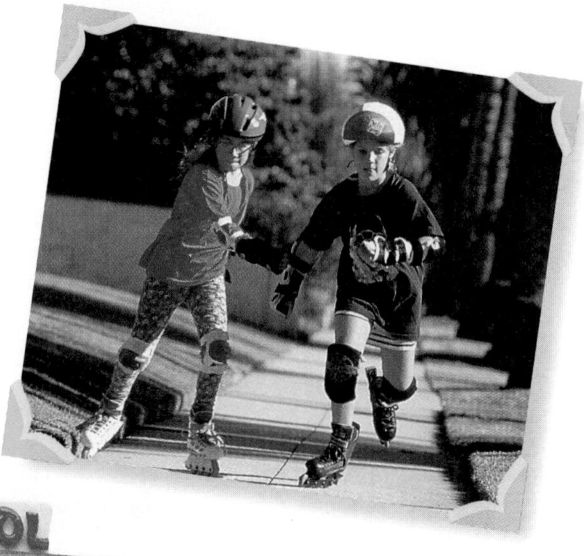

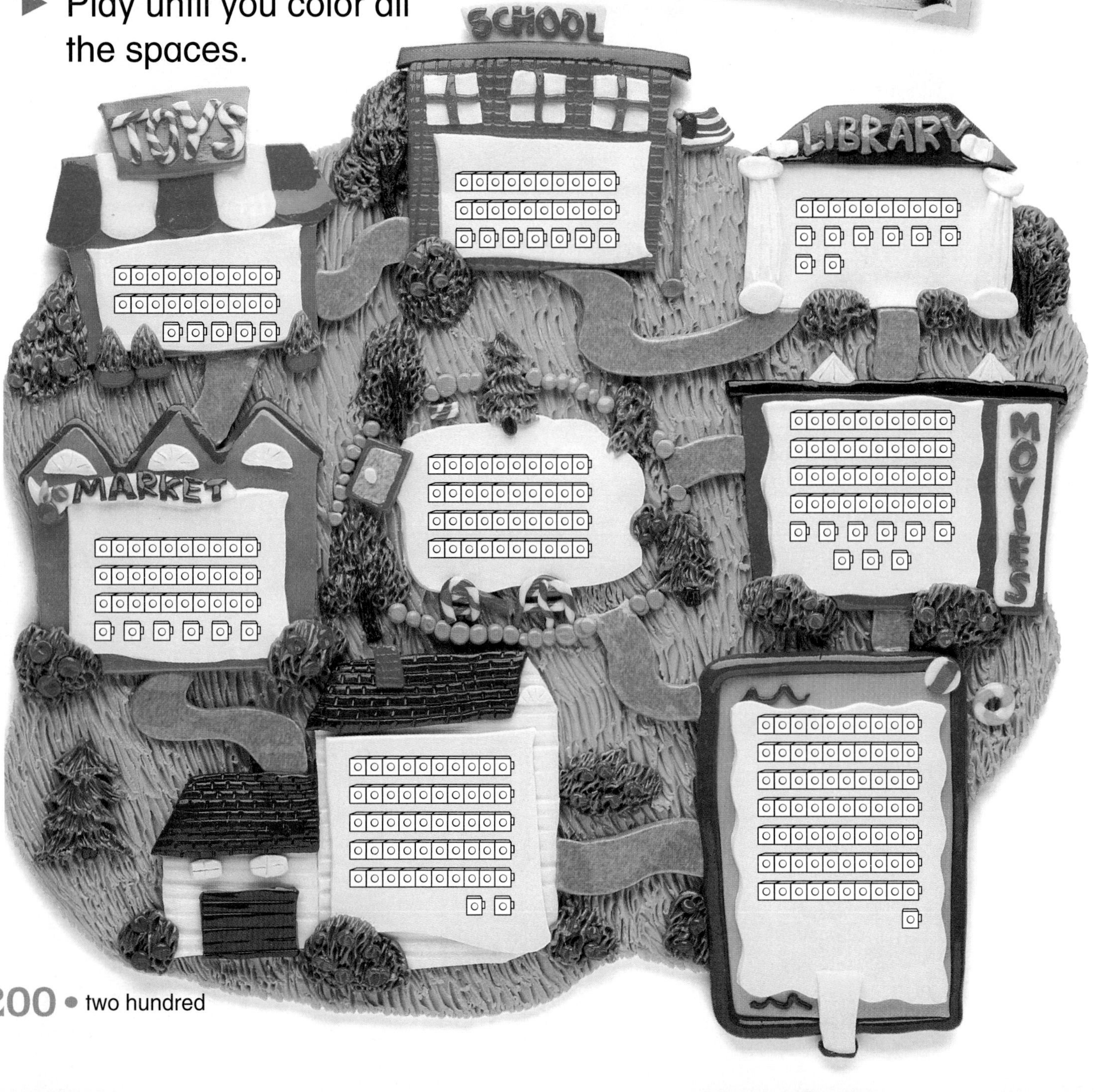

SCHOOL

TOYS

LIBRARY

MARKET

MOVIES

Name

Container Collections

Talk — Tell what you know about 100. Is 100 a lot? Is 100 a little?

Working Together

Work in small groups.

▶ Talk about what you want to count.

▶ Choose an object.

▶ Find different ways to count 100 objects.

Decision Making

1 Choose a container that you think will hold 100. Then see if it does.

2 How many objects did the container hold?

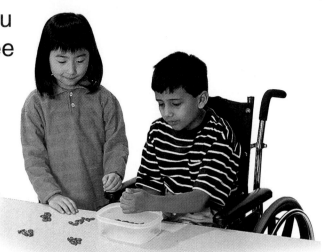

_____

Write a report.

3 Tell what you collected. Tell how you counted.

4 Describe how your collection fit in the container you chose.

More to Investigate

PREDICT Can your collection fit in a smaller container?

EXPLORE Choose a smaller container. Then try it.

FIND How did your collection fit in the container you chose?

Glossary

order

Count.
Write the numbers in **order**.

1	2	3							10
11				15			18		
	22		24					29	
		33			36				40
	42			45				49	
51					56		58		
		64				67			
	73		75					79	
		84		86		88			
	93				97				100

PATTERNS What patterns do you see?

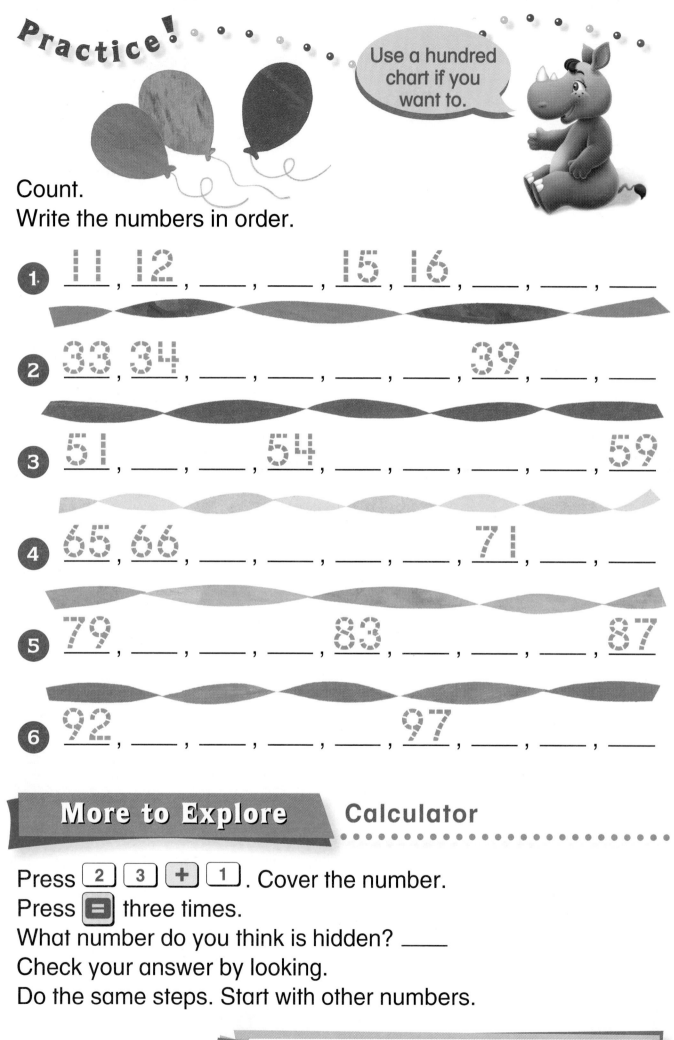

Practice!

Use a hundred chart if you want to.

Count.
Write the numbers in order.

1. 11, 12, ___, ___, 15, 16, ___, ___, ___

2. 33, 34, ___, ___, ___, ___, 39, ___, ___

3. 51, ___, ___, 54, ___, ___, ___, ___, 59

4. 65, 66, ___, ___, ___, ___, 71, ___, ___

5. 79, ___, ___, ___, 83, ___, ___, ___, 87

6. 92, ___, ___, ___, ___, 97, ___, ___, ___

More to Explore Calculator

Press ⟨2⟩ ⟨3⟩ ⟨+⟩ ⟨1⟩. Cover the number.
Press ⟨=⟩ three times.
What number do you think is hidden? ___
Check your answer by looking.
Do the same steps. Start with other numbers.

At Home

Ask your child to count on from numbers such as 11, 32, 69, and 90.

Name _____

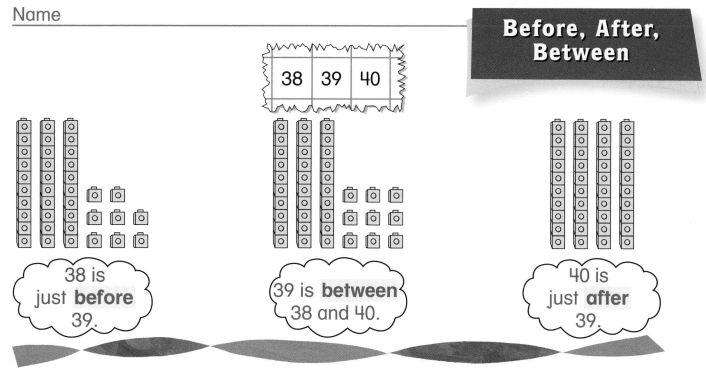

38 is just **before** 39.

39 is **between** 38 and 40.

40 is just **after** 39.

Use models. Write the number that comes just before.

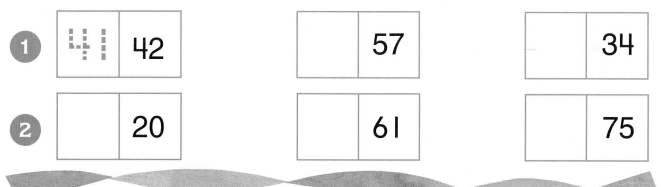

1. | 41 | 42 |

   | | 57 |

   | | 34 |

2. | | 20 |

   | | 61 |

   | | 75 |

Use models. Write the number that comes just after.

3. | 89 | |

   | 14 | |

   | 97 | |

4. | 50 | |

   | 29 | |

   | 22 | |

Use models. Write the number that comes between.

5. | 71 | | 73 |

   | 48 | | 50 |

6. | 98 | | 100 |

   | 69 | | 71 |

Glossary
before
after
between

McGraw-Hill School Division

Count.
Connect the dots.   What do you see? _____

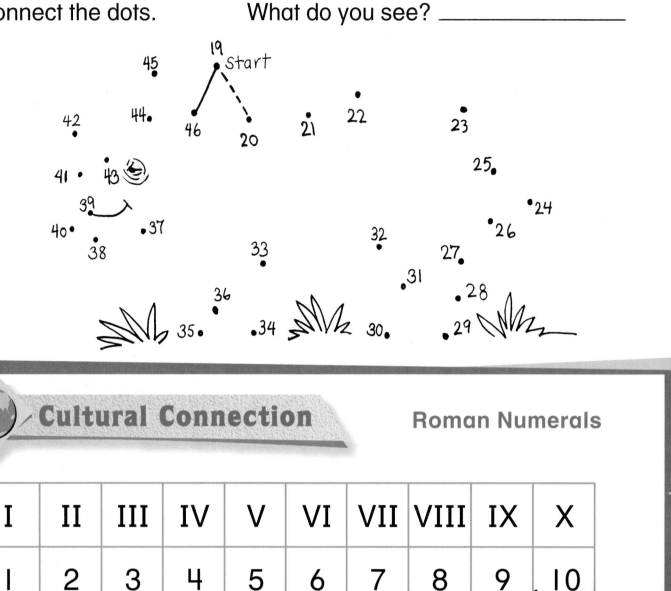

Cultural Connection   Roman Numerals

I	II	III	IV	V	VI	VII	VIII	IX	X
1	2	3	4	5	6	7	8	9	10

Write the Roman numeral that comes
just after.

III IV   VI ___   II ___

IX ___   VIII ___   V ___

At
Home   Pick a number from 10 to 99. Ask your child what number
comes just before and just after the number you pick.

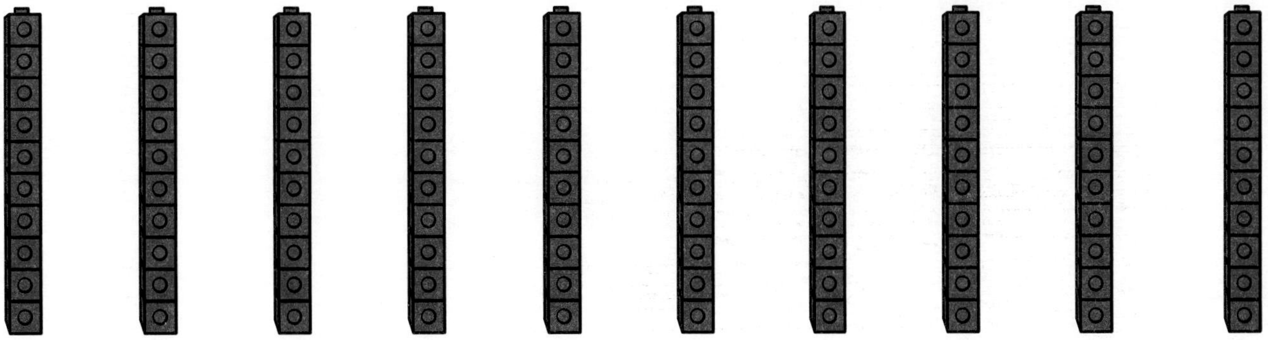

| 10 | 20 | 30 | 40 | 50 | 60 | 70 | 80 | 90 | 100 |

| 5 | 10 | 15 | 20 | 25 | 30 | 35 | 40 | 45 | 50 |

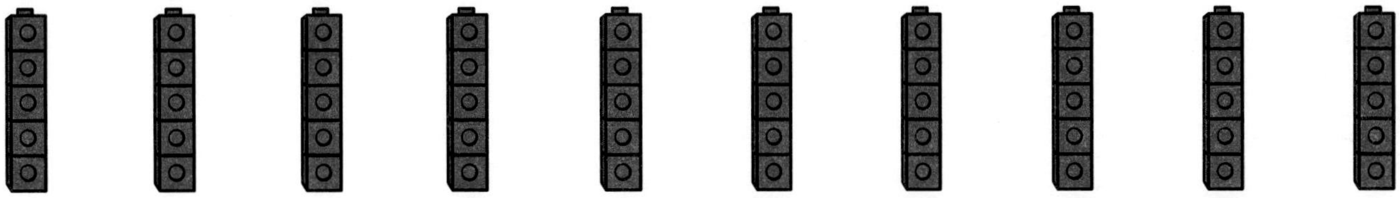

a Algebra **PATTERNS** How many? **Skip-count** by tens.

Glossary
skip-count

1 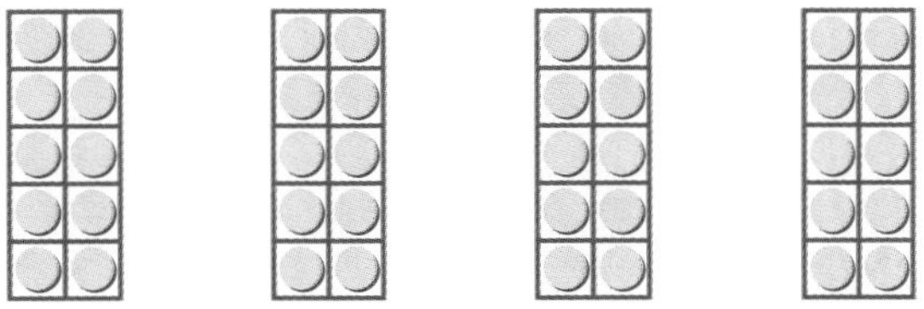 ___ ___ ___ ___   _____ in all
   10

2    _____ in all

How many? Skip-count by fives.

3 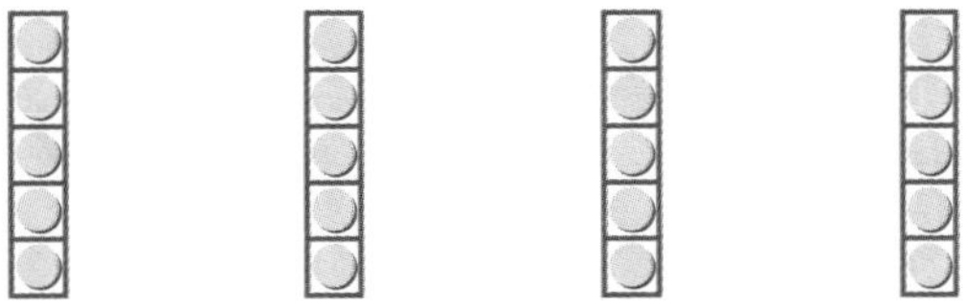 ___ ___ ___ ___   _____ in all
   5

4    _____ in all

How much money? Skip-count by tens.

1

__10__ ____ ____ ____ ____ ____ ____¢

How much money? Skip-count by fives.

2

__5__ ____ ____ ____ ____ ____¢

Skip-count by tens. Color the boxes yellow .
Skip-count by fives. Color the boxes red .

3

1	2	3	4	5	6	7	8	9	10
11	12	13	14	15	16	17	18	19	20
21	22	23	24	25	26	27	28	29	30
31	32	33	34	35	36	37	38	39	40
41	42	43	44	45	46	47	48	49	50

Talk Tell a partner about what happened when you colored the chart.

 At Home Help your child practice skip-counting by fives.

These **pairs** of children are twins.
How many children?

Glossary

pair

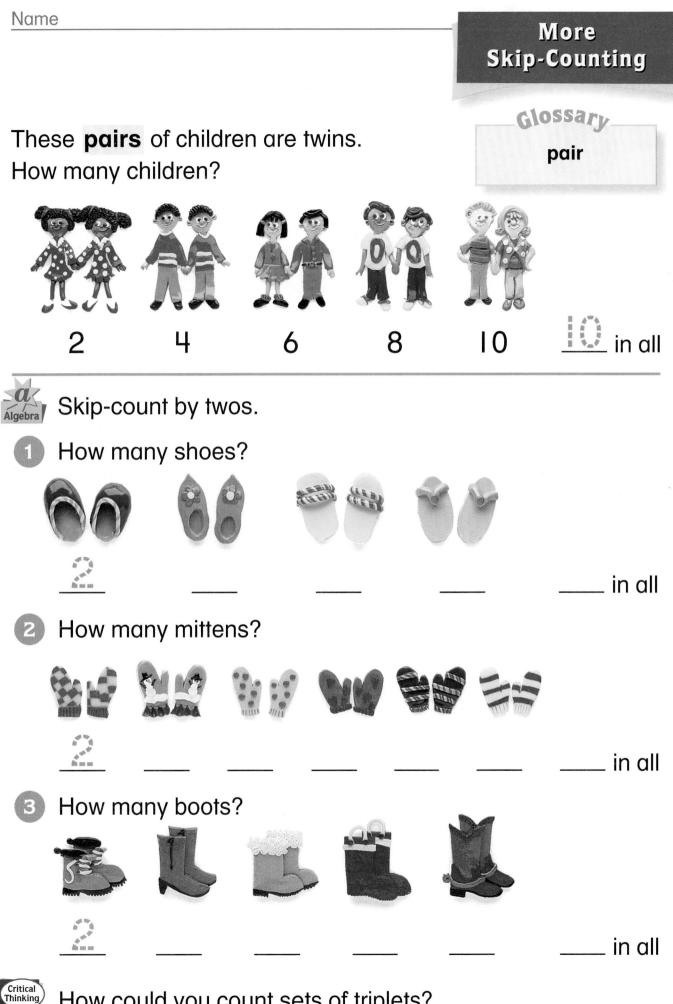

2   4   6   8   10   10 in all

a Algebra Skip-count by twos.

1 How many shoes?

2 ____ ____ ____ ____ in all

2 How many mittens?

2 ____ ____ ____ ____ ____ ____ in all

3 How many boots?

2 ____ ____ ____ ____ ____ in all

Critical Thinking How could you count sets of triplets?

McGraw-Hill School Division

Practice!

Skip-count by twos. How much money?

1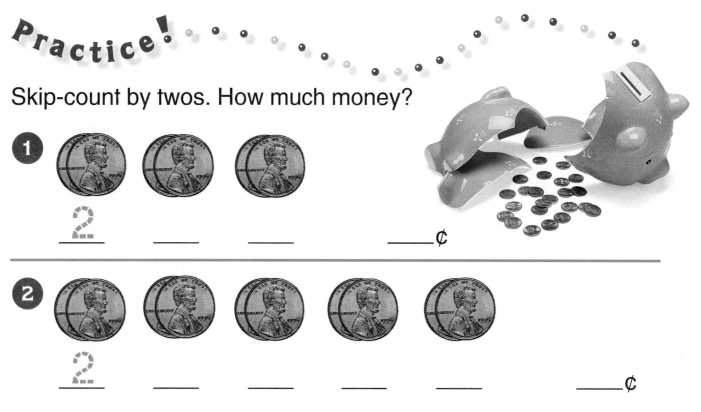

2 ____ ____ ____ ¢

2

2 ____ ____ ____ ____ ____ ¢

Skip-count by twos. Color the boxes))) blue))).

3

1	2	3	4	5	6	7	8	9	10
11	12	13	14	15	16	17	18	19	20
21	22	23	24	25	26	27	28	29	30

More to Explore Patterns

a Algebra **PATTERNS** Complete.

even numbers   *odd numbers*

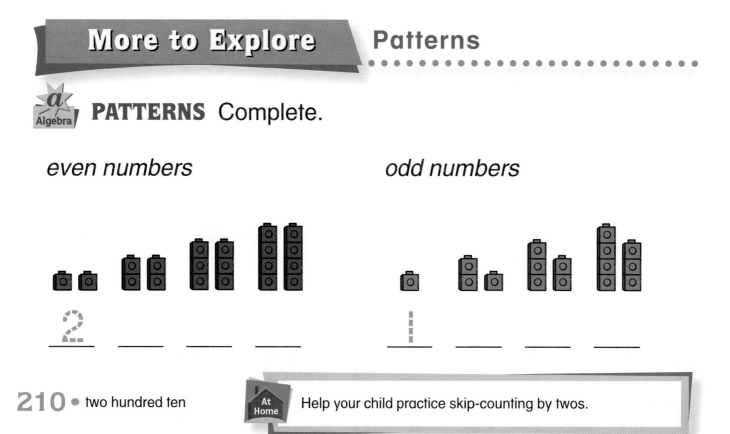

2 ____ ____ ____   1 ____ ____ ____

Name _____

Working Together

Your group needs 50 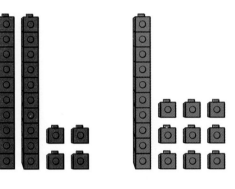 and 50 □.

Take turns.

▶ Pick up a handful of ☐.

▶ Pick up a handful of ☐.

▶ Complete the chart.

Glossary
is greater than
is less than

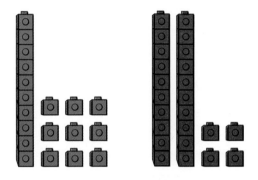

24 **is greater than** 19.   19 **is less than** 24.

	Estimate which is more. Ring.	Count how many.		Write the greater number.
1	🔲 🔲	____ 🔲	____ 🔲	____
2	🔲 🔲	____ 🔲	____ 🔲	____
3	🔲 🔲	____ 🔲	____ 🔲	____
4	🔲 🔲	____ 🔲	____ 🔲	____

Critical Thinking Show 14 ☐ and 14 ☐. Make tens and ones.
When is one number equal to another number?

McGraw-Hill School Division

Practice!

Ring the number that is less.

1 24   ⟨19⟩

> 19 is less than 24.

2

| 16 | 12 | | 17 | 20 | | 31 | 29 |

3

| 27 | 24 | | 15 | 19 | | 34 | 43 |

Ring the number that is greater.

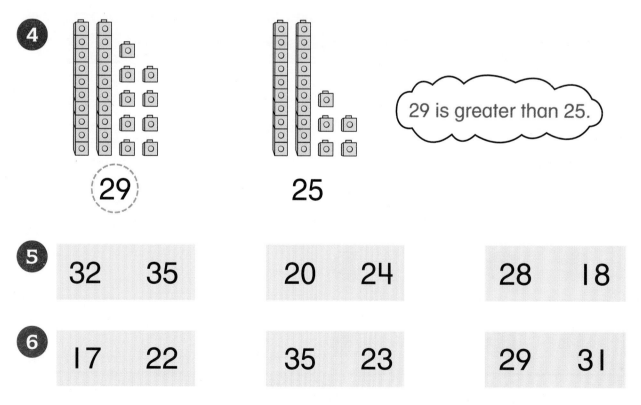

4 ⟨29⟩   25

> 29 is greater than 25.

5

| 32 | 35 | | 20 | 24 | | 28 | 18 |

6

| 17 | 22 | | 35 | 23 | | 29 | 31 |

At Home Ask your child to tell you if 25 is *less than* or *greater than* 52.

Name _____

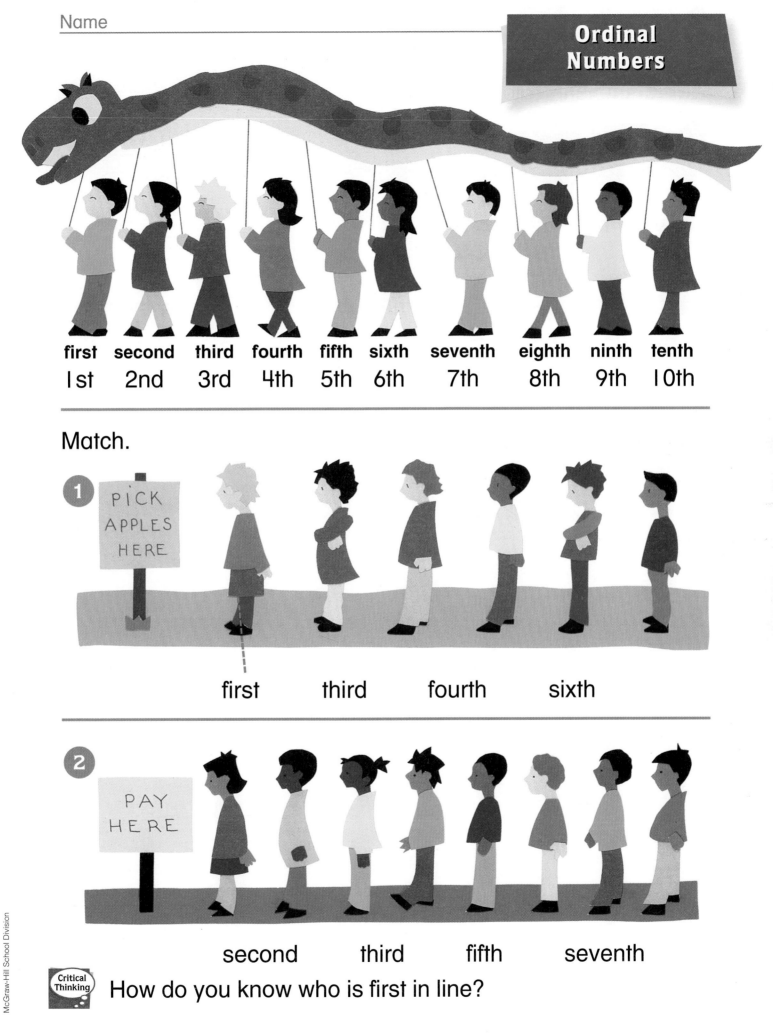

first	second	third	fourth	fifth	sixth	seventh	eighth	ninth	tenth
1st	2nd	3rd	4th	5th	6th	7th	8th	9th	10th

Match.

1 PICK APPLES HERE

first   third   fourth   sixth

2 PAY HERE

second   third   fifth   seventh

Critical Thinking How do you know who is first in line?

Practice!

Start at the left. Color.

1 second ⟩⟩ red ⟩⟩ ►   fourth ⟩⟩ yellow ⟩⟩ ►   eighth ⟩⟩ blue ⟩⟩ ►

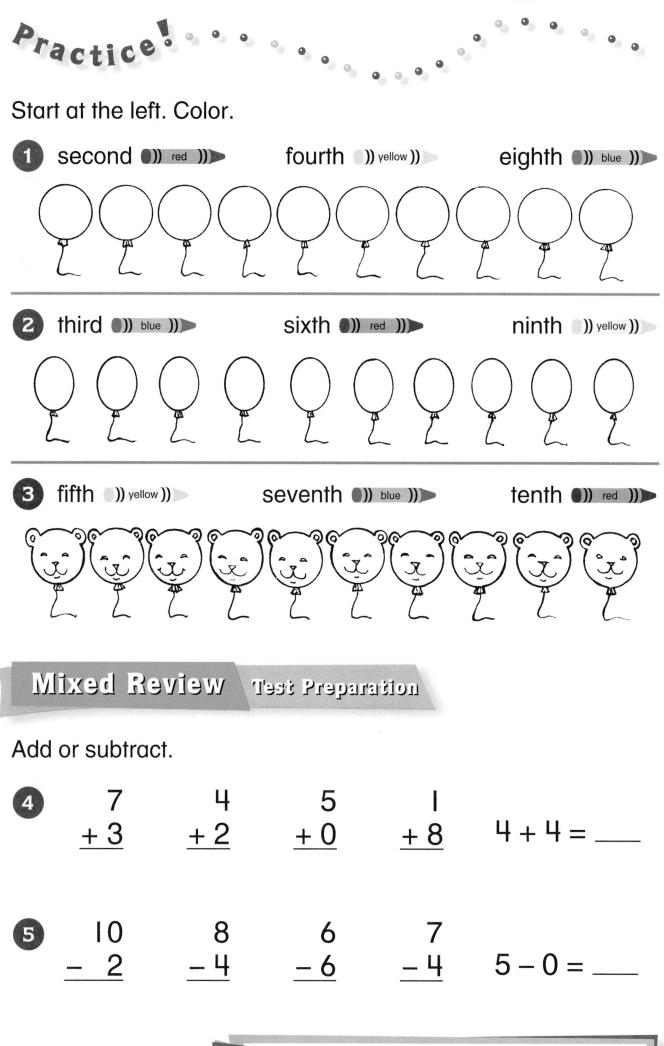

2 third ⟩⟩ blue ⟩⟩ ►   sixth ⟩⟩ red ⟩⟩ ►   ninth ⟩⟩ yellow ⟩⟩

3 fifth ⟩⟩ yellow ⟩⟩ ►   seventh ⟩⟩ blue ⟩⟩ ►   tenth ⟩⟩ red ⟩⟩ ►

Mixed Review Test Preparation

Add or subtract.

4

$$7 + 3 \qquad 4 + 2 \qquad 5 + 0 \qquad 1 + 8 \qquad 4 + 4 = \underline{\quad}$$

5

$$10 - 2 \qquad 8 - 4 \qquad 6 - 6 \qquad 7 - 4 \qquad 5 - 0 = \underline{\quad}$$

 At Home Line up some objects. Ask your child which is *first, second,* and so on.

Name _____

Working Together

You need ▲, ■, and ▰.

Glossary
picture graph

Make a **picture graph**.
Draw to show each block.
Start at the bottom.

PATTERN BLOCKS		
green	orange	blue

Each picture stands for 1 block.

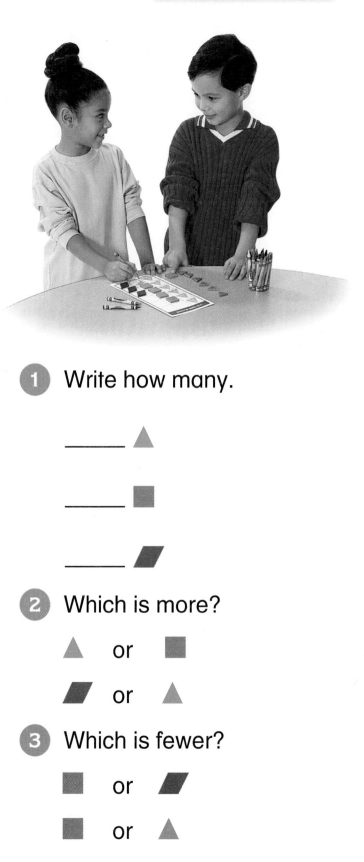

1 Write how many.

_____ ▲

_____ ■

_____ ▰

2 Which is more?

▲ or ■

▰ or ▲

3 Which is fewer?

■ or ▰

■ or ▲

McGraw-Hill School Division

Talk Tell a partner what this picture graph shows.

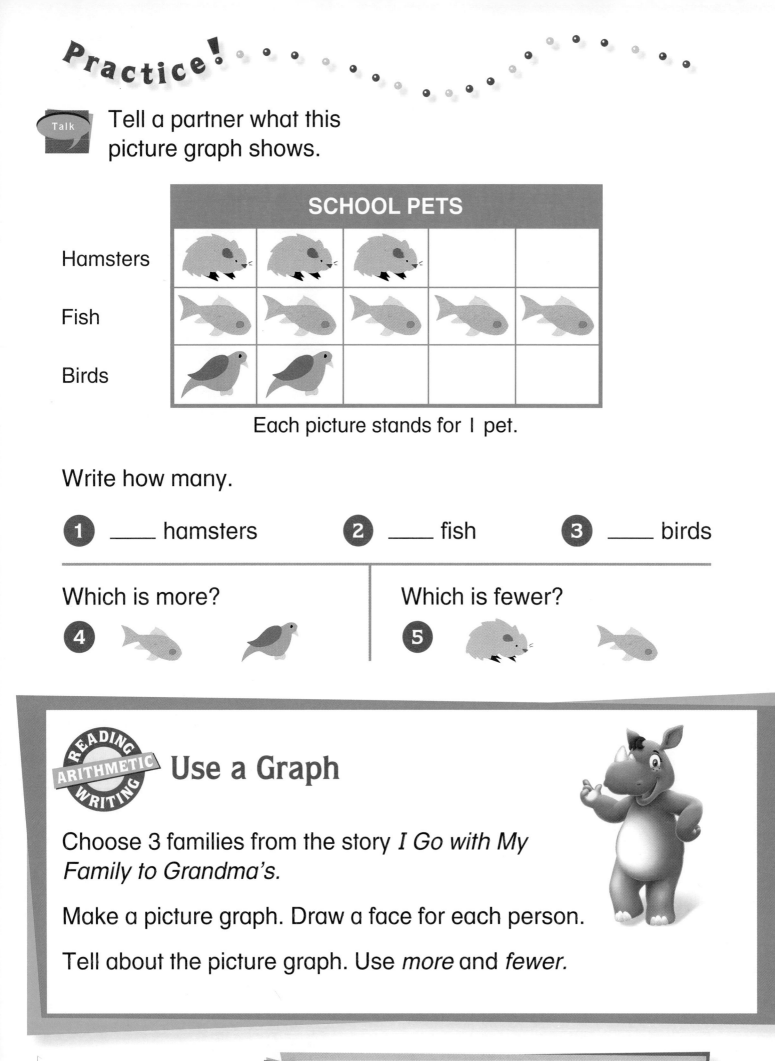

SCHOOL PETS

Hamsters

Fish

Birds

Each picture stands for 1 pet.

Write how many.

1 ____ hamsters   **2** ____ fish   **3** ____ birds

Which is more?	Which is fewer?
4	**5**

Use a Graph

READING ARITHMETIC WRITING

Choose 3 families from the story *I Go with My Family to Grandma's.*

Make a picture graph. Draw a face for each person.

Tell about the picture graph. Use *more* and *fewer.*

 At Home Have your child tell you about the picture graph.

Name _____

Working Together

You need , and .

Make a **bar graph**.
Color 1 box for each counter.
Start at the bottom.

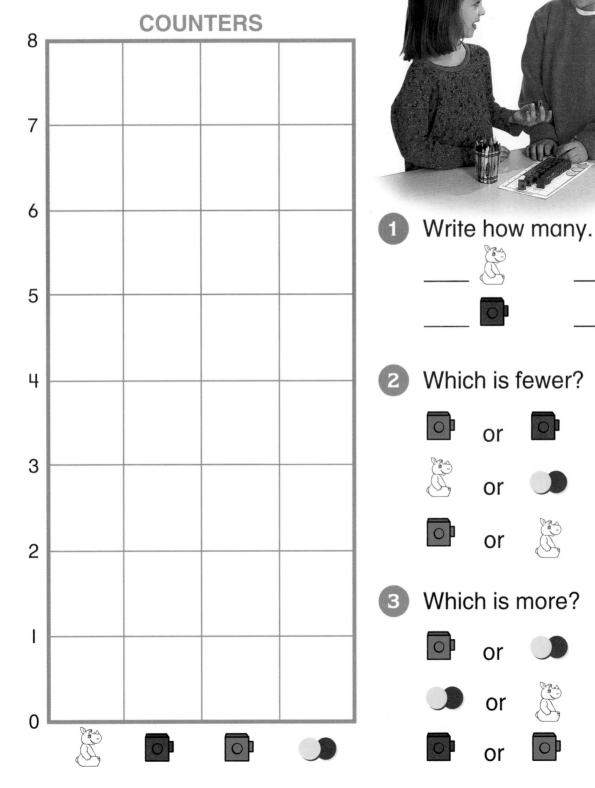

COUNTERS

1. Write how many.

   ____ 🐴   ____ 📷

   ____ 📷   ____ ⚫

2. Which is fewer?

   📷 or 📷

   🐴 or ⚫

   📷 or 🐴

3. Which is more?

   📷 or ⚫

   ⚫ or 🐴

   📷 or 📷

McGraw-Hill School Division

Tell a partner what the tally marks show.

Use the tally marks to finish the graph.

OUR FAVORITE COLORS
yellow /III
Blue LHT
Red LHT III

OUR FAVORITE COLORS

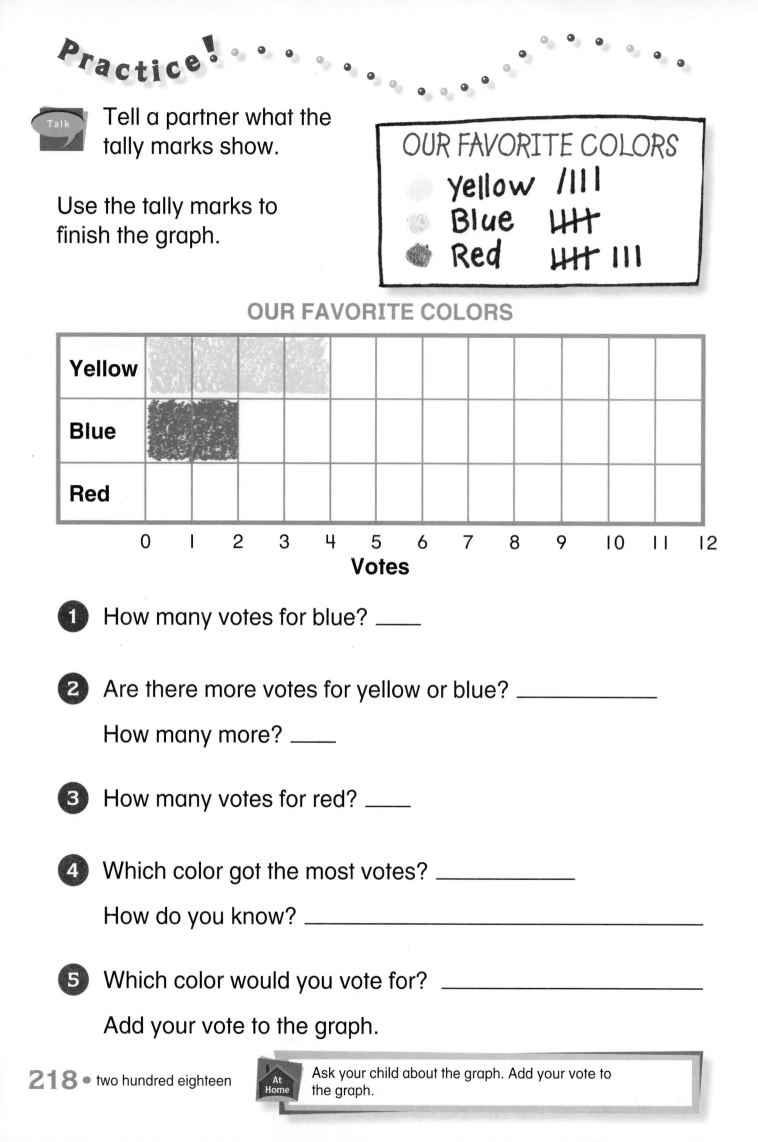

Votes

1 How many votes for blue? ____

2 Are there more votes for yellow or blue? _____

How many more? ____

3 How many votes for red? ____

4 Which color got the most votes? _____

How do you know? _____

5 Which color would you vote for? _____

Add your vote to the graph.

At Home — Ask your child about the graph. Add your vote to the graph.

Name _____

Use a Graph

Nicole made a graph about some of her family.

Read
Plan
Solve
Look Back

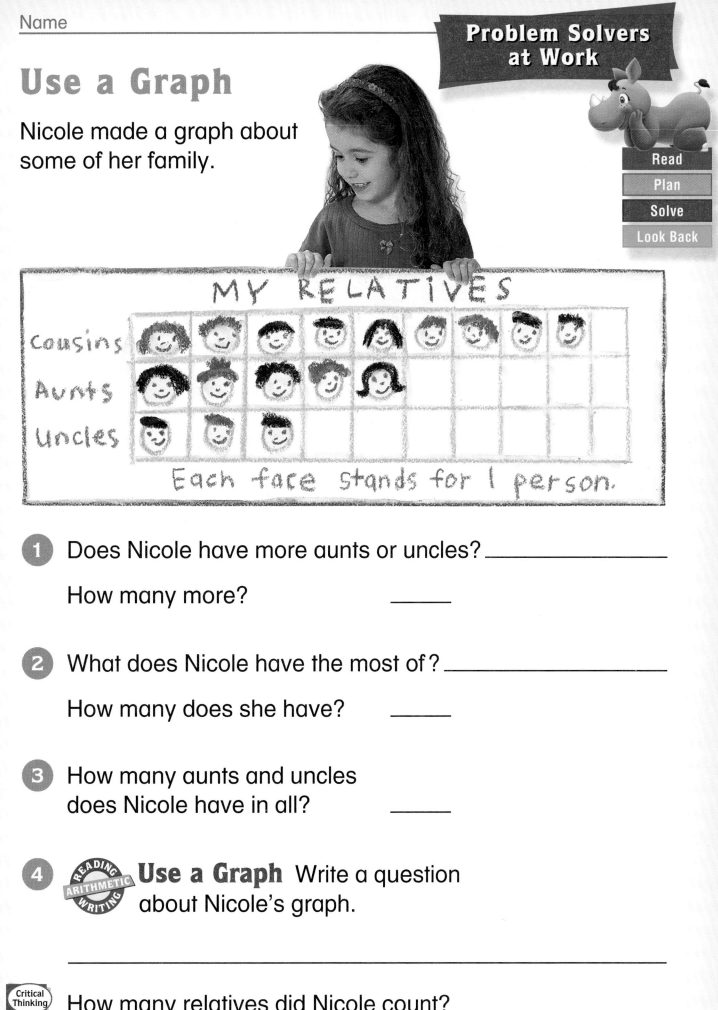

MY RELATIVES

Cousins
Aunts
Uncles

Each face stands for 1 person.

1 Does Nicole have more aunts or uncles? _____

How many more?   _____

2 What does Nicole have the most of? _____

How many does she have?   _____

3 How many aunts and uncles
   does Nicole have in all?   _____

4 **READING ARITHMETIC WRITING** **Use a Graph** Write a question
   about Nicole's graph.

_____

Critical Thinking How many relatives did Nicole count?

McGraw-Hill School Division

Practice!

Fred asked his family how many books they read. Then he made a graph.

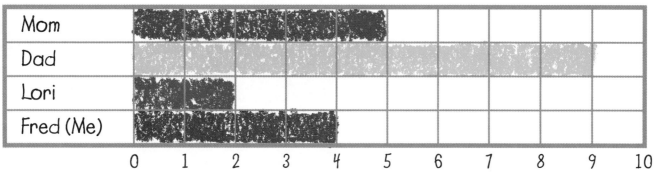

BOOKS WE READ IN JANUARY

Mom											
Dad											
Lori											
Fred (Me)											
	0	1	2	3	4	5	6	7	8	9	10

1 How many books did Lori and Fred read in all? _____ books

2 Did they read more books than their mom? _____

How many more? _____ more

Write and Share

Tearna wrote this problem.

Who read more books than Mom?

Tearna Powell
Elephant's Fork School
Suffolk, Virginia

3 Solve Tearna's problem. _____

Talk How did you solve Tearna's problem?

Use your own paper.

4 Write a problem. Have a partner solve it.

Name _____

Language and Mathematics

Choose the correct word to complete the sentence.

1 5, 10, 15, 20 shows
_____ by fives.

2 The number 73 has
7 _____.

tens
estimate
between
skip-counting

Concepts and Skills

Write the number.

3 ____

4 ____

5 ____

Ring the number that is less.

6 13   31   **7** 87   79   **8** 15   25

Write the numbers in order.

9 22, 23, ___, ___, ___, 27, ___

10 47, 48, ___, ___, ___, ___, ___

Skip-count.

11 2, 4, ___, ___, ___   **12** 5, 10, ___, ___, ___

13 Match.

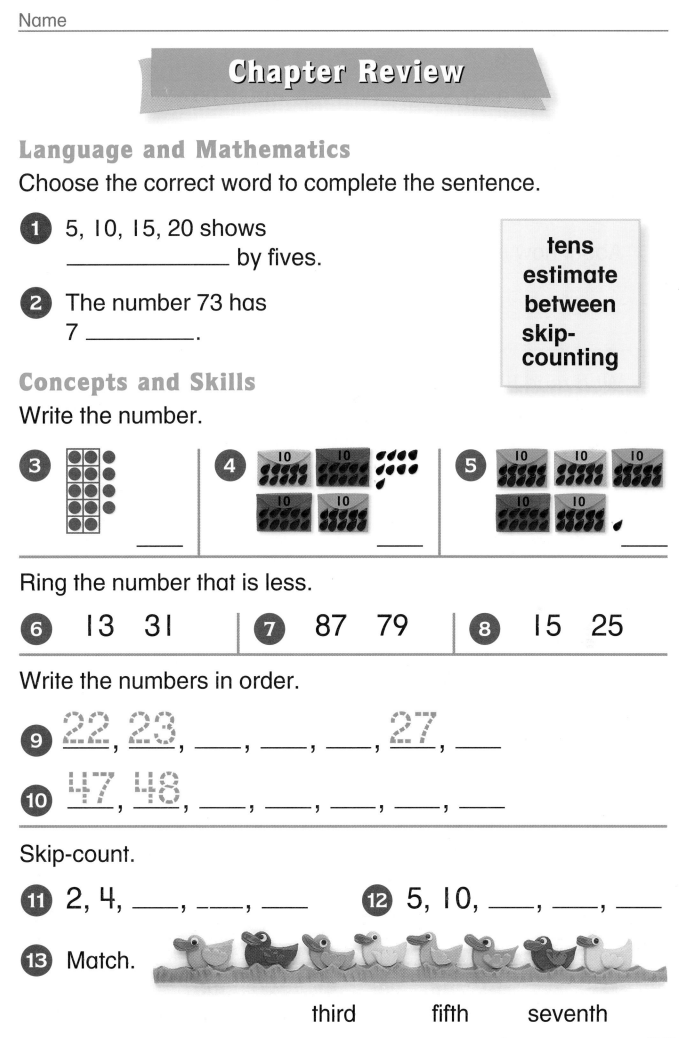

third   fifth   seventh

McGraw-Hill School Division

Problem Solving

Estimate to solve.

14 About how many?

about 10   about 20

15 About how many?

about 20   about 50

16 About how many?

about 10   about 20

---

17 Who read 4 books? _____

18 Who read the fewest books? _____

BOOKS

| | Sara | Anne | Larry |

0 1 2 3 4 5 6 7 8 9 10

19 How many books did Larry read? _____

20 Who read the most books? _____

What Do You Think?

How do you like to count?
✔ Check one.

☐ By ones ☐ By tens ☐ By fives ☐ By twos

Why? _____

Journal Show what you know about 100.

Chapter Test

1 Write the number.

_____

2 Ring the number that is greater.

58   39

3 Write the numbers in order.

68, 69, ___, ___, ___, 73, ___

Skip-count.

4 2, 4, 6, 8, 10, ___, ___, ___

5 5, 10, 15, ___, ___, ___, ___

6 10, 20, 30, ___, ___, ___, ___

7 Match.

second   fourth   eighth

8 How many cousins does Lani have?

_____

9 Who has the fewest cousins?

_____

COUSINS

Maria
Gene
Lani

0 1 2 3 4 5 6 7 8 9 10

Estimate to solve.

10 About how many fish?

about 30   about 50

What Did You Learn?

You need 30 , 30 ■, and 30 ▢.

Take a big handful of each color ▢.

Count how many of each color.
Write the number.

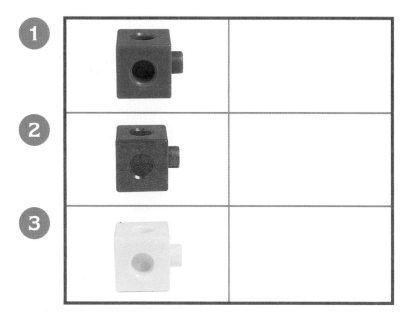

1		
2		
3		

4 Do you have more ▢ or ▢? _____

5 Do you have fewer ▢ or ▢? _____

6 About how many ▢ do you have in all?

Estimate. _____ Count how many. _____

 You may want to put this page in your portfolio.

Name

Skip-Count

How much does the necklace cost?

Algebra **PATTERNS** You can skip-count by fives to find out.

Press [ON/AC] [+] [5].
How many beads? __5__

Press [=] 5 times.
Write each number
you see. ___ ___ ___ ___ ___

The necklace costs __25__ ¢.

Talk Which keys would you press if each bead cost 10¢?

Find the cost of each necklace.

1. 10¢ a bead

   __7__ beads   ___ ¢

2. 5¢ a bead

   ___ beads   ___ ¢

3. 2¢ a bead

   ___ beads   ___ ¢

4. 6¢ a bead

   ___ beads   ___ ¢

McGraw-Hill School Division

Use a Graph

Talk Are there more toy vans or police cars? How do you know?

1 Which number of vehicles is the least?

_____

2 Which number is the greatest?

_____

Vehicles	
Vans	19
Police Cars	22
Trucks	18
Race Cars	20
Sports Cars	21

At the Computer

3 Put the numbers in the table in order.

4 Link the table to a bar graph. What do you see?

5 Change the numbers in the table. What happens to the graph?

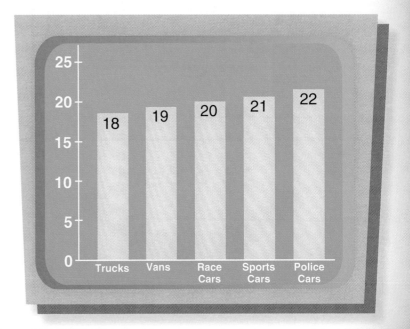

Name _____

Mark your answer.

1 9 + 1 = ___?___

   ◯ 4
   ◯ 5
   ◯ 6
   ◯ 10

2   6¢
   + 3¢

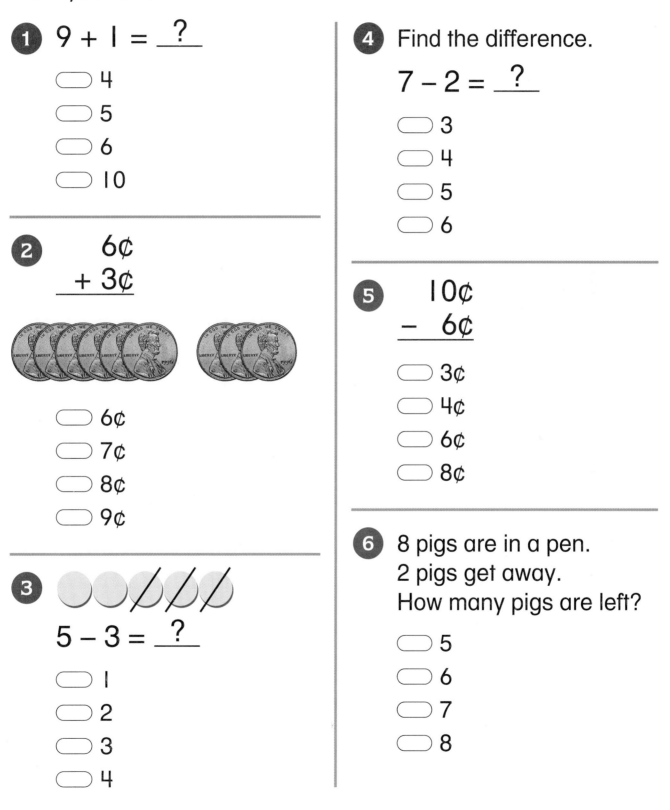

   ◯ 6¢
   ◯ 7¢
   ◯ 8¢
   ◯ 9¢

3

5 − 3 = ___?___

   ◯ 1
   ◯ 2
   ◯ 3
   ◯ 4

4 Find the difference.

7 − 2 = ___?___

   ◯ 3
   ◯ 4
   ◯ 5
   ◯ 6

5   10¢
  − 6¢

   ◯ 3¢
   ◯ 4¢
   ◯ 6¢
   ◯ 8¢

6 8 pigs are in a pen.
2 pigs get away.
How many pigs are left?

   ◯ 5
   ◯ 6
   ◯ 7
   ◯ 8

TEST PREPARATION

7 How many seeds are there?

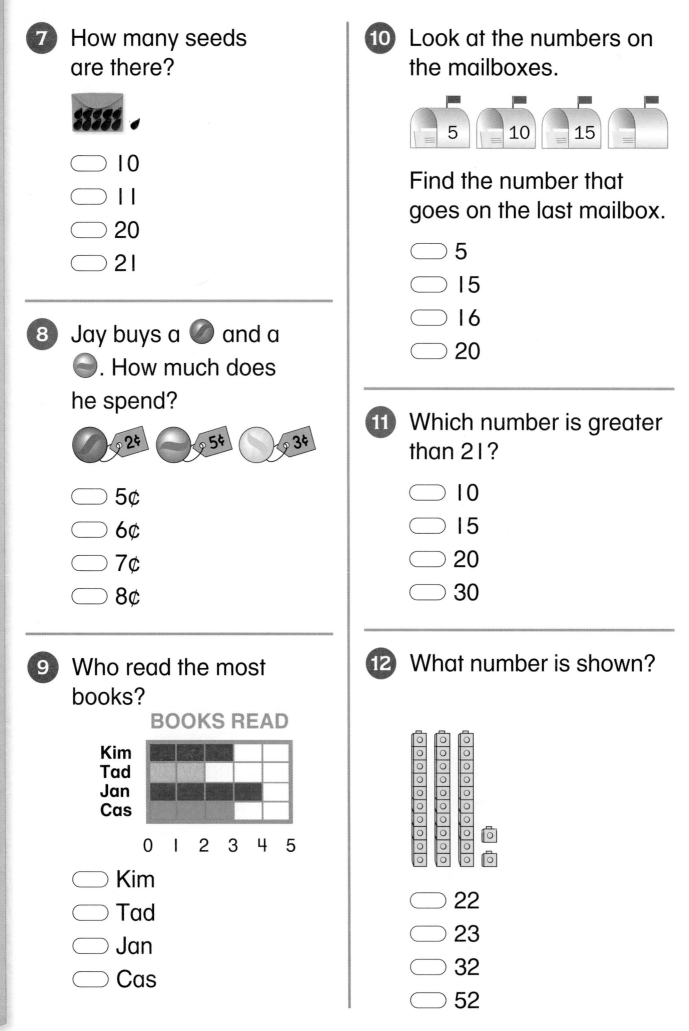

- ⚪ 10
- ⚪ 11
- ⚪ 20
- ⚪ 21

8 Jay buys a ● and a ●. How much does he spend?

2¢   5¢   3¢

- ⚪ 5¢
- ⚪ 6¢
- ⚪ 7¢
- ⚪ 8¢

9 Who read the most books?

BOOKS READ

Kim					
Tad					
Jan					
Cas					

0 1 2 3 4 5

- ⚪ Kim
- ⚪ Tad
- ⚪ Jan
- ⚪ Cas

10 Look at the numbers on the mailboxes.

5   10   15

Find the number that goes on the last mailbox.

- ⚪ 5
- ⚪ 15
- ⚪ 16
- ⚪ 20

11 Which number is greater than 21?

- ⚪ 10
- ⚪ 15
- ⚪ 20
- ⚪ 30

12 What number is shown?

- ⚪ 22
- ⚪ 23
- ⚪ 32
- ⚪ 52

Name

Every Penny Counts

MATERIALS 100 pennies, paper and pencil

DIRECTIONS Take turns. Find different ways to group 100 pennies in order to make it easy to count them. Keep a record of the ways you group.

How many ways did you group pennies? Which grouping made counting the easiest?

 At Home As you engage in this activity with your child, let your child make the grouping decisions. He or she will probably make groups, or stacks, of 2, 5, or 10. You may also choose to make groups of 20 or 25. Then discuss and have your child answer the two questions.

McGraw-Hill School Division

Dear Family,

My new chapter in mathematics is about shapes and parts of shapes.

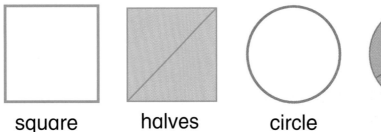

square   halves   circle   thirds

I will also be looking for shapes around me, especially how shapes are used in kites.

Learning about Kites

Let's talk about kites we have seen. We can make a list of the different shapes of kites.

My Math Words

I am going to use these and other words in this chapter.

Please help me make word cards for these math words. I can use the word cards when I practice geometry and fractions.

cube
cone
cylinder
sphere
rectangular prism
circle
square
triangle
rectangle
equal parts
halves
one half
fraction

Your child,

_____
Signature

Geometry and Fractions

Theme: High-Flying Kites

Visualize Choose a kite from the story *The Sea-Breeze Hotel*. Tell how you think it looks.

Talk about kites you have seen. What shapes did you see?

What Do You Know?

Use a))) yellow)) to color shapes with 4 sides.
Use a))) red))) to color shapes with 3 sides.

1 Which shapes do not have a color? _____

2 How many squares did you color? _____

Portfolio

Draw a kite.
Use different shapes.
Tell about the shapes.

Name _____

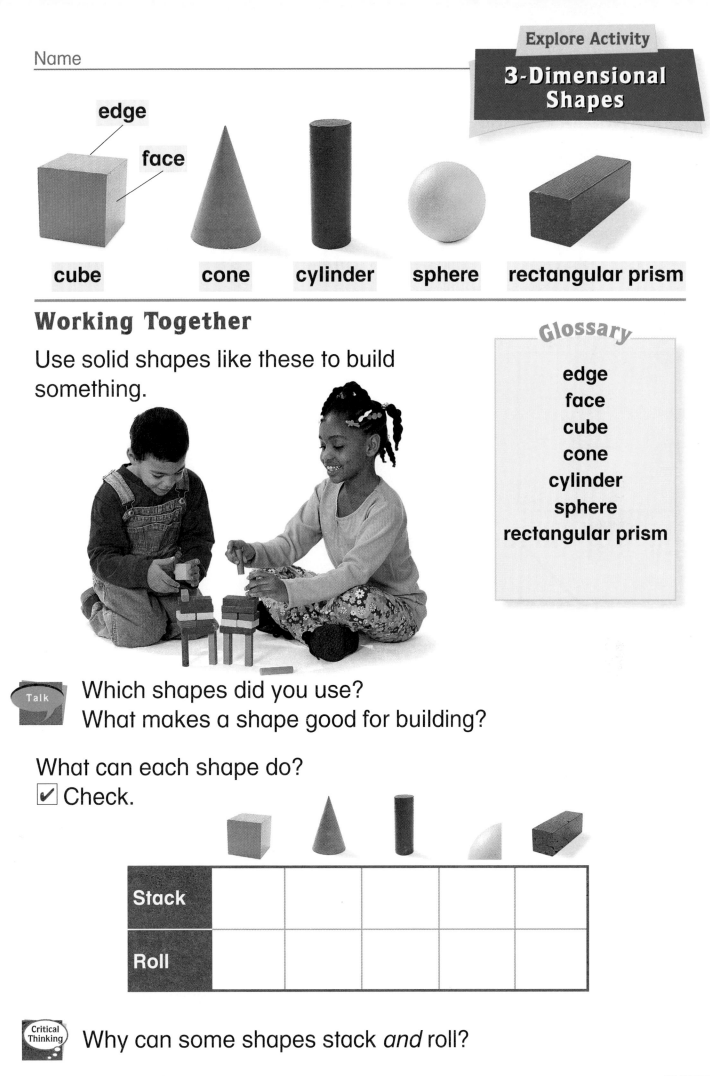

edge

face

cube   cone   cylinder   sphere   rectangular prism

Working Together

Use solid shapes like these to build something.

Glossary

edge
face
cube
cone
cylinder
sphere
rectangular prism

Talk
Which shapes did you use?
What makes a shape good for building?

What can each shape do?
☑ Check.

Stack					
Roll					

Critical Thinking Why can some shapes stack *and* roll?

McGraw-Hill School Division

Practice!

Show what the shapes do.

Color.))) blue)))))) orange)))))) green)))
stack **roll** **stack and roll**

1

2

3

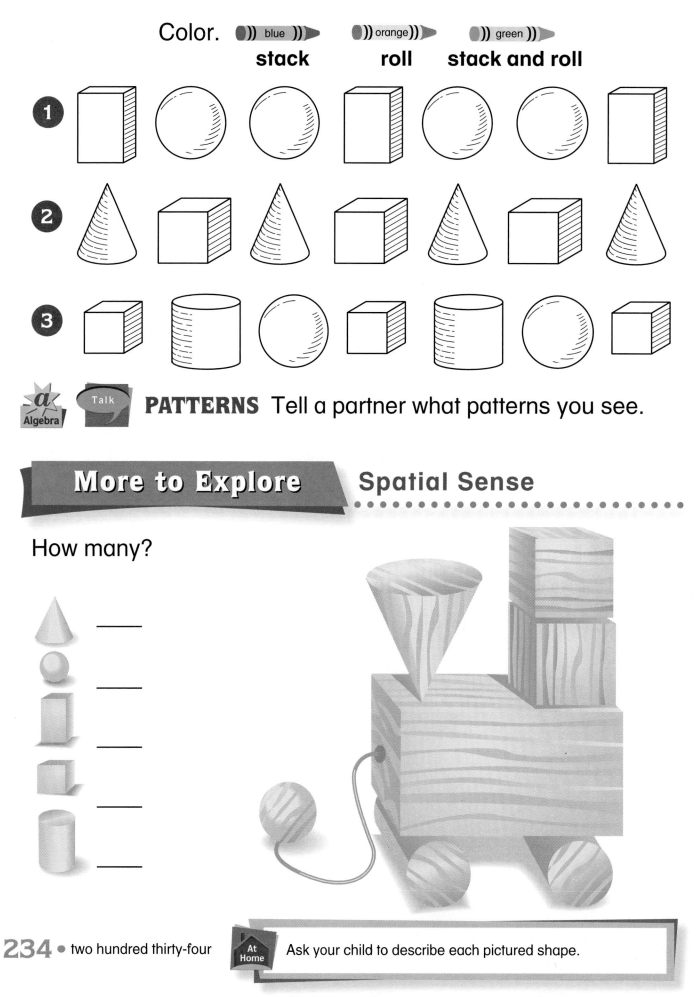

a Algebra | Talk | **PATTERNS** Tell a partner what patterns you see.

More to Explore — Spatial Sense

How many?

_____

_____

_____

_____

_____

At Home — Ask your child to describe each pictured shape.

Working Together

You and your partner need solid shapes.

Take turns.

▶ Place a solid shape on paper.

▶ Trace around the edges.

▶ Ring the shape you see.

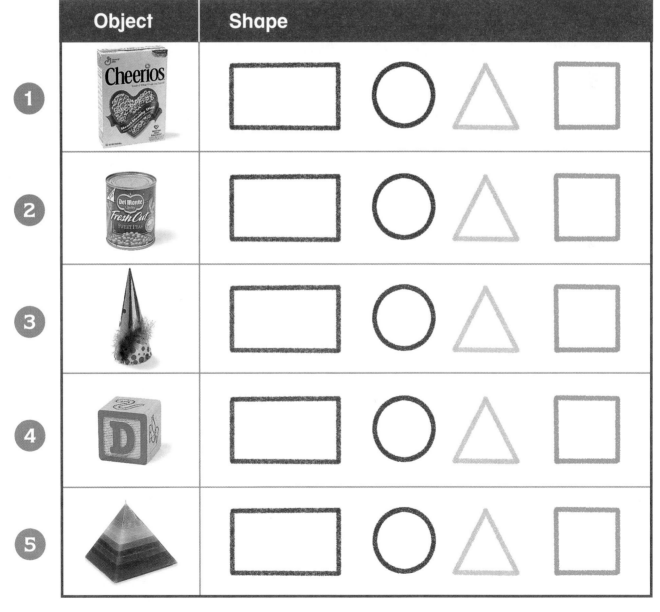

Object	Shape
1	▭ ◯ △ ☐
2	▭ ◯ △ ☐
3	▭ ◯ △ ☐
4	▭ ◯ △ ☐
5	▭ ◯ △ ☐

 Critical Thinking How many shapes can you trace from a cereal box?

McGraw-Hill School Division

Practice!

Color objects that make each shape.

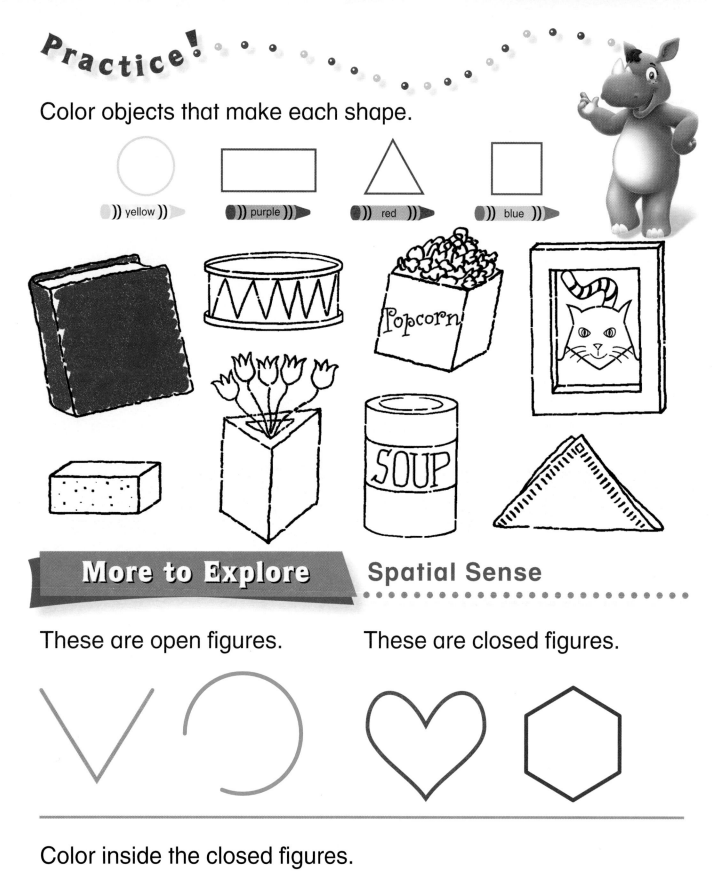

)) yellow))   )) purple))   )) red))   )) blue))

More to Explore   **Spatial Sense**

These are open figures.   These are closed figures.

Color inside the closed figures.

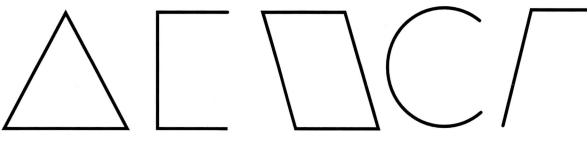

At Home Ask your child to talk about the shapes found in your kitchen.

Name _____

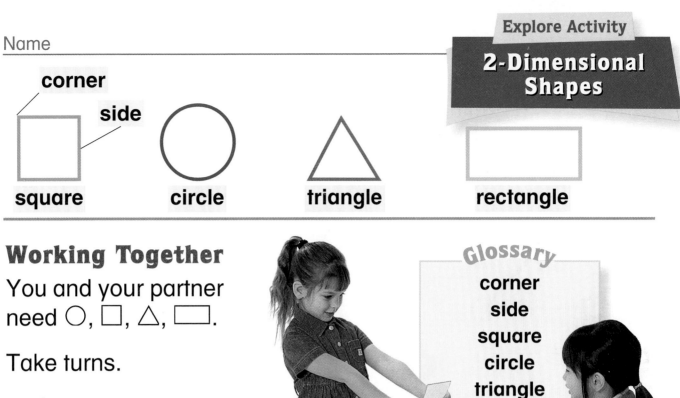

corner
side

square   circle   triangle   rectangle

Working Together

You and your partner need ○, □, △, ▭.

Take turns.

▶ Choose a shape.

▶ Say how many sides.

▶ Your partner says how many corners.

Glossary

corner
side
square
circle
triangle
rectangle

Complete the chart together.

	Shape	How many sides?	How many corners?
1	△	____	____
2	▭	____	____
3	□	____	____
4	○	____	____

Critical Thinking What if a shape has 5 sides. How many corners does it have?

McGraw-Hill School Division

Practice!

Trace the sides with a 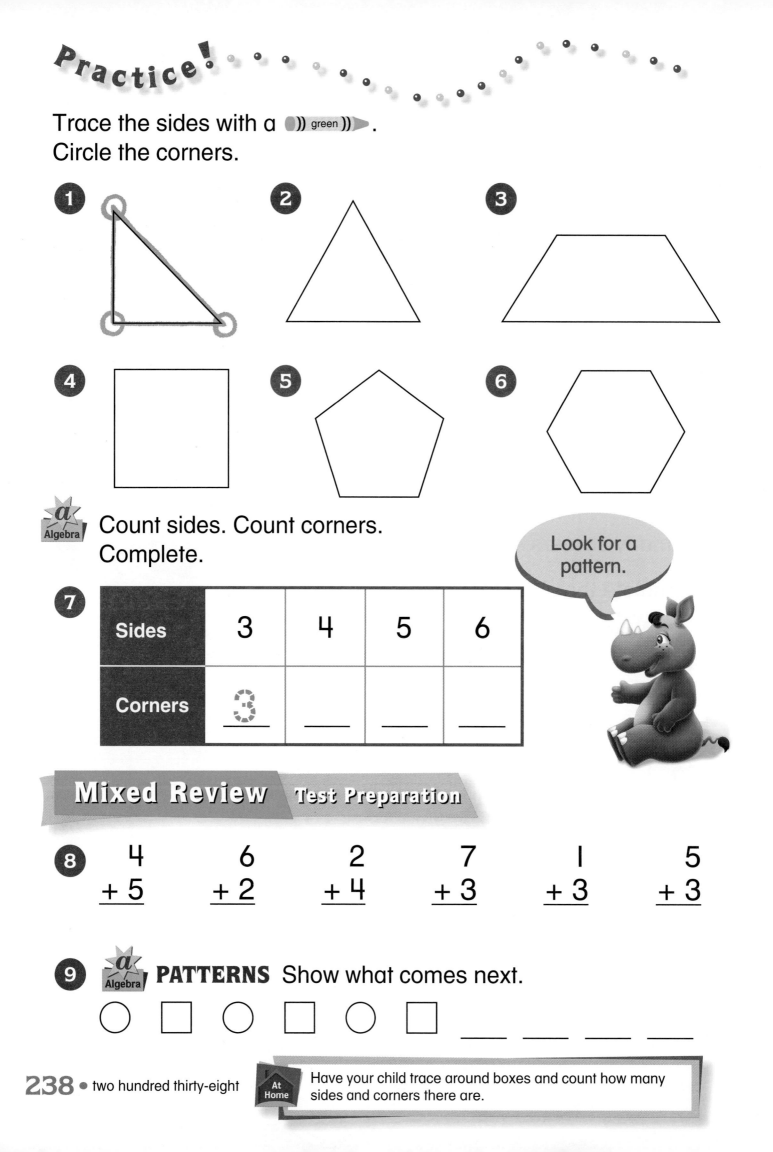 green .
Circle the corners.

1

2

3

4

5

6

a **Algebra** Count sides. Count corners.
Complete.

Look for a pattern.

7

Sides	3	4	5	6
Corners	3	__	__	__

Mixed Review Test Preparation

8

$$\begin{array}{r} 4 \\ +5 \\ \hline \end{array}$$
$$\begin{array}{r} 6 \\ +2 \\ \hline \end{array}$$
$$\begin{array}{r} 2 \\ +4 \\ \hline \end{array}$$
$$\begin{array}{r} 7 \\ +3 \\ \hline \end{array}$$
$$\begin{array}{r} 1 \\ +3 \\ \hline \end{array}$$
$$\begin{array}{r} 5 \\ +3 \\ \hline \end{array}$$

9 *a* **Algebra** **PATTERNS** Show what comes next.

○ □ ○ □ ○ □ __ __ __ __

At Home Have your child trace around boxes and count how many sides and corners there are.

Name _____

Use a Physical Model

You need 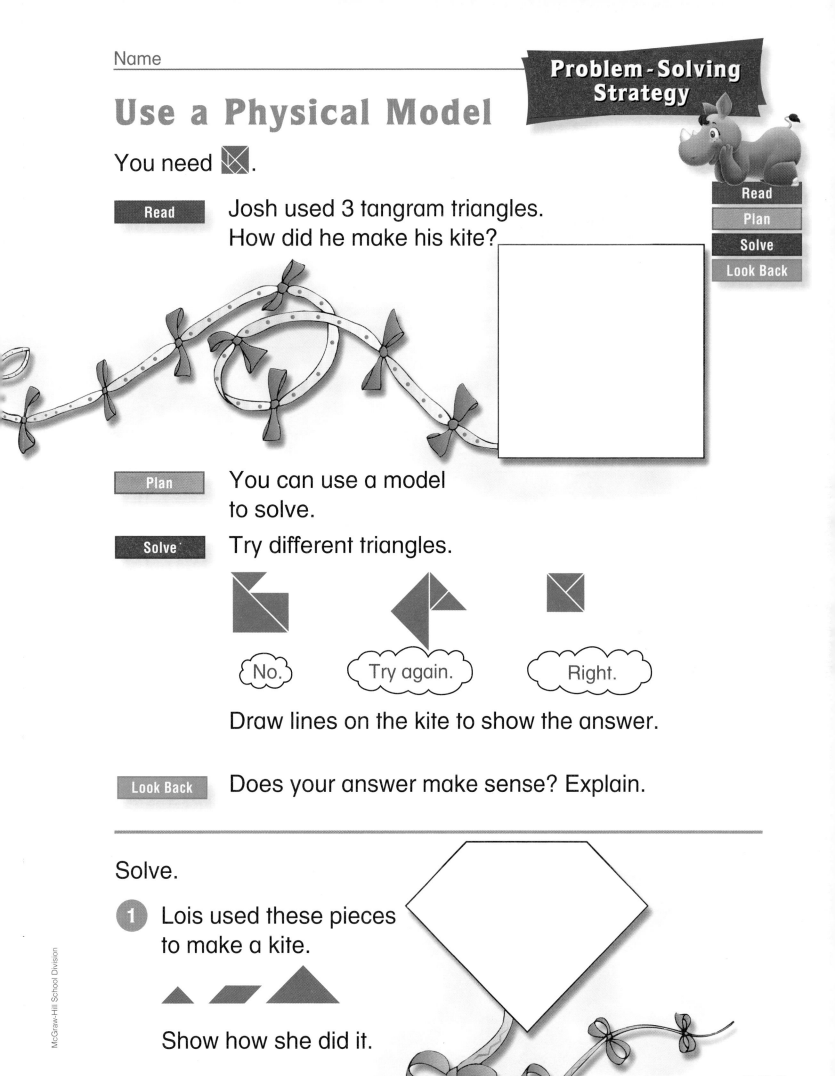.

Read   Josh used 3 tangram triangles.
How did he make his kite?

Plan   You can use a model
to solve.

Solve   Try different triangles.

No.   Try again.   Right.

Draw lines on the kite to show the answer.

Look Back   Does your answer make sense? Explain.

Solve.

1. Lois used these pieces
to make a kite.

Show how she did it.

McGraw-Hill School Division

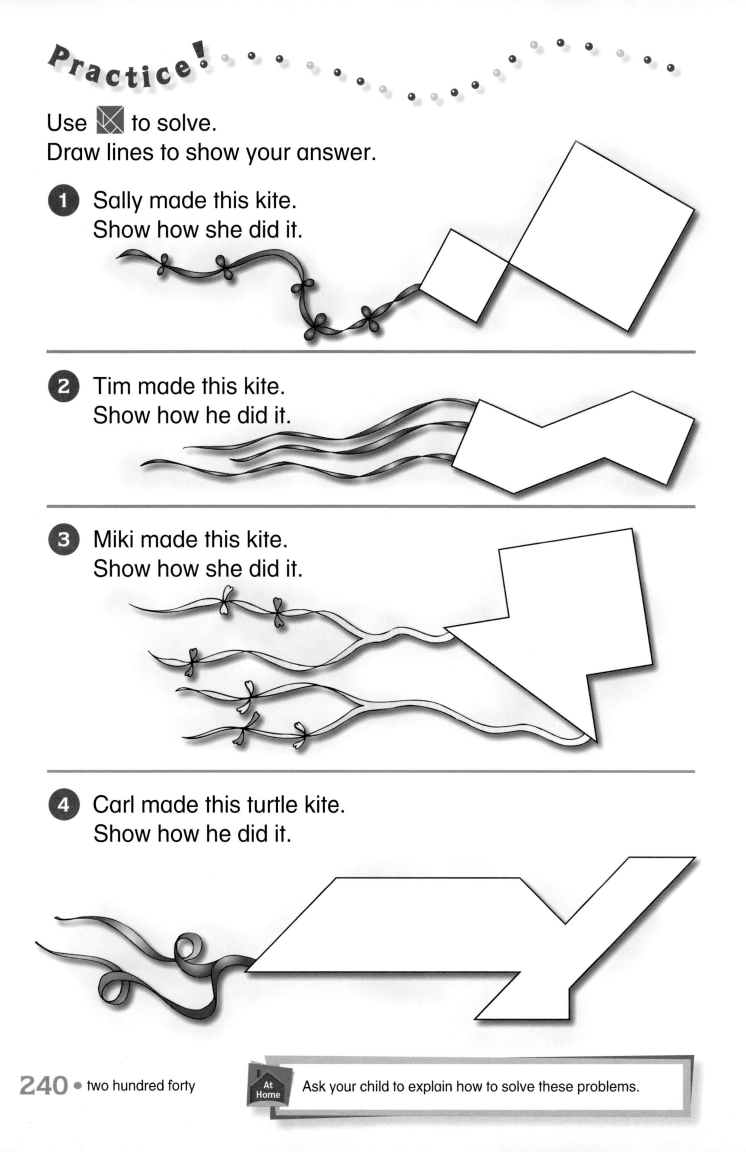

Practice!

Use ◩ to solve.
Draw lines to show your answer.

1 Sally made this kite.
Show how she did it.

2 Tim made this kite.
Show how he did it.

3 Miki made this kite.
Show how she did it.

4 Carl made this turtle kite.
Show how he did it.

At Home   Ask your child to explain how to solve these problems.

Name _____

Do your best!

Match.

Complete.

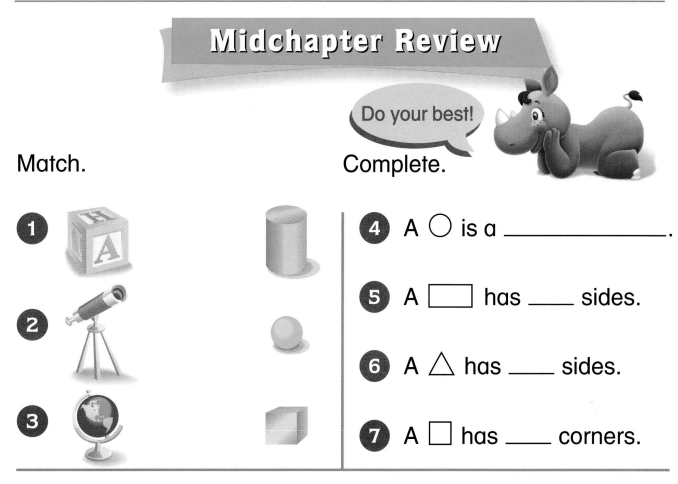

1

2

3

4 A ○ is a _____.

5 A ▭ has ___ sides.

6 A △ has ___ sides.

7 A □ has ___ corners.

Ring the shape made by the solid shape.

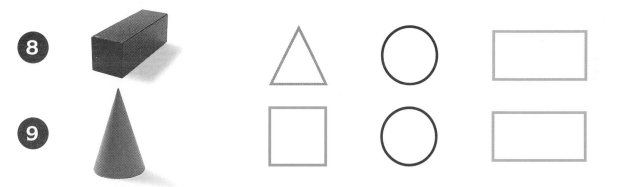

8

9

Use a model.
Draw lines to show your answer.

10 Elly made this kite.
Show how she did it.

Draw some shapes. Tell what you
know about the shapes.

Fly a Kite!

You and your partner need 2 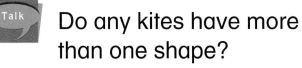 and a ⊕.

Take turns.

▶ Spin for a shape.

▶ Move your 🐴 to the first kite with that shape.

The first player to reach the *Park* wins.

Talk Do any kites have more than one shape?

Name

Making a Kite

Listen to
The Sea-Breeze Hotel.

Talk   Tell what you know about kites.

Working Together

You and your partner will make a kite.

You need paper, tape, sticks, string, and a tail.

MAKING A KITE

1. Decide what shape kite to make.

2. Draw or paste a picture.

3. Tape on two sticks.

4. Make four holes. Tie on a string.

5. Put on a tail.

243

Decision Making

1 Look at the kites you made.
Which kite do you like best? _____

_____.

2 If you made another kite,
would you choose another shape? _____.

Why? _____

Write a report

3 Draw your kite.
Tell how you decided
on a shape.

4 Tell how you made
your kite.

More to Investigate

Have a kite-flying day.

PREDICT Which kites will fly?

EXPLORE Try it. Stand with the wind at your back.

FIND Talk about the kites that fly. What is alike
about them? What is different?

Name _____

You need I ◯, 2 ▢, 2 △.

Fold a ◯ to make 2 parts that match.

Cut on the fold.

Both parts are the same size and shape.

Parts that match are **equal parts**.

Glossary

equal parts

Working Together

▶ Fold a ▢ into 2 equal parts.

▶ Fold a ▢ another way to make 2 equal parts.

▶ Draw a line to show each fold.

Talk Tell about the equal parts you made.

▶ Fold a △ into 2 equal parts.

▶ Fold a △ into 2 parts that are not equal.

▶ Ring the △ that shows equal parts.

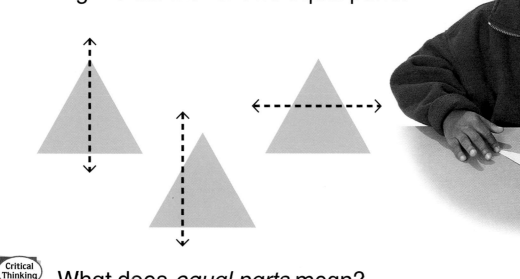

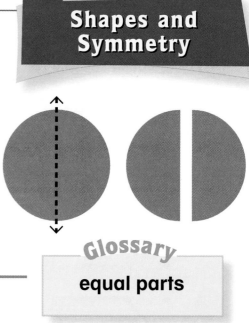

Critical Thinking What does *equal parts* mean?

Practice!

Draw a line to show 2 equal parts.

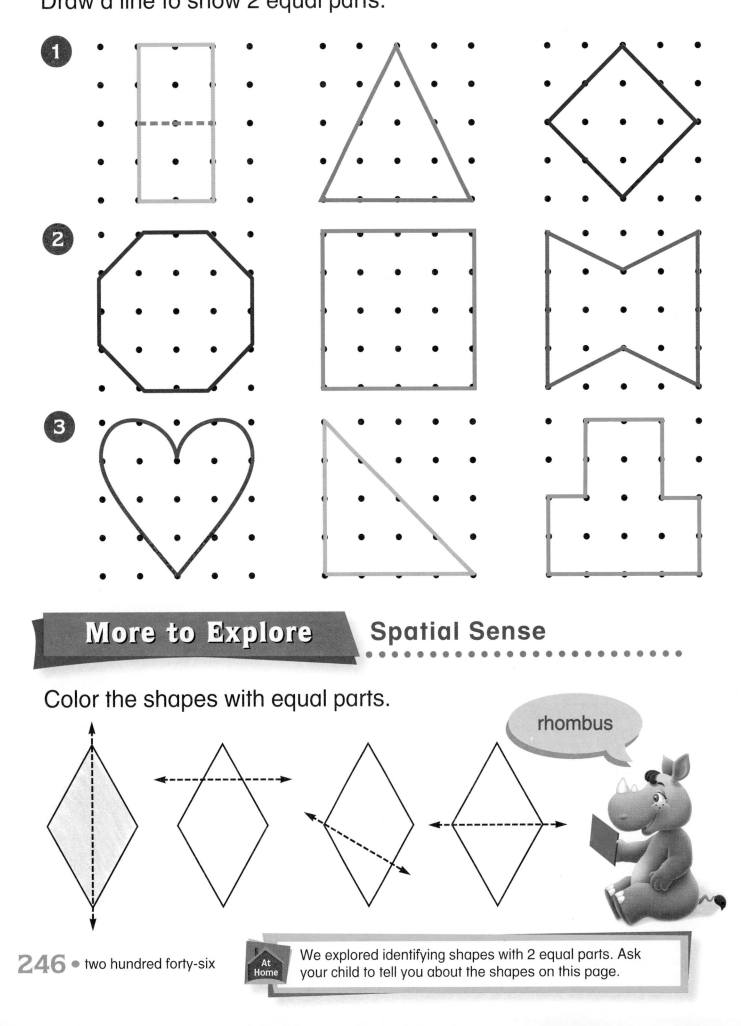

1

2

3

More to Explore · Spatial Sense

Color the shapes with equal parts.

rhombus

At Home We explored identifying shapes with 2 equal parts. Ask your child to tell you about the shapes on this page.

Working Together

You need paper shapes.

▶ Fold a ◯ into 2 equal parts to show **halves.**

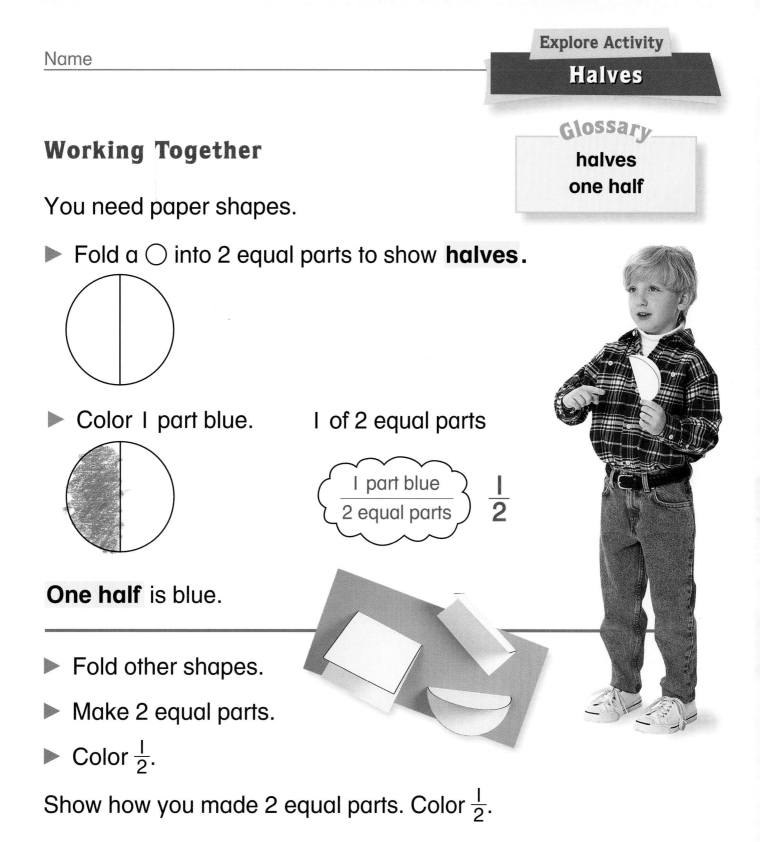

▶ Color 1 part blue.   1 of 2 equal parts

$\frac{1 \text{ part blue}}{2 \text{ equal parts}}$ $\frac{1}{2}$

One half is blue.

▶ Fold other shapes.

▶ Make 2 equal parts.

▶ Color $\frac{1}{2}$.

Show how you made 2 equal parts. Color $\frac{1}{2}$.

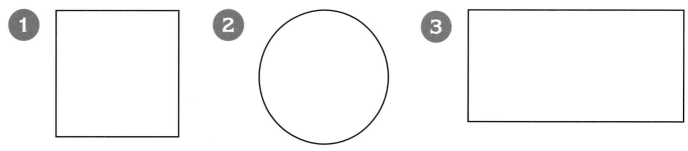

1 **2** **3**

Critical Thinking How many halves make a whole?
What is each half called?

Practice!

Only color the kites that show halves.

Color $\frac{1}{2}$.

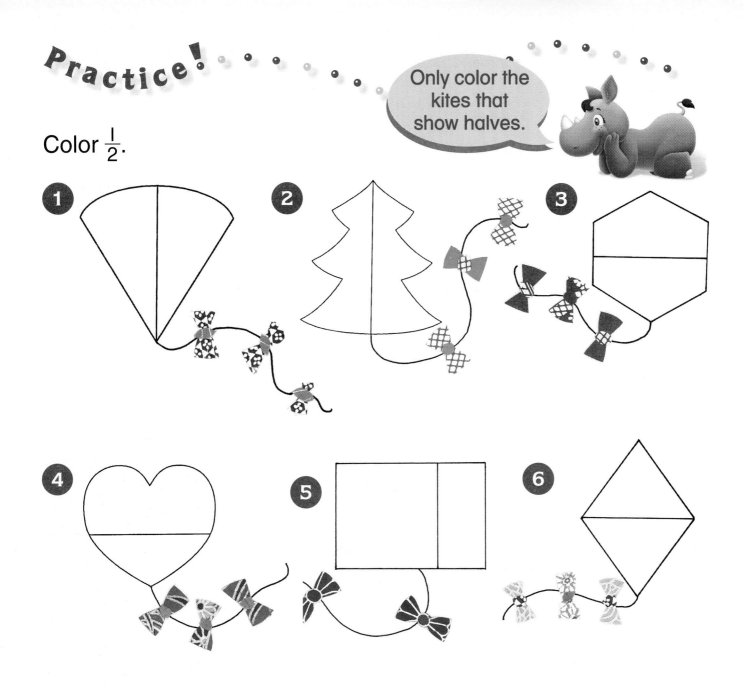

1 2 3

4 5 6

READING ARITHMETIC WRITING **Visualize**

Cover the picture. Listen to your teacher tell about a kite. Picture the kite in your mind. Uncover the picture. Ring the kite.

Journal Draw a kite. Color $\frac{1}{2}$.

At Home We learned about halves and one half. Ask your child to tell you about the pictures on this page.

Explore Activity

Fourths

Working Together

You need paper shapes.

▶ Fold a ○ into 4 equal parts to make **fourths**.

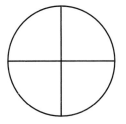

▶ Color 1 part blue.   1 of 4 equal parts

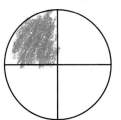

$$\frac{1 \text{ part blue}}{4 \text{ equal parts}} \quad \frac{1}{4}$$

One fourth is blue.

▶ Fold other shapes.

▶ Make 4 equal parts.

▶ Color $\frac{1}{4}$.

Show how you made 4 equal parts.
Color $\frac{1}{4}$.

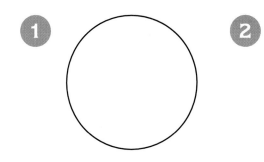

1   2   3

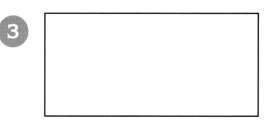

Critical Thinking How many fourths make a whole?
What is each fourth called?

McGraw-Hill School Division

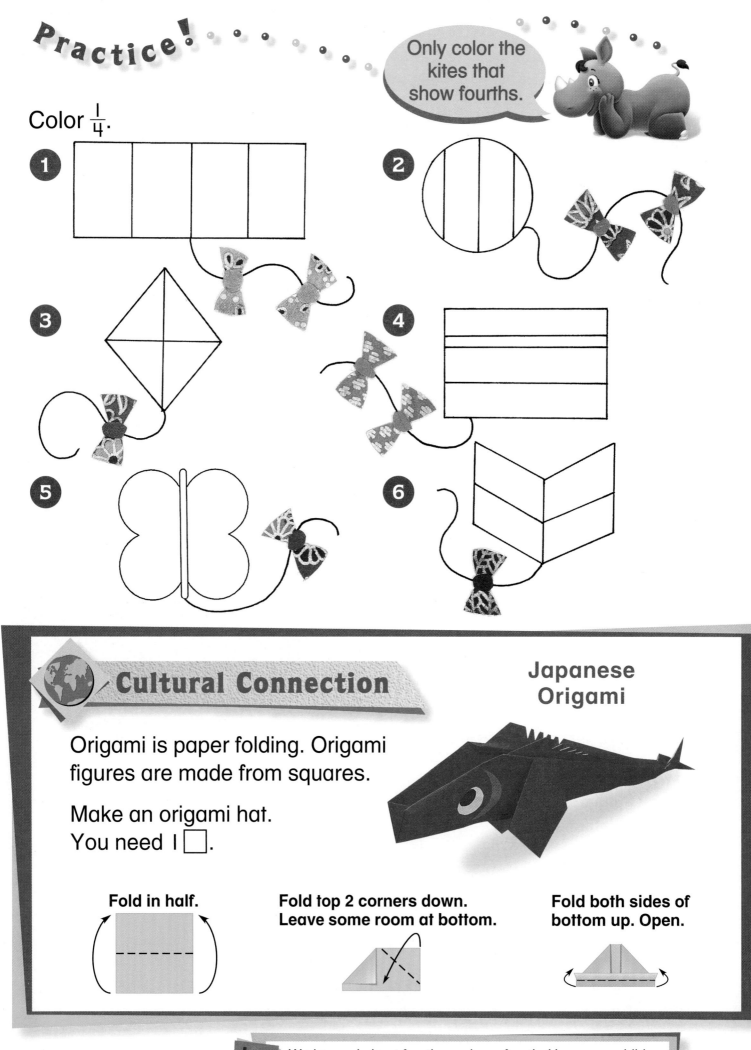

Practice!

Only color the kites that show fourths.

Color $\frac{1}{4}$.

1

2

3

4

5

6

Cultural Connection

Japanese Origami

Origami is paper folding. Origami figures are made from squares.

Make an origami hat.
You need 1 ☐.

Fold in half.

Fold top 2 corners down. Leave some room at bottom.

Fold both sides of bottom up. Open.

At Home

We learned about fourths and one fourth. Have your child show how to fold a sheet of paper into fourths.

thirds

3 equal parts

I of 3 equal parts

One third is green.

Glossary
thirds
one third
fraction

I part green
3 equal parts

$\frac{1}{3}$

$\frac{1}{3}$ is a **fraction**.

Working Together

You need paper shapes.

▶ Fold a ☐ into thirds.
Fold another ☐ in half.

▶ Cut on the folds.

▶ Look at $\frac{1}{3}$ and $\frac{1}{2}$.

▶ Fold other shapes.

▶ Make 3 equal parts.

▶ Color $\frac{1}{3}$.

Show how you made 3 equal parts. Color $\frac{1}{3}$.

1 ☐ **2** ☐ **3** ☐

Practice!

The speech bubble $\frac{1}{2}$, $\frac{1}{4}$, and $\frac{1}{3}$ are fractions.

Ring the fraction.

1

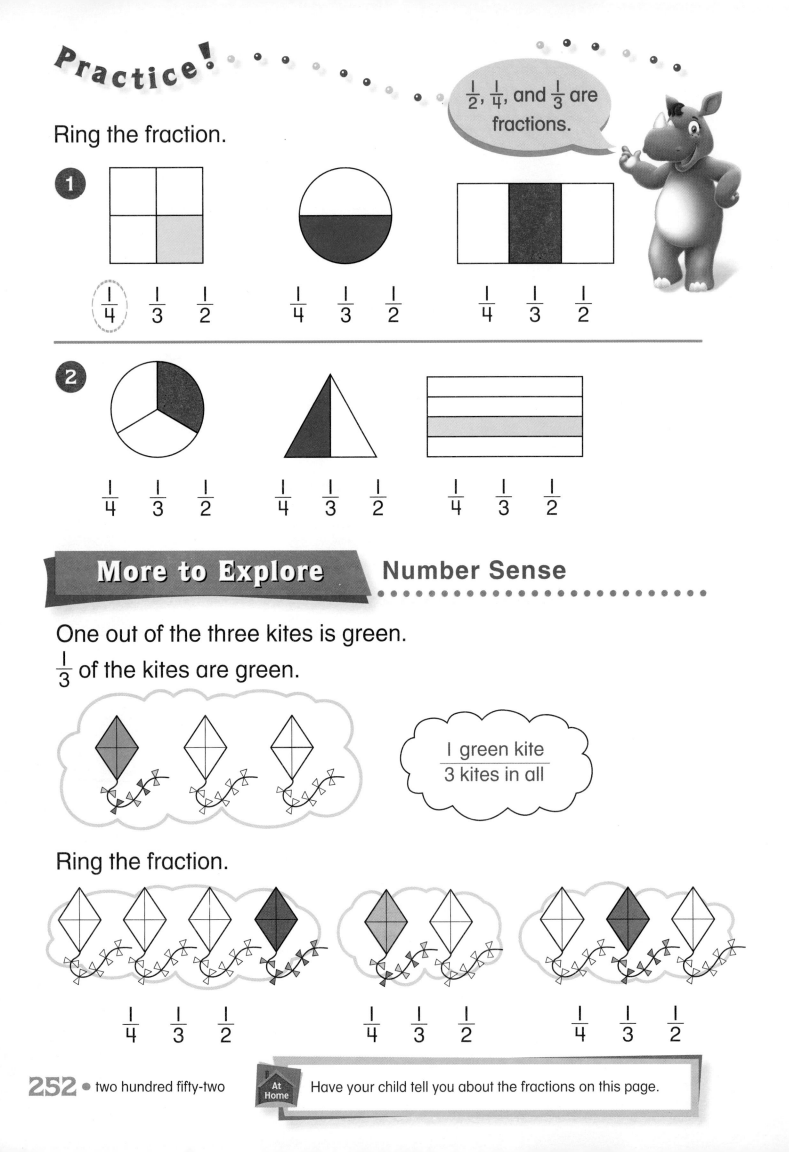

$\frac{1}{4}$ $\frac{1}{3}$ $\frac{1}{2}$ $\frac{1}{4}$ $\frac{1}{3}$ $\frac{1}{2}$ $\frac{1}{4}$ $\frac{1}{3}$ $\frac{1}{2}$

2

$\frac{1}{4}$ $\frac{1}{3}$ $\frac{1}{2}$ $\frac{1}{4}$ $\frac{1}{3}$ $\frac{1}{2}$ $\frac{1}{4}$ $\frac{1}{3}$ $\frac{1}{2}$

More to Explore   Number Sense

One out of the three kites is green.
$\frac{1}{3}$ of the kites are green.

$\frac{\text{I green kite}}{\text{3 kites in all}}$

Ring the fraction.

$\frac{1}{4}$ $\frac{1}{3}$ $\frac{1}{2}$ $\frac{1}{4}$ $\frac{1}{3}$ $\frac{1}{2}$ $\frac{1}{4}$ $\frac{1}{3}$ $\frac{1}{2}$

At Home   Have your child tell you about the fractions on this page.

Draw a Picture

Meg and Jon share a pie.
How can they divide the pie so that
each child gets an equal part?

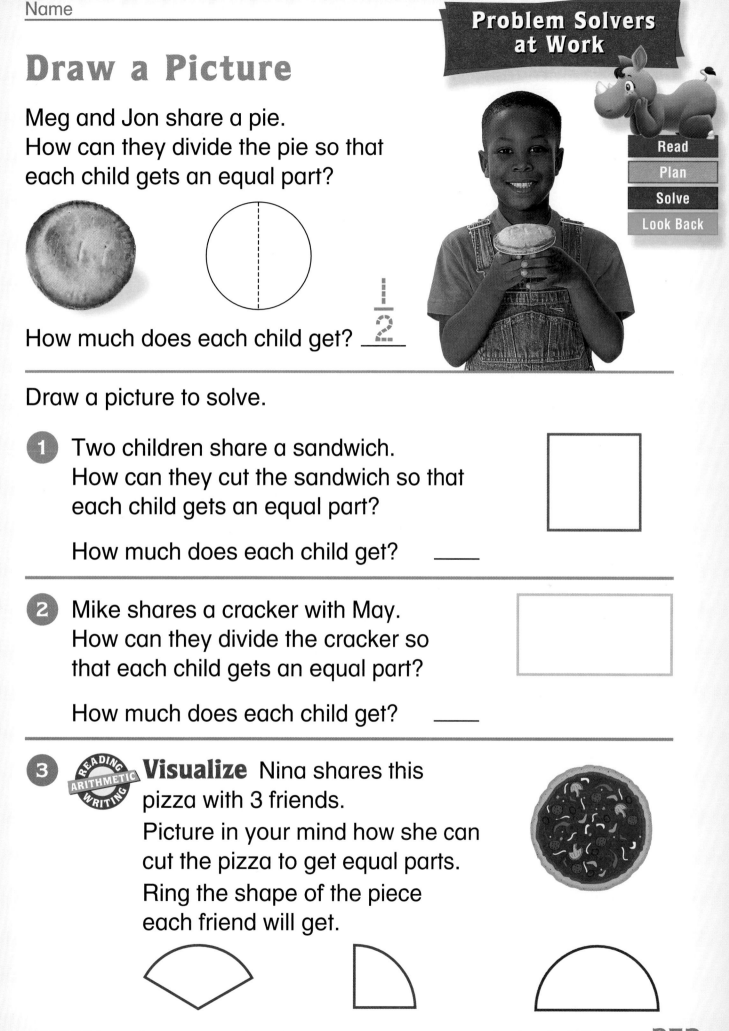

How much does each child get? $\frac{1}{2}$

Draw a picture to solve.

1 Two children share a sandwich.
How can they cut the sandwich so that
each child gets an equal part?

How much does each child get? _____

---

2 Mike shares a cracker with May.
How can they divide the cracker so
that each child gets an equal part?

How much does each child get? _____

---

3 READING ARITHMETIC WRITING **Visualize** Nina shares this
pizza with 3 friends.
Picture in your mind how she can
cut the pizza to get equal parts.
Ring the shape of the piece
each friend will get.

Practice!

Draw a picture to solve.

1 Four friends share a snack bar.
How can they divide the bar so that
each friend gets an equal part?

How much does each friend get? _____

2 What if only 3 friends share the bar?
How can they divide the bar so that
each friend gets an equal part?

How much does each friend get? _____

 Talk Would you like to have a part of the
snack bar in problem 1 or in 2? Why?

Write and Share

Randy wrote this problem.

*Randy and Casey share a
mango. How can they cut
the mango so that each
child gets an equal part?*

Randy Hall
Mandarin Oaks School
Jacksonville, Florida

3 Solve Randy's problem.
How much does each child get? _____

4 Write Write a problem about sharing.
Have a partner solve it.

Use your own paper.

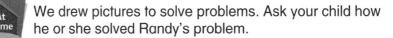 **At Home** We drew pictures to solve problems. Ask your child how
he or she solved Randy's problem.

Chapter Review

Language and Mathematics

Choose the correct word to complete the sentence.

1 ☐ is a _____.

2 ⊕ shows _____.

> edge
> square
> one half
> fourths

Concepts and Skills

Draw lines to match.

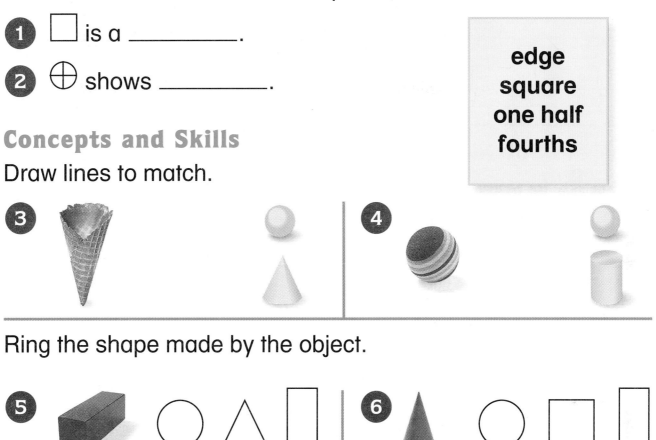

Ring the shape made by the object.

Complete.

7 A △ has _____ corners.

8 A ○ has _____ corners.

9 A ☐ has _____ sides.

10 A ☐ has _____ sides.

Does the shape have equal parts?

11   yes   no

12   yes   no

13   yes   no

Color to show the fraction.

14 $\frac{1}{3}$

15 $\frac{1}{4}$

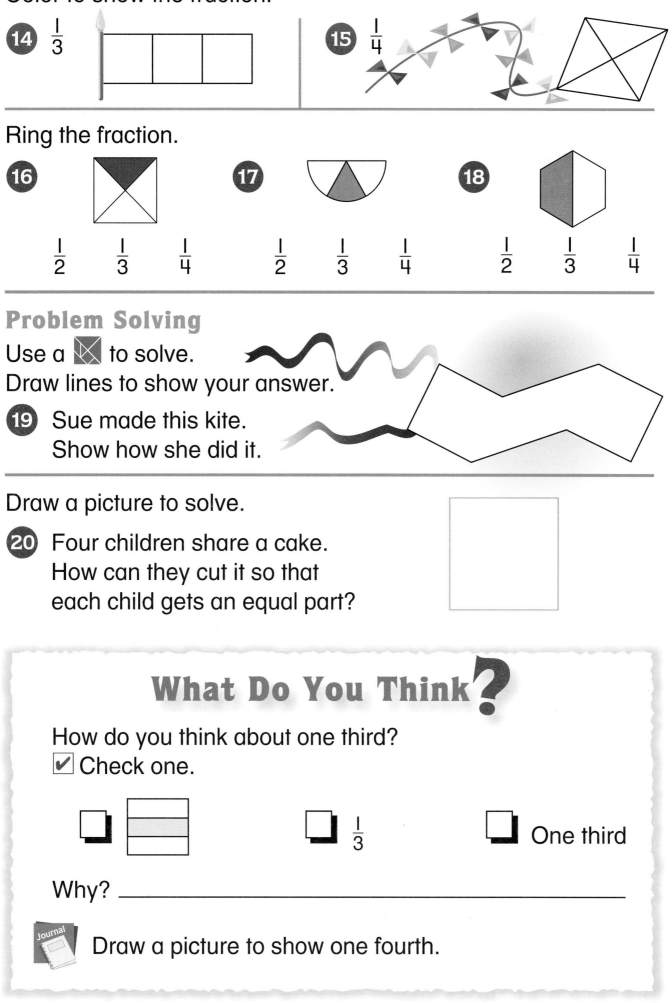

Ring the fraction.

16 $\frac{1}{2}$ $\frac{1}{3}$ $\frac{1}{4}$

17 $\frac{1}{2}$ $\frac{1}{3}$ $\frac{1}{4}$

18 $\frac{1}{2}$ $\frac{1}{3}$ $\frac{1}{4}$

Problem Solving

Use a ▨ to solve.
Draw lines to show your answer.

19 Sue made this kite.
Show how she did it.

Draw a picture to solve.

20 Four children share a cake.
How can they cut it so that
each child gets an equal part?

What Do You Think?

How do you think about one third?
☑ Check one.

☐   ☐ $\frac{1}{3}$ ☐ One third

Why? _____

Journal Draw a picture to show one fourth.

Name _____

Draw lines to match.

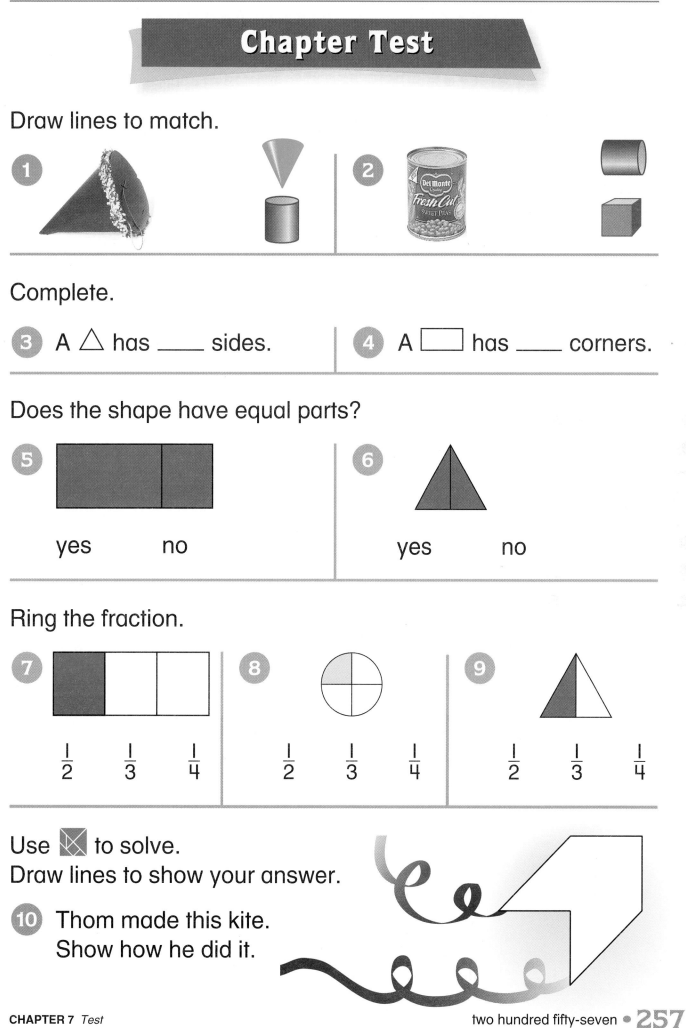

1

2

Complete.

3 A △ has ____ sides.

4 A ▭ has ____ corners.

Does the shape have equal parts?

5

yes   no

6

yes   no

Ring the fraction.

7

$\frac{1}{2}$ $\frac{1}{3}$ $\frac{1}{4}$

8

$\frac{1}{2}$ $\frac{1}{3}$ $\frac{1}{4}$

9

$\frac{1}{2}$ $\frac{1}{3}$ $\frac{1}{4}$

Use ◻ to solve.
Draw lines to show your answer.

10 Thom made this kite.
Show how he did it.

What Did You Learn?

Draw lines in each shape.
Color to show the fraction.

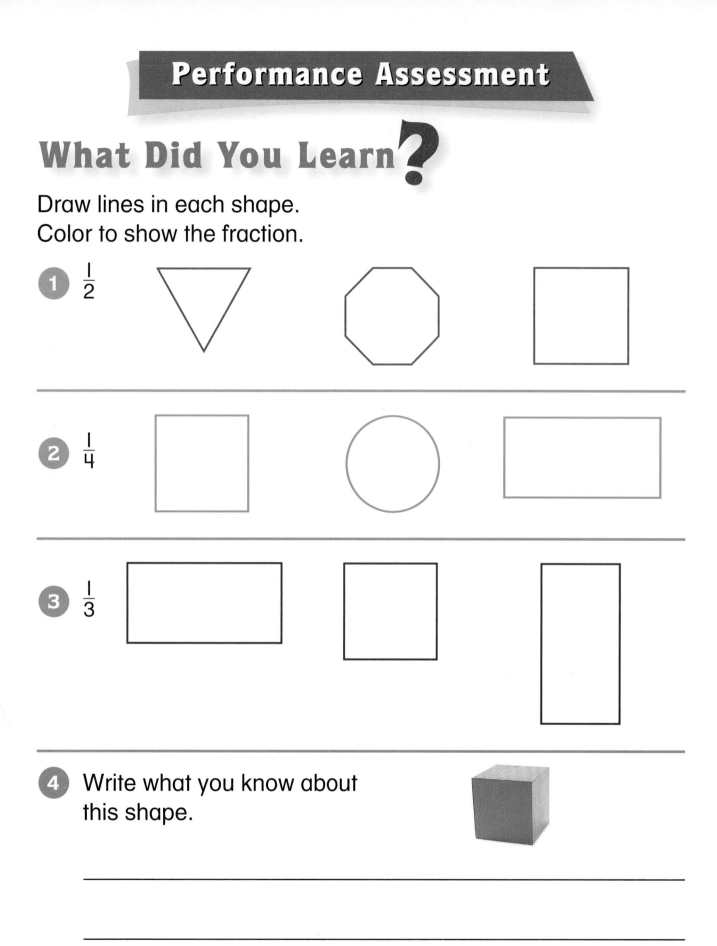

1. $\frac{1}{2}$

2. $\frac{1}{4}$

3. $\frac{1}{3}$

4. Write what you know about this shape.

_____

_____

You may want to put this page in your portfolio.

Name

Likely/Unlikely

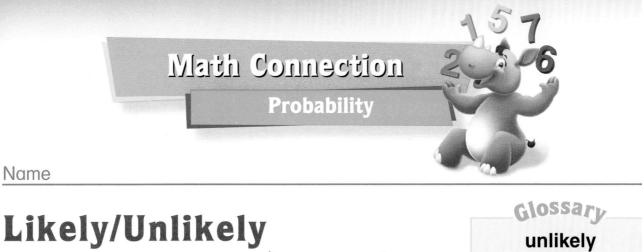

unlikely

likely

Mark an X if the picture shows what is unlikely.
Mark an O if the picture shows what is likely.

1

2

Shapes and Fractions

Talk How many small squares were used to make the larger square?

1 What fraction of the large square is one small square?

_____

At the Computer

2 Draw a triangle like the one shown. Makes copies of it to build the larger triangle.

3 What fraction of the large triangle is one small triangle?

_____

4 This triangle is $\frac{1}{2}$ of another triangle. Draw that triangle.

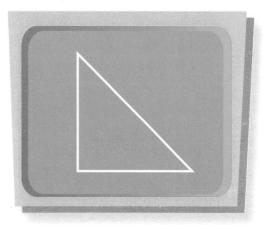

Name

Shape Riddles

PLAYERS	2 or more
MATERIALS	different-shaped toys or other objects
DIRECTIONS	Place all of the objects on the table. The first player

describes one of the objects. The other player guesses what it is and names the geometric shape.

I am thinking of an object that rolls and doesn't have flat faces.

Sphere?

At Home
Play this game with your child. It will help your child become more familiar with 3-dimensional shape names.

Dear Family,

I am beginning a new chapter in mathematics. I will be learning about money and will be counting pennies, nickels, dimes, and quarters.

I will also learn about stores and how money is used.

Learning about Stores and Money

Let's talk about different kinds of stores. We can name a store that we go to and make a list of things we can buy there.

My Math Words

I am going to use these math words in this chapter.

Please help me make word cards for these math words. I can use the word cards when I practice using money.

nickel
dime
price
guess and test
quarter
amount
certain
impossible

Your child,

_____
Signature

Money
Theme: Our Store

GENERAL STORE

by Rachel Field · illustrated by Nancy Winslow Parker

READING
ARITHMETIC
WRITING

Write How-To Directions

After you listen to the story *General Store,* tell how you would set up a store. What would you do first, next, and last?

Tell how people use money at a store.

263

What Do You Know?

Jill saves pennies.

The table shows how many pennies Jill saved in one week.

JILL'S PENNIES	
Monday	🪙🪙
Tuesday	🪙🪙🪙🪙🪙
Wednesday	🪙🪙🪙
Thursday	🪙🪙🪙🪙🪙🪙🪙🪙
Friday	🪙

1 How many pennies did Jill save on Monday and Tuesday? ____

How many cents is that? ____¢

2 How many cents for the two days with the most pennies? ____¢

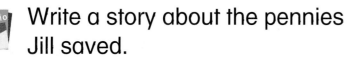 Write a story about the pennies Jill saved.

Name _____

I penny
I cent
I ¢

5 pennies
5 cents
5¢

I **nickel**
5 cents
5¢

Count by fives.
Then count on by ones.
Write how much money.

Glossary

nickel

1. 5¢ 10¢ 15¢ 16¢ 17¢   17¢

2.   ____¢

3.   ____¢

4.   ____¢

Critical Thinking Why can you count by fives to count nickels?

McGraw-Hill School Division

Write the ¢.

Count.
Write how much money.

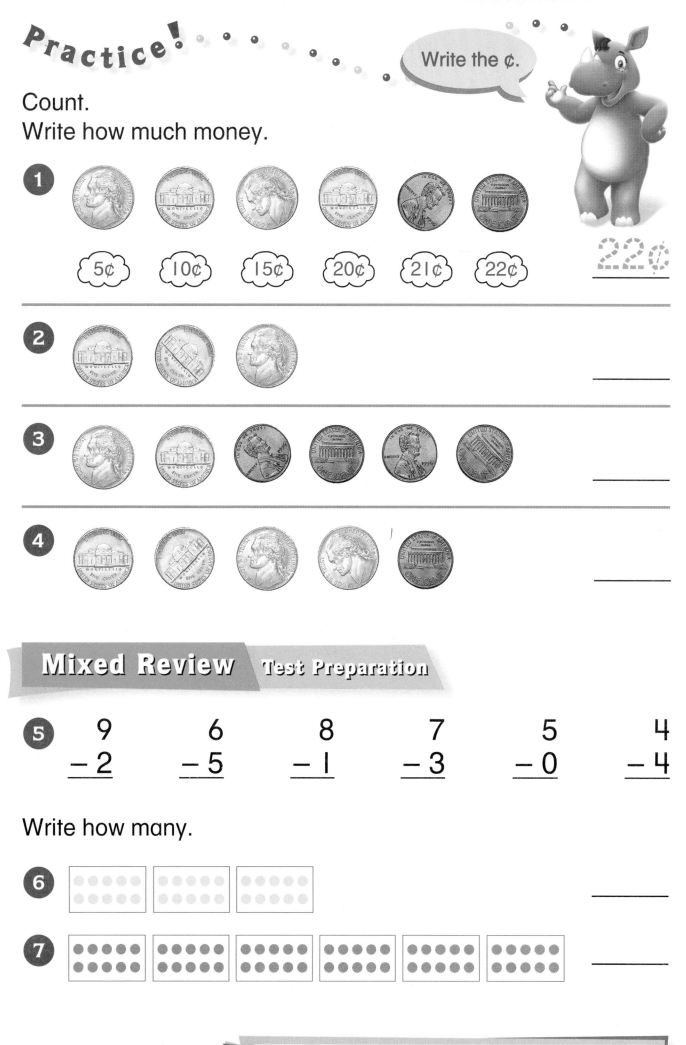

1 5¢   10¢   15¢   20¢   21¢   22¢

22¢ _____

2 _____

3 _____

4 _____

Mixed Review   Test Preparation

5
$$9 - 2$$ $$6 - 5$$ $$8 - 1$$ $$7 - 3$$ $$5 - 0$$ $$4 - 4$$

Write how many.

6 _____

7 _____

At Home

We counted pennies and nickels. Have your child count 5 nickels to find how many cents.

Name _____

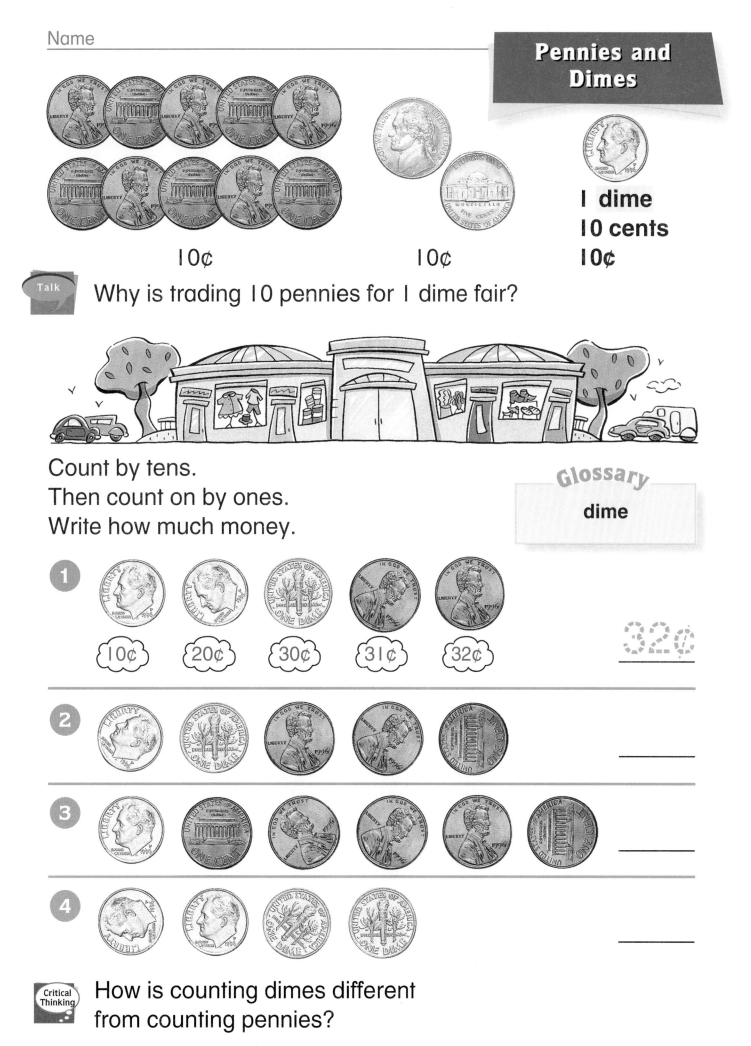

1 **dime**
10 cents
10¢

10¢   10¢

Talk Why is trading 10 pennies for 1 dime fair?

Count by tens.
Then count on by ones.
Write how much money.

Glossary

dime

1
⟨10¢⟩ ⟨20¢⟩ ⟨30¢⟩ ⟨31¢⟩ ⟨32¢⟩   32¢ _____

2   _____

3   _____

4   _____

Critical Thinking How is counting dimes different from counting pennies?

Practice!

Count. Write how much money.

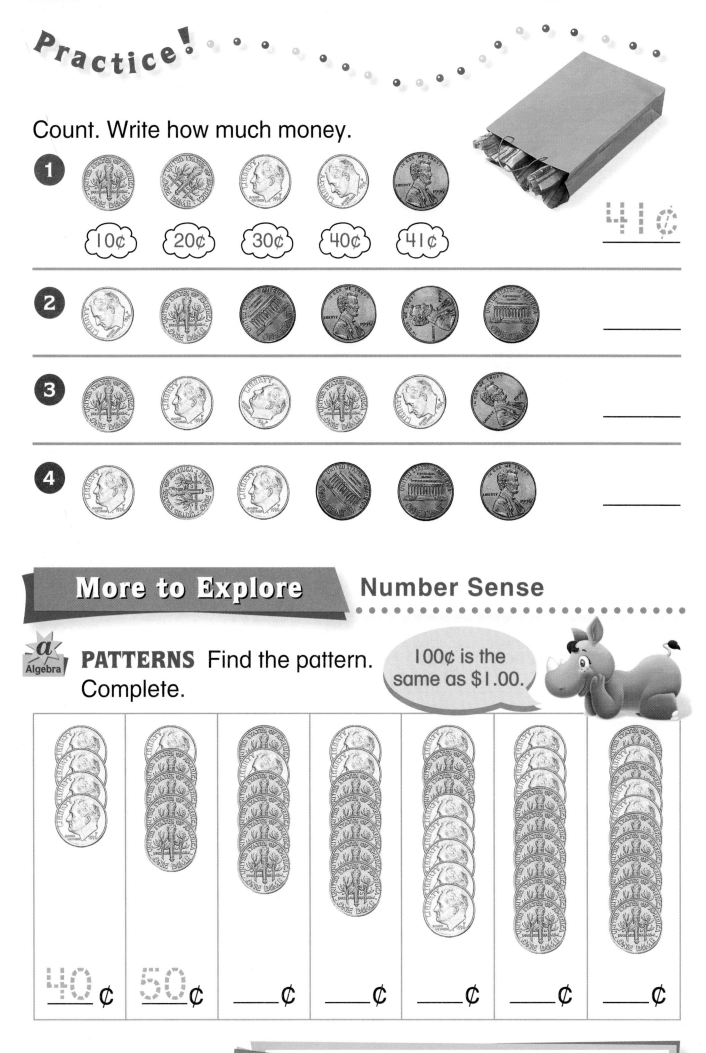

1 10¢ 20¢ 30¢ 40¢ 41¢   **41¢**

2 _____

3 _____

4 _____

More to Explore   Number Sense

a **Algebra** **PATTERNS** Find the pattern. Complete.

100¢ is the same as $1.00.

40¢   50¢   ___¢   ___¢   ___¢   ___¢   ___¢

At Home Have your child show you how to count a set of dimes and pennies.

Working Together

You and your partner need 9 ,
9 🪙, and 9 🪙.

Write a **price** for each toy.

Take turns.

Glossary
price

▶ Pretend to buy a toy.

▶ Show the price with coins.

▶ Your partner checks.

▶ Show how many of each coin you use.

🏀 **27** ¢	◯ ◯	◯	◯ ◯
🧒 _____ ¢			
🚤 _____ ¢			
🕷 _____ ¢			
🦫 _____ ¢			

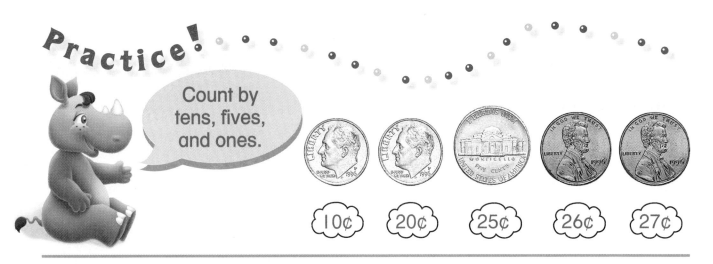

| 10¢ | 20¢ | 25¢ | 26¢ | 27¢ |

Count the coins.
Match each set to a price.

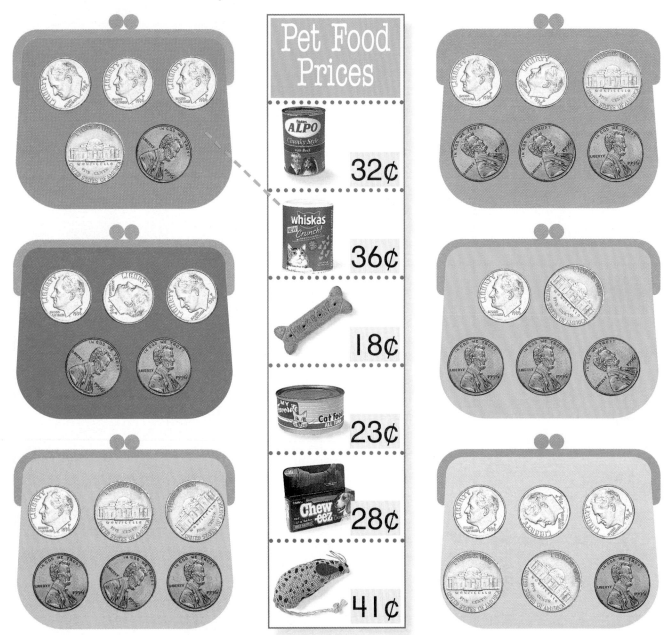

Pet Food Prices

ALPO Chunky Style with Beef — 32¢

whiskas NEW Crunch! — 36¢

(dog bone) — 18¢

Cat Food — 23¢

Chew-eez — 28¢

(mouse toy) — 41¢

 Journal

Show how you count a set of dimes, nickels, and pennies.

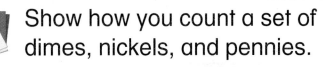

At Home Have your child show you how to count a set of dimes, nickels, and pennies.

Name _____

Tad buys soap.
Mark the coins he needs.

Mark the coins each child needs.

1 Chris buys soap.

41¢

2 May buys a bag.

35¢

3 Ed buys a cup.

27¢

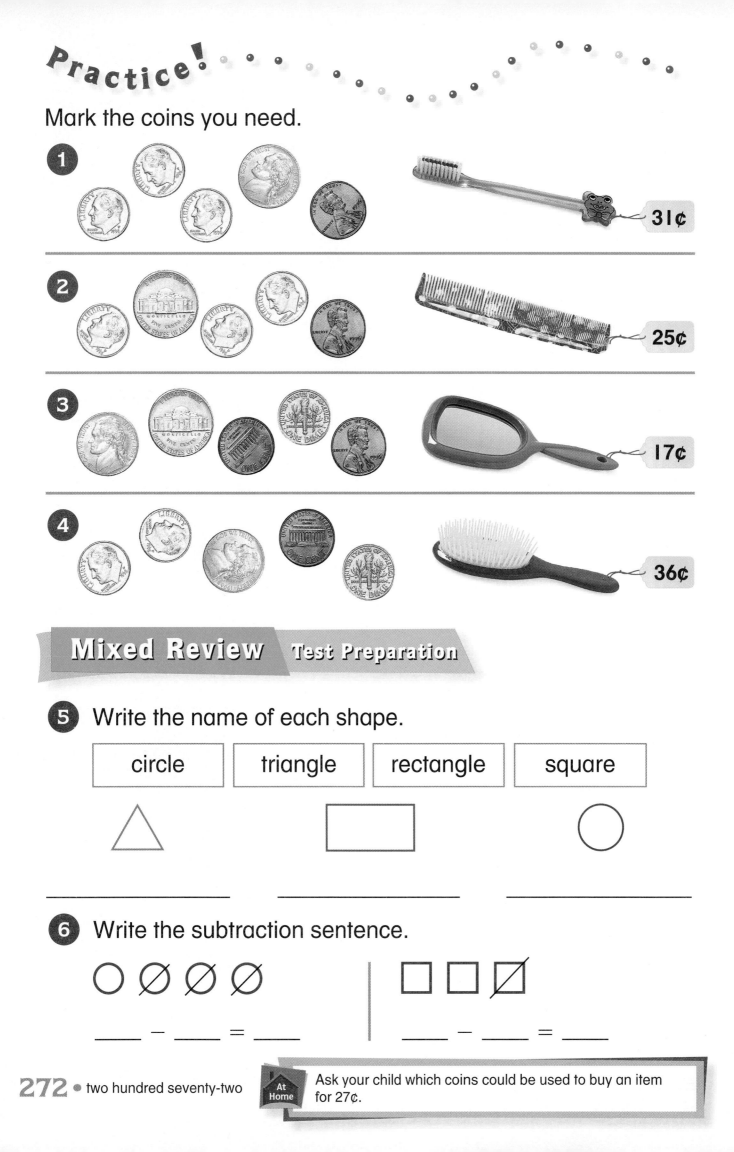

Practice!

Mark the coins you need.

1 31¢

2 25¢

3 17¢

4 36¢

5 Write the name of each shape.

circle	triangle	rectangle	square

_____   _____   _____

6 Write the subtraction sentence.

○ ⊘ ⊘ ⊘   □ □ ▢

____ – ____ = ____   ____ – ____ = ____

At Home Ask your child which coins could be used to buy an item for 27¢.

Guess and Test

Read   Lin buys 2 cards.
She spends 9¢.
Which 2 cards does she buy?

3¢   4¢   5¢

Plan   You can **guess and test** to solve.
Guess which 2 cards.
Test your guess by adding.

Glossary

guess and test

Solve   4¢ + 3¢ = 7¢   (No.)
3¢ + 5¢ = 8¢   (No.)
4¢ + 5¢ = 9¢   (Yes.)

Lin buys these cards.   4¢   5¢

Look Back   Does the answer make sense? Explain.

Guess and test to solve.
Which 2 cards does Lin buy?

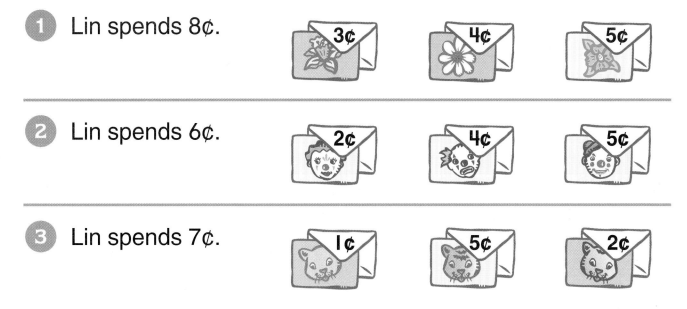

1   Lin spends 8¢.   3¢   4¢   5¢

2   Lin spends 6¢.   2¢   4¢   5¢

3   Lin spends 7¢.   1¢   5¢   2¢

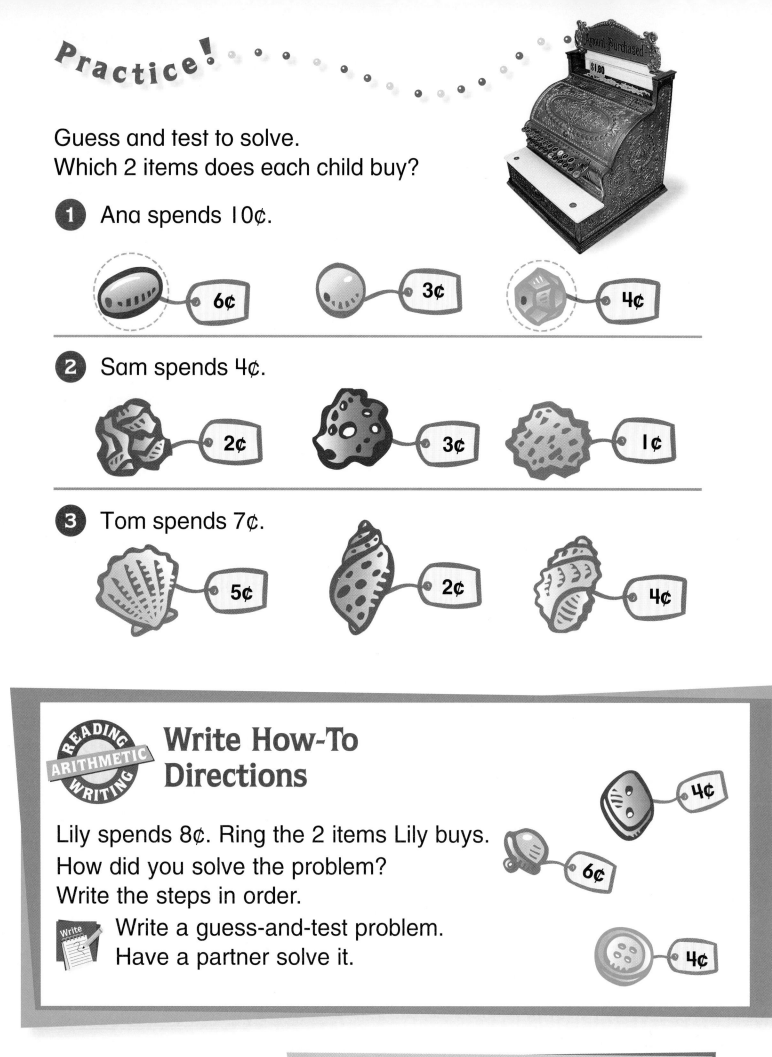

Practice!

Guess and test to solve.
Which 2 items does each child buy?

1 Ana spends 10¢.

6¢   3¢   4¢

2 Sam spends 4¢.

2¢   3¢   1¢

3 Tom spends 7¢.

5¢   2¢   4¢

READING ARITHMETIC WRITING Write How-To Directions

Lily spends 8¢. Ring the 2 items Lily buys.
How did you solve the problem?
Write the steps in order.

4¢

6¢

Write Write a guess-and-test problem.
Have a partner solve it.

4¢

274 • two hundred seventy-four

 At Home

We used the guess-and-test strategy to solve a problem.
Ask your child how to solve problem 3.

Midchapter Review

Do your best!

Write how much money.

1 _____

2 _____

3 _____

4 _____

5 _____

6 _____

Mark the coins you need.

7   20¢

8   17¢

Solve.

3¢   6¢   2¢

9 Max spends 8¢.
Which 2 books does he buy?

_____

10 How did you solve problem 9?

_____

_____

 Journal Show all the ways that you could have
20¢ in coins.

Play and Pay

You and your partner need a 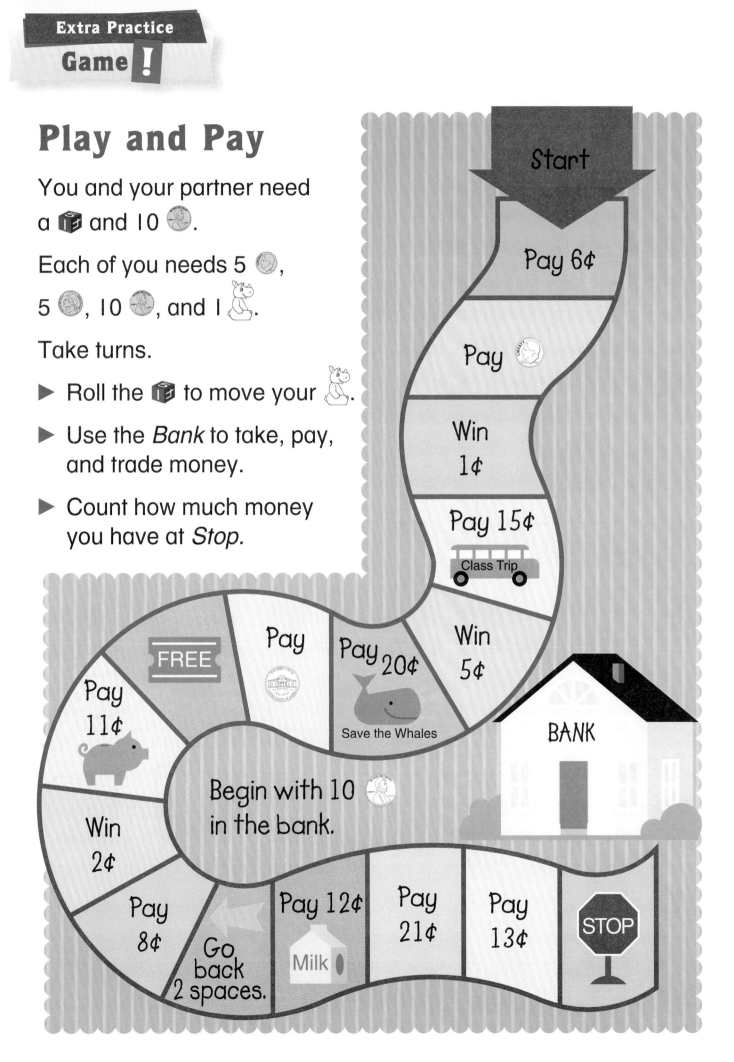 and 10 🪙.

Each of you needs 5 🪙,

5 🪙, 10 🪙, and 1 🦛.

Take turns.

▶ Roll the 🎲 to move your 🦛.

▶ Use the *Bank* to take, pay, and trade money.

▶ Count how much money you have at *Stop.*

Start

Pay 6¢

Pay 🪙

Win 1¢

Pay 15¢
Class Trip

Win 5¢

Pay 20¢
Save the Whales

Pay 🪙

FREE

Pay 11¢

Win 2¢

Pay 8¢

Go back 2 spaces.

Pay 12¢
Milk

Pay 21¢

Pay 13¢

Begin with 10 🪙 in the bank.

BANK

STOP

Name _____

100 Years Ago

Listen to
General Store.

The story takes place 100 years ago.
Many things cost pennies then.

Working Together

You need index cards, , , and .

5¢

2¢
for a
dozen

Make an
Old Fashioned Store
1. Choose items to sell.
2. Draw or paste pictures of items on cards.
3. Make up prices.
4. What can you buy with 25¢?
Go Shopping!

Decision Making

1 Decide what to buy at the store. Take a card. Leave the correct amount of money.

2 Compare what you buy with your partner. Did you spend the same amount? _____

3 Did you buy the same things? _____

 Write a report.

4 Tell about the store. What did you buy?

5 What do things cost now? Tell what you know.

More to Investigate

PREDICT What do you think things will cost 100 years from now?

EXPLORE How do stores decide on prices?

FIND Find today's price of three of the things you bought.

Name _____

**I quarter
25 cents
25¢**

Glossary

quarter

Working Together

You and your partner need

2 , 5 , and 25 .

▶ Find ways to show 25¢.

▶ Show as many different
ways as you can.

25¢	◯ ◯	◯	
25¢			
25¢			
25¢			

 Critical Thinking Did you and your class find all the ways
to show 25¢?
How can you check?

McGraw-Hill School Division

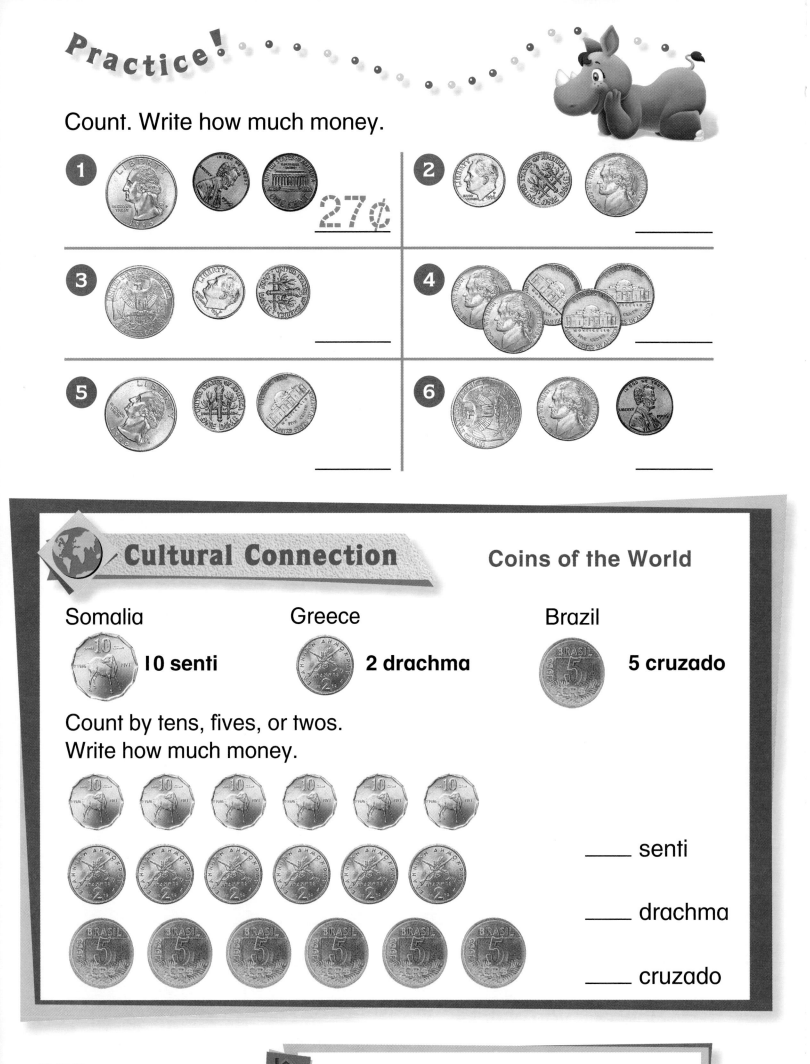

Practice!

Count. Write how much money.

1 **27¢**

2 _____

3 _____

4 _____

5 _____

6 _____

Cultural Connection

Coins of the World

Somalia	Greece	Brazil
10 senti	**2 drachma**	**5 cruzado**

Count by tens, fives, or twos.
Write how much money.

_____ senti

_____ drachma

_____ cruzado

At Home Ask your child to show you two ways to make 25¢.

Working Together

You and your partner need
4 , 10 🪙, 10 🪙, 20 🪙.

Take turns.

▶ Show the **amount**.

▶ Your partner shows the
amount a different way.

▶ Write how many of each coin.

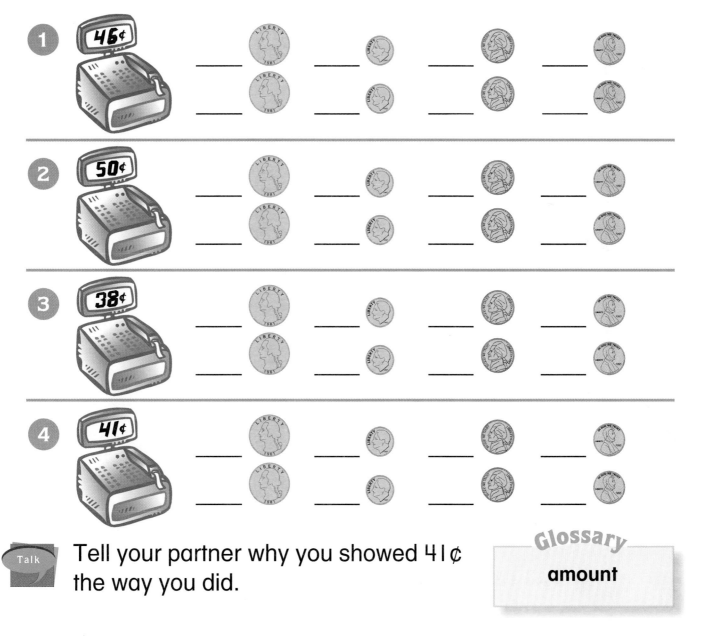

1 46¢ ____ ____ ____ ____
     ____ ____ ____ ____

2 50¢ ____ ____ ____ ____
     ____ ____ ____ ____

3 38¢ ____ ____ ____ ____
     ____ ____ ____ ____

4 41¢ ____ ____ ____ ____
     ____ ____ ____ ____

Talk — Tell your partner why you showed 41¢
the way you did.

Glossary
amount

McGraw-Hill School Division

Practice!

Count each set of coins.
Write how much money.
Color the shapes with
the same amounts the
same color.

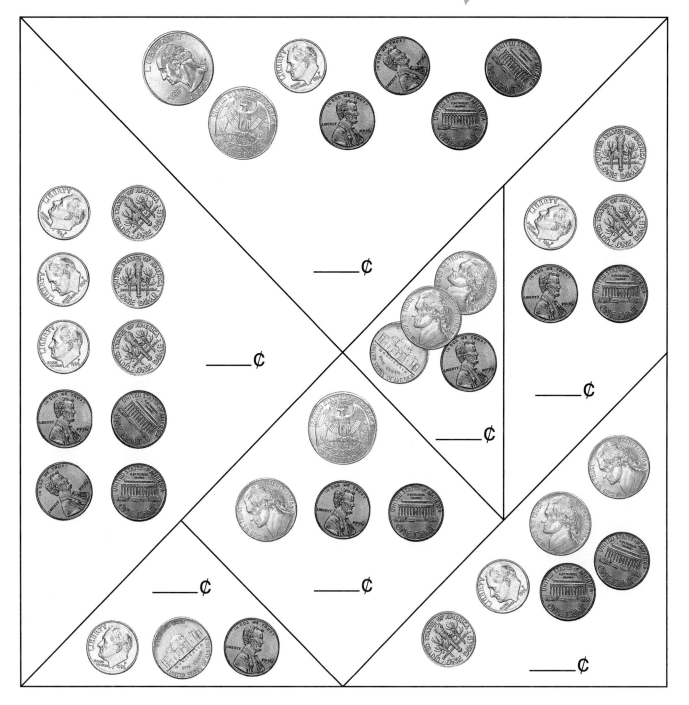

  PATTERNS Tell a partner about any patterns
you found.

At Home   Have your child show you two ways to make 31¢.

Name _____

Who has more money?

Compare.

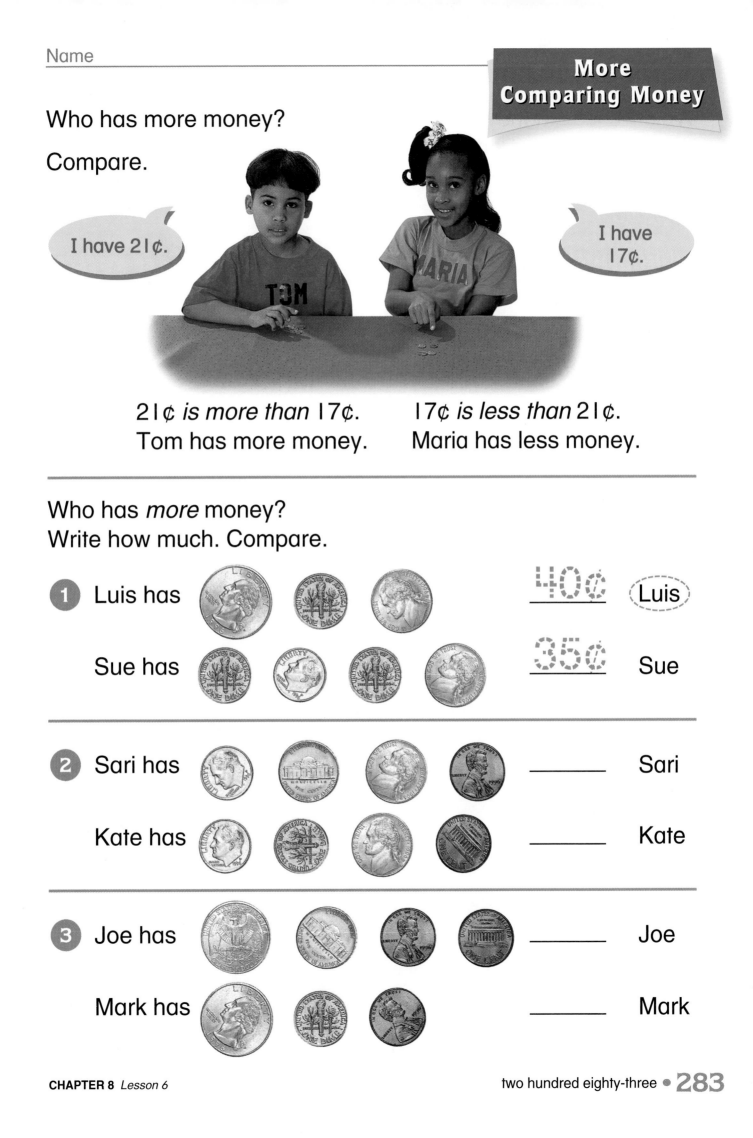

I have 21¢.

I have 17¢.

21¢ *is more than* 17¢.
Tom has more money.

17¢ *is less than* 21¢.
Maria has less money.

Who has *more* money?
Write how much. Compare.

1 Luis has ___40¢___ (Luis)

Sue has ___35¢___ Sue

2 Sari has _____ Sari

Kate has _____ Kate

3 Joe has _____ Joe

Mark has _____ Mark

McGraw-Hill School Division

Practice!

Which is *less* money?
Write how much. Compare.

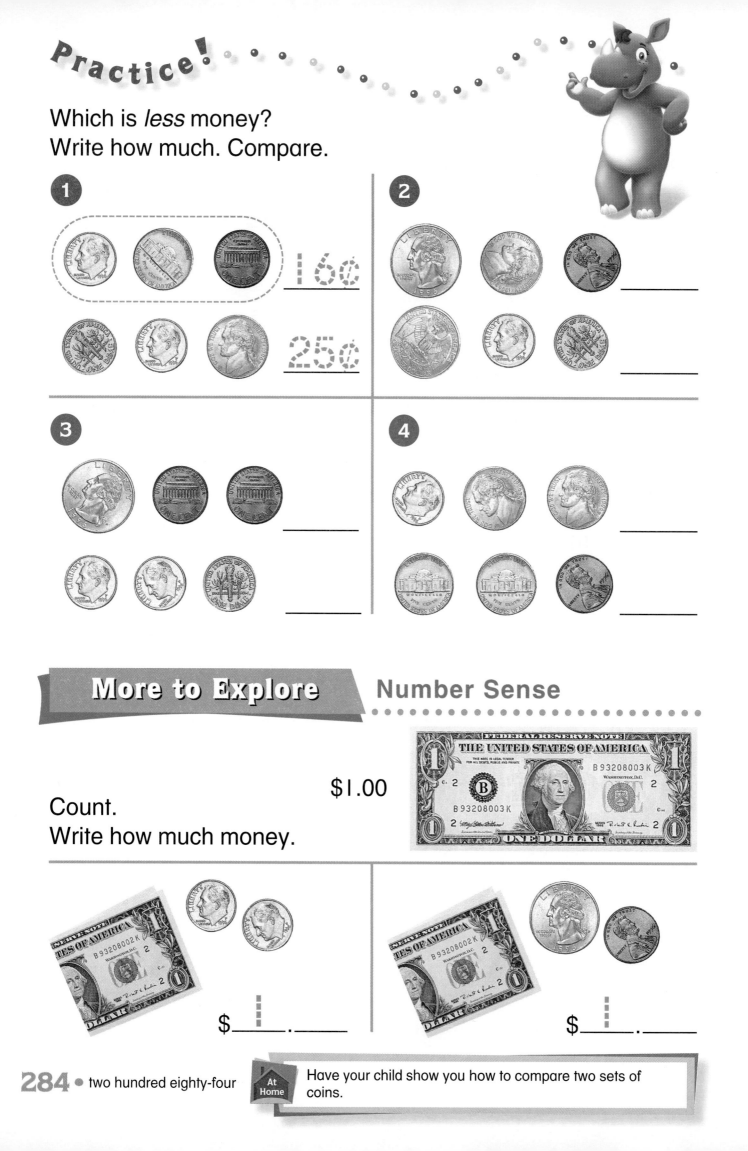

1

16¢

25¢

2

_____

_____

3

_____

_____

4

_____

_____

More to Explore — Number Sense

$1.00

Count.
Write how much money.

$_____ . _____

$_____ . _____

At Home

Have your child show you how to compare two sets of coins.

Trade Up to Quarters

You and your partner need 20 ,
4 , 4 , 8 , 2 , and 1 .

Take turns.

▶ Roll the to move your .

▶ Take money to match the
amount on the space.

▶ Trade coins when you can.

▶ Play until each of you has 2 .

START
6¢ ▶ 14¢ 7¢ 9¢ 5¢
21¢ 25¢
8¢ 3¢
10¢ 1¢ 12¢ 4¢ 11¢

McGraw-Hill School Division

Which is *more* money?
Write how much. Compare.

1

21¢

45¢

2

_____

_____

3

_____

_____

4

_____

_____

Match sets of coins that are the same amount.

5

6

Guess and test to solve.

7 Ann spends 9¢.
Which 2 fish does she buy?

4¢   3¢   5¢

Name _____

Use Data from a Table

1 You have

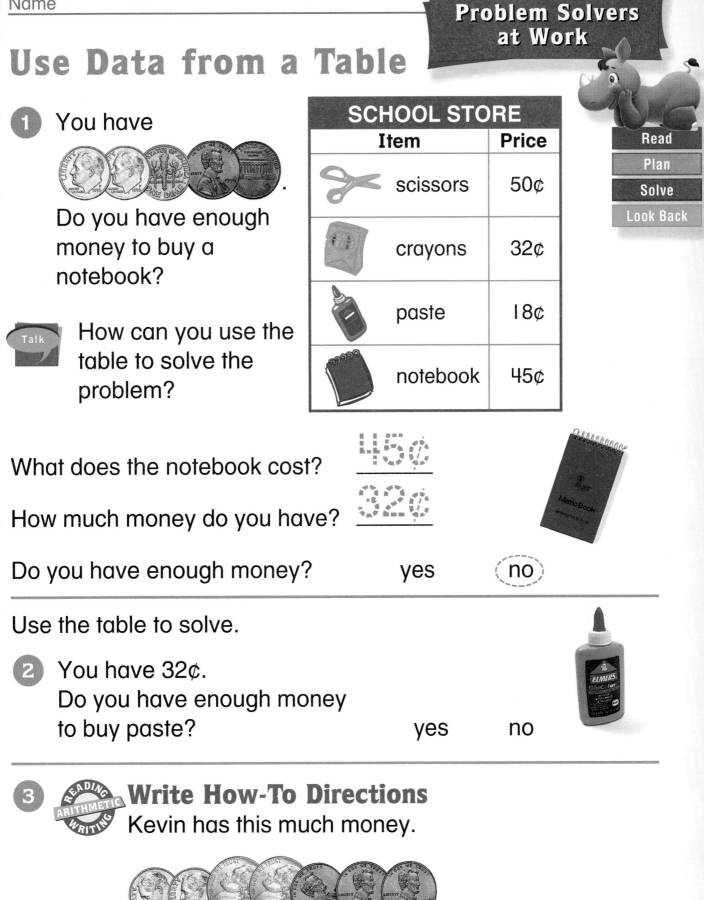

Do you have enough money to buy a notebook?

SCHOOL STORE

Item		Price
✂	scissors	50¢
	crayons	32¢
	paste	18¢
	notebook	45¢

Read
Plan
Solve
Look Back

Talk How can you use the table to solve the problem?

What does the notebook cost? ___45¢___

How much money do you have? ___32¢___

Do you have enough money? yes (no)

Use the table to solve.

2 You have 32¢.
Do you have enough money
to buy paste? yes no

---

3 **READING ARITHMETIC WRITING** **Write How-To Directions**
Kevin has this much money.

Write He can use the table to choose something to buy. Write the steps he can follow.

Use the table to solve.
Write *yes* or *no*.

1 You have 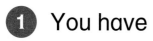.
Do you have enough money
to buy paint?

_____

2 You have 29¢.
Can you buy glue? _____

3 You have 18¢.
Can you buy paint? _____

SCHOOL STORE	
Item	Price
 paint	20¢
glue	25¢
chalk	35¢

Write and Share

Jessica wrote this problem.
You have 28¢. Can you
buy the chalk?

Jessica Castillo
Ogden School
San Antonio, Texas

4 Solve Jessica's problem. _____
How did you solve Jessica's problem? _____

5 Use the table to write a problem.
Have a partner solve it.

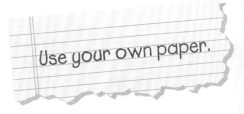
Use your own paper.

 At Home   Try to solve your child's word problem.

Name _____

Chapter Review

Language and Mathematics

Choose the correct word to complete the sentence.

1 A _____ is worth 25¢.

2 The price of 🔘 ─ 5¢ is five _____.

nickel
cents
quarter
amount

Concepts and Skills

Write how much money.

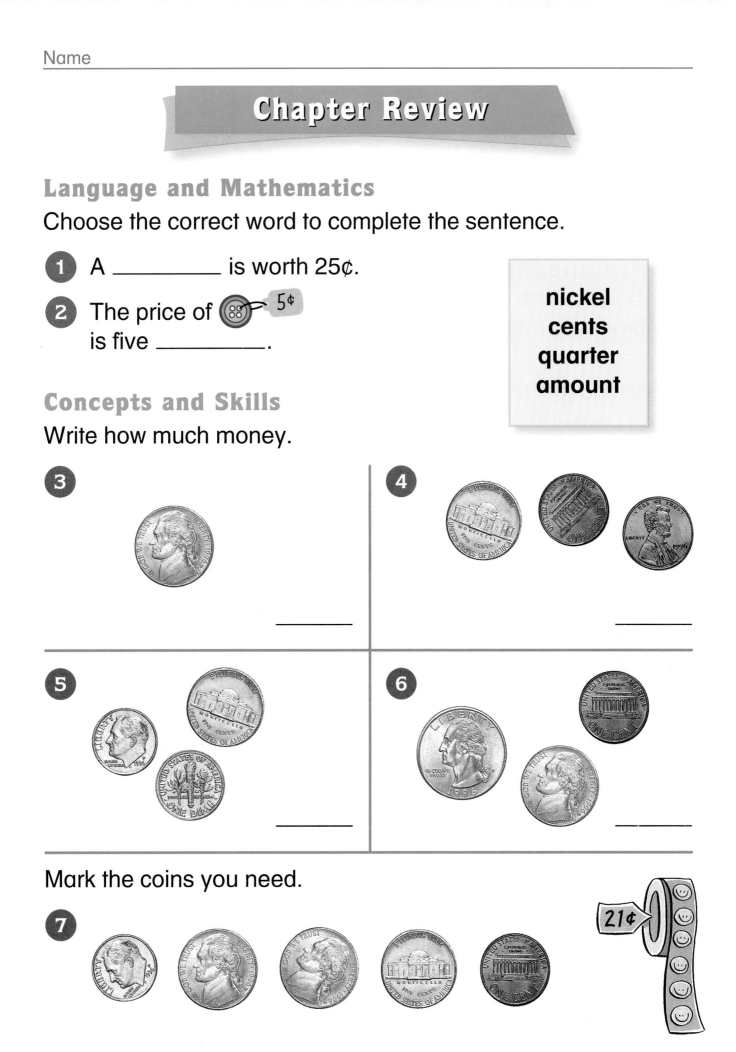

3 _____

4 _____

5 _____

6 _____

Mark the coins you need.

7

21¢

McGraw-Hill School Division

Problem Solving

Use the table to solve.
Write *yes* or *no*.

Item	Price
ball	25¢
car	39¢

8 You have 35¢.
Do you have enough
money to buy a toy car? _____

9 You have 29¢.
Do you have enough
money to buy a ball? _____

Guess and test to solve.

10 Mike spends 7¢.
Which 2 bags does he buy?

5¢   4¢   3¢

What Do You Think?

Which would you rather count?
☑ Check one.

☐ Nickels and pennies   ☐ Dimes   ☐ Pennies

Why? _____

 What did you learn about money? Draw. Write.

Name _____

Chapter Test

Write how much money.

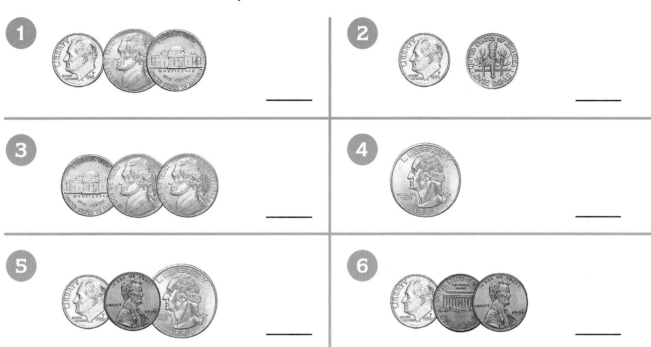

1 _____

2 _____

3 _____

4 _____

5 _____

6 _____

Mark the coins you need.

7 32¢

8 40¢

Guess and test to solve.

9 Lucy spends 9¢. Which 2 stickers does she buy?

5¢   8¢   4¢

10 Vince spends 10¢. Which 2 cards does he buy?

5¢   4¢   6¢

What Did You Learn?

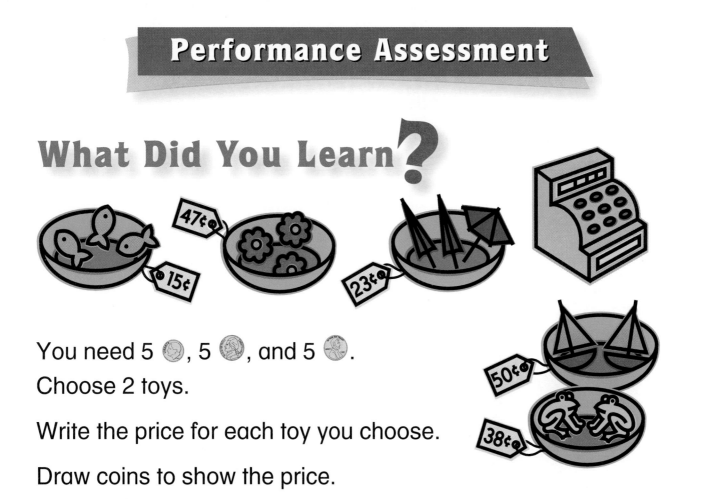

You need 5 ⊙, 5 ◎, and 5 ⊙.

Choose 2 toys.

Write the price for each toy you choose.

Draw coins to show the price.

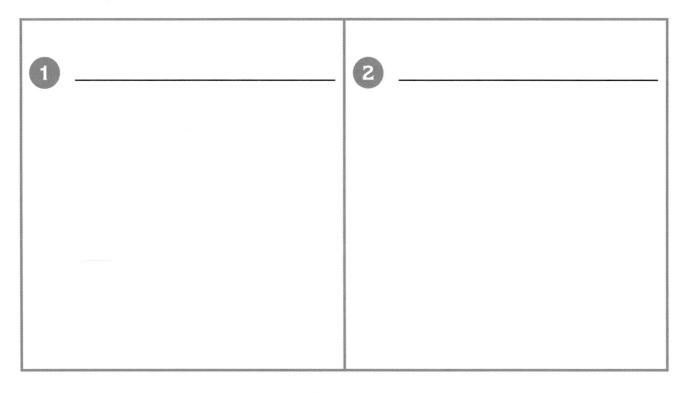

1 _____

2 _____

 3 How much money do you have left? _____

You may want to put this page in your portfolio.

Name

Certain/Impossible

I can take out a penny.

I can take out a dime.

certain   impossible

Choose the answer that makes sense.

1 You can take out a penny.

certain   impossible

2 You can take out a triangle.

certain   impossible

3 You can take out a red crayon.

Blue Crayons

certain   impossible

4 You can take out a quarter.

certain   impossible

Healthful Snacks

Talk   What are some healthful snacks?

Make a sign for a new snack bar.

▶ Choose some healthful snacks.

▶ Write a price for each snack.

SNACK BAR			
Item	Price	Item	Price

Write a word problem about the snack-bar prices.

Have a partner solve it.

Use your own paper.

Name

Money Riddles!

| **PLAYERS** | 2 |

MATERIALS pennies, nickels, dimes, quarters, 2 cups

DIRECTIONS Hide some coins under a cup. (Count them first!) Make up a riddle about your coins. Have your partner guess which coins you have hidden.

3 nickels?

I have 3 coins. They equal 15¢. Which coins do I have?

I have 4 coins. They equal 40¢. Which coins do I have?

At Home Play this riddle game with your child. Play in turns and limit the number of coins to four or fewer. You may want to start with simple combinations.

At Home

Dear Family,

I am beginning a new chapter in mathematics. I will be learning about time and how to use clocks and calendars.

March calendar

✳ **March** ✳						
Sun	**Mon**	**Tue**	**Wed**	**Thu**	**Fri**	**Sat**
1	2	3	4	5	6	7
8	9	10	11	12	13	14
15	16	17	18	19	20	21
22	23	24	25	26	27	28
29	30	31				

I will also learn about games and other ways to have fun.

Learning about Games

Let's talk about different ways we have fun. We can draw a picture of our favorite sport, activity, or hobby.

My Math Words

I am going to use these and other math words in this chapter.

Please help me make word cards for these math words. I can use the word cards when I practice telling time.

clock
o'clock
minute hand
hour hand
hour
half hour
minute
calendar
day
week
month
date
pictograph

Your child,

_____
Signature

Time

Theme: Fun and Games

by Pat Cummings

Summarize Listen to the story *Clean Your Room, Harvey Moon.*

How did Harvey clean his room?

Tell about the things Harvey found in his room.

What Do You Know?

Draw lines to match.

first   second   last

2 How did you choose which came
first, second, and last?

_____

_____

Portfolio

What do you do after school?
Write or draw a picture.
Tell the time.

Working Together

Talk Which do you think takes *more* time?

☐ Write the alphabet. ☐ Write the numbers 1 to 10.

1 Try it.
Number 1 for more time. Number 2 for less time.

Talk Which do you think takes *the most* time?

☐ Connect 10 ☐. ☐ Write your first name. ☐ Write the numbers 1 to 10.

2 Try it.
Number 1 for the most time. Number 2 for less time.
Number 3 for the least time.

Critical Thinking Why do some things take longer to do than others?

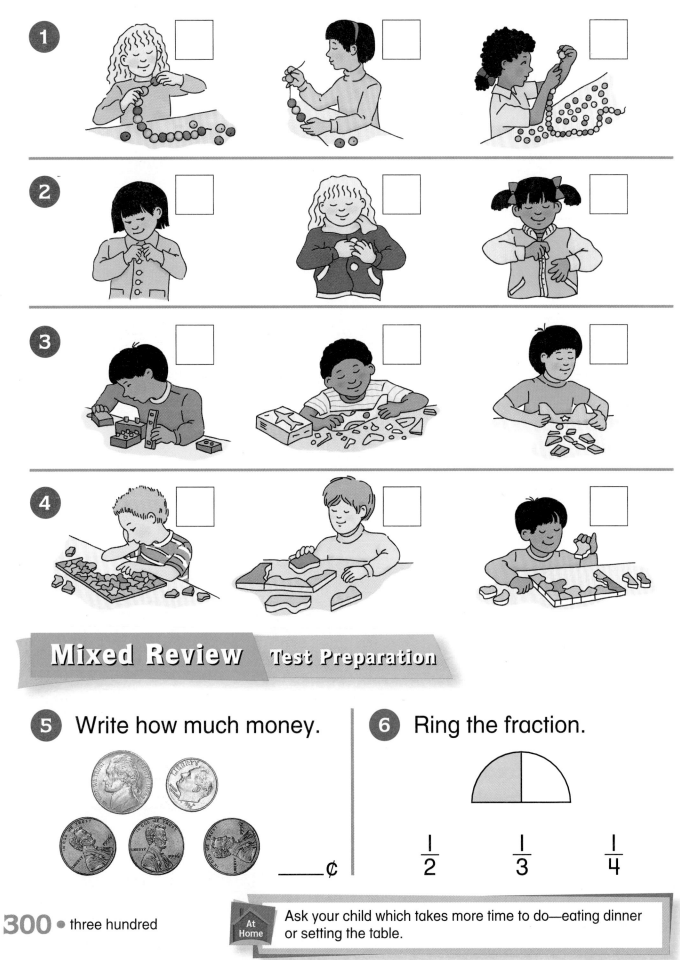

Practice!

Number 1 for the most time. Number 2 for less time.
Number 3 for the least time.

1

2

3

4

Mixed Review   Test Preparation

5 Write how much money.

_____ ¢

6 Ring the fraction.

$\dfrac{1}{2}$ $\dfrac{1}{3}$ $\dfrac{1}{4}$

At Home — Ask your child which takes more time to do—eating dinner or setting the table.

This **clock** shows
7 **o'clock**.

minute hand

hour hand

clock
o'clock
minute hand
hour hand
hour

Working Together

You and your partner need a 🕐.

Take turns.

▶ Show a time on the 🕐.

▶ Your partner draws the hour hand.

▶ Your partner writes the time to the **hour**.

1 ___ o'clock

2 ___ o'clock

3 ___ o'clock

4 ___ o'clock

Critical Thinking Where are the clock hands when the time is 12 o'clock?

Practice! • • • • •

Show the time on a 🕐.
Then write the time.

1 _7_ o'clock

2 ____ o'clock

3 ____ o'clock

4 ____ o'clock

5 ____ o'clock

6 ____ o'clock

At Home We are learning to tell time to the hour. Set a watch or clock to the hour and ask your child what time it is.

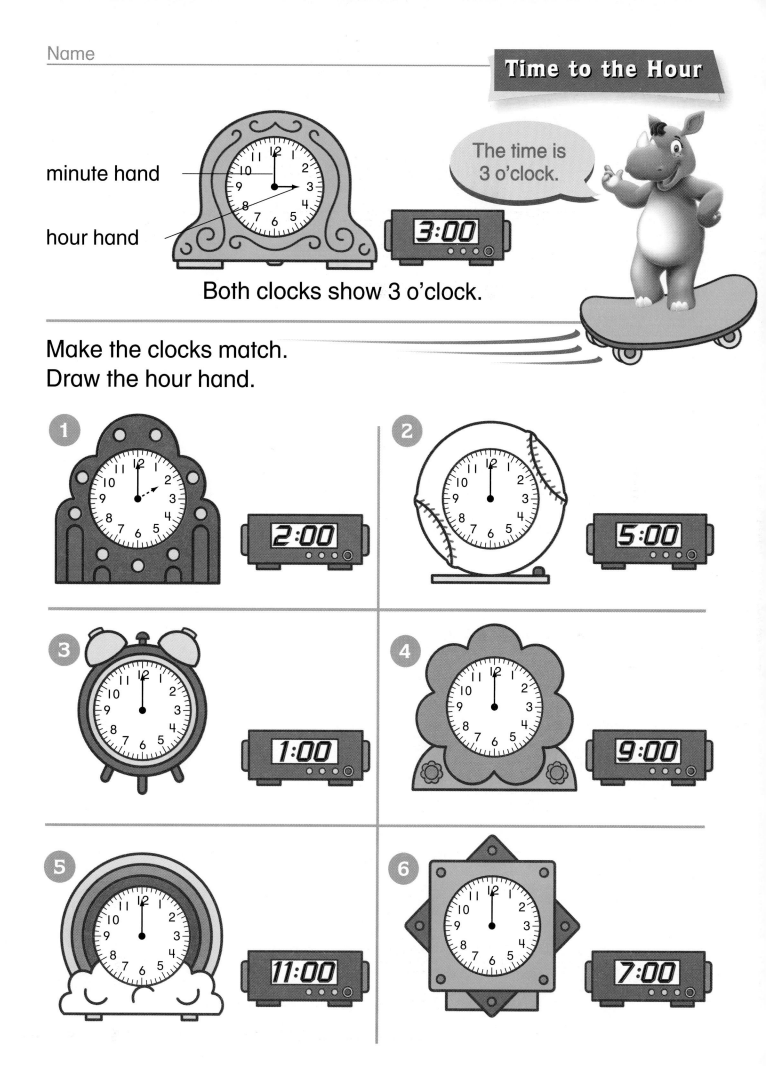

minute hand

hour hand

The time is
3 o'clock.

3:00

Both clocks show 3 o'clock.

Make the clocks match.
Draw the hour hand.

1 2:00

2 5:00

3 1:00

4 9:00

5 11:00

6 7:00

McGraw-Hill School Division

Write the time.

1 10:00

10:00

2 4:00

3 6:00

4 12:00

Talk What do you notice about the way you write the time?

More to Explore Number Sense

Draw the hour hand to show 1 hour later.

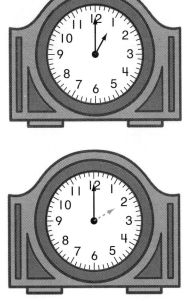

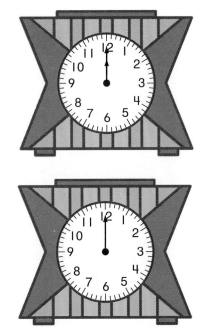

 At Home Ask your child to tell you the time on a digital clock when it shows time to the hour.

Time Is Up!

You and your partner need

2 ✏️, 1 🎲, 2 🦏, and 1 🕐.

Move clockwise!

Start

- ▶ Roll the 🎲 and move that many spaces.

- ▶ Show the time on the 🕐. Your partner checks.

- ▶ If you are correct, color the number on this clock.

- ▶ Play until all the numbers are colored in.

12 11 1 10 2 9 3 8 4 7 5 6

Show the time on each clock.

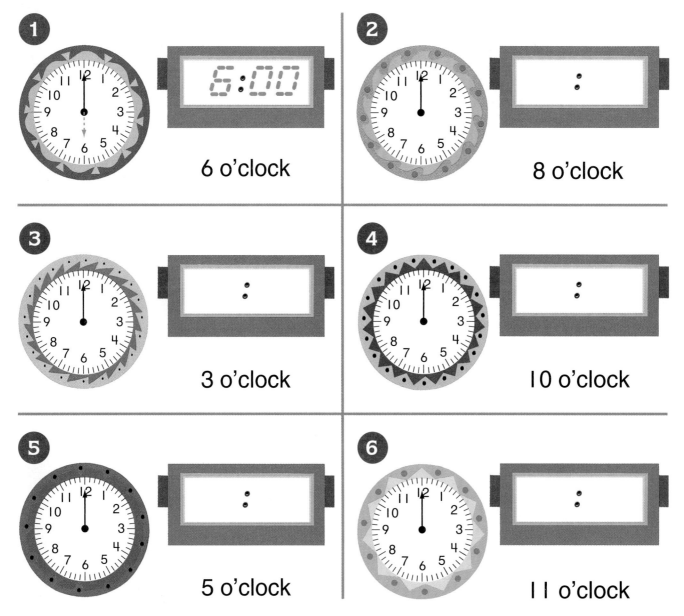

1. 6 o'clock

2. 8 o'clock

3. 3 o'clock

4. 10 o'clock

5. 5 o'clock

6. 11 o'clock

 **Summarize**

Tell a partner about things you do at 8 o'clock and other times each morning.

Write a summary that tells about what your partner does.
Use time in your summary.

Use your own paper.

minute hand

hour hand

9:00
9 o'clock

9:30
nine-thirty
30 **minutes**
after 9 o'clock

Talk

Where is the hour hand at 9:00?
Where is the hour hand at 9:30?

Glossary

half hour
minute

Working Together

You and your partner need a .

Take turns.

▶ Show a time to the **half hour** on the ⏲.

▶ Your partner draws the hands.

▶ Your partner writes the time.

1

___ : ___

2

___ : ___

3

___ : ___

4

___ : ___

Practice!

Show the time on a .
Then write the time.

1 7:30

2 __:__

3 __:__

4 __:__

5 __:__

6 __:__

Journal Draw pictures of two things you do.
Write the time you do each thing.

At Home Discuss with your child what time he or she does the activity shown in exercise 1.

Time to the Half Hour

10:30

The time is ten-thirty.

Both clocks show 30 minutes after 10 o'clock.

Match.

1 5:30

9 o'clock

2 1:30

3 3:30

4 8:30

Critical Thinking Where do the hands of a clock point at 30 minutes after 4?

Write the time.

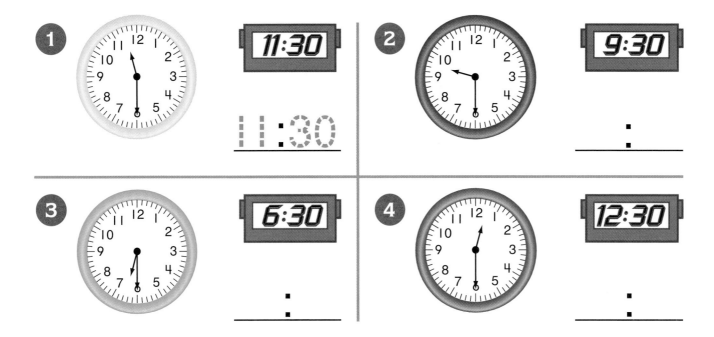

1 11:30

11:30

2 9:30

___:___

3 6:30

___:___

4 12:30

___:___

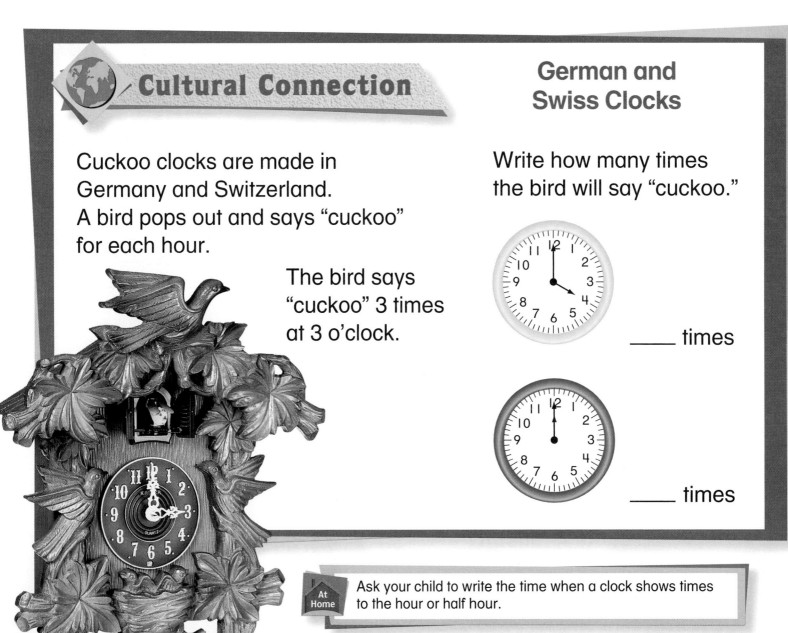

Cultural Connection

German and Swiss Clocks

Cuckoo clocks are made in Germany and Switzerland. A bird pops out and says "cuckoo" for each hour.

The bird says "cuckoo" 3 times at 3 o'clock.

Write how many times the bird will say "cuckoo."

_____ times

_____ times

At Home Ask your child to write the time when a clock shows times to the hour or half hour.

Name _____

Midchapter Review

Do your best!

Show the time on each clock.

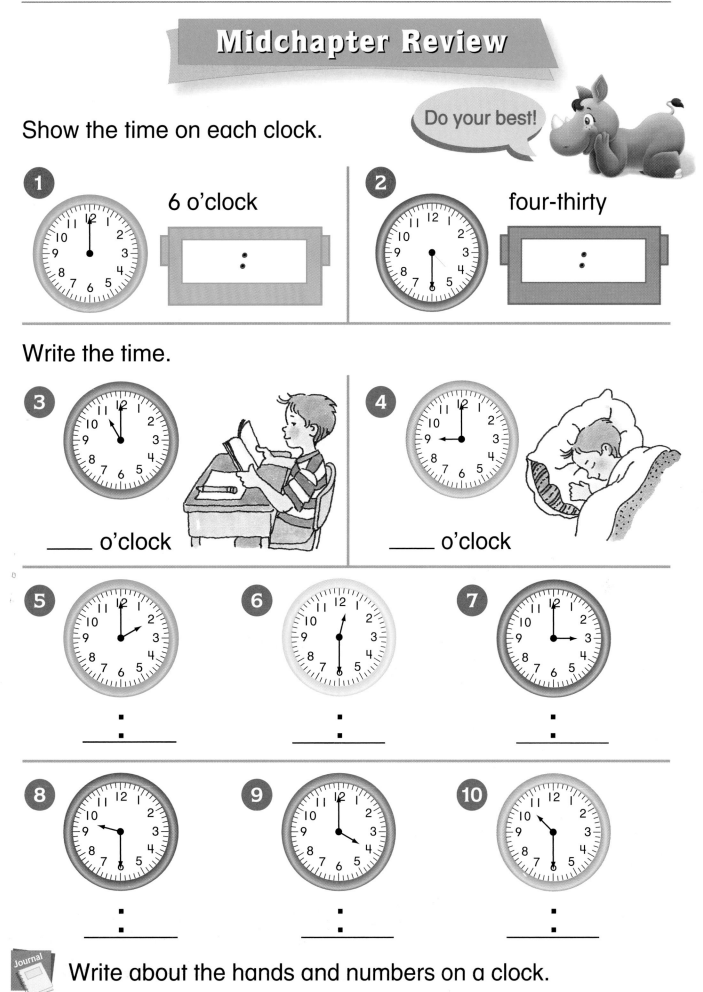

1 6 o'clock

2 four-thirty

Write the time.

3 _____ o'clock

4 _____ o'clock

5

6

7

8

9

10

Journal Write about the hands and numbers on a clock.

Time to Remember

You and a partner need clock cards.

Put all cards facedown.

Take turns.

▶ Turn two cards over.

▶ Keep the cards if the times match.

▶ Turn the cards over again if the times do not match.

The player with more cards wins.

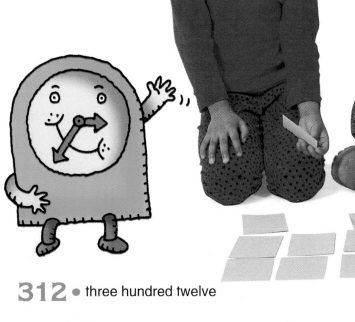

Name

In a Minute

 What can you do in 1 minute?

Working Together

▶ Think of something you can do quickly.

▶ Estimate how many times you can do it in 1 minute.

▶ Try it. Your teacher will time you.

▶ Take turns counting how many. Record your work.

Decision Making

1 Decide on another thing to do for a minute. Try it. Count how many.

2 Make a graph. Show this count and your first count.

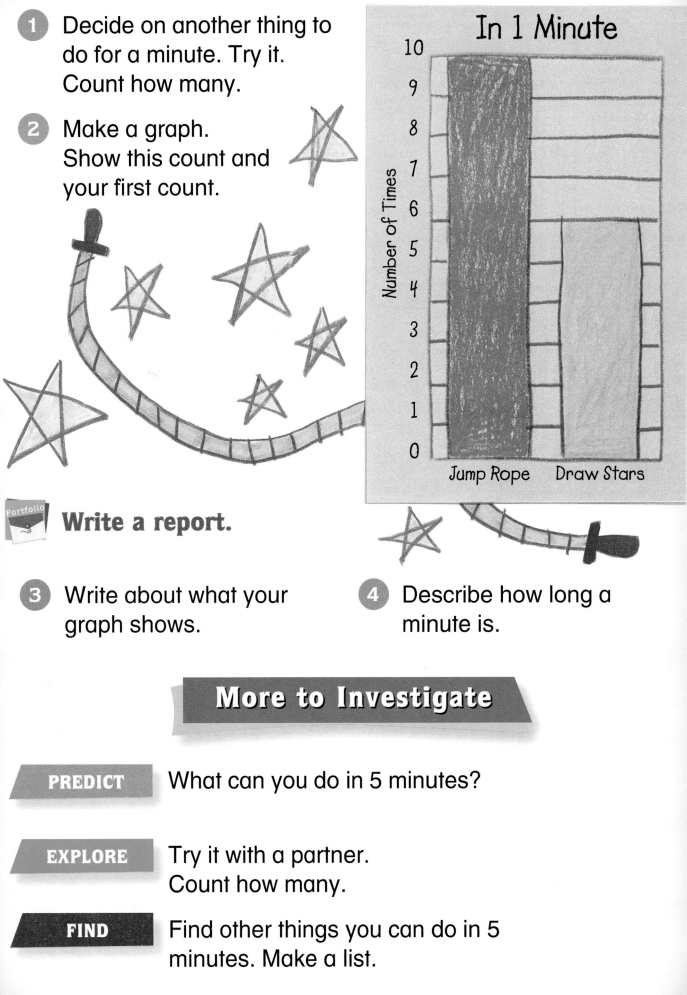

In 1 Minute

Number of Times

10 9 8 7 6 5 4 3 2 1 0

Jump Rope   Draw Stars

Portfolio

Write a report.

3 Write about what your graph shows.

4 Describe how long a minute is.

More to Investigate

PREDICT What can you do in 5 minutes?

EXPLORE Try it with a partner. Count how many.

FIND Find other things you can do in 5 minutes. Make a list.

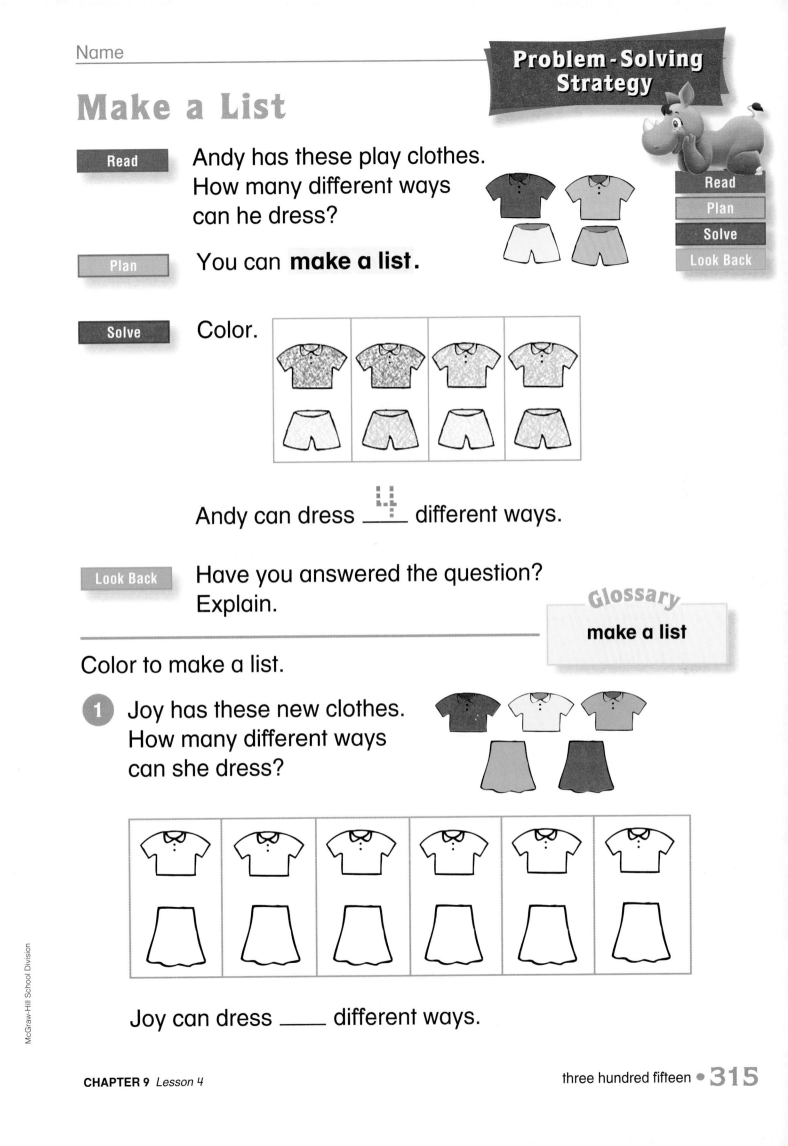

Make a List

Read   Andy has these play clothes. How many different ways can he dress?

Read
Plan
Solve
Look Back

Plan   You can **make a list.**

Solve   Color.

Andy can dress __4__ different ways.

Look Back   Have you answered the question? Explain.

Glossary

make a list

Color to make a list.

1 Joy has these new clothes. How many different ways can she dress?

Joy can dress _____ different ways.

Color to make a list.

1 Cindy has these shoes and socks. Show the different ways she can wear them.

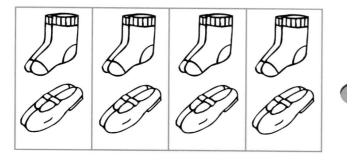

Talk — Tell about other ways to wear these shoes and socks.

2 Karl got these new clothes. Show the different ways he can wear them.

3 Lisa has these hats and mittens. Show the different ways she can wear them.

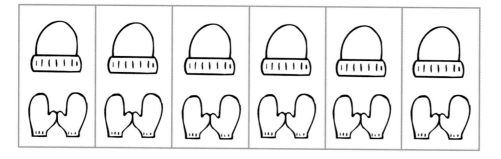

Talk — Show and tell about problem 3.

 At Home — Have your child use clothing similar to the pictures above to find different combinations.

Name ______________________

Use a Calendar

Write the missing numbers on the **calendar**.

January

Sunday	Monday	Tuesday	Wednesday	Thursday	Friday	Saturday
				1	2	3
4	5	6	7	8	9	10
11						
18						
					30	31

Talk Which **day** of the **week** is your favorite? Why?

1. How many days are in a week? ____ days

2. How many days are in January? ____ days

3. What day comes after Monday?

   ____

4. What day comes before Thursday?

   ____

Algebra Critical Thinking **PATTERNS** What patterns do you see on the calendar?

Glossary

calendar
day
week
month
today
tomorrow

Make a calendar for this **month**.

Month: _____

Sunday	Monday	Tuesday	Wednesday	Thursday	Friday	Saturday

Use the calendar to solve.

1. How many days are in this month?   ____ days

2. What day of the week is **today**?   _____

3. What day of the week is **tomorrow**? _____

4. What day of the week is the last day
   of the month?   _____

Mixed Review   Test Preparation

5. Subtract.

   $$9 - 1$$ $$4 - 4$$ $$10 - 3$$

6. Ring the number that
   is greater.

   40   67

At Home   We are learning to read a calendar. Ask your child what day of the week comes after Sunday.

☀ June ☀

Sunday	Monday	Tuesday	Wednesday	Thursday	Friday	Saturday
	1	2	3	4	5	6
7	8	9	10	11 Class field trip	12	13
14 Flag Day	15	16	17	18	19	20
21 Father's Day	22	23	24	25	26	27
28	29	30				

Glossary

date

The **date** of the first Friday is June 5.

1 What is the date of the class field trip?

June 11

2 What is the date of the last day of the month?

_____

3 What date is Flag Day?

_____

4 What date is Father's Day?

_____

5 Summer vacation starts on June 25. What day of the week is that?

_____

6 Jill's birthday is the second Tuesday of the month. What is the date of Jill's birthday?

_____

✳ January ✳

Sunday	Monday	Tuesday	Wednesday	Thursday	Friday	Saturday
				1 New Year's Day	2	3
4	5	6	7	8	9 School Play	10
11	12	13	14	15	16	17
18	19 Martin Luther King, Jr., Day	20	21	22	23	24
25	26	27	28	29	30	31

1 What is the date of the school play?

January 9

2 What date is New Year's Day?

_____

3 What is the date of the last Sunday of the month?

_____

4 What is the date of Martin Luther King, Jr., Day?

_____

More to Explore   Problem Solving

Dan is going to the circus the Sunday after the school play. What date is that?

_____

What day of the week will February 1 be?

_____

 At Home Use the calendar on this page. Ask your child the date of the last day of the month.

Name _____

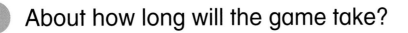
Use Estimation

1 About how long will the game take?

Read
Plan
Solve
Look Back

I minute   I hour

 Talk Why is I hour a good estimate?

Solve.

2 About how long will it take to eat?

I minute   I hour

3 About how long will it take to read?

I minute   I hour

Solve.

1 About how long to watch a movie?

2 minutes

2 hours

2 About how long to brush your teeth?

3 minutes

3 hours

Write and Share

Josh wrote this problem.

About how long would it take to line up for a fire drill?

1 minute

1 hour

Josh Steen
West Lake School
Apex, North Carolina

3 Solve Josh's problem.

4 READING ARITHMETIC WRITING **Summarize** Make a list of things you can do on Saturday morning. Which takes the most time? Which takes the least time?

Use your own paper.

 At Home Talk with your child about how long it would take to do certain chores around the house.

Name _____

Chapter Review

Language and Mathematics

Choose the correct word to complete the sentence.

1 At 7 o'clock the _____ points to the 7.

2 There are 7 _____ in a week.

> hour hand
> half hour
> days
> date

Concepts and Skills

Show the time on each clock.

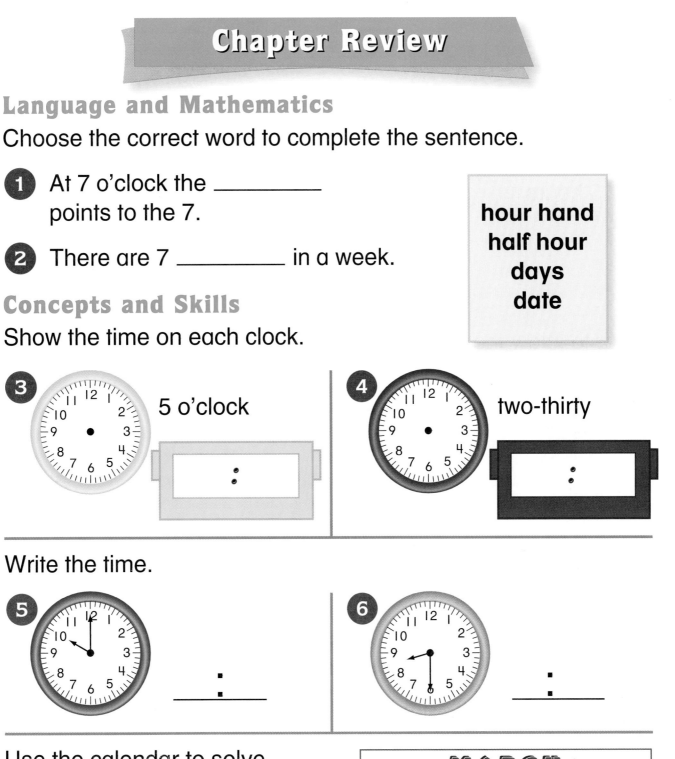

3 5 o'clock

4 two-thirty

Write the time.

5 _____ : _____

6 _____ : _____

Use the calendar to solve.

7 How many days in a week? _____ days

8 What day comes after Tuesday?

_____

✳ MARCH ✳						
Sun	**Mon**	**Tue**	**Wed**	**Thu**	**Fri**	**Sat**
1	2	3	4	5	6	7
8	9	10	11	12	13	14
15	16	17	18	19	20	21
22	23	24	25	26	27	28
29	30	31				

Problem Solving

Solve.

9 About how long will it take?

3 minutes

3 hours

Color to show the different ways to wear the clothes.

10

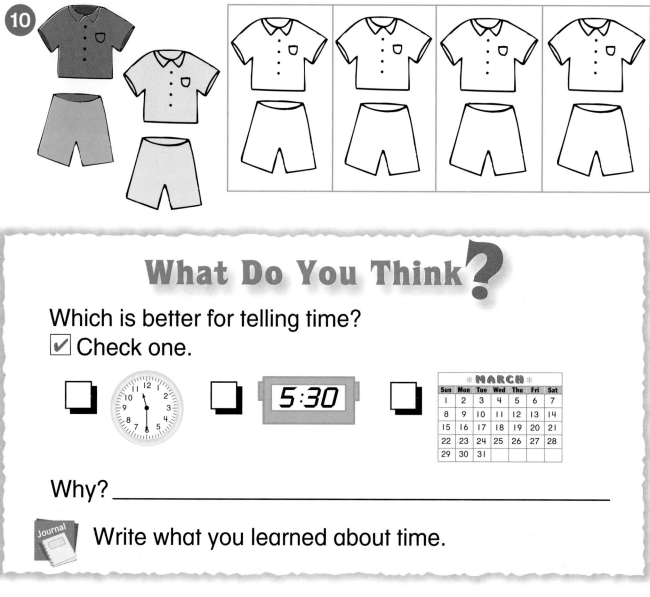

What Do You Think?

Which is better for telling time?
☑ Check one.

☐ ☐ 5:30 ☐

☀ MARCH ☀						
Sun	Mon	Tue	Wed	Thu	Fri	Sat
1	2	3	4	5	6	7
8	9	10	11	12	13	14
15	16	17	18	19	20	21
22	23	24	25	26	27	28
29	30	31				

Why? _____

Write what you learned about time.

Chapter Test

Show the time on each clock.

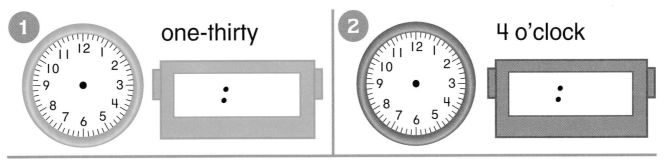

1 one-thirty

2 4 o'clock

Write the time.

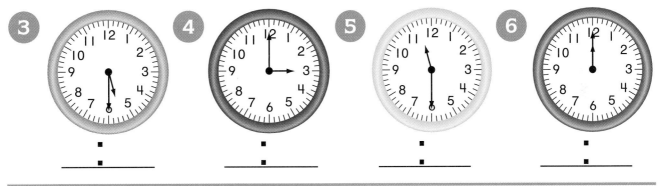

3 :____

4 :____

5 :____

6 :____

Use the calendar to solve.

7 How many days in October? _____

8 What is the first Friday in October? _____

9 What day comes after Thursday? _____

✳ October ✳						
Sun	**Mon**	**Tue**	**Wed**	**Thu**	**Fri**	**Sat**
				1	2	3
4	5	6	7	8	9	10
11	12	13	14	15	16	17
18	19	20	21	22	23	24
25	26	27	28	29	30	31

Color to show different ways to wear the clothes.

10

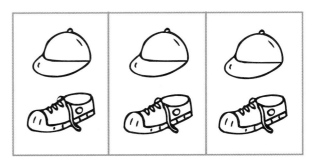

What Did You Learn?

Draw lines to match.

Tell what happens first, second, third, last.

You may want to put this page in your portfolio.

Math Connection

Graphs

Name _____

Pictographs

Rosa asked some friends what time they eat dinner. Rosa made a chart.

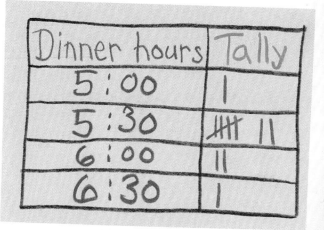

Dinner hours	Tally
5:00	I
5:30	IIII III
6:00	II
6:30	I

Talk What does the chart show?

1 Make a **pictograph** using the information in the chart.

DINNER TIMES	
5:00	☺
5:30	
6:00	
6:30	

☺ **stands for I friend.**

2 How many friends did Rosa ask? _____

3 What time do most of Rosa's friends eat dinner? _____ : _____

4 **Write** Write a problem about the information in the graph. Have a partner solve it.

Use your own paper.

Glossary

pictograph

Make Graphs

A computer helps you show information on a graph.

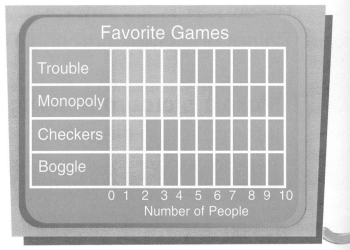

Favorite Games

Trouble	😊😊😊😊
Monopoly	😊😊😊😊😊😊
Checkers	😊😊
Boggle	😊😊😊

😊 stands for one person

Favorite Games

(bar graph showing games by Number of People, scale 0–10)

 What do these graphs show?

Which graph do you think is better? Why?

At the Computer

1. Ask 10 people what game they like best. Put the information in a chart.

2. Use the chart to make a pictograph.

3. Then use the chart to make a bar graph.

4. Write about your graphs.

Cumulative Review

Mark your answer.

1
$$\begin{array}{r} 8 \\ -3 \\ \hline \end{array}$$

⊂⊃ 5

⊂⊃ 6

⊂⊃ 10

⊂⊃ 11

2 What is the missing number?

10, 20, __?__, 40

⊂⊃ 21

⊂⊃ 25

⊂⊃ 30

⊂⊃ 50

3 Which number is just before?

	41

⊂⊃ 43

⊂⊃ 40

⊂⊃ 39

⊂⊃ 31

4 What number is shown by the cubes?

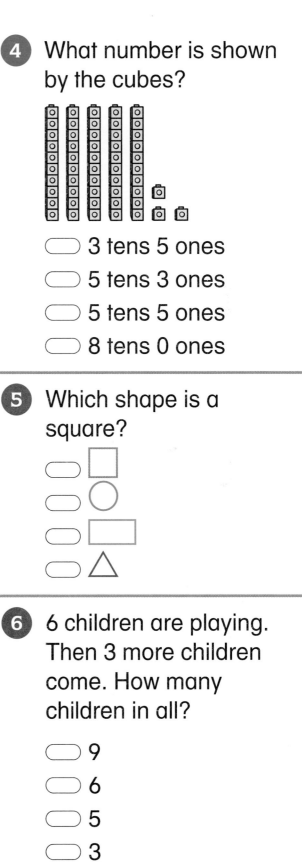

⊂⊃ 3 tens 5 ones

⊂⊃ 5 tens 3 ones

⊂⊃ 5 tens 5 ones

⊂⊃ 8 tens 0 ones

5 Which shape is a square?

⊂⊃ □

⊂⊃ ○

⊂⊃ ▭

⊂⊃ △

6 6 children are playing. Then 3 more children come. How many children in all?

⊂⊃ 9

⊂⊃ 6

⊂⊃ 5

⊂⊃ 3

7 4 friends share a pizza. How much does each get?

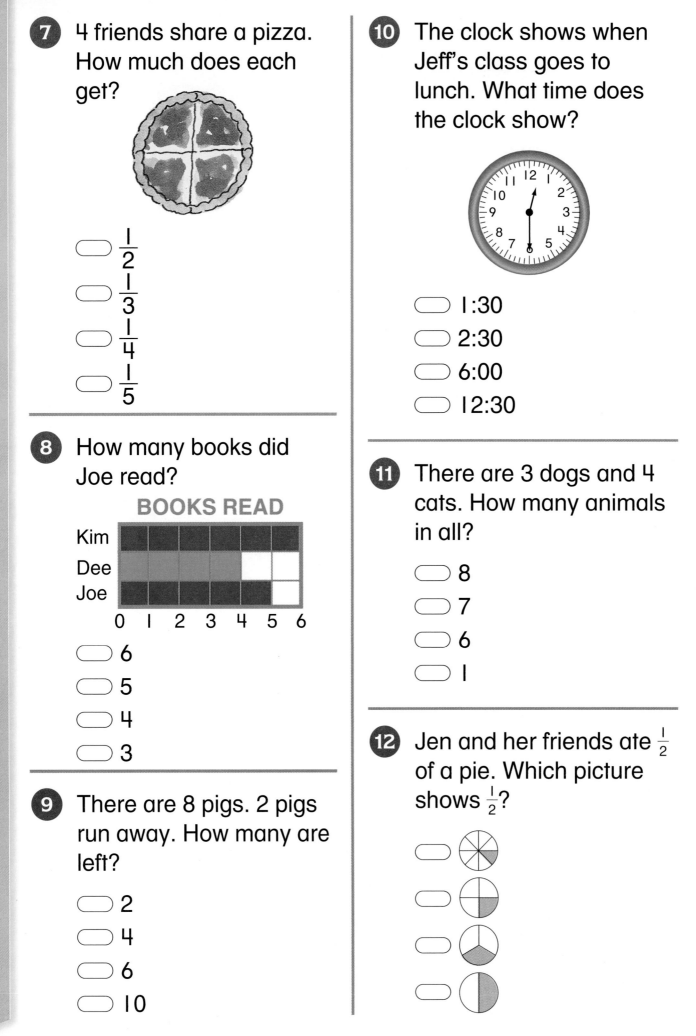

⬭ $\frac{1}{2}$

⬭ $\frac{1}{3}$

⬭ $\frac{1}{4}$

⬭ $\frac{1}{5}$

8 How many books did Joe read?

BOOKS READ

	0	1	2	3	4	5	6
Kim							
Dee							
Joe							

⬭ 6

⬭ 5

⬭ 4

⬭ 3

9 There are 8 pigs. 2 pigs run away. How many are left?

⬭ 2

⬭ 4

⬭ 6

⬭ 10

10 The clock shows when Jeff's class goes to lunch. What time does the clock show?

⬭ 1:30

⬭ 2:30

⬭ 6:00

⬭ 12:30

11 There are 3 dogs and 4 cats. How many animals in all?

⬭ 8

⬭ 7

⬭ 6

⬭ 1

12 Jen and her friends ate $\frac{1}{2}$ of a pie. Which picture shows $\frac{1}{2}$?

⬭

⬭

⬭

⬭

T E S T   P R E P A R A T I O N

Name _____

Make a Water Clock

paper cup

MATERIALS Small paper or plastic cup, masking tape, pin (for small hole), watch, small glass jar.

tape scale

DIRECTIONS Poke a small hole in the cup. Put the clock together (see picture). Fill the cup with water. Every 5 minutes, draw a line to show where the water is.

glass jar

For how many minutes will your water clock run?

_____ minutes

Which activity can you do before the water runs out?

☑ Check them.

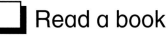 Read a book

Clean your room

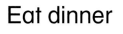 Eat dinner

At Home

The duration of the clock will depend on the size of the container and the hole made in the bottom of the cup. A 6-ounce plastic yogurt cup pierced with a sewing needle and filled halfway with warm water will drip for about 30 minutes.

At Home

Dear Family,

I am beginning a new chapter in mathematics. I will be learning about strategies to help me add and subtract.

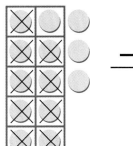

$$\begin{array}{r} 13 \\ -\ 9 \\ \hline 4 \end{array}$$

$$\begin{array}{r} 6 \\ +\ 6 \\ \hline 12 \end{array}$$

$$\begin{array}{r} 6 \\ +\ 7 \\ \hline 13 \end{array}$$

I will also learn about different kinds of water, and animals and fish that live there.

Learning about Water Environments

Let's talk about fun things we can do on or near water. We can describe animals that live in water.

My Math Words

I am going to use these math words in this chapter.

Please help me make word cards for these math words. I can use the word cards when I practice addition and subtraction.

doubles
strategy
related facts
fact family

Your child,

_____
Signature

Adding and Subtracting to 18

Theme: Under the Water

READING · ARITHMETIC · WRITING

Reread You may have questions after you listen to a story. Listen again to find the answers.

Listen to the story *Splash.*

How many times did a frog jump into the pond? Go back to the story. Read to find out.

What Do You Know?

Solve.

1 Sue caught 9 fish.
She threw 6 fish back
into the water.
How many fish did
Sue keep?

____ fish

Show or write about how you
solved the problem.

2 Dan had 4 fish
in his bowl. One
morning there were 3
baby fish in the bowl.
How many fish does
Dan have now?

____ fish

Show or write about how you
solved the problem.

Write a problem that uses addition or
subtraction. Show how to solve it.

Doubles

7
+ 7
14

14
− 7
7

7 + 7 is a **double.**

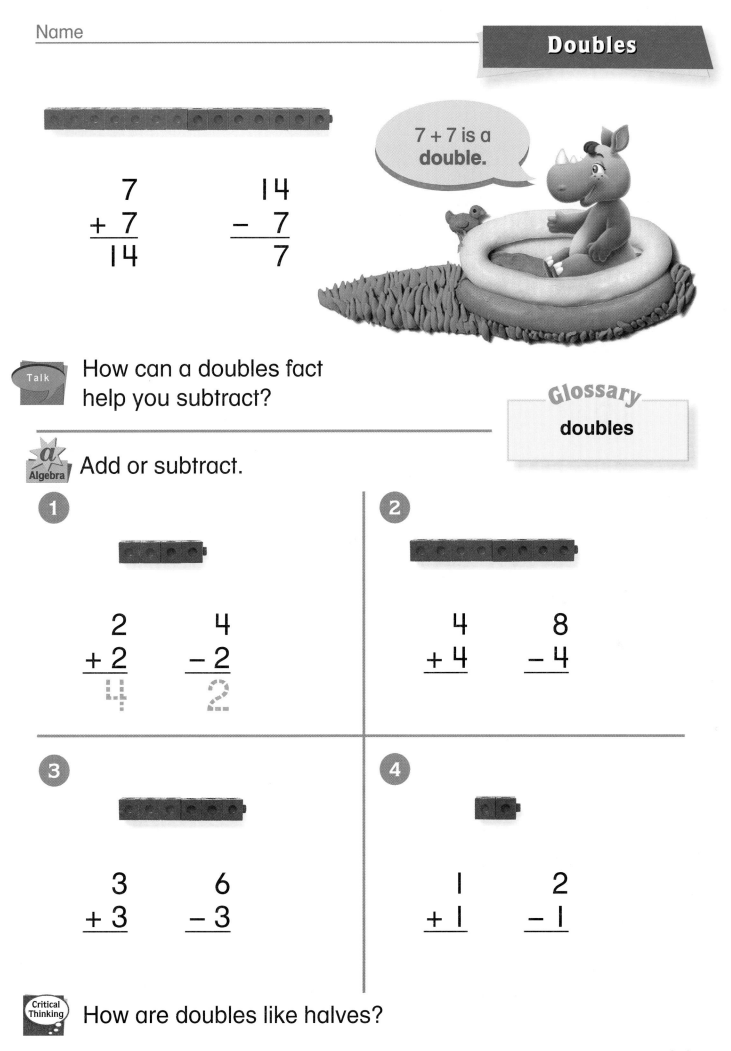

Talk How can a doubles fact help you subtract?

Glossary
doubles

Algebra Add or subtract.

1

2
+ 2
4

4
− 2
2

2

4
+ 4

8
− 4

3

3
+ 3

6
− 3

4

1
+ 1

2
− 1

Critical Thinking How are doubles like halves?

McGraw-Hill School Division

Add or subtract.

1

$$\begin{array}{r} 6 \\ + 6 \\ \hline 12 \end{array}$$

$$\begin{array}{r} 12 \\ - 6 \\ \hline 6 \end{array}$$

2

$$\begin{array}{r} 5 \\ + 5 \\ \hline \end{array}$$

$$\begin{array}{r} 10 \\ - 5 \\ \hline \end{array}$$

3

$$\begin{array}{r} 9 \\ + 9 \\ \hline \end{array} \qquad \begin{array}{r} 3 \\ + 3 \\ \hline \end{array} \qquad \begin{array}{r} 14¢ \\ - 7¢ \\ \hline \end{array} \qquad \begin{array}{r} 1¢ \\ + 1¢ \\ \hline \end{array} \qquad \begin{array}{r} 6 \\ - 3 \\ \hline \end{array} \qquad \begin{array}{r} 8 \\ + 8 \\ \hline \end{array}$$

4

$$\begin{array}{r} 2¢ \\ + 2¢ \\ \hline \end{array} \qquad \begin{array}{r} 8 \\ - 4 \\ \hline \end{array} \qquad \begin{array}{r} 10 \\ - 5 \\ \hline \end{array} \qquad \begin{array}{r} 18 \\ - 9 \\ \hline \end{array} \qquad \begin{array}{r} 4 \\ + 4 \\ \hline \end{array} \qquad \begin{array}{r} 7¢ \\ + 7¢ \\ \hline \end{array}$$

5

$$\begin{array}{r} 12 \\ - 6 \\ \hline \end{array} \qquad \begin{array}{r} 2¢ \\ - 1¢ \\ \hline \end{array} \qquad \begin{array}{r} 4¢ \\ - 2¢ \\ \hline \end{array} \qquad \begin{array}{r} 5 \\ + 5 \\ \hline \end{array} \qquad \begin{array}{r} 6 \\ + 6 \\ \hline \end{array} \qquad \begin{array}{r} 16 \\ - 8 \\ \hline \end{array}$$

More to Explore   Algebra Sense

a Algebra Complete.

$$3 + \underline{\hspace{1cm}} = 6 \qquad 5 + \underline{\hspace{1cm}} = 10 \qquad 8 + \underline{\hspace{1cm}} = 16$$

At Home — Ask your child to tell you the addition doubles facts: $1 + 1$, $2 + 2$, $3 + 3$, and so on.

Doubles Plus One

5 + 5 = 10
5 + 6 is 1 more.
So 5 + 6 = 11.

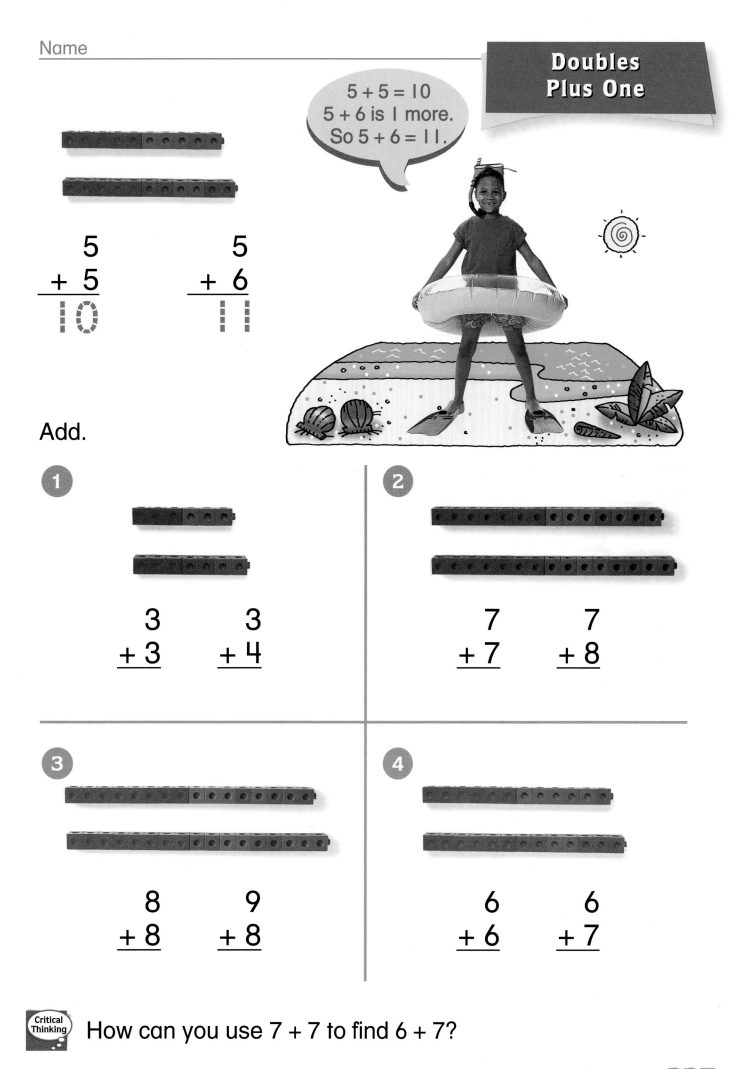

```
    5          5
  + 5        + 6
  ----       ----
   10         11
```

Add.

1

```
    3          3
  + 3        + 4
```

2

```
    7          7
  + 7        + 8
```

3

```
    8          9
  + 8        + 8
```

4

```
    6          6
  + 6        + 7
```

Critical Thinking How can you use 7 + 7 to find 6 + 7?

Add.

1

$$\begin{array}{r} 4 \\ +4 \\ \hline 8 \end{array}$$

$$\begin{array}{r} 4 \\ +5 \\ \hline 9 \end{array}$$

2

$$\begin{array}{r} 2 \\ +2 \\ \hline \end{array}$$

$$\begin{array}{r} 2 \\ +3 \\ \hline \end{array}$$

3
$$\begin{array}{r} 3 \\ +3 \\ \hline \end{array} \qquad \begin{array}{r} 4 \\ +3 \\ \hline \end{array}$$

4
$$\begin{array}{r} 7 \\ +7 \\ \hline \end{array} \qquad \begin{array}{r} 7 \\ +8 \\ \hline \end{array}$$

5
$$\begin{array}{r} 5 \\ +5 \\ \hline \end{array} \qquad \begin{array}{r} 6 \\ +5 \\ \hline \end{array}$$

6
$$\begin{array}{r} 6 \\ +6 \\ \hline \end{array} \quad \begin{array}{r} 3 \\ +2 \\ \hline \end{array} \quad \begin{array}{r} 8¢ \\ +8¢ \\ \hline \end{array} \quad \begin{array}{r} 1 \\ +2 \\ \hline \end{array} \quad \begin{array}{r} 4¢ \\ +5¢ \\ \hline \end{array} \quad \begin{array}{r} 9 \\ +9 \\ \hline \end{array}$$

7
$$\begin{array}{r} 8 \\ +9 \\ \hline \end{array} \quad \begin{array}{r} 5¢ \\ +4¢ \\ \hline \end{array} \quad \begin{array}{r} 4¢ \\ +4¢ \\ \hline \end{array} \quad \begin{array}{r} 6 \\ +7 \\ \hline \end{array} \quad \begin{array}{r} 2 \\ +1 \\ \hline \end{array} \quad \begin{array}{r} 4¢ \\ +3¢ \\ \hline \end{array}$$

Journal

Write all the doubles you know.
Tell how you use doubles.

At Home · Ask your child which double he or she can use to add 7 + 8.

Explore Activity

Add 9

Working Together

You and your partner

need 18 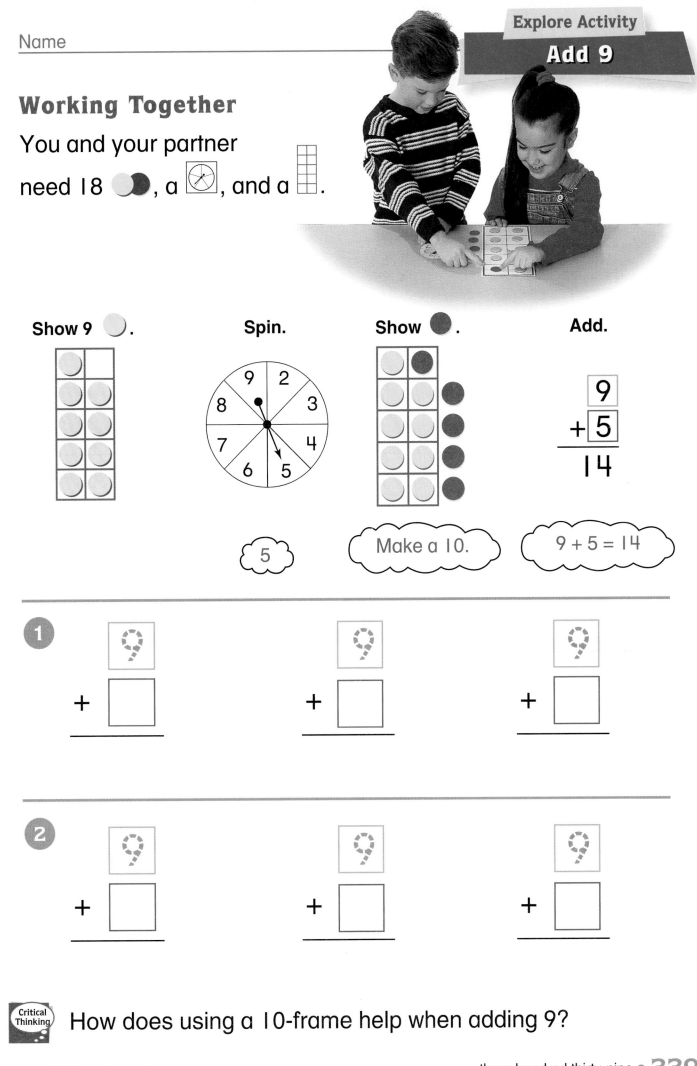, a ⊕, and a ☐.

Show 9 ○.

Spin.

5

Show ●.

Make a 10.

Add.

9
+ 5
——
14

9 + 5 = 14

1

9
+ ☐
———

9
+ ☐
———

9
+ ☐
———

2

9
+ ☐
———

9
+ ☐
———

9
+ ☐
———

Critical Thinking How does using a 10-frame help when adding 9?

Practice!

Draw the ●.
Write the sum.

1

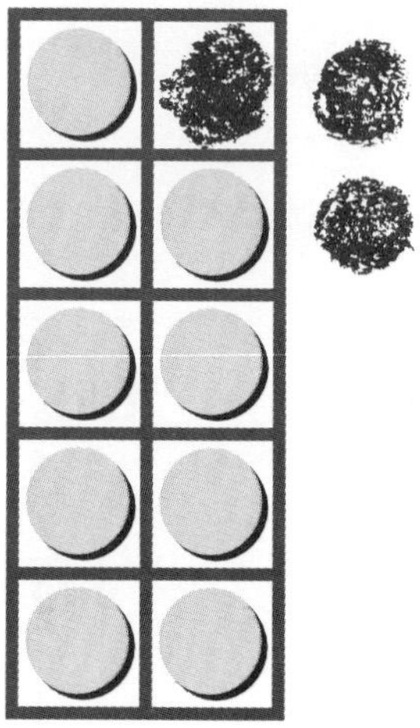

$$\begin{array}{r} 9 \\ +\ 3 \\ \hline 12 \end{array}$$

2

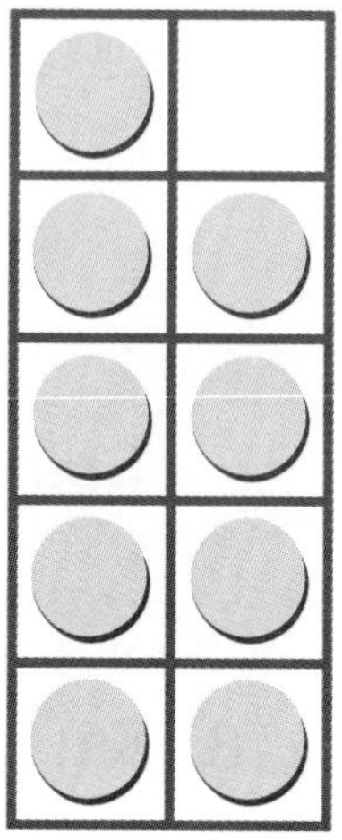

$$\begin{array}{r} 9 \\ +\ 6 \\ \hline \end{array}$$

3

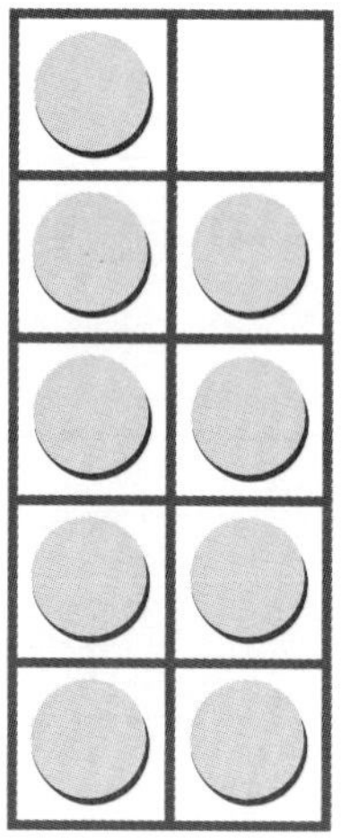

$$\begin{array}{r} 9 \\ +\ 4 \\ \hline \end{array}$$

4

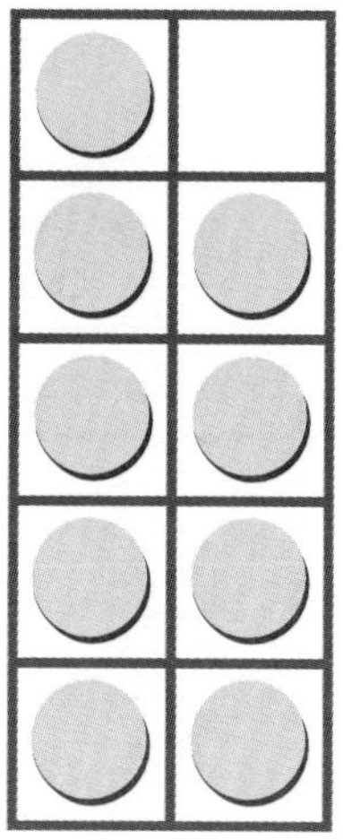

$$\begin{array}{r} 9 \\ +\ 8 \\ \hline \end{array}$$

5

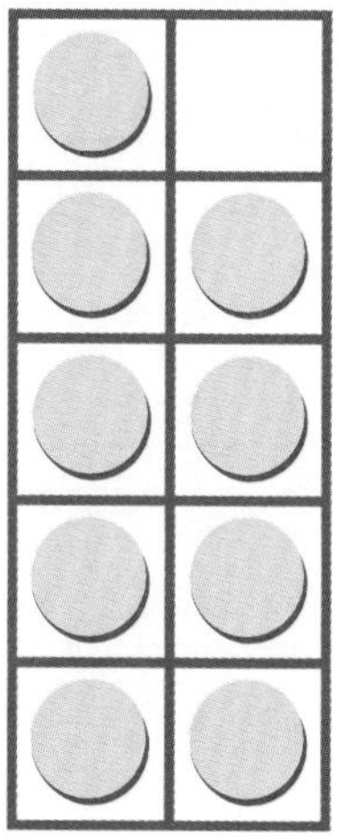

$$\begin{array}{r} 9 \\ +\ 2 \\ \hline \end{array}$$

6

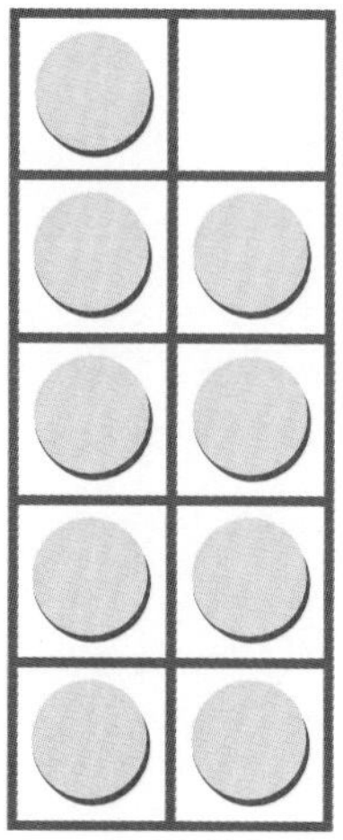

$$\begin{array}{r} 9 \\ +\ 7 \\ \hline \end{array}$$

At Home   Ask your child to explain how to add 9 on a 10-frame.

Add

Kim saw 9 sunfish in the pond.
Brian saw 8 goldfish in the pond.
How many fish did they see?

 Talk Which **strategies** can you
use to add 9 + 8?

There are __17__ fish
in the pond.

Find the sum.

1

2	6	7	9	7¢	7
+ 9	+ 6	+ 8	+ 3	+ 7¢	+ 9

2

3	4	9¢	6	3	5
+ 8	+ 8	+ 9¢	+ 7	+ 9	+ 7

3

9	8	7	5	5¢	8
+ 5	+ 9	+ 4	+ 8	+ 6¢	+ 8

4

8	9	7	9¢	5	8
+ 6	+ 6	+ 6	+ 2¢	+ 9	+ 7

Critical Thinking Why is it useful to know different strategies for addition?

Practice!

Add.

1
$$\begin{array}{r} 9 \\ +\ 3 \\ \hline 12 \end{array}$$

Adding 9

2
$$\begin{array}{r} 7 \\ +\ 8 \\ \hline 15 \end{array}$$

Doubles plus one
$7 + 7 = 14$
$7 + 8$ is one more.

3

$$\begin{array}{r} 9 \\ +\ 7 \\ \hline \end{array} \qquad \begin{array}{r} 6 \\ +\ 8 \\ \hline \end{array} \qquad \begin{array}{r} 8 \\ +\ 4 \\ \hline \end{array} \qquad \begin{array}{r} 7 \\ +\ 5 \\ \hline \end{array} \qquad \begin{array}{r} 4¢ \\ +\ 9¢ \\ \hline \end{array} \qquad \begin{array}{r} 9 \\ +\ 7 \\ \hline \end{array}$$

4

$$\begin{array}{r} 6 \\ +\ 5 \\ \hline \end{array} \qquad \begin{array}{r} 8 \\ +\ 5 \\ \hline \end{array} \qquad \begin{array}{r} 6¢ \\ +\ 9¢ \\ \hline \end{array} \qquad \begin{array}{r} 9 \\ +\ 4 \\ \hline \end{array} \qquad \begin{array}{r} 4 \\ +\ 7 \\ \hline \end{array} \qquad \begin{array}{r} 5¢ \\ +\ 8¢ \\ \hline \end{array}$$

5

$$\begin{array}{r} 5 \\ +\ 9 \\ \hline \end{array} \qquad \begin{array}{r} 8 \\ +\ 3 \\ \hline \end{array} \qquad \begin{array}{r} 9 \\ +\ 8 \\ \hline \end{array} \qquad \begin{array}{r} 6 \\ +\ 7 \\ \hline \end{array} \qquad \begin{array}{r} 5 \\ +\ 6 \\ \hline \end{array} \qquad \begin{array}{r} 8¢ \\ +\ 7¢ \\ \hline \end{array}$$

Mixed Review Test Preparation

6 _____

7 _____

8 _____ ¢

At Home We used strategies to add. Have your child explain how to add 6 + 7.

Add Three Numbers

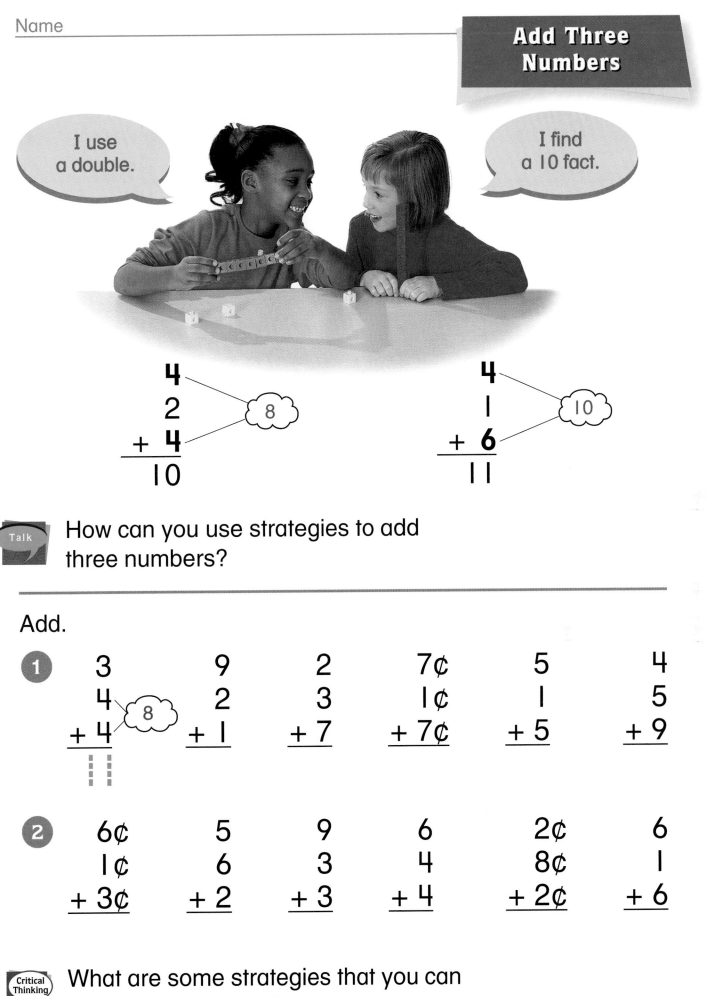

I use a double.

I find a 10 fact.

$$\begin{array}{r} 4 \\ 2 \\ + \ 4 \\ \hline 10 \end{array}$$ 8

$$\begin{array}{r} 4 \\ 1 \\ + \ 6 \\ \hline 11 \end{array}$$ 10

Talk How can you use strategies to add three numbers?

Add.

1

$$\begin{array}{r} 3 \\ 4 \\ + \ 4 \\ \hline \end{array}$$ 8

$$\begin{array}{r} 9 \\ 2 \\ + \ 1 \\ \hline \end{array}$$

$$\begin{array}{r} 2 \\ 3 \\ + \ 7 \\ \hline \end{array}$$

$$\begin{array}{r} 7¢ \\ 1¢ \\ + \ 7¢ \\ \hline \end{array}$$

$$\begin{array}{r} 5 \\ 1 \\ + \ 5 \\ \hline \end{array}$$

$$\begin{array}{r} 4 \\ 5 \\ + \ 9 \\ \hline \end{array}$$

2

$$\begin{array}{r} 6¢ \\ 1¢ \\ + \ 3¢ \\ \hline \end{array}$$

$$\begin{array}{r} 5 \\ 6 \\ + \ 2 \\ \hline \end{array}$$

$$\begin{array}{r} 9 \\ 3 \\ + \ 3 \\ \hline \end{array}$$

$$\begin{array}{r} 6 \\ 4 \\ + \ 4 \\ \hline \end{array}$$

$$\begin{array}{r} 2¢ \\ 8¢ \\ + \ 2¢ \\ \hline \end{array}$$

$$\begin{array}{r} 6 \\ 1 \\ + \ 6 \\ \hline \end{array}$$

Critical Thinking What are some strategies that you can use to add $3 + 3 + 7$?

Practice!

Find the sum.

1

2	3	1	2	4¢	8
5	7	5	5	4¢	1
+ 3	+ 3	+ 5	+ 8	+ 4¢	+ 7
10					

2

1	2	5	3¢	5	7
2	2	4	4¢	4	0
+ 9	+ 6	+ 3	+ 7¢	+ 5	+ 4

Cultural Connection

Korea

Numbers can look the same all around the world. You can read numbers in Korea. But this is how you say the numbers.

1	2	3	4	5	6	7	8	9
yil	yee	sam	sa	oh	yuk	chil	par	goo

10	11	12	13	14	15	16	17	18
ship	ship yil	ship yee	ship sam	ship sa	ship oh	ship yuk	ship chil	ship par

At Home Have your child add 4 pennies plus 5 pennies plus 3 pennies.

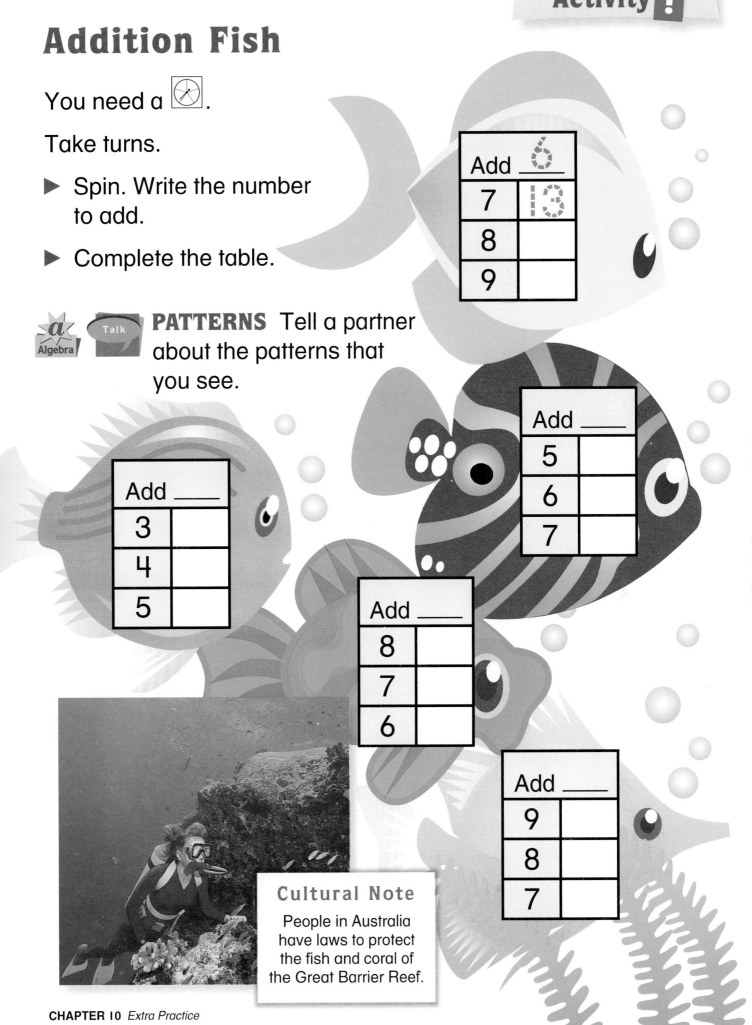

Name _____

Addition Fish

You need a ⊘.

Take turns.

▶ Spin. Write the number to add.

▶ Complete the table.

PATTERNS Tell a partner about the patterns that you see.

a Algebra Talk

Add __6__

7	13
8	
9	

Add _____

3	
4	
5	

Add _____

5	
6	
7	

Add _____

8	
7	
6	

Add _____

9	
8	
7	

Cultural Note
People in Australia have laws to protect the fish and coral of the Great Barrier Reef.

Add.

Use strategies to help you add.

1

5	4	7	9	8¢	8
+ 9	+ 8	+ 6	+ 3	+ 3¢	+ 9

14

2

7	5	4	5¢	8	7
+ 7	+ 6	+ 9	+ 7¢	+ 5	+ 9

3

9	8	9¢	6	6	8
+ 6	+ 8	+ 8¢	+ 7	+ 8	+ 7

4

2	5¢	1	4	6	4
4	4¢	3	0	2	4
+ 8	+ 6¢	+ 9	+ 7	+ 6	+ 8

Workspace

Solve.

5 7 angelfish are eating.
8 more angelfish come to eat.
How many angelfish
are eating?   _____ angelfish

6 3 lionfish swim into a cave.
8 butterfly fish join them.
How many fish are in
the cave?   _____ fish

• three hundred forty-six

Name

Sue had 13 shells.
She gave away 9 shells.
How many shells does she
have left?

Show 13.   Subtract 9.

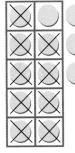

3 and
1 more

Sue has ___ shells left.

Working Together

You and your partner need a ▦, a ⊗, and 18 ◖.

▶ Spin to find how many shells.

▶ Show the number with ◖ and the ▦.

▶ Subtract 9.

▶ Write the subtraction.

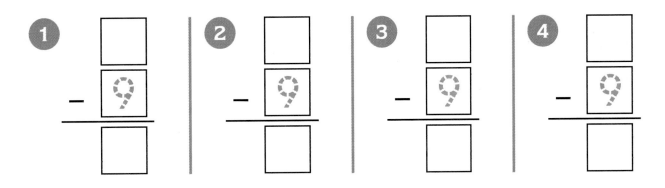

1 □ − 9 □ = □

2 □ − 9 □ = □

3 □ − 9 □ = □

4 □ − 9 □ = □

Talk How does using a 10-frame help you subtract 9?

Practice!

Cross out 9.
Write how many are left.

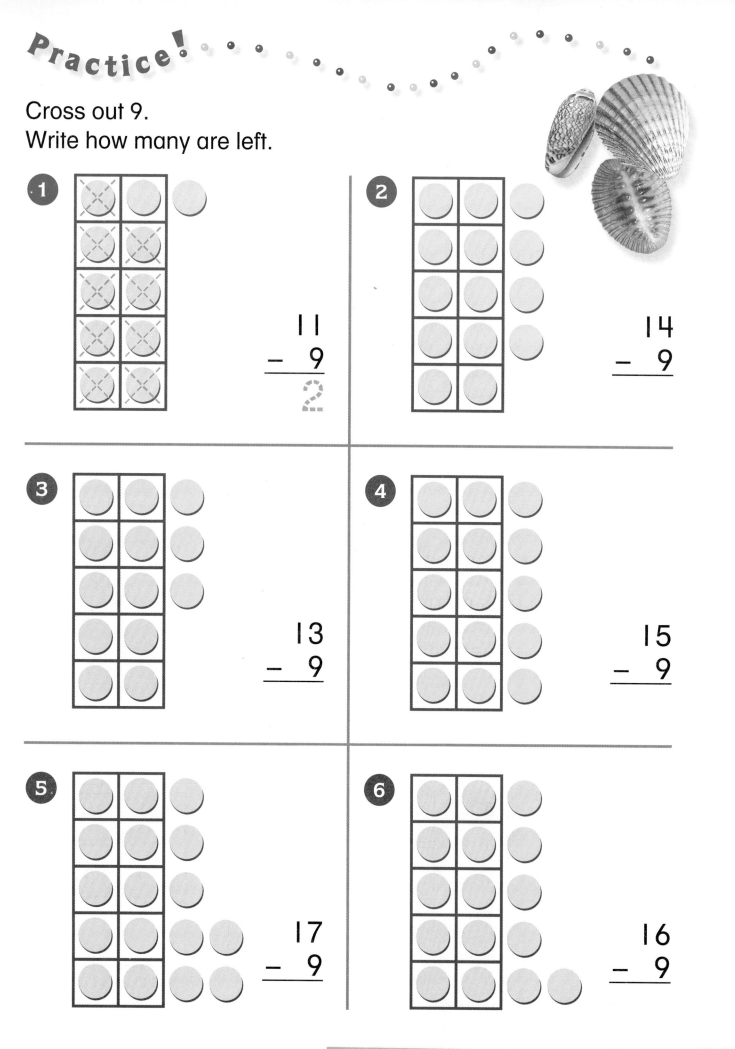

1

$$\begin{array}{r} 11 \\ -9 \\ \hline 2 \end{array}$$

2

$$\begin{array}{r} 14 \\ -9 \\ \hline \end{array}$$

3

$$\begin{array}{r} 13 \\ -9 \\ \hline \end{array}$$

4

$$\begin{array}{r} 15 \\ -9 \\ \hline \end{array}$$

5

$$\begin{array}{r} 17 \\ -9 \\ \hline \end{array}$$

6

$$\begin{array}{r} 16 \\ -9 \\ \hline \end{array}$$

At Home

We learned how to use a 10-frame to subtract. Ask your child how to subtract 9.

Subtract

13   13
− 5   − 8
  8   5

Talk Why do you think these are called **related facts**?

Glossary

related facts

a Algebra Subtract.
Use ◐ if you want to.

1. 11   11   12   12   13   13
   − 4   − 7   − 5   − 7   − 4   − 9
    7   4

2. 12   12   11   11   13   13
   − 3   − 9   − 8   − 3   − 6   − 7

3. 10   10   12   12   11   11
   − 4   − 6   − 8   − 4   − 9   − 2

Critical Thinking How do you use 11 − 5 = 6 to help you subtract 11 − 6?

Practice!

Subtract.

1

$$\begin{array}{r} 11 \\ -\ 9 \\ \hline 2 \end{array}$$
$$\begin{array}{r} 11 \\ -\ 2 \\ \hline 9 \end{array}$$

2

$$\begin{array}{r} 12 \\ -\ 4 \\ \hline \end{array}$$
$$\begin{array}{r} 12 \\ -\ 8 \\ \hline \end{array}$$

3

$$\begin{array}{r} 12 \\ -\ 7 \\ \hline \end{array}$$
$$\begin{array}{r} 13 \\ -\ 4 \\ \hline \end{array}$$
$$\begin{array}{r} 12¢ \\ -\ 8¢ \\ \hline \end{array}$$
$$\begin{array}{r} 11 \\ -\ 4 \\ \hline \end{array}$$
$$\begin{array}{r} 12 \\ -\ 3 \\ \hline \end{array}$$
$$\begin{array}{r} 11¢ \\ -\ 2¢ \\ \hline \end{array}$$

4

$$\begin{array}{r} 11 \\ -\ 5 \\ \hline \end{array}$$
$$\begin{array}{r} 12 \\ -\ 5 \\ \hline \end{array}$$
$$\begin{array}{r} 11¢ \\ -\ 7¢ \\ \hline \end{array}$$
$$\begin{array}{r} 13¢ \\ -\ 8¢ \\ \hline \end{array}$$
$$\begin{array}{r} 13¢ \\ -\ 5¢ \\ \hline \end{array}$$
$$\begin{array}{r} 11 \\ -\ 6 \\ \hline \end{array}$$

READING ARITHMETIC WRITING Reread

Read the story.
How many gulls are left on the beach?
Read the story again.
Answer the question. ____ gulls
Ask a question for your partner
to answer.

On the Beach
12 gulls were walking
on the beach.
They walked past
6 puffins.
Soon 5 gulls flew away.
Then 2 puffins swam away.

350 • three hundred fifty

 At Home We learned about related facts. Have your child find the related subtraction facts in exercise 4 above.

Name _____

$$
\begin{array}{r} 15 \\ -\ 6 \\ \hline 9 \end{array}
\qquad
\begin{array}{r} 15 \\ -\ 9 \\ \hline 6 \end{array}
$$

Algebra

Subtract.
Use ◖ if you want to.

1
$$
\begin{array}{r} 17 \\ -\ 8 \\ \hline 9 \end{array}
\quad
\begin{array}{r} 17 \\ -\ 9 \\ \hline 8 \end{array}
\quad
\begin{array}{r} 14 \\ -\ 6 \\ \hline \end{array}
\quad
\begin{array}{r} 14 \\ -\ 8 \\ \hline \end{array}
\quad
\begin{array}{r} 15 \\ -\ 7 \\ \hline \end{array}
\quad
\begin{array}{r} 15 \\ -\ 8 \\ \hline \end{array}
$$

2
$$
\begin{array}{r} 14 \\ -\ 5 \\ \hline \end{array}
\quad
\begin{array}{r} 14 \\ -\ 9 \\ \hline \end{array}
\quad
\begin{array}{r} 16 \\ -\ 7 \\ \hline \end{array}
\quad
\begin{array}{r} 16 \\ -\ 9 \\ \hline \end{array}
\quad
\begin{array}{r} 13 \\ -\ 4 \\ \hline \end{array}
\quad
\begin{array}{r} 13 \\ -\ 9 \\ \hline \end{array}
$$

3
$$
\begin{array}{r} 11 \\ -\ 3 \\ \hline \end{array}
\quad
\begin{array}{r} 11 \\ -\ 8 \\ \hline \end{array}
\quad
\begin{array}{r} 13 \\ -\ 8 \\ \hline \end{array}
\quad
\begin{array}{r} 13 \\ -\ 5 \\ \hline \end{array}
\quad
\begin{array}{r} 15 \\ -\ 9 \\ \hline \end{array}
\quad
\begin{array}{r} 15 \\ -\ 6 \\ \hline \end{array}
$$

Critical Thinking Which subtraction facts do not have related subtraction facts? Why?

Practice!

Subtract.

1

$$\begin{array}{r} 14 \\ -\ 6 \\ \hline 8 \end{array}$$

$$\begin{array}{r} 14 \\ -\ 8 \\ \hline 6 \end{array}$$

2

$$\begin{array}{r} 13 \\ -\ 7 \\ \hline \end{array}$$

$$\begin{array}{r} 13 \\ -\ 6 \\ \hline \end{array}$$

3

$$\begin{array}{r} 16 \\ -\ 7 \\ \hline \end{array}$$

$$\begin{array}{r} 17 \\ -\ 8 \\ \hline \end{array}$$

$$\begin{array}{r} 16 \\ -\ 9 \\ \hline \end{array}$$

$$\begin{array}{r} 14¢ \\ -\ 8¢ \\ \hline \end{array}$$

$$\begin{array}{r} 15 \\ -\ 7 \\ \hline \end{array}$$

$$\begin{array}{r} 18 \\ -\ 9 \\ \hline \end{array}$$

4

$$\begin{array}{r} 15 \\ -\ 8 \\ \hline \end{array}$$

$$\begin{array}{r} 17 \\ -\ 9 \\ \hline \end{array}$$

$$\begin{array}{r} 14¢ \\ -\ 6¢ \\ \hline \end{array}$$

$$\begin{array}{r} 14 \\ -\ 9 \\ \hline \end{array}$$

$$\begin{array}{r} 16 \\ -\ 8 \\ \hline \end{array}$$

$$\begin{array}{r} 14 \\ -\ 5 \\ \hline \end{array}$$

Solve.

5 Kate has 14 shells.
8 of the shells are white.
How many shells are
not white?

_____ shells

6 Write a subtraction word
problem. Have a partner solve it.

Use your own paper.

At Home Ask your child how to solve problem 5 above.

Ocean Colors

Subtract. Color to match differences.

5	6	7	8	9
))) yellow)))	)) red))	)) orange)))	)) green)))	)) blue))

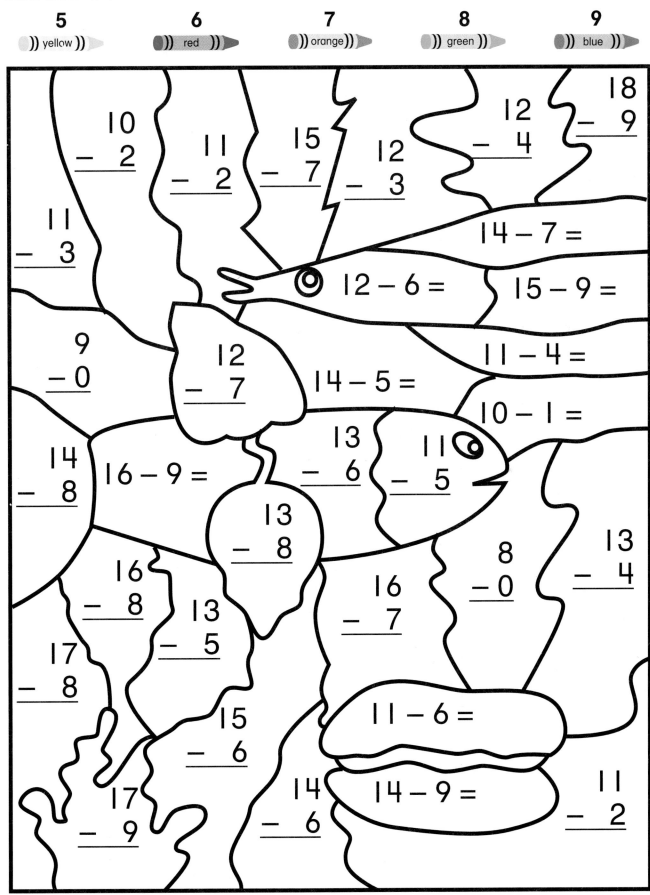

10
− 2

11
− 2

15
− 7

12
− 3

12
− 4

18
− 9

11
− 3

14 − 7 =

12 − 6 =

15 − 9 =

9
− 0

12
− 7

14 − 5 =

11 − 4 =

10 − 1 =

14
− 8

16 − 9 =

13
− 6

11
− 5

13
− 8

13
− 4

16
− 8

13
− 5

16
− 7

8
− 0

17
− 8

15
− 6

11 − 6 =

17
− 9

14
− 6

14 − 9 =

11
− 2

Subtract.

1

$$\begin{array}{r} 11 \\ -\ 4 \\ \hline 7 \end{array}$$
$$\begin{array}{r} 12 \\ -\ 5 \\ \hline \end{array}$$
$$\begin{array}{r} 18 \\ -\ 9 \\ \hline \end{array}$$
$$\begin{array}{r} 15 \\ -\ 7 \\ \hline \end{array}$$

2

$$\begin{array}{r} 16 \\ -\ 8 \\ \hline \end{array}$$
$$\begin{array}{r} 13 \\ -\ 4 \\ \hline \end{array}$$
$$\begin{array}{r} 12¢ \\ -\ 4¢ \\ \hline \end{array}$$
$$\begin{array}{r} 17 \\ -\ 9 \\ \hline \end{array}$$
$$\begin{array}{r} 14 \\ -\ 5 \\ \hline \end{array}$$

3

$$\begin{array}{r} 15 \\ -\ 9 \\ \hline \end{array}$$
$$\begin{array}{r} 13 \\ -\ 6 \\ \hline \end{array}$$
$$\begin{array}{r} 14 \\ -\ 7 \\ \hline \end{array}$$
$$\begin{array}{r} 12 \\ -\ 3 \\ \hline \end{array}$$
$$\begin{array}{r} 11¢ \\ -\ 5¢ \\ \hline \end{array}$$

4

$$\begin{array}{r} 16 \\ -\ 9 \\ \hline \end{array}$$
$$\begin{array}{r} 12 \\ -\ 6 \\ \hline \end{array}$$
$$\begin{array}{r} 17 \\ -\ 8 \\ \hline \end{array}$$
$$\begin{array}{r} 15¢ \\ -\ 8¢ \\ \hline \end{array}$$
$$\begin{array}{r} 15 \\ -\ 6 \\ \hline \end{array}$$

5

$$\begin{array}{r} 14 \\ -\ 6 \\ \hline \end{array}$$
$$\begin{array}{r} 13¢ \\ -\ 5¢ \\ \hline \end{array}$$
$$\begin{array}{r} 14 \\ -\ 9 \\ \hline \end{array}$$
$$\begin{array}{r} 11 \\ -\ 2 \\ \hline \end{array}$$
$$\begin{array}{r} 16 \\ -\ 7 \\ \hline \end{array}$$

Solve.

Workspace

6 12 fish are in a cave.
3 swim away.
How many fish are left? _____ fish

7 13 sea turtles are on the beach.
5 walk into the water.
How many sea turtles
are left on the beach? _____ sea turtles

Midchapter Review

Do your best!

1 Find the sum and difference.

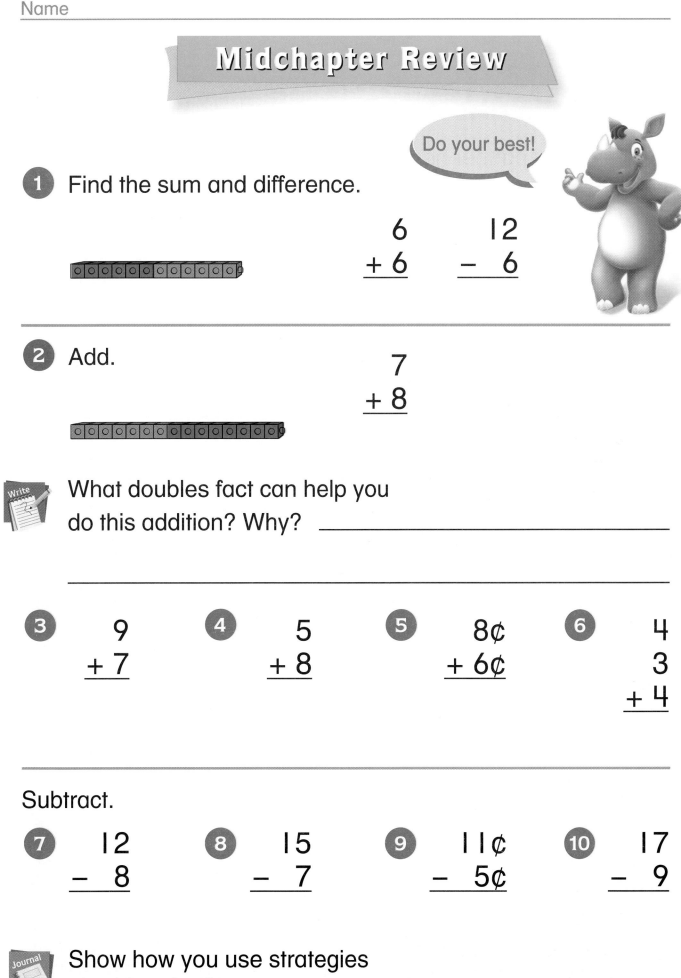

$$\begin{array}{r} 6 \\ +\ 6 \\ \hline \end{array} \qquad \begin{array}{r} 12 \\ -\ 6 \\ \hline \end{array}$$

2 Add.

$$\begin{array}{r} 7 \\ +\ 8 \\ \hline \end{array}$$

Write What doubles fact can help you do this addition? Why? _____

_____

3
$$\begin{array}{r} 9 \\ +\ 7 \\ \hline \end{array}$$

4
$$\begin{array}{r} 5 \\ +\ 8 \\ \hline \end{array}$$

5
$$\begin{array}{r} 8\cent \\ +\ 6\cent \\ \hline \end{array}$$

6
$$\begin{array}{r} 4 \\ 3 \\ +\ 4 \\ \hline \end{array}$$

Subtract.

7
$$\begin{array}{r} 12 \\ -\ 8 \\ \hline \end{array}$$

8
$$\begin{array}{r} 15 \\ -\ 7 \\ \hline \end{array}$$

9
$$\begin{array}{r} 11\cent \\ -\ 5\cent \\ \hline \end{array}$$

10
$$\begin{array}{r} 17 \\ -\ 9 \\ \hline \end{array}$$

Journal Show how you use strategies to add and subtract.

Fill the Fish Tank

You and your partner need 18  and a .

Take turns.

► Put some  in the .

► Shake and spill.

► Write the addition and subtraction.

► Your partner finds the sum and the difference.

Play until you fill the fish tank.

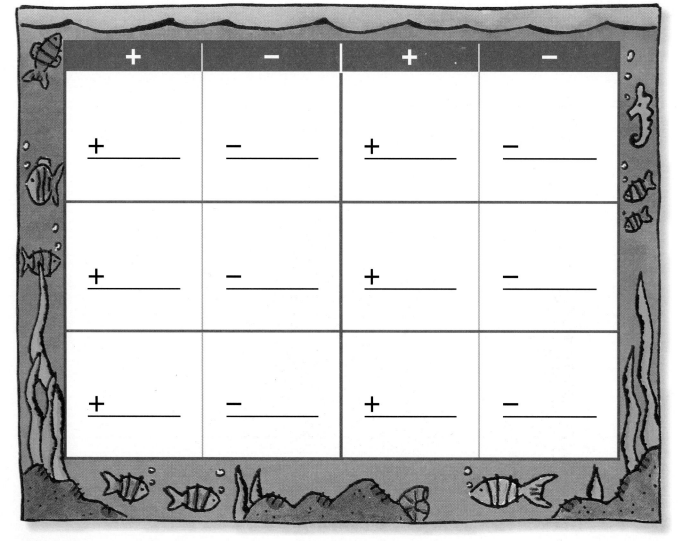

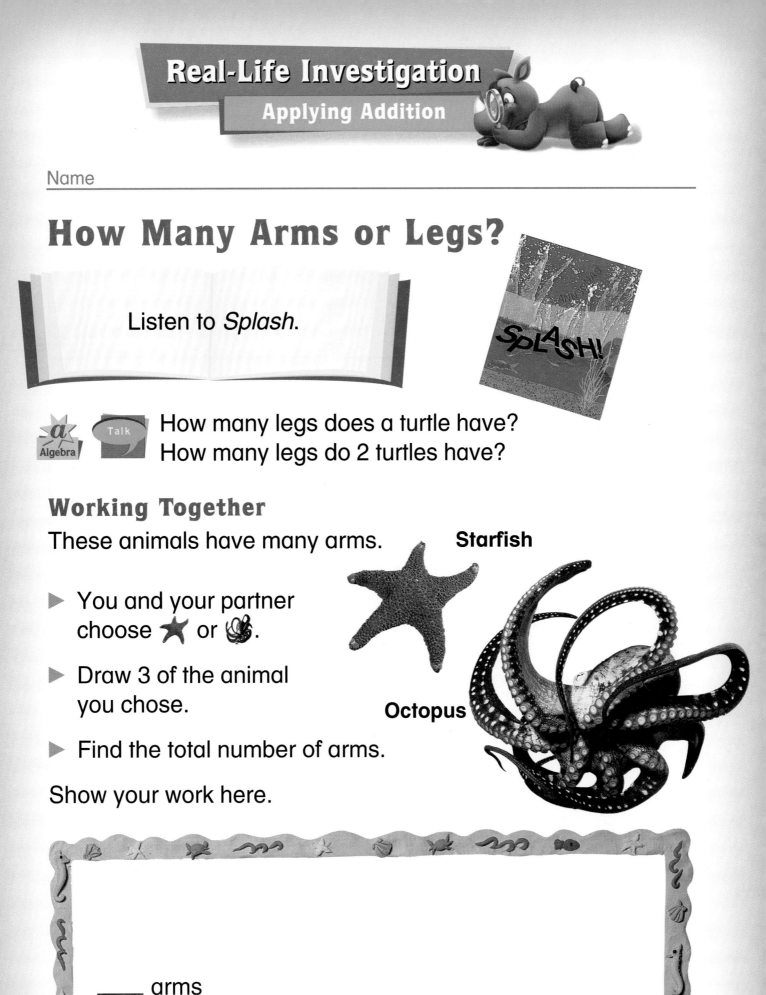

Name _____

How Many Arms or Legs?

Listen to *Splash*.

a Algebra **Talk** How many legs does a turtle have?
How many legs do 2 turtles have?

Working Together

These animals have many arms.

Starfish

Octopus

▶ You and your partner choose ⭐ or 🐙.

▶ Draw 3 of the animal you chose.

▶ Find the total number of arms.

Show your work here.

_____ arms

Decision Making

PATTERNS

1 Complete the table. Find how many legs for each number of turtles.

Number of Turtles	1	2	3	4	5
Number of Legs	4	8			

2 Choose another animal. Complete the table.

Number of _____	1	2	3	4	5
Number of _____					

 Write a report.

3 Tell how you completed the tables.

4 Describe any patterns you see in the tables.

More to Investigate

PREDICT How many starfish are in a group with a total of 20 arms?

EXPLORE Try it. Use counters, draw pictures, or make a table.

FIND Find how many starfish are in the group.

Name _____

Choose the Operation

Read
Plan
Solve
Look Back

Read Meg has 8 goldfish. Alex has 5 goldfish. How many more goldfish does Meg have than Alex?

What do you know?

What do you need to find out?

Plan Do you add or subtract to compare?   add   (subtract)

Solve

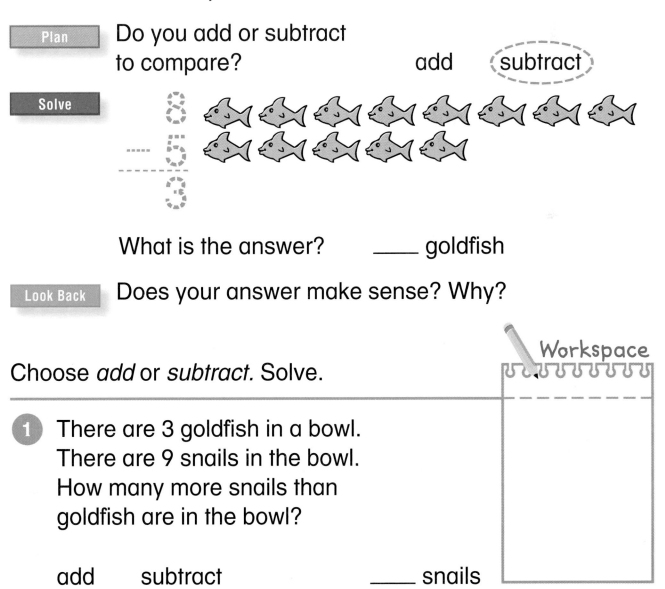

$$\begin{array}{r} 8 \\ -5 \\ \hline 3 \end{array}$$

What is the answer?   _____ goldfish

Look Back Does your answer make sense? Why?

Workspace

Choose *add* or *subtract*. Solve.

1 There are 3 goldfish in a bowl. There are 9 snails in the bowl. How many more snails than goldfish are in the bowl?

add   subtract   _____ snails

McGraw-Hill School Division

Practice!

Choose *add* or *subtract.* Solve.

1 Lee buys a shell for 7¢.
Then she buys a rock for 5¢.
How much money does Lee spend?

add   subtract   ___¢

2 There are 13 fish in a tank.
9 are goldfish and the rest are angelfish.
How many angelfish are in the tank?

add   subtract   ___ angelfish

3 Vic buys 12 fish. Joe buys 6 fish.
How many more fish does
Vic buy than Joe?

add   subtract   ___ fish

4 The store has 8 large fish tanks
and 6 small fish tanks.
How many fish tanks are in the store?

add   subtract   ___ fish tanks

At Home   Ask your child to explain how to solve these problems.

Add and Subtract

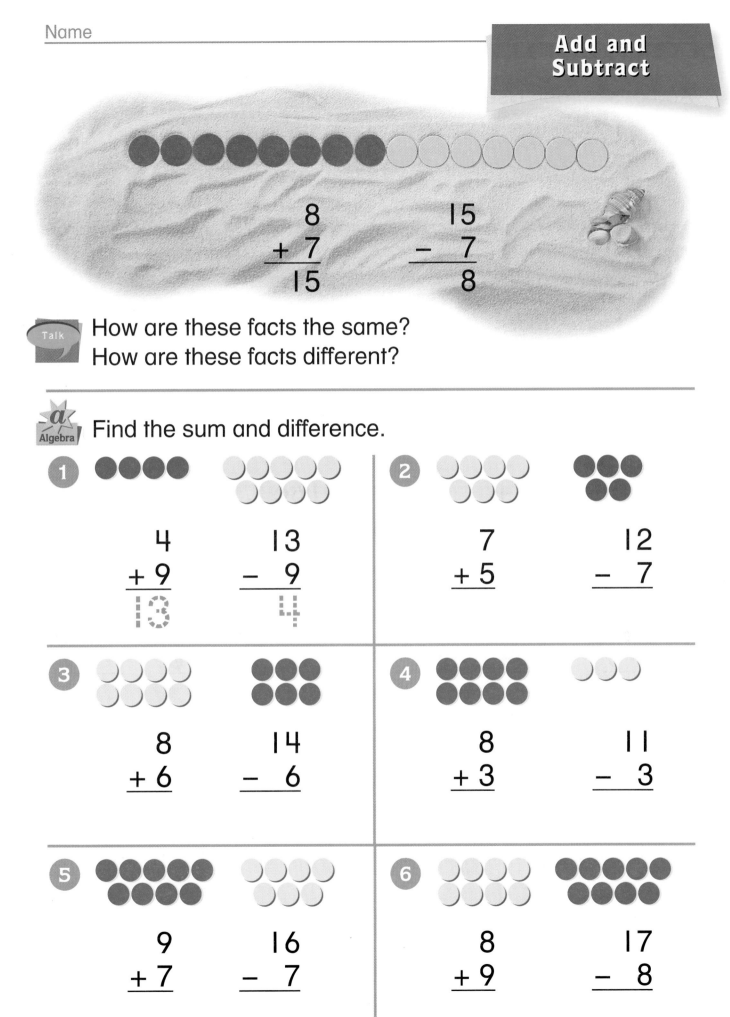

$$\begin{array}{r} 8 \\ + 7 \\ \hline 15 \end{array}$$
$$\begin{array}{r} 15 \\ - 7 \\ \hline 8 \end{array}$$

Talk How are these facts the same?
How are these facts different?

Algebra Find the sum and difference.

1
$$\begin{array}{r} 4 \\ + 9 \\ \hline 13 \end{array}$$
$$\begin{array}{r} 13 \\ - 9 \\ \hline 4 \end{array}$$

2
$$\begin{array}{r} 7 \\ + 5 \\ \hline \end{array}$$
$$\begin{array}{r} 12 \\ - 7 \\ \hline \end{array}$$

3
$$\begin{array}{r} 8 \\ + 6 \\ \hline \end{array}$$
$$\begin{array}{r} 14 \\ - 6 \\ \hline \end{array}$$

4
$$\begin{array}{r} 8 \\ + 3 \\ \hline \end{array}$$
$$\begin{array}{r} 11 \\ - 3 \\ \hline \end{array}$$

5
$$\begin{array}{r} 9 \\ + 7 \\ \hline \end{array}$$
$$\begin{array}{r} 16 \\ - 7 \\ \hline \end{array}$$

6
$$\begin{array}{r} 8 \\ + 9 \\ \hline \end{array}$$
$$\begin{array}{r} 17 \\ - 8 \\ \hline \end{array}$$

Practice!

Add or subtract. Use ⬤◐ if you want to.

1 ⬤⬤⬤⬤⬤ ○○○○○
        ○○○○

$$\begin{array}{r} 4 \\ +\ 8 \\ \hline 12 \end{array}$$
$$\begin{array}{r} 12 \\ -\ 8 \\ \hline 4 \end{array}$$

2 ⬤⬤⬤⬤ ○○○○
       ⬤⬤⬤

$$\begin{array}{r} 7 \\ +\ 4 \\ \hline \end{array}$$
$$\begin{array}{r} 11 \\ -\ 4 \\ \hline \end{array}$$

3
$$\begin{array}{r} 8 \\ +\ 5 \\ \hline \end{array}$$
$$\begin{array}{r} 13 \\ -\ 5 \\ \hline \end{array}$$
$$\begin{array}{r} 9 \\ +\ 6 \\ \hline \end{array}$$
$$\begin{array}{r} 15 \\ -\ 6 \\ \hline \end{array}$$
$$\begin{array}{r} 3¢ \\ +\ 8¢ \\ \hline \end{array}$$
$$\begin{array}{r} 11¢ \\ -\ 8¢ \\ \hline \end{array}$$

4
$$\begin{array}{r} 5 \\ +\ 9 \\ \hline \end{array}$$
$$\begin{array}{r} 14 \\ -\ 9 \\ \hline \end{array}$$
$$\begin{array}{r} 9¢ \\ +\ 7¢ \\ \hline \end{array}$$
$$\begin{array}{r} 16¢ \\ -\ 7¢ \\ \hline \end{array}$$
$$\begin{array}{r} 3 \\ +\ 9 \\ \hline \end{array}$$
$$\begin{array}{r} 12 \\ -\ 9 \\ \hline \end{array}$$

5
$$\begin{array}{r} 9 \\ +\ 9 \\ \hline \end{array}$$
$$\begin{array}{r} 18 \\ -\ 9 \\ \hline \end{array}$$
$$\begin{array}{r} 6 \\ +\ 5 \\ \hline \end{array}$$
$$\begin{array}{r} 11 \\ -\ 5 \\ \hline \end{array}$$
$$\begin{array}{r} 7¢ \\ +\ 6¢ \\ \hline \end{array}$$
$$\begin{array}{r} 13¢ \\ -\ 6¢ \\ \hline \end{array}$$

Mixed Review   Test Preparation

Complete.

6

(clock showing 6:00)

____ : ____

7
$$\begin{array}{r} 3¢ \\ +\ 5¢ \\ \hline \end{array}$$
$$\begin{array}{r} 8¢ \\ +\ 1¢ \\ \hline \end{array}$$
$$\begin{array}{r} 2¢ \\ +\ 4¢ \\ \hline \end{array}$$

At Home — Ask your child to write a subtraction fact related to $3 + 7 = 10$.

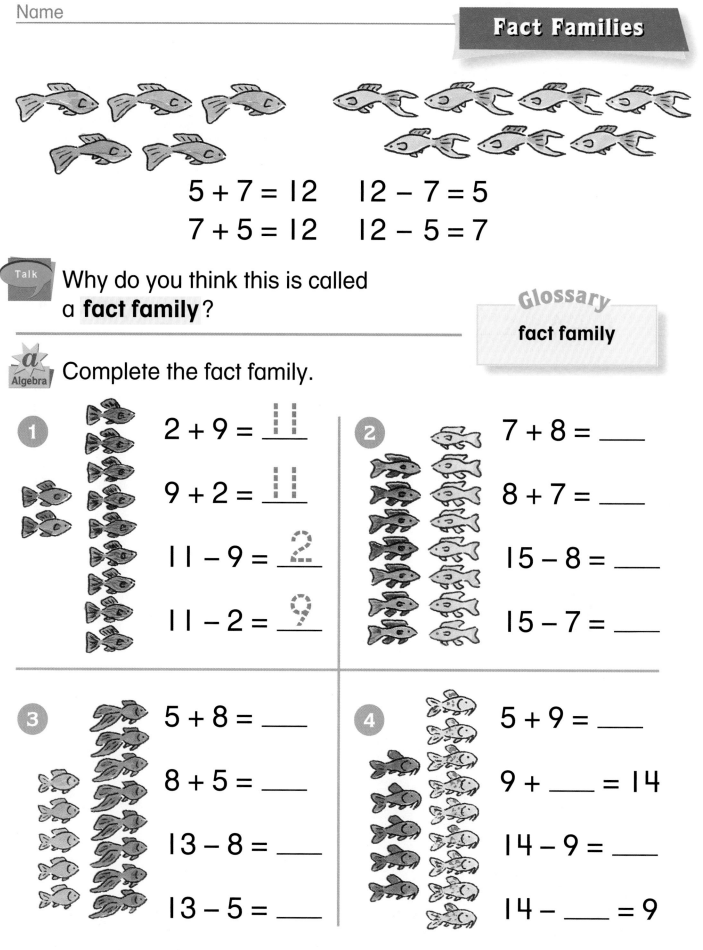

$$5 + 7 = 12 \qquad 12 - 7 = 5$$
$$7 + 5 = 12 \qquad 12 - 5 = 7$$

Talk Why do you think this is called
a **fact family**?

Glossary
fact family

a Algebra Complete the fact family.

1
$2 + 9 = 11$

$9 + 2 = 11$

$11 - 9 = 2$

$11 - 2 = 9$

2
$7 + 8 = \underline{}$

$8 + 7 = \underline{}$

$15 - 8 = \underline{}$

$15 - 7 = \underline{}$

3
$5 + 8 = \underline{}$

$8 + 5 = \underline{}$

$13 - 8 = \underline{}$

$13 - 5 = \underline{}$

4
$5 + 9 = \underline{}$

$9 + \underline{} = 14$

$14 - 9 = \underline{}$

$14 - \underline{} = 9$

Critical Thinking How many facts are in the $7 + 7 = 14$
family? Why?

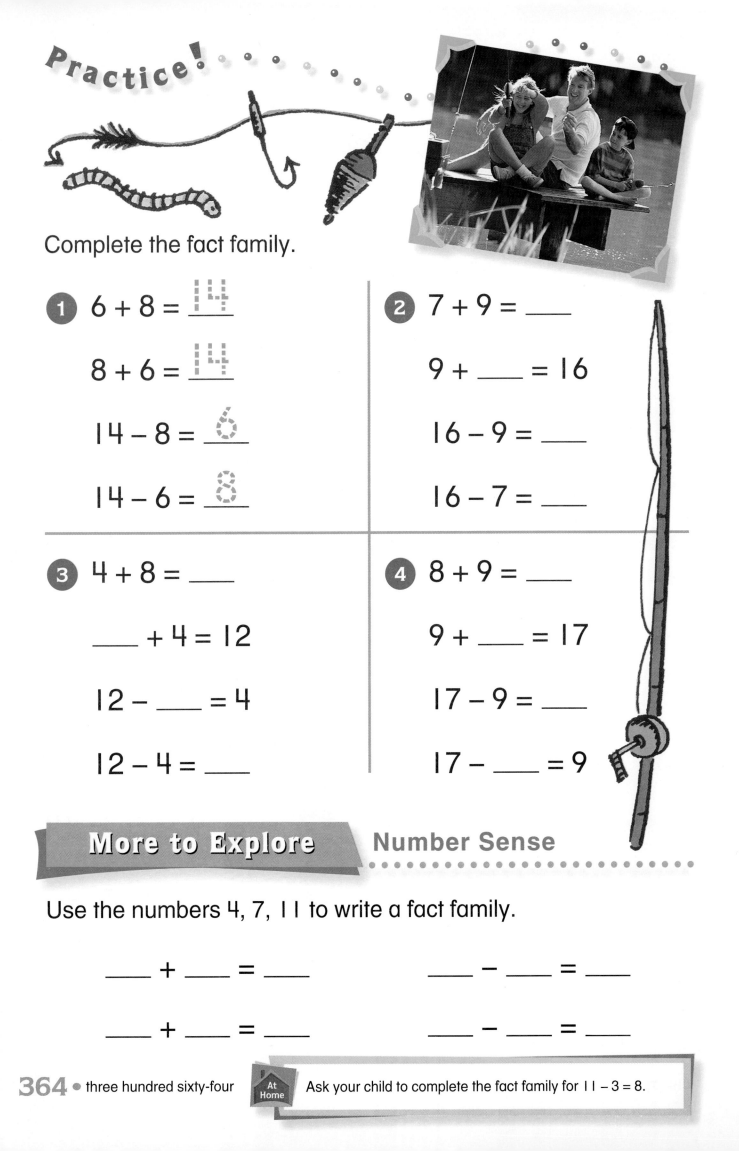

Practice!

Complete the fact family.

1 $6 + 8 = 14$

$8 + 6 = 14$

$14 - 8 = 6$

$14 - 6 = 8$

2 $7 + 9 = \_\_\_$

$9 + \_\_\_ = 16$

$16 - 9 = \_\_\_$

$16 - 7 = \_\_\_$

3 $4 + 8 = \_\_\_$

$\_\_\_ + 4 = 12$

$12 - \_\_\_ = 4$

$12 - 4 = \_\_\_$

4 $8 + 9 = \_\_\_$

$9 + \_\_\_ = 17$

$17 - 9 = \_\_\_$

$17 - \_\_\_ = 9$

More to Explore   Number Sense

Use the numbers 4, 7, 11 to write a fact family.

$\_\_\_ + \_\_\_ = \_\_\_$ $\_\_\_ - \_\_\_ = \_\_\_$

$\_\_\_ + \_\_\_ = \_\_\_$ $\_\_\_ - \_\_\_ = \_\_\_$

At Home   Ask your child to complete the fact family for $11 - 3 = 8$.

Choose a Strategy

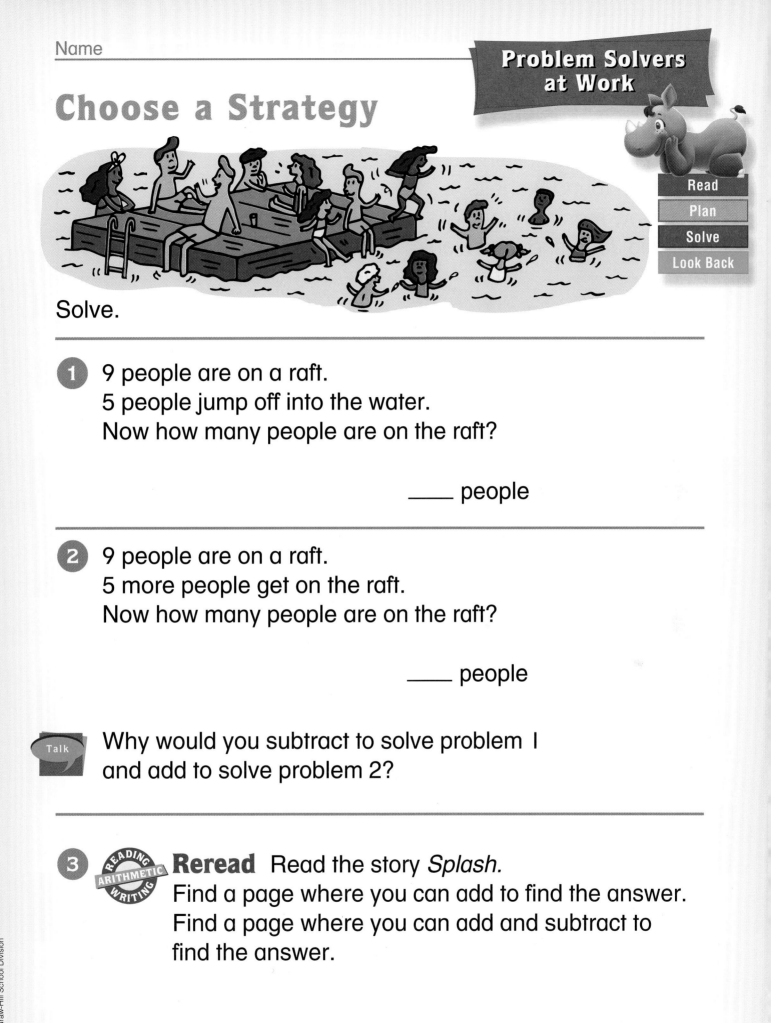

Read
Plan
Solve
Look Back

Solve.

1 9 people are on a raft.
5 people jump off into the water.
Now how many people are on the raft?

_____ people

2 9 people are on a raft.
5 more people get on the raft.
Now how many people are on the raft?

_____ people

Talk Why would you subtract to solve problem 1
and add to solve problem 2?

3 READING ARITHMETIC WRITING **Reread** Read the story *Splash.*
Find a page where you can add to find the answer.
Find a page where you can add and subtract to
find the answer.

Practice!

Solve.

1 Jean found 17 shells.
Ron found 8 shells.
How many more shells
did Jean find than Ron? _____ shells

9¢   8¢   6¢

2 Helen buys a 🐚 and a 🐚.
How much money does
she spend? _____ ¢

Write and Share

Bobby wrote this problem.

Ten people were having
pizza and two joined in.
Now how many people
are there?

Bobby Wiggins
Mandarin Oaks School
Jacksonville, Florida

3 Solve Bobby's problem. _____ people

4 Write a word problem.
Have a partner solve it.

Use your own paper.

What strategy did your partner use? _____

What strategy would you use? _____

At Home   Have your child tell how to solve problem 2 above.

Chapter Review

Language and Mathematics

Choose the correct word to complete the sentence.

1 You can use the numbers 3, 9, and 12 to write a _____.

2 5 + 5 = 10 is a _____ fact.

> doubles
> strategy
> fact family

Concepts and Skills

Find the sum or difference.

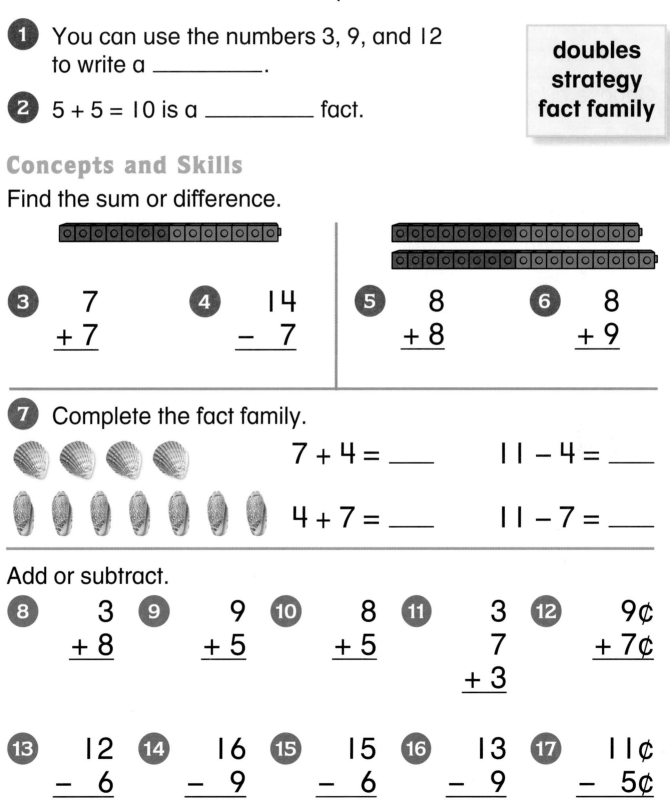

3 7
+ 7

4 14
− 7

5 8
+ 8

6 8
+ 9

7 Complete the fact family.

$7 + 4 =$ ___ $11 - 4 =$ ___

$4 + 7 =$ ___ $11 - 7 =$ ___

Add or subtract.

8 3
+ 8

9 9
+ 5

10 8
+ 5

11 3
7
+ 3

12 9¢
+ 7¢

13 12
− 6

14 16
− 9

15 15
− 6

16 13
− 9

17 11¢
− 5¢

Problem Solving

Solve.

Workspace

---

18 There are 17 fish in a cave.
8 fish swim away.
How many fish are left
in the cave? _____ fish

Choose *add* or *subtract*. Solve.

19 Ben had 12 fish. He gave
8 fish to Kim. Now how
many fish does Ben have?

add   subtract   _____ fish

---

20 Eric has 5 brown shells and
9 white shells. How many
shells does Eric have in all?

add   subtract   _____ shells

What Do You Think?

Which strategy do you like to use?
☑ Check one.

☐ Adding 9   ☐ Subtracting 9   ☐ Fact families

Why? _____

Tell what you learned about adding and subtracting.

Chapter Test

Find the sum and difference.

1

$$\begin{array}{cc} 5 & 10 \\ +5 & -5 \end{array}$$

2

$$\begin{array}{cc} 9 & 18 \\ +9 & -9 \end{array}$$

Complete the fact family.

3

$7 + 6 =$ ___

$6 + 7 =$ ___

$13 - 7 =$ ___

$13 - 6 =$ ___

4

$8 + 3 =$ ___

$3 + 8 =$ ___

$11 - 8 =$ ___

$11 - 3 =$ ___

Add.

5

$$\begin{array}{c} 5¢ \\ +7¢ \end{array}$$

6

$$\begin{array}{c} 9 \\ +6 \end{array}$$

Subtract.

7

$$\begin{array}{c} 16¢ \\ -8¢ \end{array}$$

8

$$\begin{array}{c} 17 \\ -9 \end{array}$$

Choose *add* or *subtract*. Solve.

9 Lucas has 9 fish. He catches 5 more. How many fish does Lucas have now?

add   subtract

___ fish

10 Lily sees 12 pink fish and 8 red fish. How many more pink fish than red fish does Lily see?

add   subtract

___ pink fish

What Did You Learn?

POND ANIMALS I COUNTED			
			🐟
🐸			🐟
🐸			🐟
🐸			🐟
🐸		🦐	🐟
🐸		🦐	🐟
🐸		🦐	🐟
🐸	🐢	🦐	🐟
🐸	🐢	🦐	🐟
Frogs	**Turtles**	**Crayfish**	**Minnows**

Each picture stands for 1 animal.

Use the information in the graph.

1 Make up a problem that uses addition.
Solve it.

_____

2 Make up a problem that uses subtraction.
Solve it.

_____

 You may want to put this page in your portfolio.

Name

Add and Subtract

You can use a calculator to help solve problems.

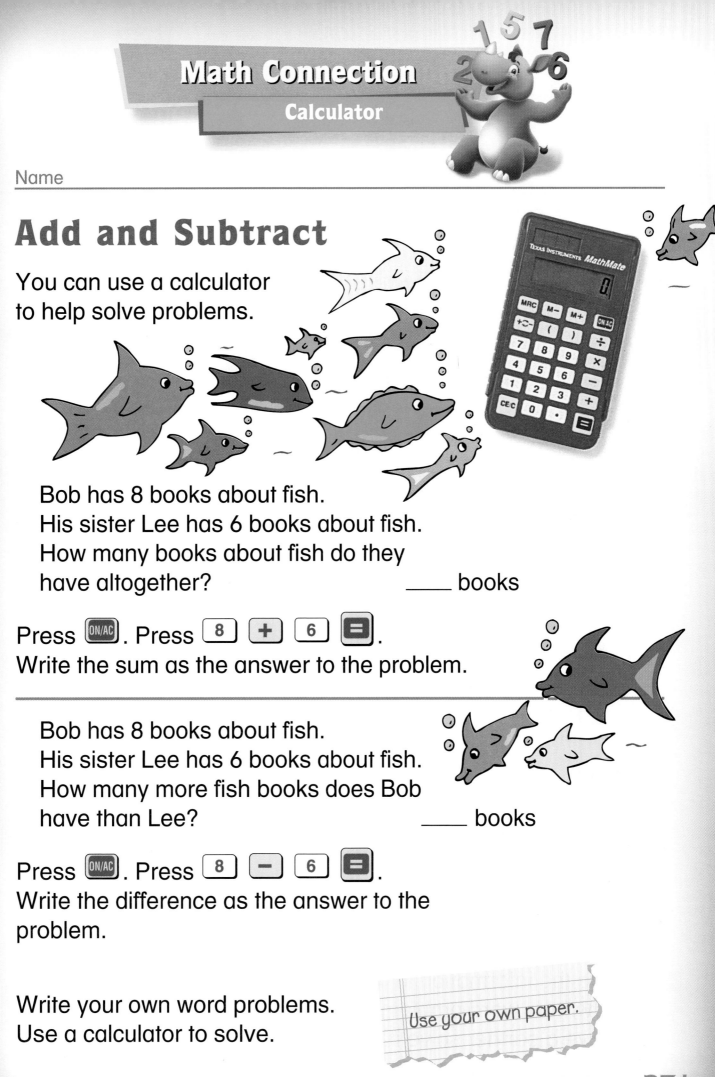

Bob has 8 books about fish.
His sister Lee has 6 books about fish.
How many books about fish do they
have altogether?   _____ books

Press ON/AC. Press 8 + 6 =.
Write the sum as the answer to the problem.

Bob has 8 books about fish.
His sister Lee has 6 books about fish.
How many more fish books does Bob
have than Lee?   _____ books

Press ON/AC. Press 8 − 6 =.
Write the difference as the answer to the
problem.

Write your own word problems.
Use a calculator to solve.

Use your own paper.

McGraw-Hill School Division

Beachcombing

Lisa and her family went to the beach.
This is what they found.

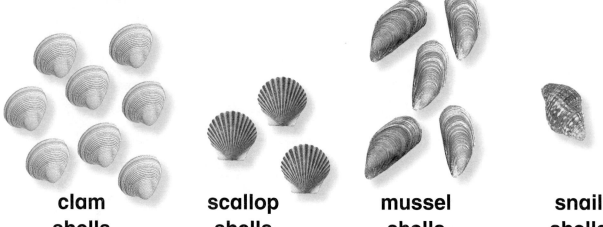

| clam shells | scallop shells | mussel shells | snail shells |

Use this information to complete the graph.

LISA'S SHELLS

	0	1	2	3	4	5	6	7	8	9	10
Clam											
Scallop											
Mussel											
Snail											

 Write

Use the information in the graph
to write a word problem.
Have a partner solve it.

Use your own paper.

Name

Hidden Pennies

PLAYERS 2

MATERIALS 18 pennies, 2 cups, pencil and paper

DIRECTIONS Put 18 pennies in the middle of the table.

Each player takes some pennies and puts them in a cup.

Use the pennies in your cup and the pennies left on the table to find out how many pennies your partner has.

Score 2 points for a correct answer. Continue playing until you have 18 points altogether.

 Play this game with your child to practice addition and to help him or her develop number sense.

At Home

Dear Family,

I am beginning a new chapter in mathematics. I will be learning about measurement. Some of the measurement tools that I will use are rulers, cups, and thermometers.

I will also learn about dinosaurs.

Learning about Dinosaurs

Let's talk about dinosaurs and describe them. We can draw a picture of a dinosaur and tell how big it was.

My Math Words

I am going to use these math words in this chapter.

Please help me make word cards for these math words. I can use the word cards when I practice measurement.

measure
long
inch
foot
centimeter
draw a picture
weigh
pound
cup
thermometer
temperature
degrees

Your child,

_____
Signature

Exploring Measurement
Theme: Dinosaurs and Me

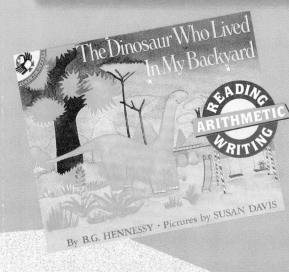

By B.G. HENNESSY · Pictures by SUSAN DAVIS

Make Inferences A story may have clues that help you answer questions. Listen to *The Dinosaur Who Lived in My Backyard.* Find clues to help answer these questions.

▶ Does the boy like dinosaurs?
▶ Does the boy like lima beans?

What Do You Know?

1 Draw a line around the dinosaur that is longer.

2 Draw a line around the dinosaur that is shortest.

3 Mark the object that is heavier.

4 Mark the object that is lighter.

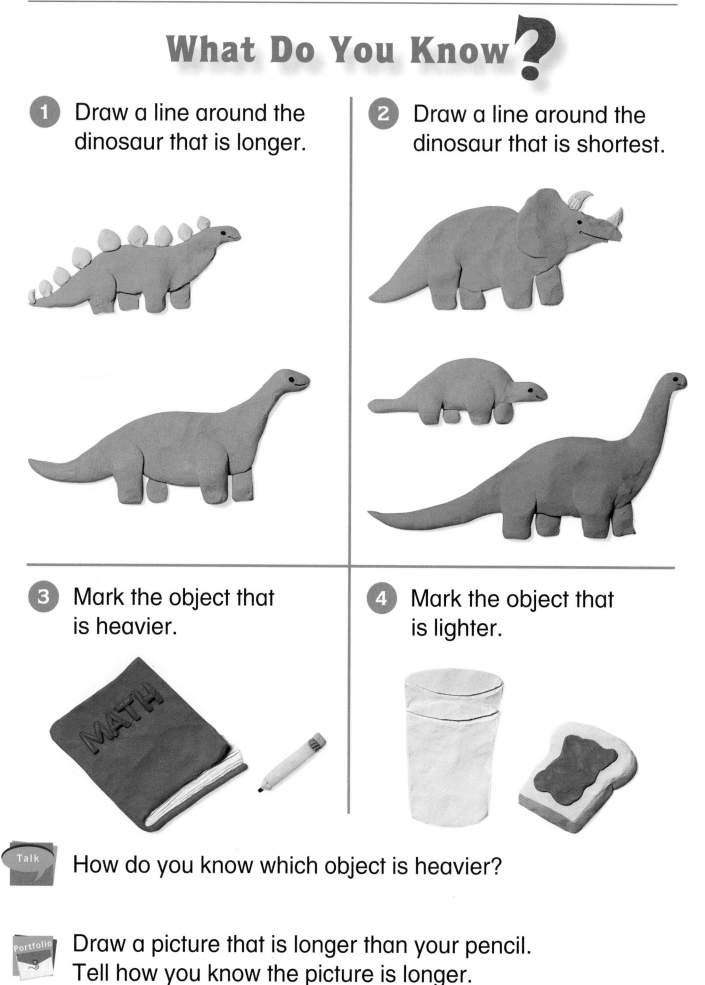

Talk   How do you know which object is heavier?

Portfolio   Draw a picture that is longer than your pencil. Tell how you know the picture is longer.

Working Together

You and your partners need 10 🐾.

▶ Find the real object.

▶ **Measure** with 🐾.

▶ Write how **long** it is.

Let's measure.

It's about 3 dinosaur feet long.

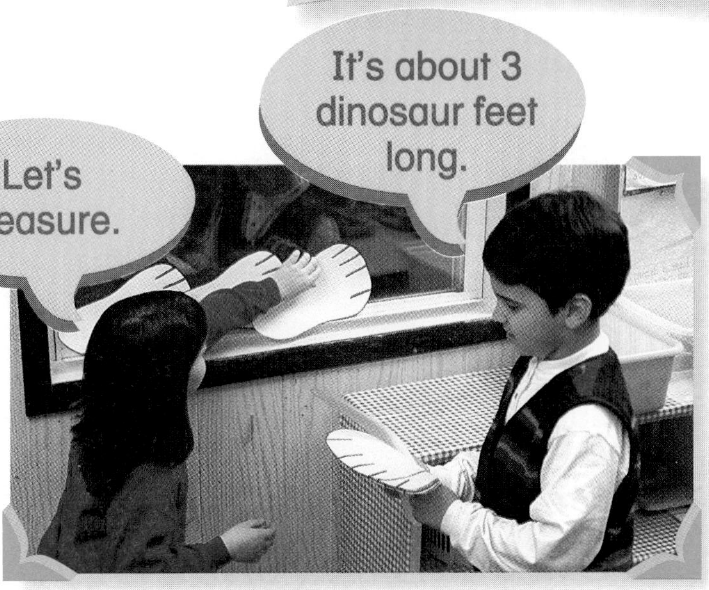

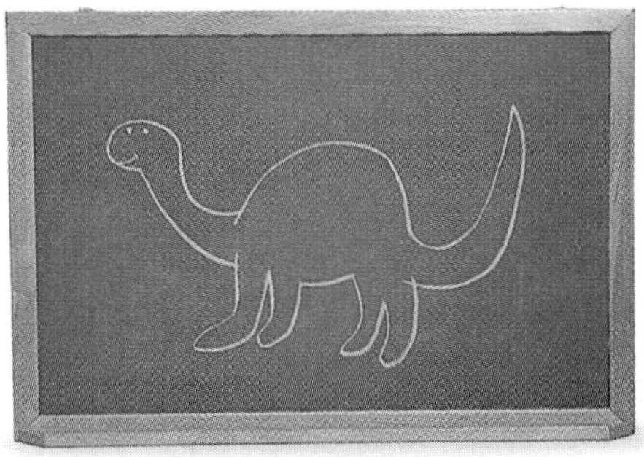

Glossary
measure
long

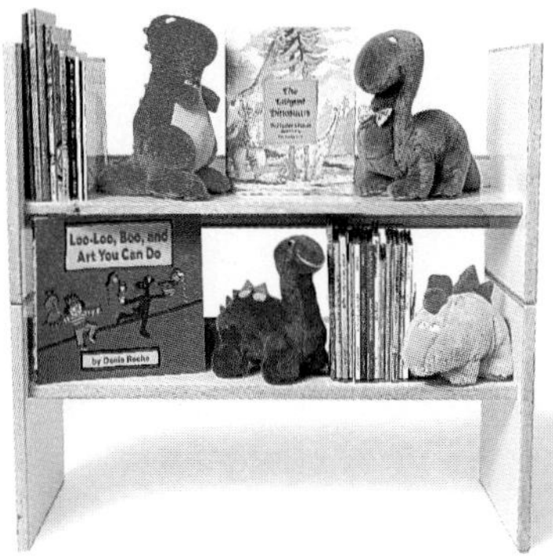

1

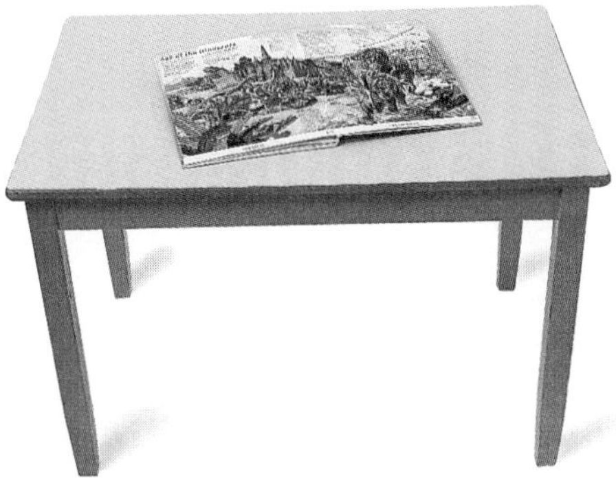

about ____ 🐾

2

about ____ 🐾

3

about ____ 🐾

Critical Thinking Does it make a difference if you use the footprints like this: 👣👣👣 ? Explain.

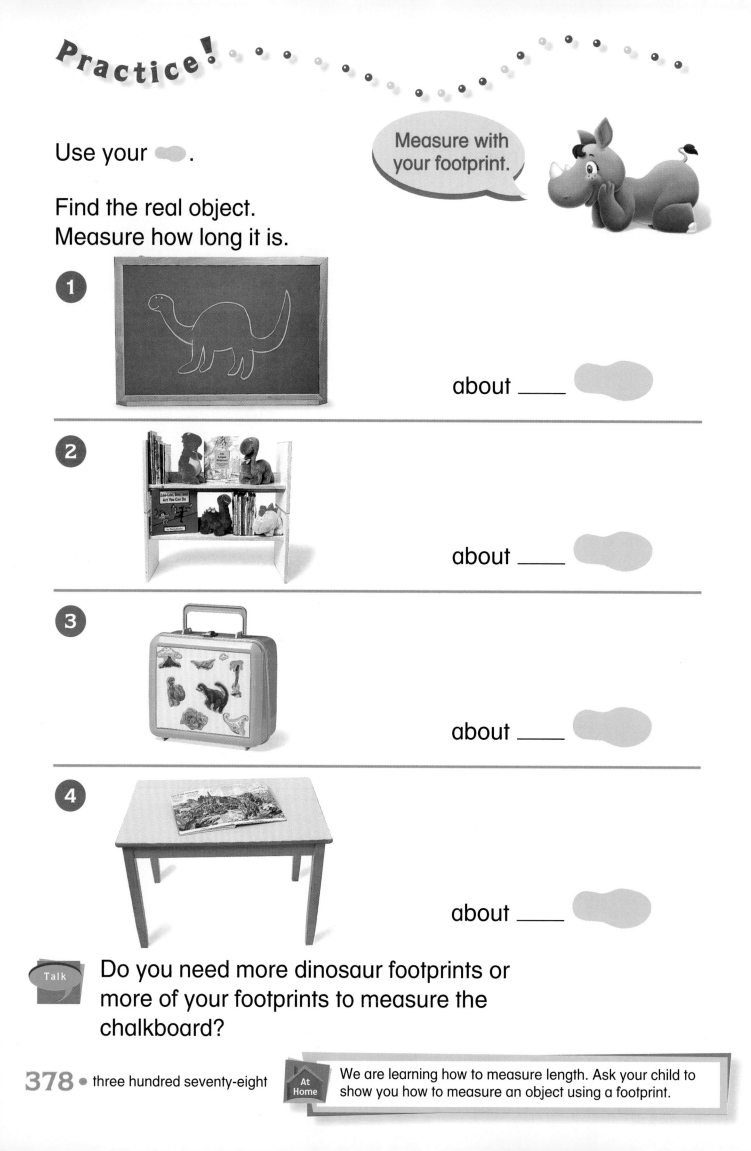

Use your 🥔 .

Measure with your footprint.

Find the real object.
Measure how long it is.

1 about ____ 🦶

2 about ____ 🦶

3 about ____ 🦶

4 about ____ 🦶

Talk Do you need more dinosaur footprints or more of your footprints to measure the chalkboard?

At Home
We are learning how to measure length. Ask your child to show you how to measure an object using a footprint.

Name _____

It's about 10 cubes long.

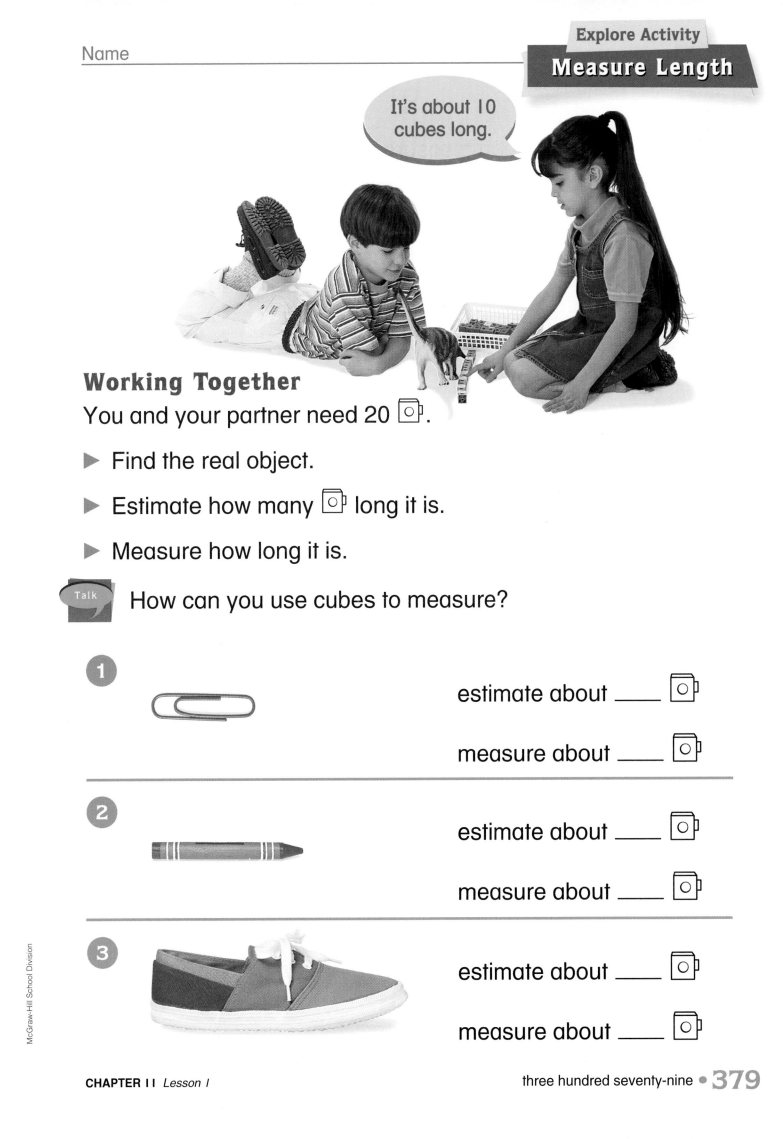

Working Together

You and your partner need 20 ▢.

▶ Find the real object.

▶ Estimate how many ▢ long it is.

▶ Measure how long it is.

Talk How can you use cubes to measure?

1

estimate about _____ ▢

measure about _____ ▢

2

estimate about _____ ▢

measure about _____ ▢

3

estimate about _____ ▢

measure about _____ ▢

McGraw-Hill School Division

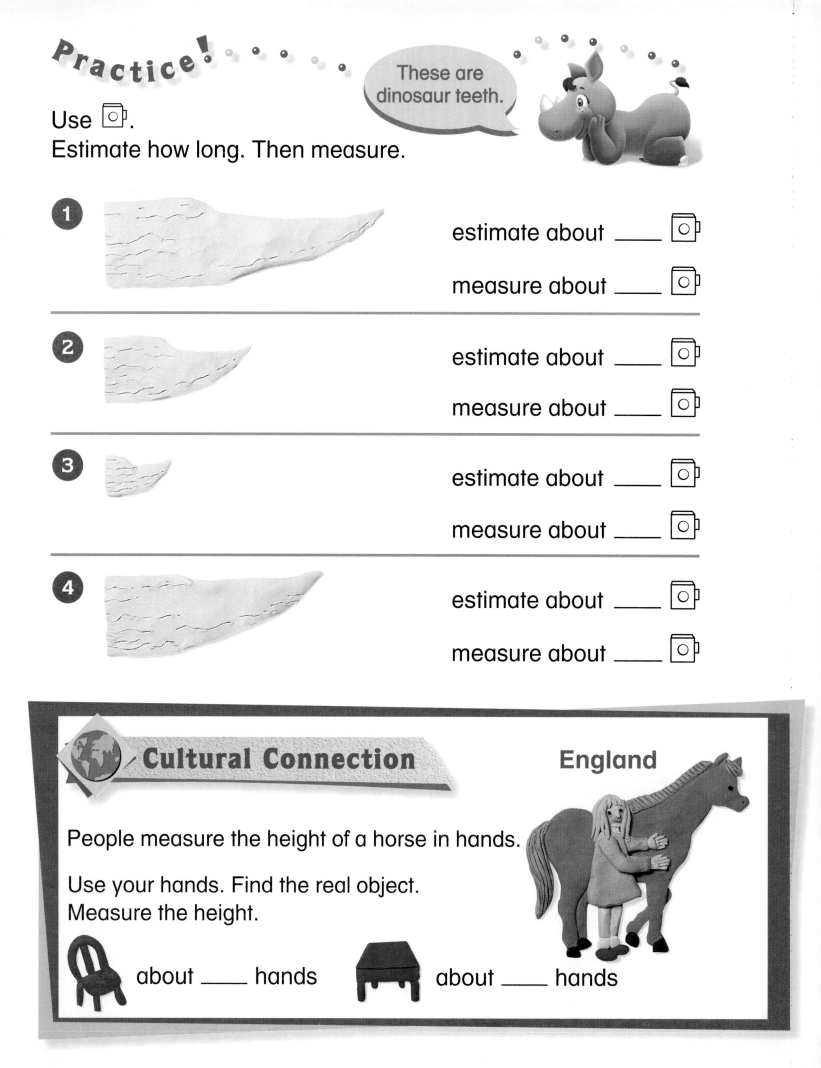

These are dinosaur teeth.

Use 🗍.
Estimate how long. Then measure.

1
estimate about _____ 🗍

measure about _____ 🗍

2
estimate about _____ 🗍

measure about _____ 🗍

3
estimate about _____ 🗍

measure about _____ 🗍

4
estimate about _____ 🗍

measure about _____ 🗍

Cultural Connection   England

People measure the height of a horse in hands.

Use your hands. Find the real object.
Measure the height.

about _____ hands   about _____ hands

Inch

You need a ▱ .

Glossary

inch

I **inch (in.)**

| 0 | I | 2 | 3 | 4 |

about 2 **inches**

▶ Find the real object.

▶ Estimate how many inches long it is.

▶ Then measure.

		Estimate	Measure
1		about ____ inches	about ____ inches
2		about ____ inches	about ____ inches
3		about ____ inches	about ____ inches
4		about ____ inches	about ____ inches

Critical Thinking Which objects are longer than your hand?
Which objects are shorter?

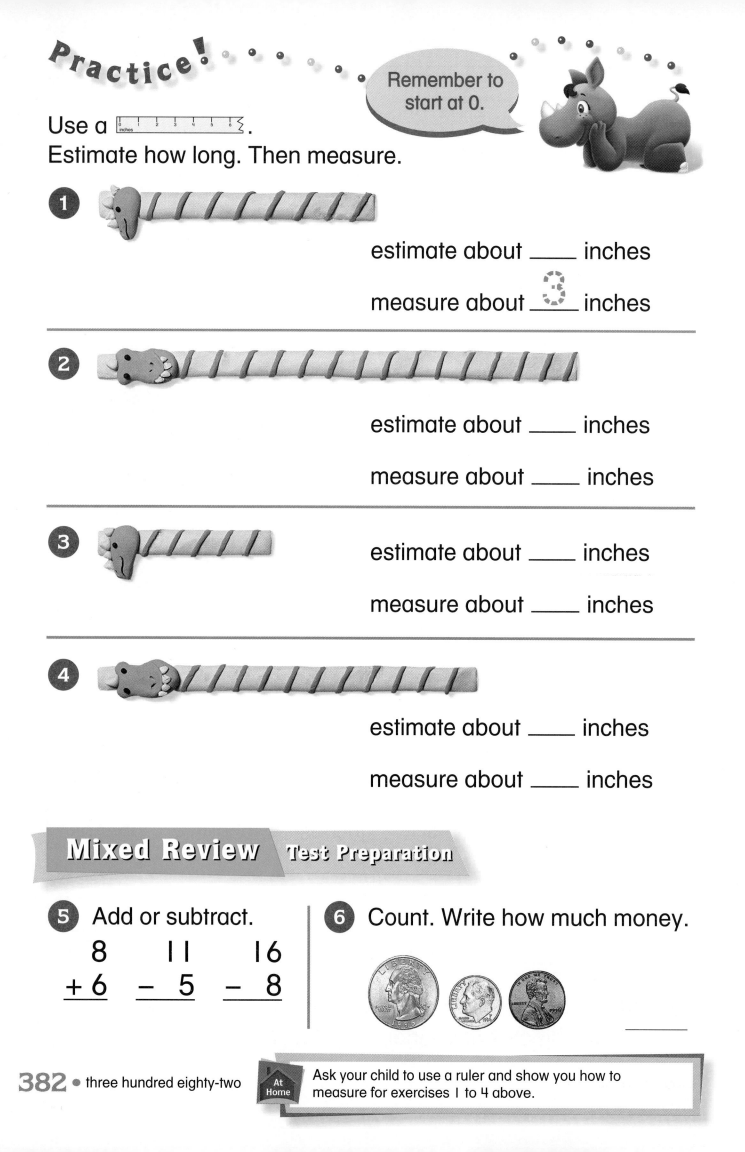

Practice!

Remember to start at 0.

Use a ⌊inches 0 1 2 3 4 5 6⌋.

Estimate how long. Then measure.

1

estimate about _____ inches

measure about __3__ inches

2

estimate about _____ inches

measure about _____ inches

3

estimate about _____ inches

measure about _____ inches

4

estimate about _____ inches

measure about _____ inches

Mixed Review   Test Preparation

5 Add or subtract.

$$\begin{array}{ccc} 8 & 11 & 16 \\ +6 & -5 & -8 \\ \hline \end{array}$$

6 Count. Write how much money.

_____

At Home — Ask your child to use a ruler and show you how to measure for exercises 1 to 4 above.

Put things back after you measure!

This math book is 1 foot long.

Working Together

You and your partner need a ⊏⊐ .

▶ Find things that look about 1 **foot (ft)** long.

▶ Measure each object.

▶ Draw or write to show things that are about 1 foot long.

Critical Thinking What did you find that is more than 1 foot long? What is less than 1 foot?

Glossary

foot

Practice!

Use a ▱inches▱.
Find the real object.
Estimate how long and record.
Measure and record.

		Estimate	Measure
1		less than 1 foot more than 1 foot	less than 1 foot more than 1 foot
2		less than 1 foot more than 1 foot	less than 1 foot more than 1 foot
3		less than 1 foot more than 1 foot	less than 1 foot more than 1 foot
4		less than 1 foot more than 1 foot	less than 1 foot more than 1 foot
5		less than 1 foot more than 1 foot	less than 1 foot more than 1 foot

 Show and write about how you measure things.

At Home Ask your child to show you an object that is more than 1 foot long and an object that is less than 1 foot long.

Name _____

You need a 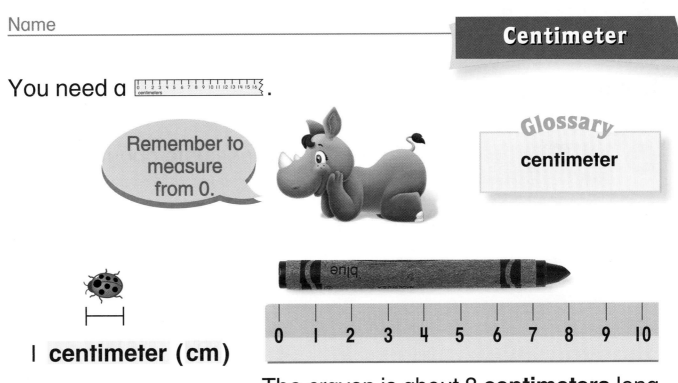 .

Remember to measure from 0.

Glossary
centimeter

l centimeter (cm)

The crayon is about 8 **centimeters** long.

▶ Find the real object.

▶ Estimate how many centimeters long it is.

▶ Then measure.

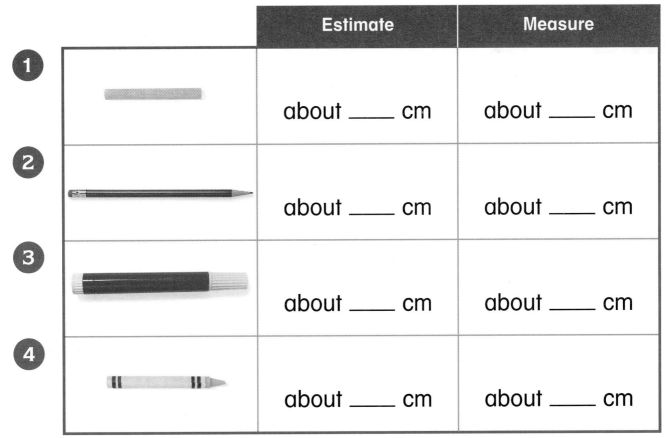

		Estimate	Measure
1		about ____ cm	about ____ cm
2		about ____ cm	about ____ cm
3		about ____ cm	about ____ cm
4		about ____ cm	about ____ cm

McGraw-Hill School Division

Practice!

Use a ⏢ centimeters ⏢ .
Estimate how long. Then measure.

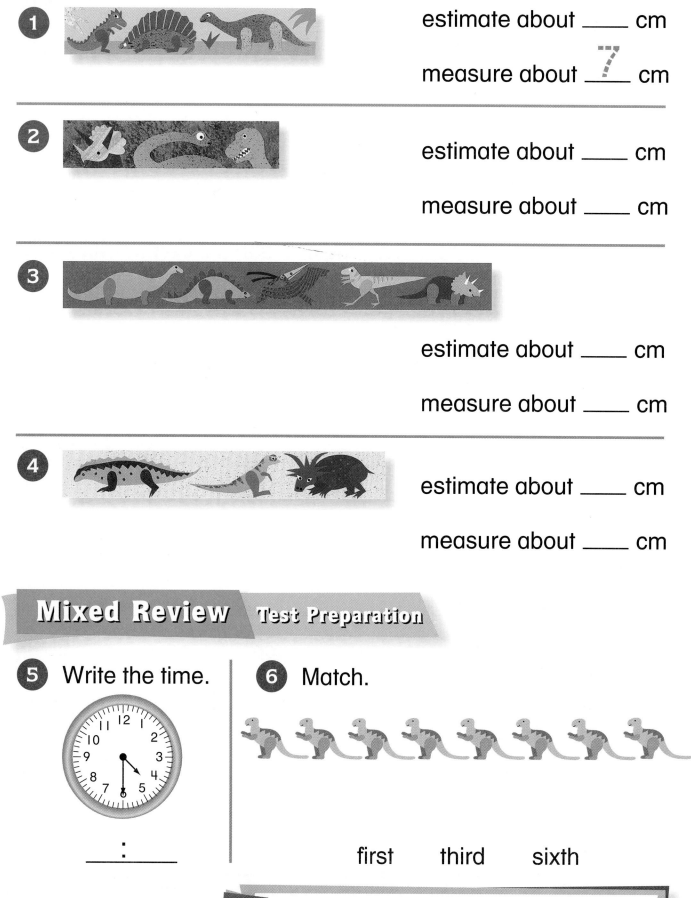

1
estimate about _____ cm

measure about _7_ cm

2
estimate about _____ cm

measure about _____ cm

3
estimate about _____ cm

measure about _____ cm

4
estimate about _____ cm

measure about _____ cm

Mixed Review Test Preparation

5 Write the time.

_____ : _____

6 Match.

first   third   sixth

At Home — Ask your child to use a centimeter ruler and show you how to measure some objects.

Name _____

Draw a Picture

You need a .

Read Annie builds a fence around her toy dinosaur. It is 4 cm on one side. It is 7 cm on another side. How many centimeters around is the fence?

Plan You can **draw a picture** to solve.

Solve Draw the two missing sides. Measure each side and add the measures.

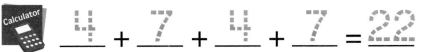 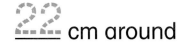

$$\underline{4} + \underline{7} + \underline{4} + \underline{7} = \underline{22}$$ $\underline{22}$ cm around

Look Back How can you check the answer?

Glossary

draw a picture

Draw a picture to solve.

1 Brad builds a square fence around his toy dinosaur. It is 6 cm on one side. How many centimeters around is the fence?

___ + ___ + ___ + ___ = ___   ___ cm around

McGraw-Hill School Division

Practice!

Draw a picture to solve.

1 Luke draws a rectangle
around a picture.
It is 6 cm on one side.
It is 3 cm on another side.
How many centimeters around
is the rectangle?

___ + ___ + ___ + ___ = ___   ___ cm around

---

2 Tess draws a triangle
around a picture.
One side is 5 cm.
Another side is 6 cm.
How many centimeters around
is the triangle?

___ + ___ + ___ = ___   ___ cm around

---

3 Lee draws a shape
with 4 sides.
Two sides are 5 cm long.
One side is 3 cm long.
How many centimeters around
is the shape?

___ + ___ + ___ + ___ = ___   ___ cm around

 At Home   Ask your child to show you how to draw a picture to solve
a problem.

Name _____

Measure how long.

Do your best!

Use 🔲.

1 about _____ 🔲

Use a 📏.

2 about _____ inches

Use a 📏.

3 about _____ cm

Estimate how long.

4

less than 1 foot

more than 1 foot

Draw a picture to solve.

5 Emily builds a square fence.
It is 3 cm on one side.
How many centimeters
around is the fence?

_____ + _____ + _____ + _____ = _____   _____ cm around

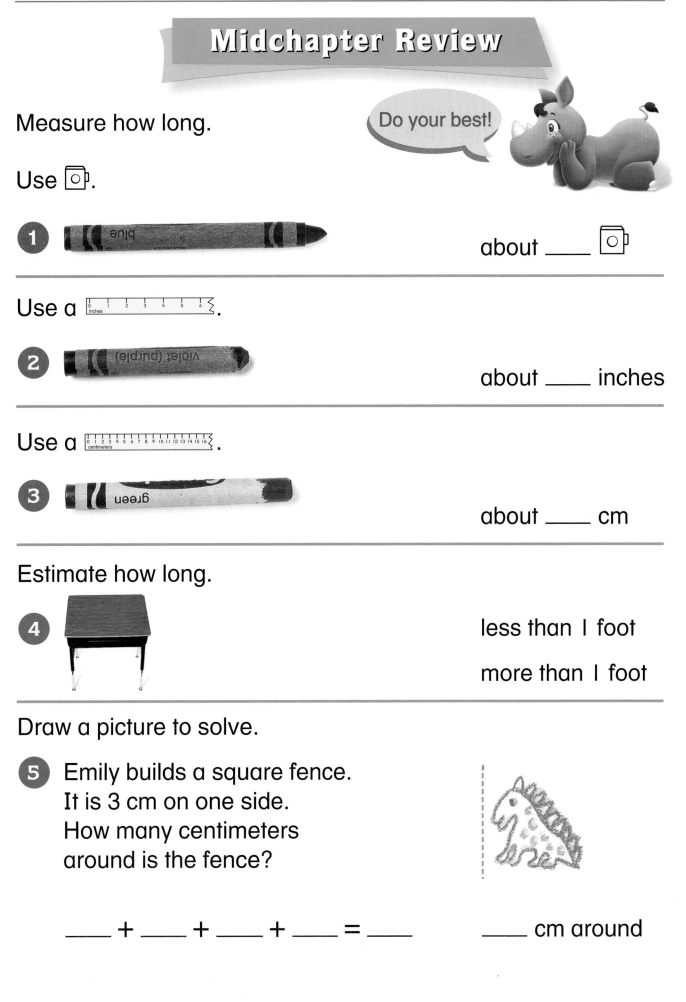

Draw Straws

You and your partner need straws,
a , and a box.

Take turns.

▶ Put your straws in a box.

▶ Close your eyes. Take 1 straw.

▶ Measure how long. Write.

▶ Compare with your partner.

▶ Color the box if your straw is longer.

Play 3 times.

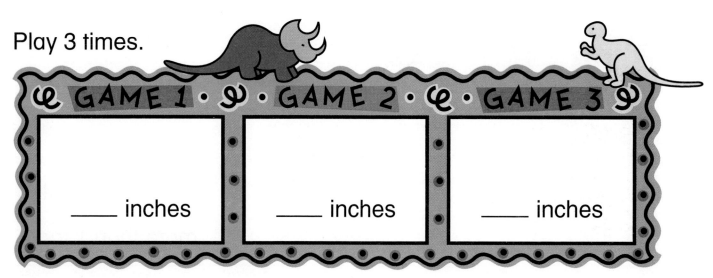

GAME 1	GAME 2	GAME 3
____ inches	____ inches	____ inches

Play again. Take 1 straw.
Color the box if your straw is shorter.

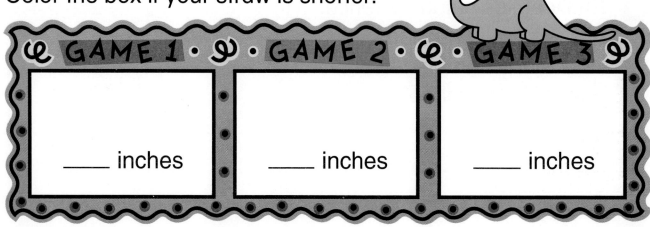

GAME 1	GAME 2	GAME 3
____ inches	____ inches	____ inches

Name

Last of the Dinosaurs

The largest living lizard is called a *komodo dragon.*

Komodo dragons are about 6 feet long and **weigh** about 60 pounds.

Glossary

weigh

Komodo dragons live on the island of Komodo and other small islands in Indonesia.

Working Together

Your group will show how long a komodo dragon is.

You need yarn.

▶ Choose a starting point.

▶ Hold the yarn at the starting point.

▶ Use a ruler to measure 6 feet.

▶ Stretch the yarn to show the length.

▶ Cut the yarn at 6 feet.

Decision Making

1 How can you find out how many children long a komodo dragon is?

 Write a report.

2 Tell how you found out how many children long a komodo dragon is.

3 Does a komodo dragon weigh more than you or less than you? Explain how you know.

More to Investigate

PREDICT A scelidosaurus was 12 feet long. About how many children long is that?

EXPLORE Try different ways to find out.

FIND Read a book about dinosaurs. How big was the biggest dinosaur?

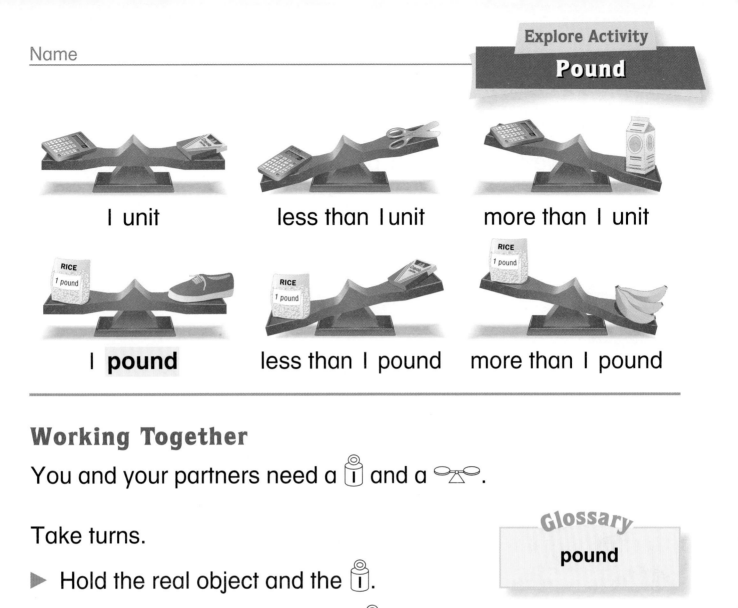

I unit   less than I unit   more than I unit

I **pound**   less than I pound   more than I pound

Working Together

You and your partners need a 🛢 and a ⚖.

Take turns.

Glossary
pound

▶ Hold the real object and the 🛢.

▶ Estimate. Choose *more than* 🛢 or *less than* 🛢.

▶ Measure and record.

		Estimate	Measure
1	stapler	less than 🛢 more than 🛢	less than 🛢 more than 🛢
2	ruler	less than 🛢 more than 🛢	less than 🛢 more than 🛢
3	Math book	less than 🛢 more than 🛢	less than 🛢 more than 🛢

Practice!

Estimate.

1 Which weigh less than 1 pound?

2 Which weigh more than 1 pound?

READING · ARITHMETIC · WRITING

Make Inferences

There are two dinosaur bones.
Each weighs about 1 pound.
What if you measured them on a balance.
Draw how the balance will look.

Tell about your drawing.

At Home Have your child hold two objects and tell which is heavier.

Name _____

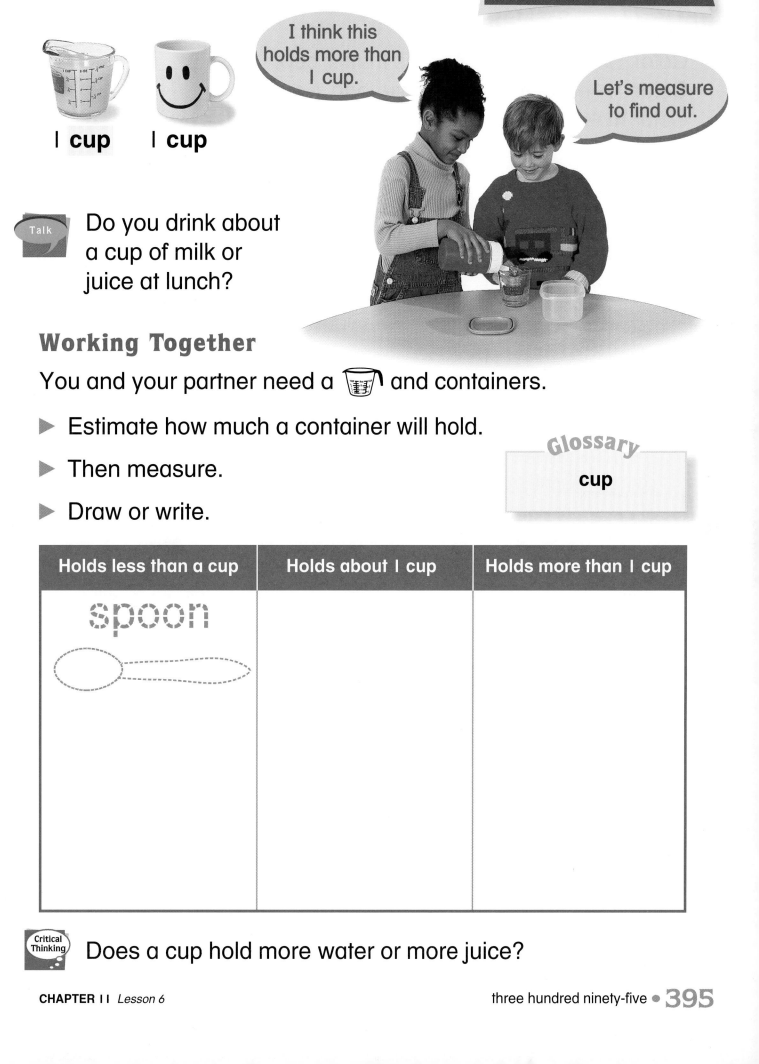

I **cup**   I **cup**

I think this holds more than I cup.

Let's measure to find out.

Talk Do you drink about a cup of milk or juice at lunch?

Working Together

You and your partner need a 🥛 and containers.

▶ Estimate how much a container will hold.

▶ Then measure.

▶ Draw or write.

Glossary

cup

Holds less than a cup	Holds about I cup	Holds more than I cup
spoon		

Critical Thinking Does a cup hold more water or more juice?

McGraw-Hill School Division

Estimate.

Color)) red)) if it holds less than 1 cup.

Color)) yellow)) if it holds more than 1 cup.

Color)) purple)) if it holds about 1 cup.

More to Explore   Measurement Sense

2 cups fill 1 pint.

Color to show the cups you can fill.

At Home Ask your child to find a container that holds about 1 cup.

Name _____

A **thermometer** measures **temperature**. Temperature is measured in **degrees**.
The sign for degrees is °.

The thermometer shows 80°F.

Glossary
thermometer
temperature
degrees

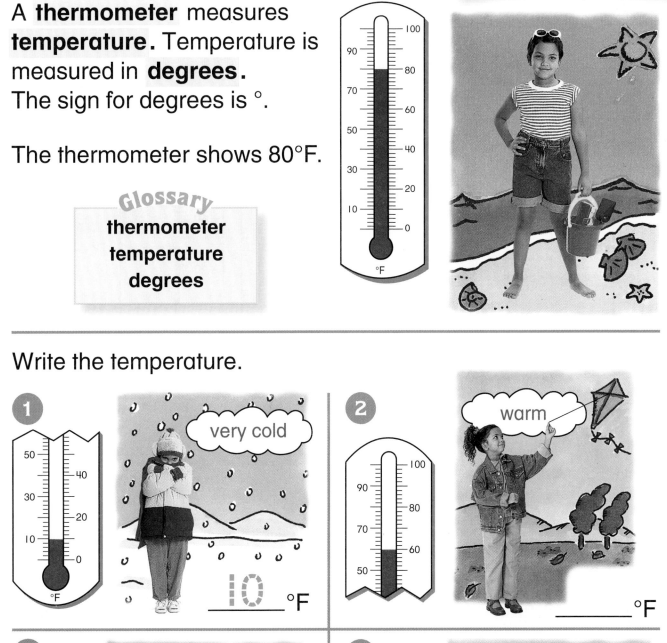

Write the temperature.

1 very cold

_10_ °F

2 warm

_____°F

3 hot

_____°F

4 cold

_____°F

Critical Thinking How can you find out what the temperature is today? Is it hot or cold?

McGraw-Hill School Division

Color the thermometer.
Show the temperature.

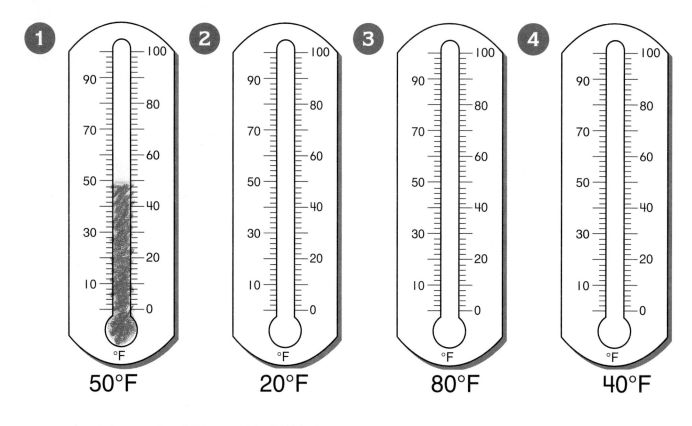

1. 50°F
2. 20°F
3. 80°F
4. 40°F

More to Explore   Measurement

Temperature can be measured another way.
Write the temperature.

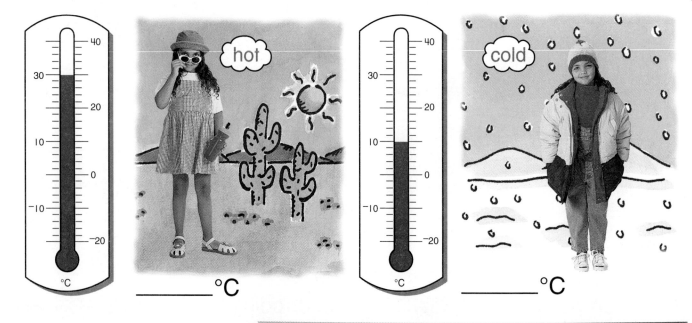

hot

_____ °C

cold

_____ °C

At Home

Ask your child to show you how to read the temperature on the thermometers above.

Choose Reasonable Answers

Read
Plan
Solve
Look Back

Yoon drinks a glass of water.
About how much does she drink?

1 cup   10 cups

Which answer makes sense?

(I cup makes sense.)   (10 cups is too much.)

Yoon drinks about 1 cup of water.

Choose the answer that makes sense.

1 Amy wants a jump rope.
About how long should the rope be?

4 pounds   (4 feet)

2 Luis weighs his backpack.
About how much does the
backpack weigh?

more than 1 pound   more than 1 foot

3 **READING ARITHMETIC WRITING** **Make Inferences** Dana makes a string
bracelet. About how long is the bracelet?

7 feet   7 inches

What clue did you use?

1 Célene measures her pencil.
About how long is her pencil?

5 centimeters   15 centimeters   5° F

---

2 Wayne eats a box of popcorn.
About how much does the
popcorn weigh?

more than 1 pound   less than 1 pound   less than 1 cup

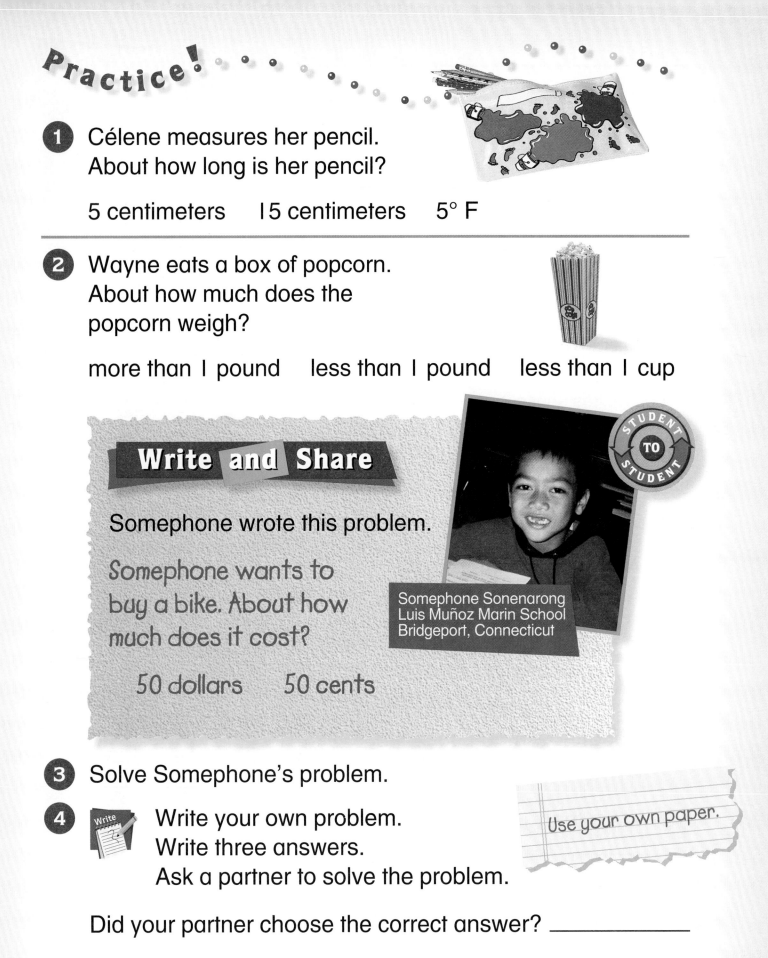

Write and Share

Somephone wrote this problem.

Somephone wants to
buy a bike. About how
much does it cost?

50 dollars   50 cents

Somephone Sonenarong
Luis Muñoz Marin School
Bridgeport, Connecticut

3 Solve Somephone's problem.

4 Write your own problem.
Write three answers.
Ask a partner to solve the problem.

Use your own paper.

Did your partner choose the correct answer? _____

Why didn't the other answers make sense? _____

_____

 At Home   Ask your child to show you how to solve problem 4 above.

Chapter Review

Language and Mathematics

Choose the correct word to complete the sentence.

1 Weight can be measured in

_____.

2 A pencil can be 8 _____ long.

measure
centimeters
pounds
thermometer

Concepts and Skills

3 Use a 🟦. Measure how long.

about ____ inches

4 Use a 🟦. Measure how long.

about ____ cm

Estimate. About how much does it weigh?

5   less than I pound   more than I pound

Estimate. About how much does it hold?

6   less than I cup   more than I cup

Write the temperature.

7 _____ °F

8 _____ °F

Problem Solving

9 Draw a picture to solve.
Use a .

Cera draws a rectangle around
her dinosaur.
It is 4 cm on one side.
It is 6 cm on another side.
How many centimeters around
is the frame?

___ + ___ + ___ + ___ = ___   ___ cm around

---

10 Choose the answer that makes sense.
Jeff measures his crayon.
About how long is his crayon?

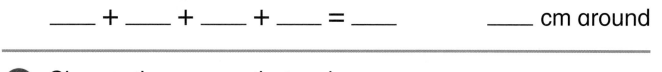

24 inches   4 inches   14° F

What Do You Think?

Which tool do you like to use to measure?
☑ Check one.

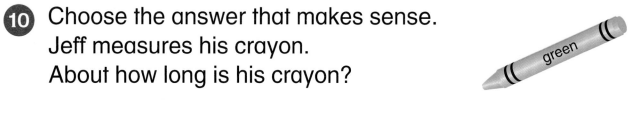

Why? _____

Journal When would you use inches to measure?
When would you use feet?

Name

Chapter Test

1 Use a 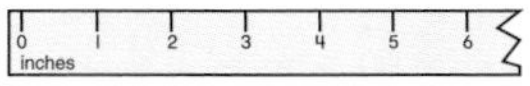

. Measure how long.

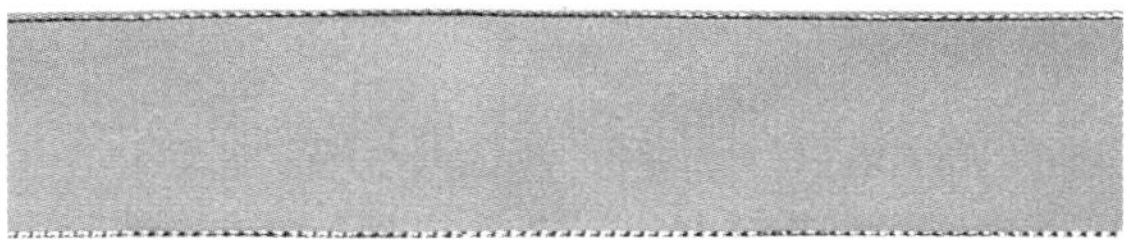

about ____ inches

Use a 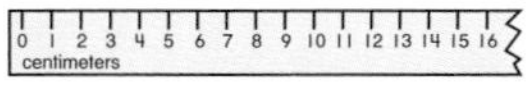

. Measure how long.

about ____ cm

Estimate. About how much does it weigh?

2 

less than 1 pound   more than 1 pound

Estimate. About how much does it hold?

3 

less than 1 cup   more than 1 cup

Write the temperature.

4 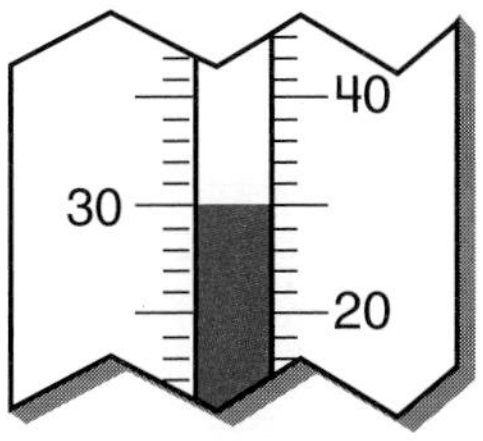

____ °F

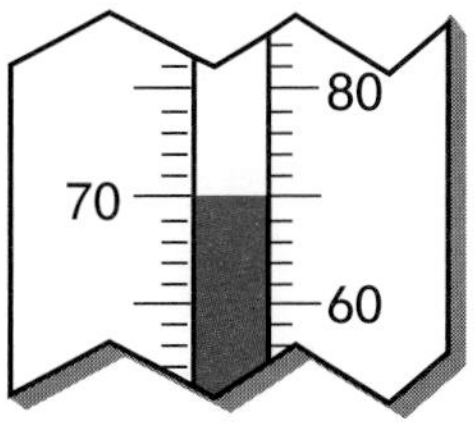

____ °F

Solve.

5 Tim draws a triangle.
One side is 4 cm.
Another side is 3 cm.
How many centimeters around
is the triangle?

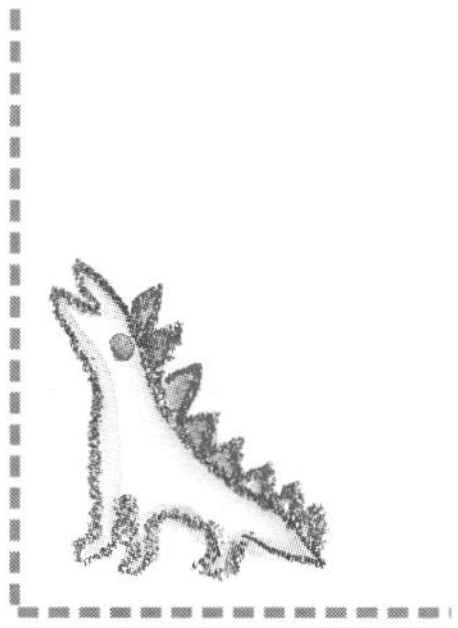

____ + ____ + ____ = ____

____ cm around

What Did You Learn?

Work with a partner.

► Choose an object to measure.

► Write about the object you chose.

We chose _____.

It is bigger than _____.

It is _____ long.

It weighs _____.

Also, _____.

Talk What did you use to measure the object? Why?
What are some other ways you could measure the object?

Portfolio You may want to put this page in your portfolio.

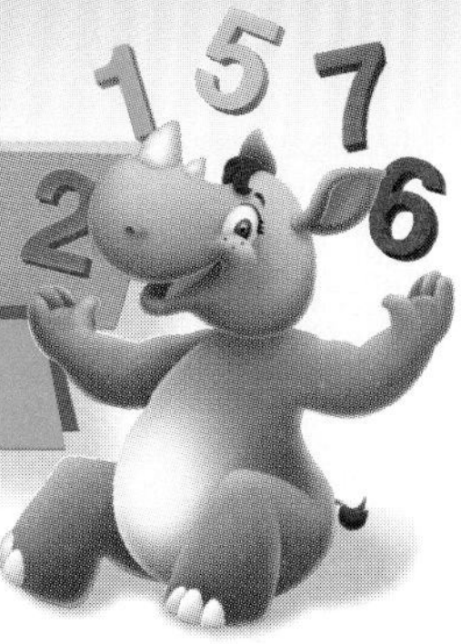

Math Connection

Algebra

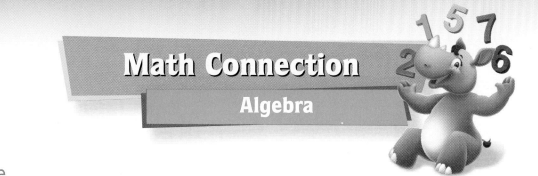

Name

Coordinate Graphs

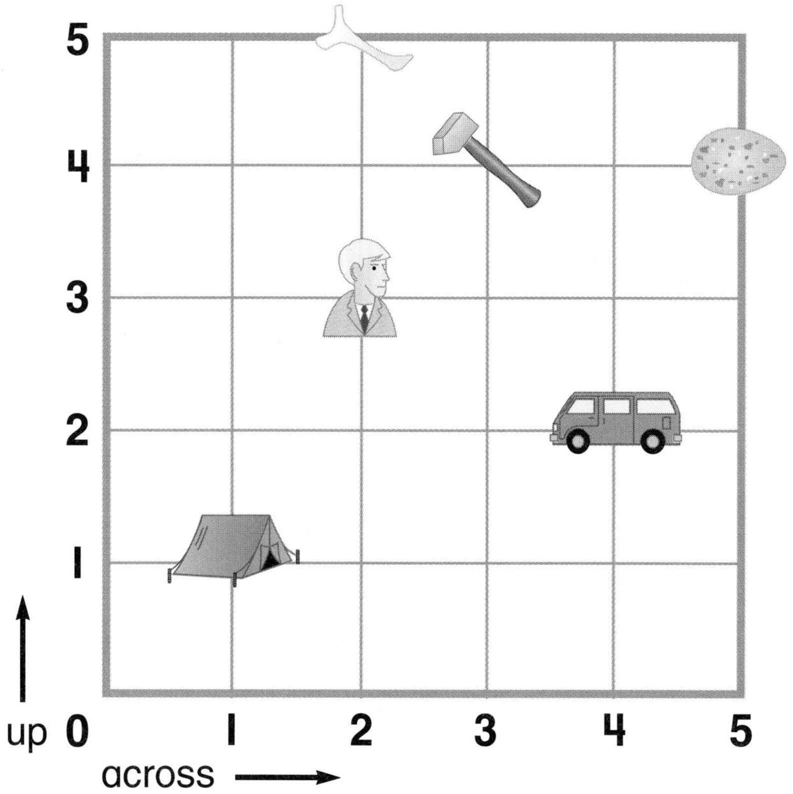

Algebra

Visit the dinosaur dig.

Start at 0.
Go across 3. Go up 4.

You found the 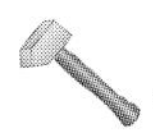.

Complete.
Show what you find.

Across	Up	
4	2	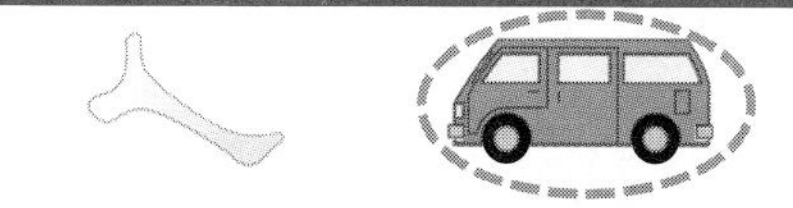
2	5	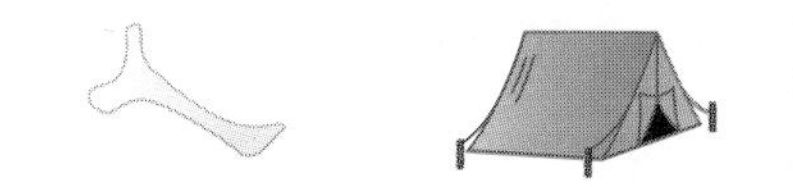
1	1	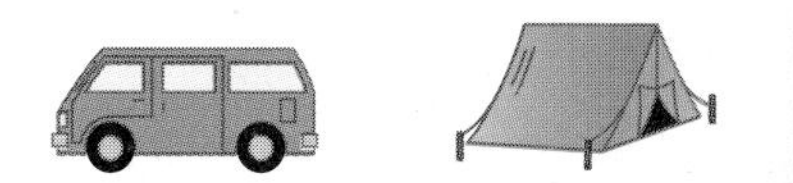
5	4	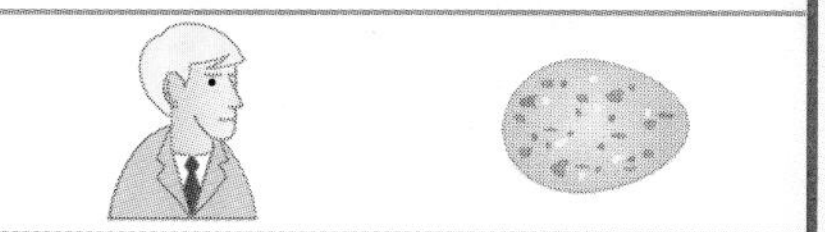
2	3	

Distance

Use a ![ruler] .
Measure each path.
Add to find how far.

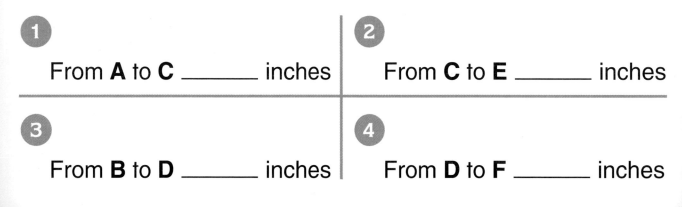

1

From **A** to **C** _____ inches

2

From **C** to **E** _____ inches

3

From **B** to **D** _____ inches

4

From **D** to **F** _____ inches

Name _____

How Many Cups?

MATERIALS   I cup measure, a variety of containers, index cards, pencil

DIRECTIONS   Put containers of different sizes on the table. Estimate how many cups each container will hold. Write your estimate on a card.

Then measure and record the number of cups each container holds.

How close are your estimates?

This activity will help your child develop an understanding of capacity.

At Home

Dear Family,

This is the last chapter in my mathematics book. I will be learning more about mental math and how to use what I know to add and subtract greater numbers.

$$20 + 30 \qquad 36 + 20 \qquad 60 - 10 \qquad 54 - 30$$

I will also learn about music and musical shows.

Learning about Music

Let's talk about the kinds of music we like to listen to. We can make a list of different instruments we know.

My Math Words

I am going to use these math words in this chapter.

Please help me make word cards for these math words. I can use the word cards when I practice addition and subtraction.

mental math
fact
count on
data
count back
method

Your child,

_____
Signature

Exploring 2-Digit Addition and Subtraction

Theme: Music

Write a Paragraph Listen to the story *Zin! Zin! Zin! a Violin.* What instruments did the trio play? How many people are in a trio?

Make a list of other words that tell how many are in a group. Use the words to write a paragraph about the concert.

What Do You Know?

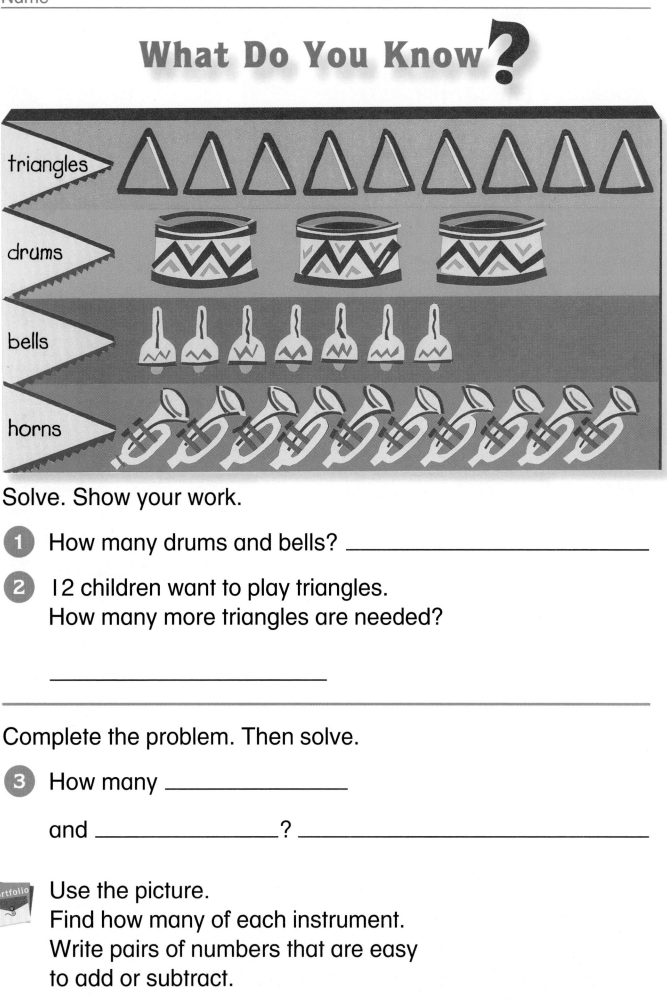

Solve. Show your work.

1. How many drums and bells? _____

2. 12 children want to play triangles.
   How many more triangles are needed?

   _____

Complete the problem. Then solve.

3. How many _____

   and _____ ? _____

Use the picture.
Find how many of each instrument.
Write pairs of numbers that are easy
to add or subtract.

Working Together

You and your partner need a ⊕.

Take turns.

▶ Spin. Write the number.

▶ Count on to add.

▶ Write the total.

You can use **mental math** to add.

Glossary

mental math

	Starting number	Count on.	Total
1	38	+ 3	41
2	26	+	
3	47	+	
4	53	+	
5	19	+	
6	35	+	
7	74	+	

Critical Thinking

Look at the starting numbers.
What is the greatest total you could get?
What is the smallest total you could get?

Use mental math.

Count on to add.

1 59 + 2 = 61

2 89 + 1 = ___

3 45 + 3 = ___

4 94 + 2 = ___

5 39 + 2 = ___

6 28 + 3 = ___

7 17 + 2 = ___

8 70 + 1 = ___

9 67 + 3 = ___

10 35 + 2 = ___

11 29 + 1 = ___

12 56 + 3 = ___

More to Explore   Algebra Sense

a Algebra

Think about how you count on.
Find the missing number.

⟨49⟩ ⟨50⟩

48 + 2 = 50   37 + ___ = 38

63 + ___ = 64   25 + ___ = 27

31 + ___ = 34   72 + ___ = 75

80 + ___ = 82   90 + ___ = 92

 At Home

We counted on to add 1, 2, and 3. Ask your child how to add 25 + 2 using mental math.

You can use addition **facts** to
help you add tens.

Glossary
fact

$$\begin{array}{r} 4 \\ +\,2 \\ \hline 6 \end{array}$$

$$\begin{array}{r} 40 \\ +\,20 \\ \hline 60 \end{array}$$

Talk How are 4 + 2 and 40 + 20 the same?
How are they different?

Add.

1

$$\begin{array}{r} 3 \\ +\,5 \\ \hline 8 \end{array}$$

$$\begin{array}{r} 30 \\ +\,50 \\ \hline 80 \end{array}$$

2

$$\begin{array}{r} 6 \\ +\,1 \\ \hline \end{array}$$

$$\begin{array}{r} 60 \\ +\,10 \\ \hline \end{array}$$

3

$$\begin{array}{r} 7 \\ +\,2 \\ \hline \end{array}$$

$$\begin{array}{r} 70 \\ +\,20 \\ \hline \end{array}$$

Critical Thinking What addition fact helps you add 20 + 30? Why?

Practice!

Add.
Use cubes if you want to.

1)

4	40		2	20		1	10
+ 4	+ 40		+ 6	+ 60		+ 5	+ 50
8	80						

2)

5	50		8	80		4	40
+ 4	+ 40		+ 1	+ 10		+ 2	+ 20

3) 17 + 1 = ___   66 + 2 = ___   71 + 3 = ___

4) 40 + 2 = ___   83 + 1 = ___   18 + 2 = ___

Mixed Review   Test Preparation

Skip-count by tens.

5) 10, 20, 30, ___, ___, ___, ___

6) 30, 40, 50, ___, ___, ___, ___

Add.

7)

4	3	6¢	7	8	3
5	4	2¢	2	4	9
+ 5	+ 8	+ 6¢	+ 4	+ 4	+ 3

At Home We used addition facts to help add tens. Ask your child how to add 50 + 30.

32 children sing in the show.
20 children dance in the show.
How many children is that in all?

You can **count on** by tens to add.

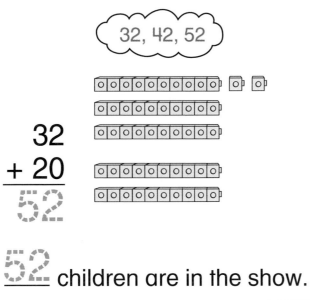

32, 42, 52

$$32 + 20 = 52$$

52 children are in the show.

Glossary

count on

Count on by tens to add.

1

$$24 + 30 = 54$$

2

$$33 + 10$$

3

$$41 + 20$$

4

$$25 + 30$$

Practice!

Use cubes or a hundred chart.
Count on by tens to add.

1
$$\begin{array}{r} 22 \\ + 30 \\ \hline 52 \end{array}$$
$$\begin{array}{r} 41 \\ + 20 \\ \hline \end{array}$$
$$\begin{array}{r} 63 \\ + 20 \\ \hline \end{array}$$
$$\begin{array}{r} 56 \\ + 30 \\ \hline \end{array}$$
$$\begin{array}{r} 72 \\ + 20 \\ \hline \end{array}$$

2
$$\begin{array}{r} 15 \\ + 30 \\ \hline \end{array}$$
$$\begin{array}{r} 45 \\ + 30 \\ \hline \end{array}$$
$$\begin{array}{r} 34 \\ + 10 \\ \hline \end{array}$$
$$\begin{array}{r} 18 \\ + 10 \\ \hline \end{array}$$
$$\begin{array}{r} 63 \\ + 20 \\ \hline \end{array}$$

Solve.

Workspace

3 15 children play triangles.
20 children play bells.
How many children
is that in all? _____ children

4 32 girls dance.
30 boys join them.
How many boys and
girls dance? _____ boys and girls

5 Write a word problem that can be
solved by counting on by tens.
Have a partner solve it.
Check your partner's answer.

Use your own paper.

At Home — We counted on by tens to add. Ask your child to add 35 + 20.

Name _____

Working Together

You and your partner need
5 , 18 ▫, and a ⊘.

Take turns.

▶ Show the number with cubes.

▶ Spin.

▶ Write the number. Show
with cubes.

▶ Combine the cubes to add.

▶ Write the total.

	Show.	Spin and show.	Total
1	26	+ ⁊	= 33
2	15	+ _____	= _____
3	37	+ _____	= _____
4	19	+ _____	= _____
5	28	+ _____	= _____
6	44	+ _____	= _____

Critical Thinking When did you make a 10-cube train?

Practice!

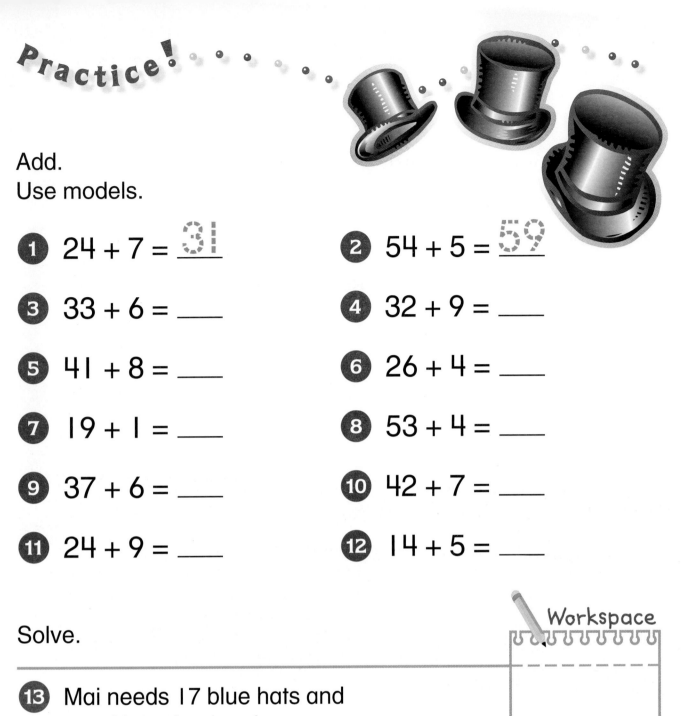

Add.
Use models.

1. 24 + 7 = 31

2. 54 + 5 = 59

3. 33 + 6 = ___

4. 32 + 9 = ___

5. 41 + 8 = ___

6. 26 + 4 = ___

7. 19 + 1 = ___

8. 53 + 4 = ___

9. 37 + 6 = ___

10. 42 + 7 = ___

11. 24 + 9 = ___

12. 14 + 5 = ___

Solve.

Workspace

13. Mai needs 17 blue hats and
5 red hats for the show.
How many hats does she need?

___ hats

14. 12 children paint posters.
8 children make signs.
How many children is that in all?

___ children

Journal Show how you add 25 + 6.
Write or draw.

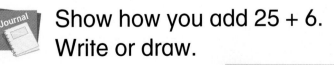

At Home — We added 2-digit and 1-digit numbers. Ask your child how to solve problems 13 and 14.

Name _____

Working Together

You and your partner need
I ⬚⬚⬚⬚⬚⬚⬚⬚⬚⬚ and 18 ▢.

Use each number once.

▶ Choose a number from ♩.

▶ Choose a number from ♩.

▶ Show them with cubes.

▶ Add. Write the addition sentence.

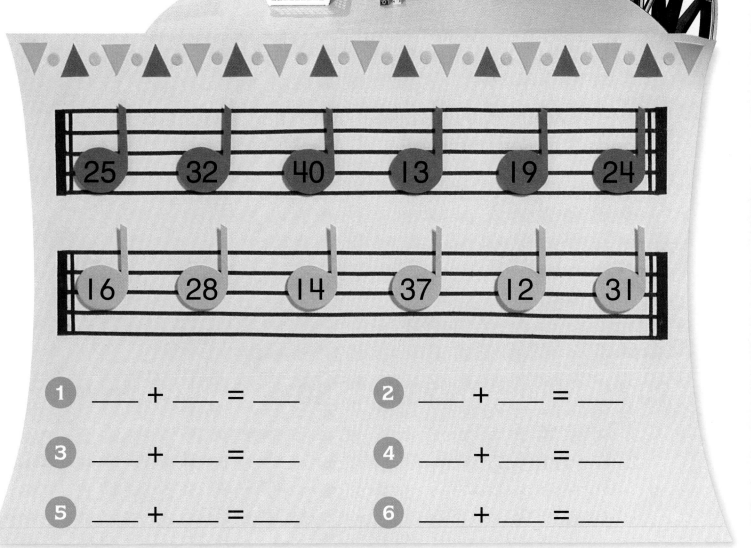

25   32   40   13   19   24

16   28   14   37   12   31

1 ___ + ___ = ___   2 ___ + ___ = ___

3 ___ + ___ = ___   4 ___ + ___ = ___

5 ___ + ___ = ___   6 ___ + ___ = ___

CHAPTER 12 *Lesson 3*

Practice!

Add. Use models to help.

1. $14 + 36 = \underline{50}$

2. $24 + 15 = \underline{39}$

3. $23 + 41 = \underline{}$

4. $17 + 12 = \underline{}$

5. $35 + 26 = \underline{}$

6. $52 + 25 = \underline{}$

7. $43 + 21 = \underline{}$

8. $29 + 11 = \underline{}$

9. $32 + 43 = \underline{}$

10. $19 + 32 = \underline{}$

11. $15 + 15 = \underline{}$

12. $28 + 14 = \underline{}$

More to Explore   Algebra Sense

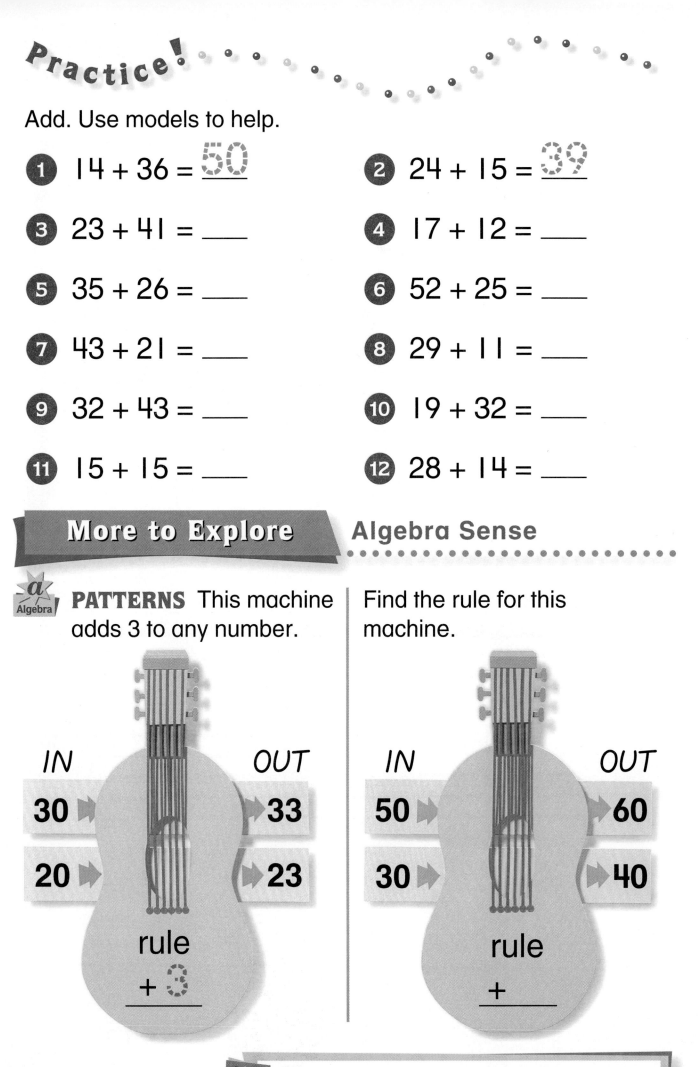

a Algebra **PATTERNS** This machine adds 3 to any number.

Find the rule for this machine.

IN	OUT
30	33
20	23

rule $+\,3$

IN	OUT
50	60
30	40

rule $+\,\underline{}$

At Home   We explored adding two 2-digit numbers. Ask your child how to solve exercise 12.

Name _____

Use Estimation

Read Kevin helps make costumes.
He spends 43¢ for glitter.
He spends 21¢ for buttons.
About how much does
he spend?

Read
Plan
Solve
Look Back

Plan You can estimate to find
about how much.

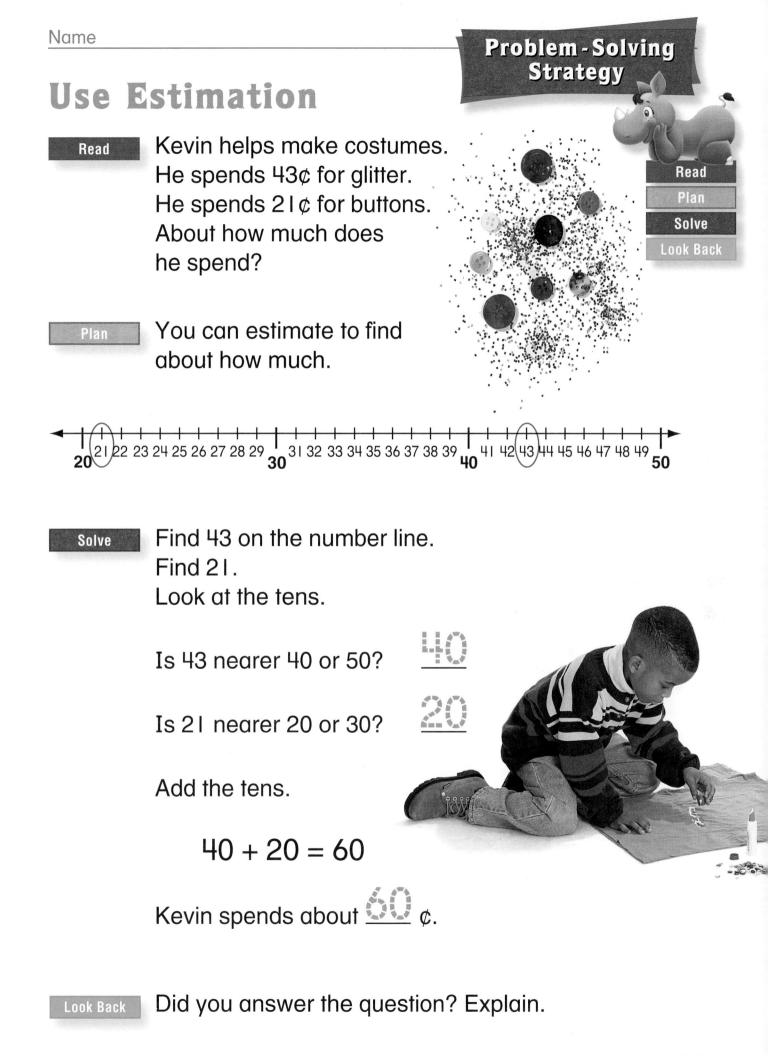

Number line: 20 21 22 23 24 25 26 27 28 29 30 31 32 33 34 35 36 37 38 39 40 41 42 43 44 45 46 47 48 49 50

Solve Find 43 on the number line.
Find 21.
Look at the tens.

Is 43 nearer 40 or 50?   40

Is 21 nearer 20 or 30?   20

Add the tens.

$$40 + 20 = 60$$

Kevin spends about 60 ¢.

Look Back Did you answer the question? Explain.

McGraw-Hill School Division

Practice!

Use the number line to find the nearest ten.

Solve. Use estimation.

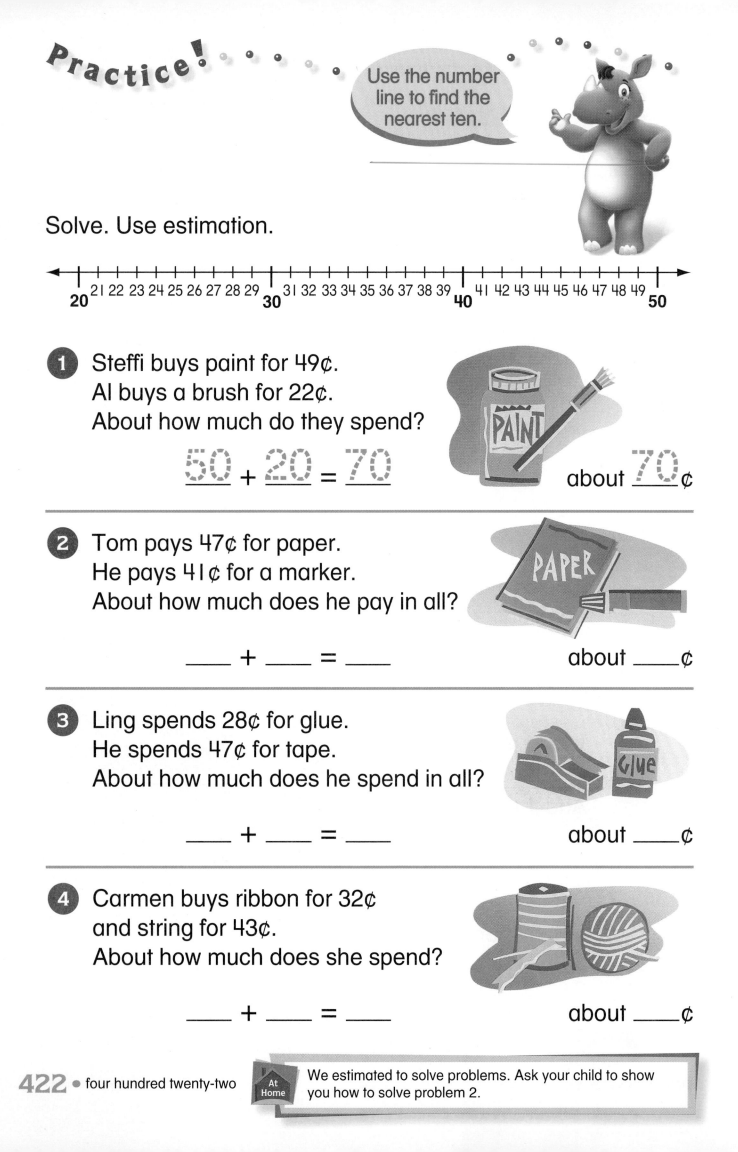

Number line: 20 21 22 23 24 25 26 27 28 29 30 31 32 33 34 35 36 37 38 39 40 41 42 43 44 45 46 47 48 49 50

1 Steffi buys paint for 49¢.
Al buys a brush for 22¢.
About how much do they spend?

$$50 + 20 = 70$$

about 70 ¢

2 Tom pays 47¢ for paper.
He pays 41¢ for a marker.
About how much does he pay in all?

____ + ____ = ____

about ____¢

3 Ling spends 28¢ for glue.
He spends 47¢ for tape.
About how much does he spend in all?

____ + ____ = ____

about ____¢

4 Carmen buys ribbon for 32¢
and string for 43¢.
About how much does she spend?

____ + ____ = ____

about ____¢

At Home — We estimated to solve problems. Ask your child to show you how to solve problem 2.

Name _____

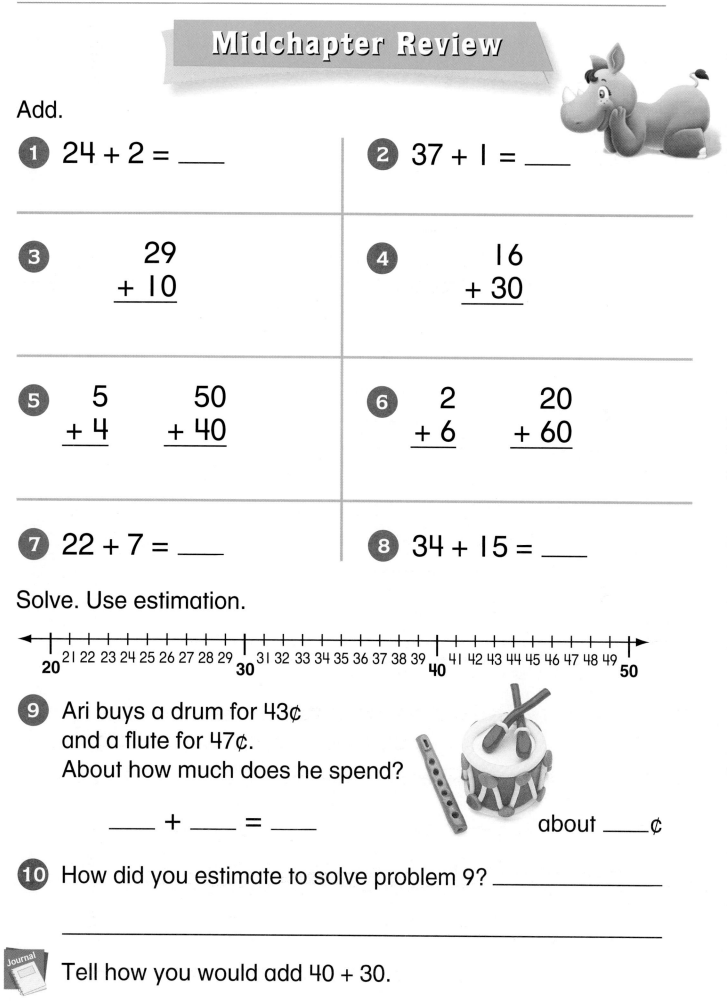

Midchapter Review

Add.

1 24 + 2 = ___

2 37 + 1 = ___

3
```
  29
+ 10
```

4
```
  16
+ 30
```

5
```
   5      50
+  4    + 40
```

6
```
   2      20
+  6    + 60
```

7 22 + 7 = ___

8 34 + 15 = ___

Solve. Use estimation.

20 21 22 23 24 25 26 27 28 29 30 31 32 33 34 35 36 37 38 39 40 41 42 43 44 45 46 47 48 49 50

9 Ari buys a drum for 43¢
and a flute for 47¢.
About how much does he spend?

___ + ___ = ___

about ___ ¢

10 How did you estimate to solve problem 9? _____

_____

Journal Tell how you would add 40 + 30.

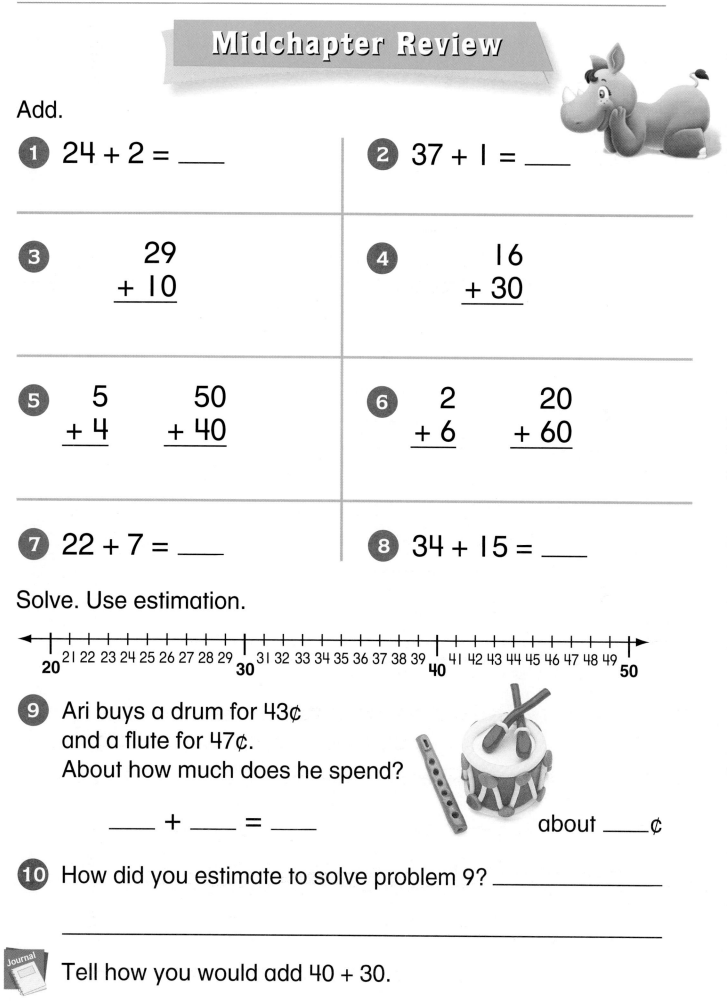

Be Seated at the Show

You and your partner
need ⊡⊡⊡⊡⊡⊡⊡⊡ and ⊡.

Take turns.

► Add. Write the sum on the seat.

► Your partner checks your answer.

► If correct, write your initials on the seat.

Play until all seats are taken.

MEOW...
NEXT SEAT!

1	2	3	4
10 + 30	12 + 8	31 + 30	20 + 10

6	7	8	9	10
40 + 11	50 + 30	76 + 2	42 + 20	54 + 9

11	12	13	14	15
18 + 30	48 + 3	30 + 20	16 + 14	25 + 15

Real-Life Investigation

Applying Addition

Name _____

Class Trip

Listen to
Zin! Zin! Zin! a Violin.

Glossary

data

Your class will go to a concert.
Two other classes will go also.

Working Together
Find out how many children
and teachers will go to
the concert. Collect **data**.

▶ Show how many children
and teachers are in your class.

▶ Show how many children and teachers
are in each of the other two classes.

CLASS TRIP	
My class	_____ children and teachers
_____	_____ children and teachers
_____	_____ children and teachers

▶ Find the total.   _____ children and teachers

McGraw-Hill School Division

Decision Making

1 Use your data. Decide how many buses you need to seat all the children and teachers going on the trip.

_____ buses

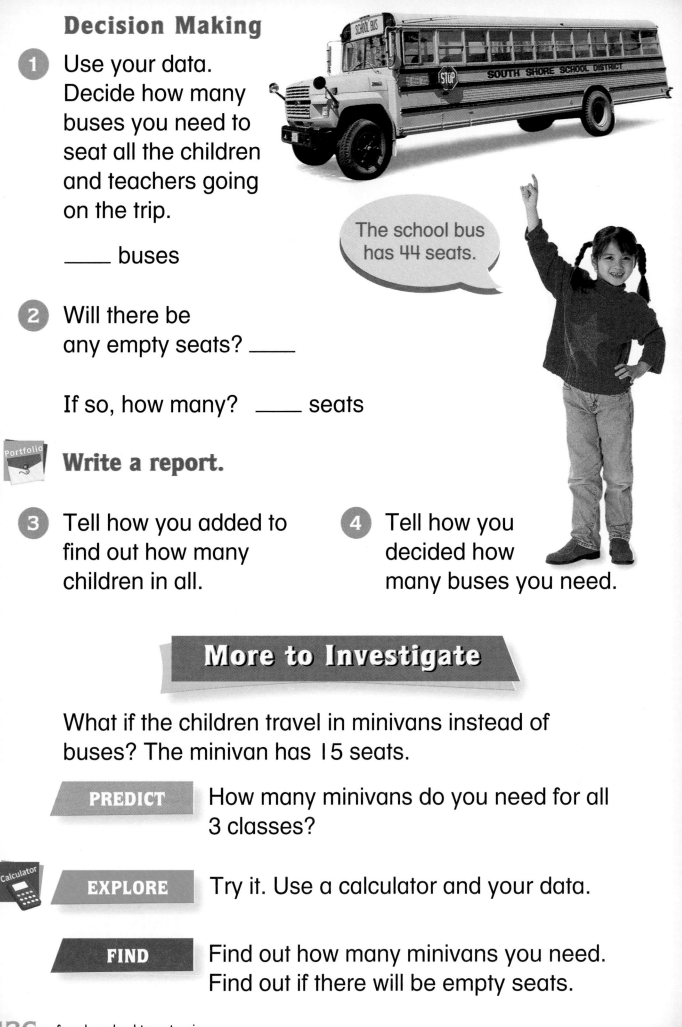

The school bus has 44 seats.

2 Will there be any empty seats? _____

If so, how many? _____ seats

Portfolio

Write a report.

3 Tell how you added to find out how many children in all.

4 Tell how you decided how many buses you need.

More to Investigate

What if the children travel in minivans instead of buses? The minivan has 15 seats.

PREDICT How many minivans do you need for all 3 classes?

Calculator

EXPLORE Try it. Use a calculator and your data.

FIND Find out how many minivans you need. Find out if there will be empty seats.

Working Together

You and your partner need a hundred chart.

You can use mental math to subtract.

Take turns.

► Pick a number from the chart.

► Write that number under *Starting number*.

► Count back to subtract.

► Write the difference.

	Starting number	Count back.	Difference
1	24	− 2	22
2		− 3	
3		− 1	
4		− 2	
5		− 3	
6		− 3	
7		− 1	

Critical Thinking Look at the charts.
What is the greatest difference you could get?
What is the smallest difference you could get?

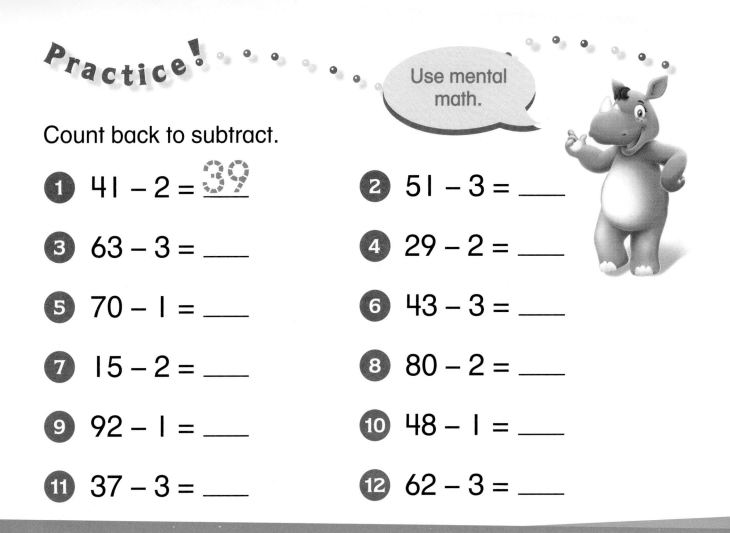

Use mental math.

Count back to subtract.

1 $41 - 2 = 39$

2 $51 - 3 =$ ___

3 $63 - 3 =$ ___

4 $29 - 2 =$ ___

5 $70 - 1 =$ ___

6 $43 - 3 =$ ___

7 $15 - 2 =$ ___

8 $80 - 2 =$ ___

9 $92 - 1 =$ ___

10 $48 - 1 =$ ___

11 $37 - 3 =$ ___

12 $62 - 3 =$ ___

READING ARITHMETIC WRITING

Write a Paragraph

Finish the report about the School Music Show. Use information from the poster.

    The School Music Show has ___ singers and ___ dancers. ___ children in all are in the show.

Write one more sentence about the School Music Show. Use numbers.

School Music Show!

Singers: 19

Dancers: 6

Place: Room 12

_____

_____

At Home

We counted back to subtract 1, 2, and 3. Ask your child how to subtract 20 – 3.

You can use subtraction facts
to help you subtract tens.

$$\begin{array}{r} 5 \\ -\,2 \\ \hline 3 \end{array}$$

$$\begin{array}{r} 50 \\ -\,20 \\ \hline 30 \end{array}$$

Talk How are 5 – 2 and 50 – 20 the same?
How are they different?

Subtract.

1
$$\begin{array}{r} 6 \\ -\,2 \\ \hline 4 \end{array}$$

$$\begin{array}{r} 60 \\ -\,20 \\ \hline 40 \end{array}$$

2
$$\begin{array}{r} 4 \\ -\,1 \\ \hline \end{array}$$

$$\begin{array}{r} 40 \\ -\,10 \\ \hline \end{array}$$

3
$$\begin{array}{r} 7 \\ -\,3 \\ \hline \end{array}$$

$$\begin{array}{r} 70 \\ -\,30 \\ \hline \end{array}$$

Critical Thinking What subtraction fact helps you subtract 60 – 30? Why?

Practice!

Subtract.
Use cubes if you want to.

1

3	30	9	90	5	50
− 1	− 10	− 4	− 40	− 3	− 30
2	20				

2

8	80	6	60	7	70
− 6	− 60	− 1	− 10	− 4	− 40

3   90 − 2 = _____   64 − 2 = _____   17 − 3 = _____

4   43 − 3 = _____   19 − 2 = _____   38 − 3 = _____

Mixed Review Test Preparation

Use a ⟨ruler⟩. Measure.

5   about _____ cm

6   about _____ cm

Ring the shape made by the solid shape.

7

☐   △   ○

Name _____

You can **count back** by tens to subtract.

42, 32, 22

$$
\begin{array}{r}
42 \\
- 20 \\
\hline
22
\end{array}
$$

Glossary

count back

Count back by tens to subtract.

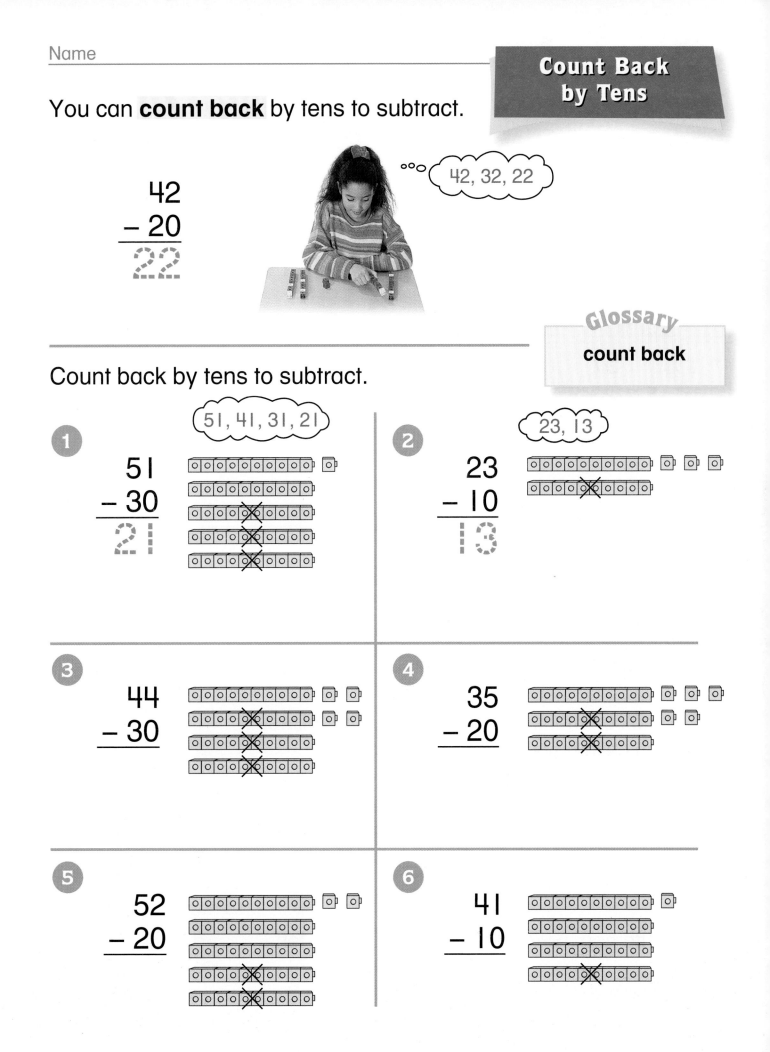

1 51, 41, 31, 21

$$
\begin{array}{r}
51 \\
- 30 \\
\hline
21
\end{array}
$$

2 23, 13

$$
\begin{array}{r}
23 \\
- 10 \\
\hline
13
\end{array}
$$

3

$$
\begin{array}{r}
44 \\
- 30 \\
\hline
\end{array}
$$

4

$$
\begin{array}{r}
35 \\
- 20 \\
\hline
\end{array}
$$

5

$$
\begin{array}{r}
52 \\
- 20 \\
\hline
\end{array}
$$

6

$$
\begin{array}{r}
41 \\
- 10 \\
\hline
\end{array}
$$

McGraw-Hill School Division

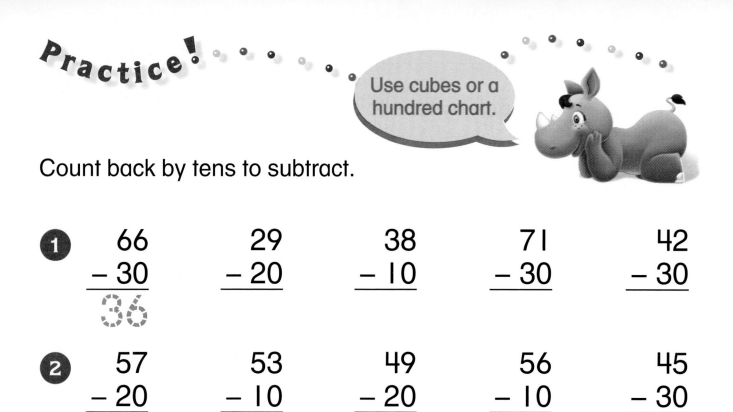

Use cubes or a hundred chart.

Count back by tens to subtract.

1
66	29	38	71	42
− 30	− 20	− 10	− 30	− 30
36				

2
57	53	49	56	45
− 20	− 10	− 20	− 10	− 30

Cultural Connection   Jamaica

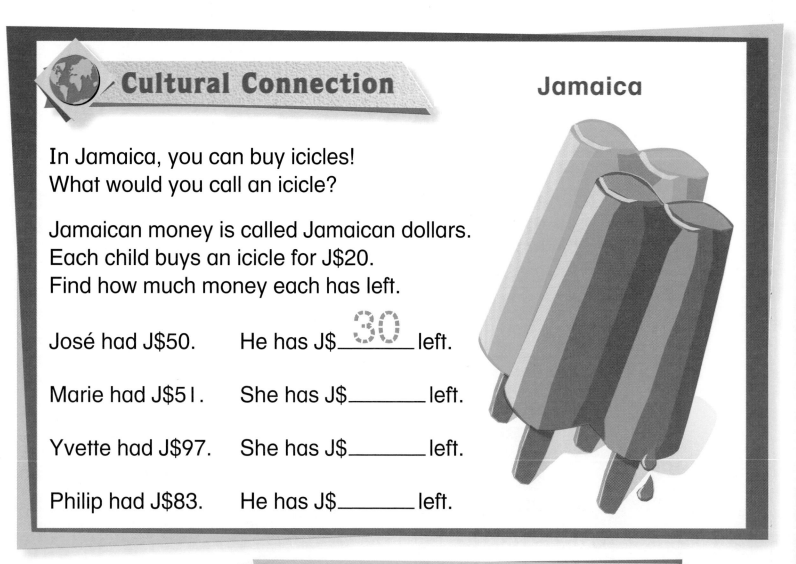

In Jamaica, you can buy icicles!
What would you call an icicle?

Jamaican money is called Jamaican dollars.
Each child buys an icicle for J$20.
Find how much money each has left.

José had J$50.   He has J$___30___ left.

Marie had J$51.   She has J$_____ left.

Yvette had J$97.   She has J$_____ left.

Philip had J$83.   He has J$_____ left.

 At Home — We counted back by tens to subtract. Ask your child to subtract 35 − 10.

Name _____

Working Together

You and your partner need

3 ▭▭▭▭▭, 9 ▱, and a ◷.

Take turns.

▶ Show the number with cubes.

▶ Spin. Write the number to subtract.

▶ Take away that number.

▶ Write the number that is left.

Show.	Spin to subtract.	Number left
1. 22 −	5 =	17
2. 28 −	_____ =	_____
3. 37 −	_____ =	_____
4. 25 −	_____ =	_____
5. 19 −	_____ =	_____
6. 36 −	_____ =	_____

Critical Thinking How did you use cubes to take away 5 from 22?

Practice!

Subtract.
Use models.

1 34 − 6 = 28

2 27 − 5 = 22

3 26 − 4 = ___

4 19 − 5 = ___

5 31 − 6 = ___

6 27 − 7 = ___

7 29 − 3 = ___

8 35 − 6 = ___

9 30 − 5 = ___

10 28 − 7 = ___

11 39 − 9 = ___

12 24 − 8 = ___

Solve.

Workspace

13 There are 21 bands on the field.
5 bands march away.
How many bands are still
on the field?   ___ bands

14 30 people watch the band.
8 of them go home.
How many people now
watch the band?   ___ people

 Journal Show how you subtract 26 − 4.
Write or draw.

Working Together

You and your partner need 4 ▭ and 9 ▢.

Take turns.

▶ Show the number with cubes.

▶ Choose a number to take away.

▶ Write the number.

▶ Subtract using the cubes.

▶ Write the number that is left.

Show.	Take away.	Number left	Choose a number.
36	– _18_	= _18_	13
29	– ____	= ____	19
34	– ____	= ____	12
45	– ____	= ____	14
26	– ____	= ____	25
47	– ____	= ____	18

Practice!

Subtract. Use models to help.

1 44 – 21 = 23

2 33 – 16 = 17

3 28 – 17 = ___

4 42 – 12 = ___

5 35 – 18 = ___

6 26 – 23 = ___

7 49 – 15 = ___

8 22 – 19 = ___

9 37 – 24 = ___

10 41 – 13 = ___

More to Explore

Number Sense

Calculator Use a calculator.
Add.

3 + 3 = ___

3 + 3 + 3 = ___

3 + 3 + 3 + 3 = ___

3 + 3 + 3 + 3 + 3 = ___

4 + 4 = ___

4 + 4 + 4 = ___

4 + 4 + 4 + 4 = ___

4 + 4 + 4 + 4 + 4 = ___

a Algebra **PATTERNS** What patterns do you see? _____

At Home Ask your child how he or she solved exercise 3.

Subtraction Race

You and your partner need a .

Take turns.

▶ Spin. Write the number.

▶ Subtract the number from 50.

▶ Spin again.

▶ Subtract from the new number.

▶ Spin and subtract until both players reach *Score.*

The player with the lowest *Score* wins.

Cultural Note
In Nigeria, people play the *kalungu*, or "talking drum." It sounds like people's voices.

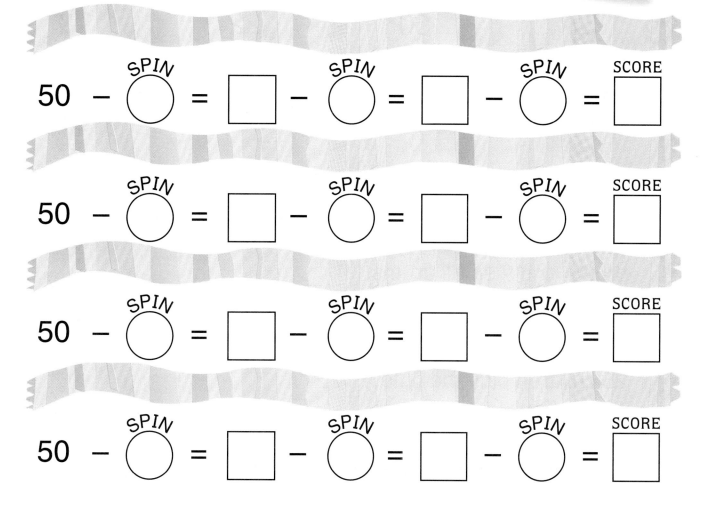

McGraw-Hill School Division

Add or subtract.
Use mental math or cubes.

1. 42 + 3 = ___

2. 43 – 2 = ___

3. 32 – 3 = ___

4. 59 + 2 = ___

5. 45 – 20 = ___

6. 13 + 8 = ___

7. 14 + 12 = ___

8. 36 – 14 = ___

9. 55 – 8 = ___

10. 20 + 60 = ___

11. 43 + 19 = ___

12. 42 – 17 = ___

13.
```
  31
+ 20
```

14.
```
  50
– 20
```

15.
```
  22
+ 30
```

16.
```
  70
– 30
```

Solve.

Workspace

17. The school has 12 large drums and 9 small drums. How many drums does the school have?   ___ drums

18. 25 children play the flute. 10 are boys, and the rest are girls. How many girls play the flute?   ___ girls

Name _____

Choose the Method

The school band had 43 triangles.
They gave 20 triangles to
another school.
How many triangles do they
have left?

Read
Plan
Solve
Look Back

triangle

drum

flute   maracas

wood block

Solve.
Choose the best **method** for you.

Mental Math

Glossary

method

1 How many triangles are left? _____ triangles

Talk   Which method did you choose?

2 27 first-grade children play drums.
14 second-grade children play drums.
How many children play drums?   _____ children

3 **Write a Paragraph** The band has
32 wood blocks and 30 flutes. How
many more wood blocks than
flutes are there?   _____ wood blocks

Write a paragraph.
Tell how you solved the problem.   Use your own paper.

McGraw-Hill School Division

Solve. Choose the best method for you.

1 What if the band had 23 triangles and got 10 more. How many triangles would they have in all? ____ triangles

2 39 third-grade children play in the band. 7 of them play the flute. How many of them do not play the flute? ____ children

Write and Share

Staci-Ann wrote this problem.

There were 19 people playing the maracas. There were 12 people playing the drums. How many more people were playing the maracas?

Staci-Ann Dias
Piney Grove School
Charlotte,
North Carolina

3 Solve Staci-Ann's problem. _____

4 Write an addition or subtraction word problem. Have a partner solve it.

Use your own paper.

  Ask your child how to solve the problem he or she wrote.

Chapter Review

Language and Mathematics

Choose the correct word to complete the sentence.

 1 When you subtract 51 − 30, you can _____ by tens.

2 You can _____ by tens to add 22 + 20.

> count on
> data
> count back
> mental math

Concepts and Skills

Add or subtract.

3 64 + 3 = ___

4 38 + 20 = ___

5
```
   3      30
 + 6    + 60
```

6
```
   4      40
 + 4    + 40
```

7 44 + 12 = ___

8 35 + 14 = ___

9 38 − 2 = ___

10 59 − 10 = ___

11 28 − 6 = ___

12 30 − 5 = ___

13 48 − 15 = ___

14 26 − 24 = ___

15
```
   8      80
 − 6    − 60
```

16
```
   5      50
 − 4    − 40
```

Problem Solving

Solve. Use estimation.

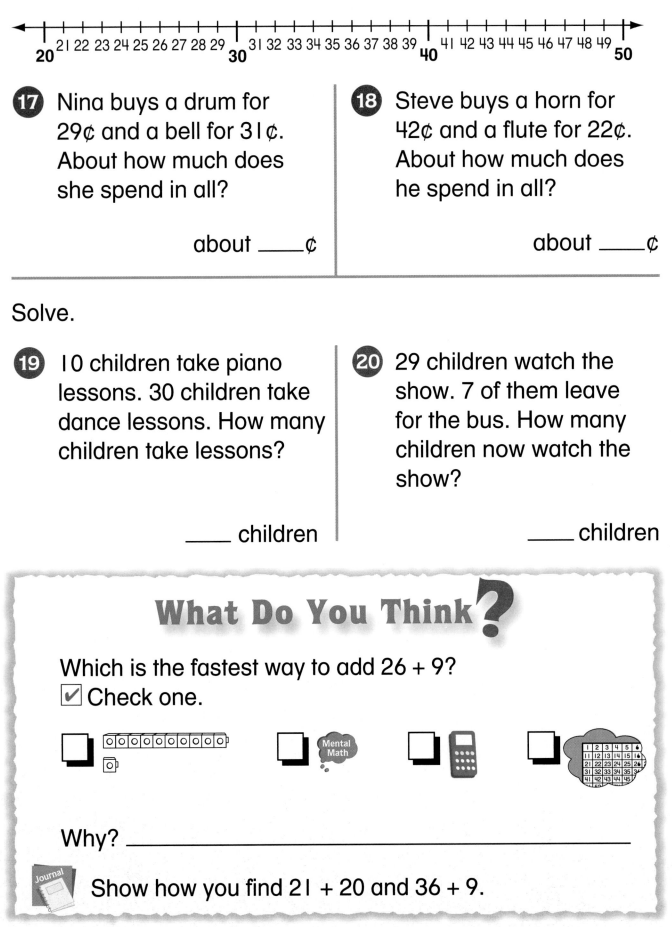

17 Nina buys a drum for 29¢ and a bell for 31¢. About how much does she spend in all?

about ____¢

18 Steve buys a horn for 42¢ and a flute for 22¢. About how much does he spend in all?

about ____¢

Solve.

19 10 children take piano lessons. 30 children take dance lessons. How many children take lessons?

____ children

20 29 children watch the show. 7 of them leave for the bus. How many children now watch the show?

____ children

What Do You Think?

Which is the fastest way to add 26 + 9?
☑ Check one.

Why? _____

Show how you find 21 + 20 and 36 + 9.

Chapter Test

Add.

1   4   40
     + 5   + 50

2   2   20
     + 6   + 60

3 75 + 2 = ___

4 18 + 30 = ___

Subtract.

5   9   90
     – 4   – 40

6   7   70
     – 3   – 30

7 83 – 2 = ___

8 32 – 10 = ___

Solve.

9 20 children take tap lessons.
     40 children take ballet lessons.
     How many children take lessons?   ___ children

Solve. Use estimation.

20 21 22 23 24 25 26 27 28 29 30 31 32 33 34 35 36 37 38 39 40 41 42 43 44 45 46 47 48 49 50

10 32 children are in the big band.
      21 children are in the jazz band.
      About how many children are in
      both bands?   about ___ children

What Did You Learn?

You and your partner need a 🎲.

Take turns.

▶ Toss the 🎲.

▶ Write the number.

▶ Add. Subtract.

65 + ___ = ___   41 + ___ = ___

30 + ___ = ___   22 + ___ = ___

Talk Tell how you added.

50 − ___ = ___   93 − ___ = ___

86 − ___ = ___   70 − ___ = ___

Talk Tell how you subtracted.

Portfolio You may want to put this page in your portfolio.

Name _____

Add and Subtract

Find 46 – 15.

> Press ⊞ to add.
> Press ⊟ to subtract.

Press [ON/AC].

Press [4] [6] [−] [1] [5] [=].

Write what the display shows. ___31___

Use the calculator to add or subtract.
Write each key you press.
Write the answer.

1 24 + 28 □ □ □ □ □ □ ___

2 52 – 19 □ □ □ □ □ □ ___

3 46 + 35 □ □ □ □ □ □ ___

4 65 – 26 □ □ □ □ □ □ ___

5 48 + 49 □ □ □ □ □ □ ___

Tens and Ones

Tapes come 10 to a box.

Mr. Neil buys 35 tapes for his class. Mrs. Lee buys 27 tapes for her class. How many tapes do they buy in all?

You can use tens and ones models to add. A computer can help you.

What numbers are on the mat?

_____

stands for 10 tapes or 1 box.

stands for 1 tape.

☐ + ☐ = ☐

At the Computer

1 Show the models. Combine them.
How many tapes do they buy in all? _____ tapes

Use models to solve.

2 Sam buys 43 tapes.
Tia buys 36 tapes.
How many tapes do they buy in all?

_____ tapes

3 Sam buys 51 tapes.
Tia buys 29 tapes.
How many tapes do they buy in all?

_____ tapes

Name _____

Cumulative Review

Mark your answer.

1 Joan has 35¢. Which item does she have enough money to buy?

Item	Price
soap	52¢
comb	34¢
brush	47¢
cup	38¢

⬭ soap
⬭ comb
⬭ brush
⬭ cup

2 Which shape shows equal parts?

⬭ △
⬭ ⊖
⬭ ▭
⬭ ⊖

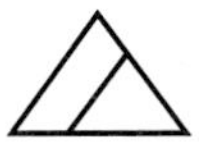

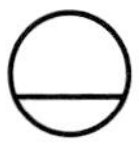

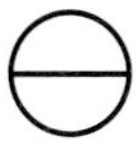

3 Which object can you use to measure temperature?

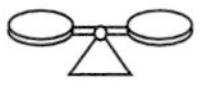

⬭ (thermometer)
⬭ (glasses)
⬭ (clock)
⬭ (ruler)

4 Which pair means the same?

⬭ 3 + 7 = 10   3 + 8 = 11
⬭ 3 + 7 = 10   7 − 3 = 4
⬭ 3 + 7 = 10   4 + 6 = 10
⬭ 3 + 7 = 10   7 + 3 = 10

5 There are 37 horns and 20 bells. How many horns and bells in all?

⬭ 17
⬭ 47
⬭ 50
⬭ 57

6 Which picture shows 6 − 2 = 4?

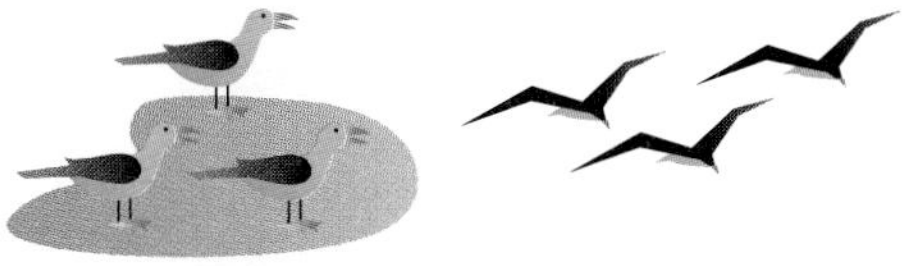

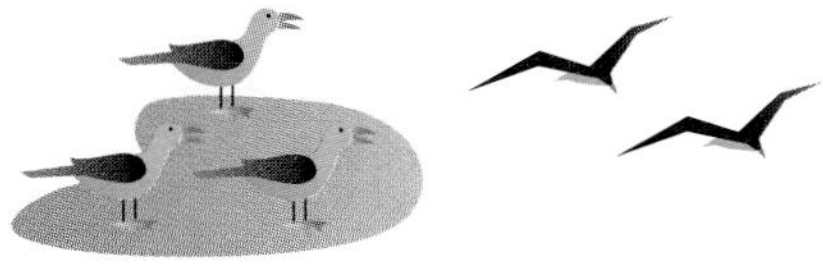

⬭ (birds picture)
⬭ (birds picture)
⬭ (birds picture)
⬭ (birds picture)

7 9 ducks are in a pond. 7 ducks fly away. Which shows how many ducks are left?

⬭ 9 − 7 = 3
⬭ 9 + 7 = 16
⬭ 9 − 2 = 7
⬭ 9 − 7 = 2

8 About how long would it take to eat?

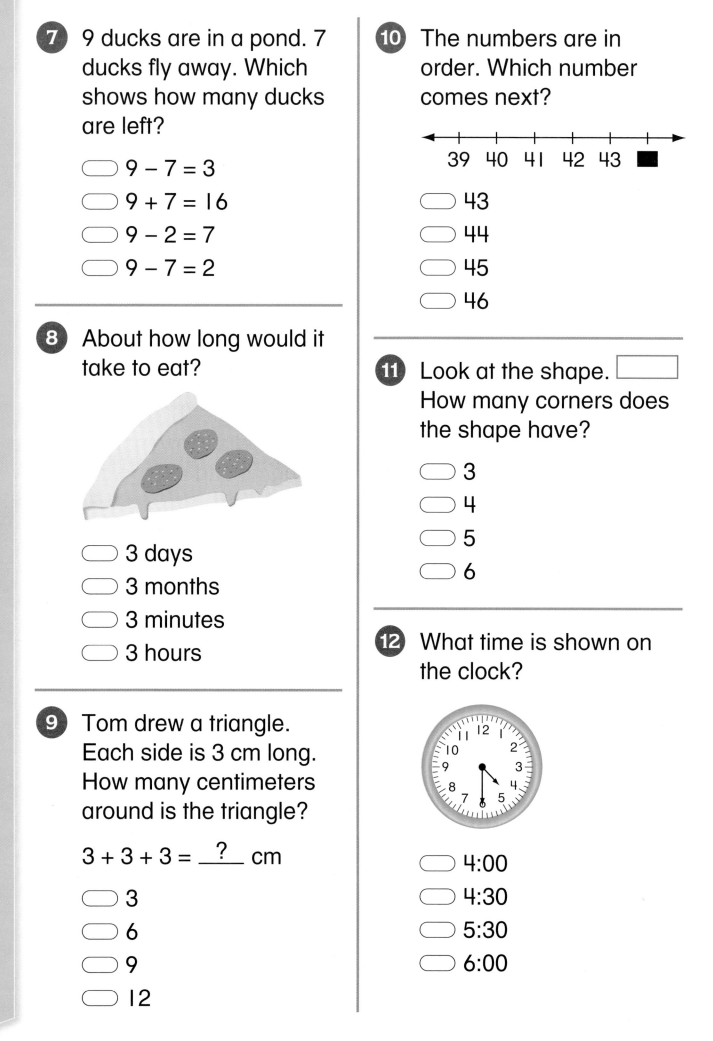

⬭ 3 days
⬭ 3 months
⬭ 3 minutes
⬭ 3 hours

9 Tom drew a triangle. Each side is 3 cm long. How many centimeters around is the triangle?

3 + 3 + 3 = ____?____ cm

⬭ 3
⬭ 6
⬭ 9
⬭ 12

10 The numbers are in order. Which number comes next?

39 40 41 42 43 ■

⬭ 43
⬭ 44
⬭ 45
⬭ 46

11 Look at the shape. ▭ How many corners does the shape have?

⬭ 3
⬭ 4
⬭ 5
⬭ 6

12 What time is shown on the clock?

⬭ 4:00
⬭ 4:30
⬭ 5:30
⬭ 6:00

Name _____

PLAYERS   2 or more

MATERIALS   index cards, pencil

DIRECTIONS   Write these numbers on separate cards. Put cards for 10, 20, and 30 in one pile. Put cards for 40, 50, and 60 in another pile.

Take turns.

► Pick a card from each pile. Add the 2 numbers.

► Score 1 point for each correct sum. Return the cards to the piles.

► Play until each player has 5 points.

Play again.

► This time subtract the lesser number from the greater number.

Make 3 cards with each number. Make 2 sets of cards if there are more than 2 players. As you play, have your child discuss what strategies he or she uses to find the answer.

Glossary

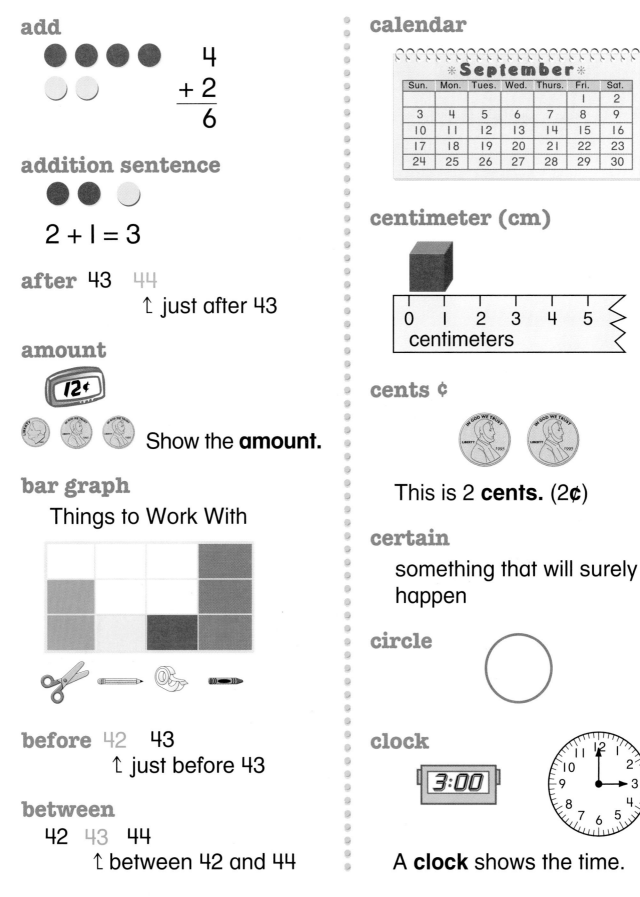

add

$$\begin{array}{r} 4 \\ + 2 \\ \hline 6 \end{array}$$

addition sentence

2 + 1 = 3

after 43 44
↑ just after 43

amount

12¢

Show the **amount.**

bar graph

Things to Work With

before 42 43
↑ just before 43

between

42 43 44
↑ between 42 and 44

calendar

* September *

Sun.	Mon.	Tues.	Wed.	Thurs.	Fri.	Sat.
					1	2
3	4	5	6	7	8	9
10	11	12	13	14	15	16
17	18	19	20	21	22	23
24	25	26	27	28	29	30

centimeter (cm)

0 1 2 3 4 5
centimeters

cents ¢

This is 2 **cents.** (2¢)

certain

something that will surely happen

circle

clock

3:00

A **clock** shows the time.

cone

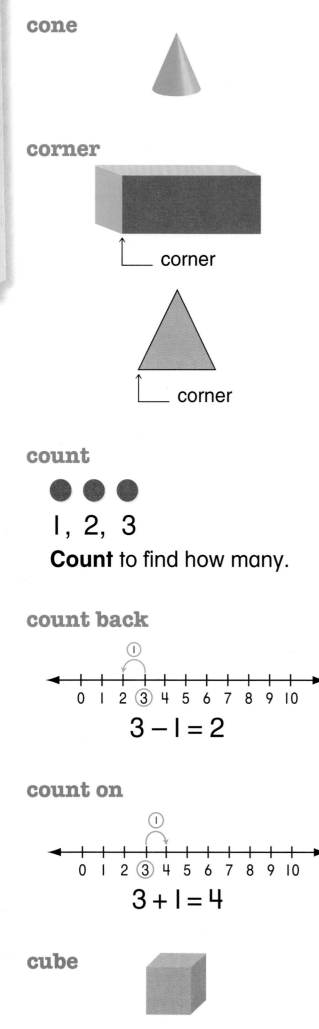

corner

corner

corner

count

1, 2, 3

Count to find how many.

count back

0 1 2 ③ 4 5 6 7 8 9 10

$$3 - 1 = 2$$

count on

0 1 2 ③ 4 5 6 7 8 9 10

$$3 + 1 = 4$$

cube

cup

cylinder

date

✹ September ✹						
Sun.	Mon.	Tues.	Wed.	Thurs.	Fri.	Sat.
					1	2
3	4	5	6	7	8	9
10	11	12	13	14	15←	16
17	18	19	20	21	22	23
24	25	26	27	28	29	30

The **date** is September 15.

day

✹ September ✹						
→Sun.	Mon.	Tues.	Wed.	Thurs.	Fri.	Sat.
					1	2
3	4	5	6	7	8	9
10	11	12	13	14	15	16
17	18	19	20	21	22	23
24	25	26	27	28	29	30

Sunday is the first **day** of the week.

degrees

60°
degrees

100
90
80
70
60
50

difference

$$7 - 6 = 1$$

difference

dime

10¢

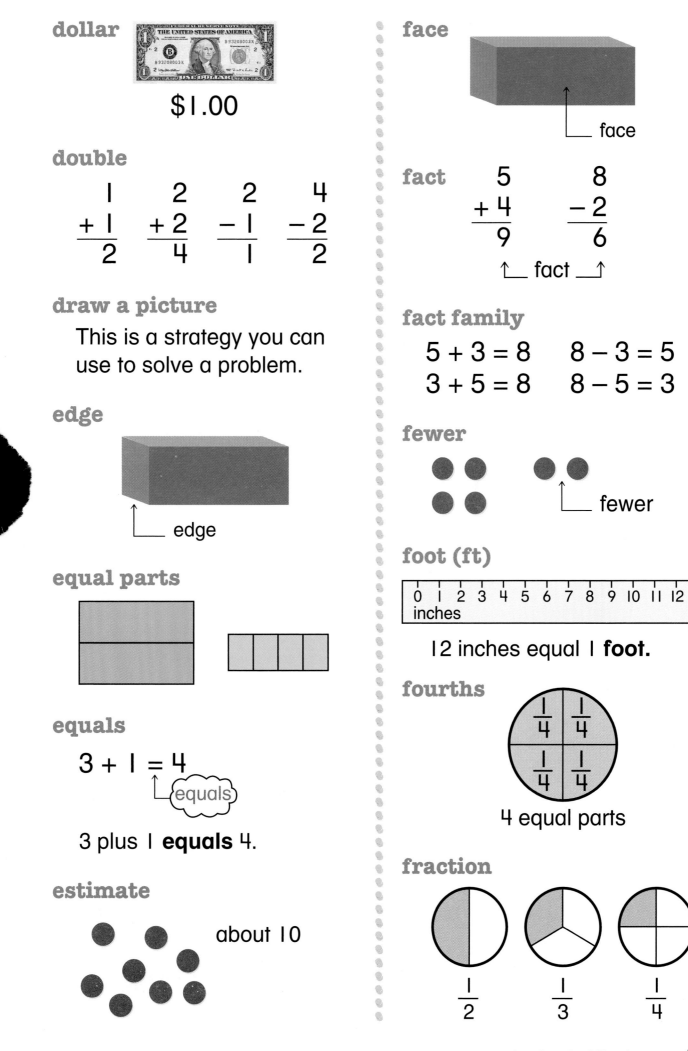

dollar

$1.00

double

$$\begin{array}{r}1\\+1\\\hline 2\end{array}\qquad\begin{array}{r}2\\+2\\\hline 4\end{array}\qquad\begin{array}{r}2\\-1\\\hline 1\end{array}\qquad\begin{array}{r}4\\-2\\\hline 2\end{array}$$

draw a picture

This is a strategy you can use to solve a problem.

edge

edge

equal parts

equals

3 + 1 = 4

equals

3 plus 1 **equals** 4.

estimate

about 10

face

face

fact

$$\begin{array}{r}5\\+4\\\hline 9\end{array}\qquad\begin{array}{r}8\\-2\\\hline 6\end{array}$$

fact

fact family

$5 + 3 = 8 \qquad 8 - 3 = 5$
$3 + 5 = 8 \qquad 8 - 5 = 3$

fewer

fewer

foot (ft)

| 0 | 1 | 2 | 3 | 4 | 5 | 6 | 7 | 8 | 9 | 10 | 11 | 12 |
inches

12 inches equal 1 **foot.**

fourths

$\frac{1}{4}$ $\frac{1}{4}$
$\frac{1}{4}$ $\frac{1}{4}$

4 equal parts

fraction

$\frac{1}{2}$ $\qquad$ $\frac{1}{3}$ $\qquad$ $\frac{1}{4}$

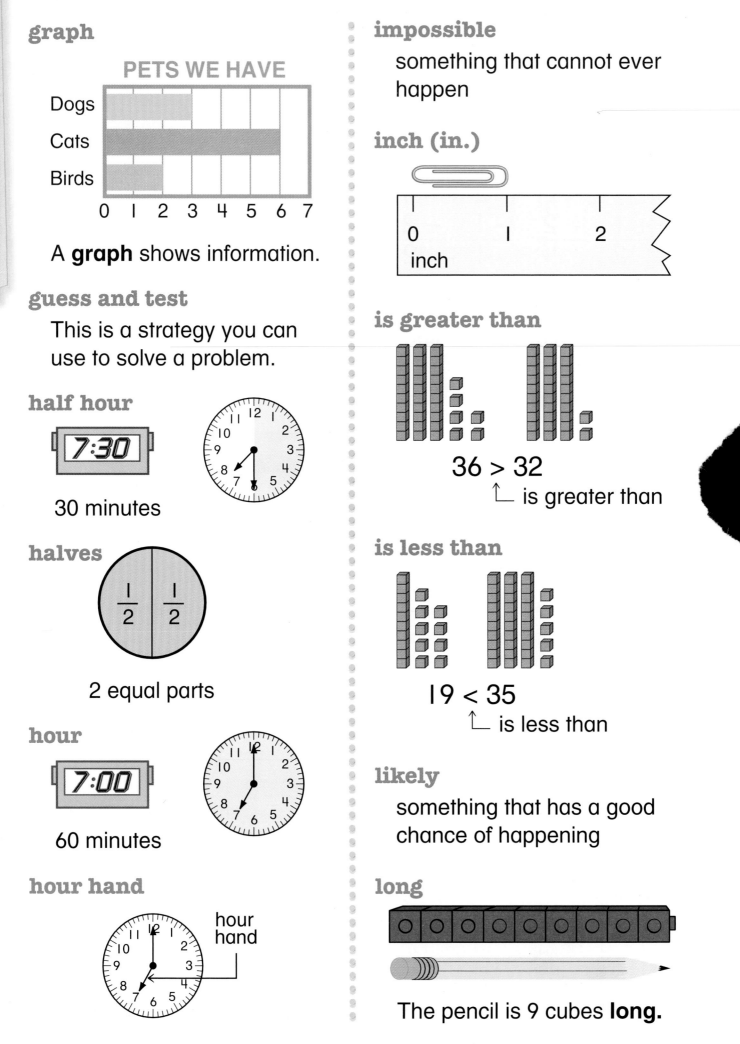

graph

PETS WE HAVE

Dogs	
Cats	
Birds	

0 1 2 3 4 5 6 7

A **graph** shows information.

guess and test

This is a strategy you can use to solve a problem.

half hour

7:30

30 minutes

halves

$\frac{1}{2}$ $\frac{1}{2}$

2 equal parts

hour

7:00

60 minutes

hour hand

hour hand

impossible

something that cannot ever happen

inch (in.)

0   1   2
inch

is greater than

36 > 32
└ is greater than

is less than

19 < 35
└ is less than

likely

something that has a good chance of happening

long

The pencil is 9 cubes **long.**

make a list

This is a strategy you can use to solve a problem.

measure

to find length, weight, or amount

mental math

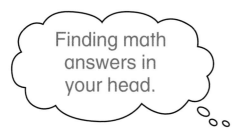

Finding math answers in your head.

method

A **method** is your way of carrying out your plan.

minus

$$4 - 1 = 3$$

minus

4 **minus** 1 equals 3.

minute

There are 60 **minutes** in one hour.

minute hand

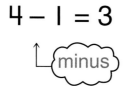

minute hand

month

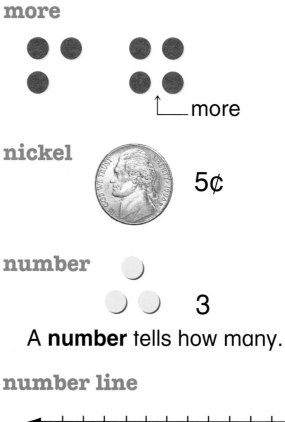

This calendar shows the **month** of September.

more

more

nickel

5¢

number

3

A **number** tells how many.

number line

0 1 2 3 4 5 6 7 8 9 10

o'clock

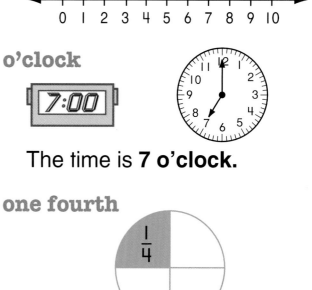

7:00

The time is **7 o'clock.**

one fourth

$\frac{1}{4}$

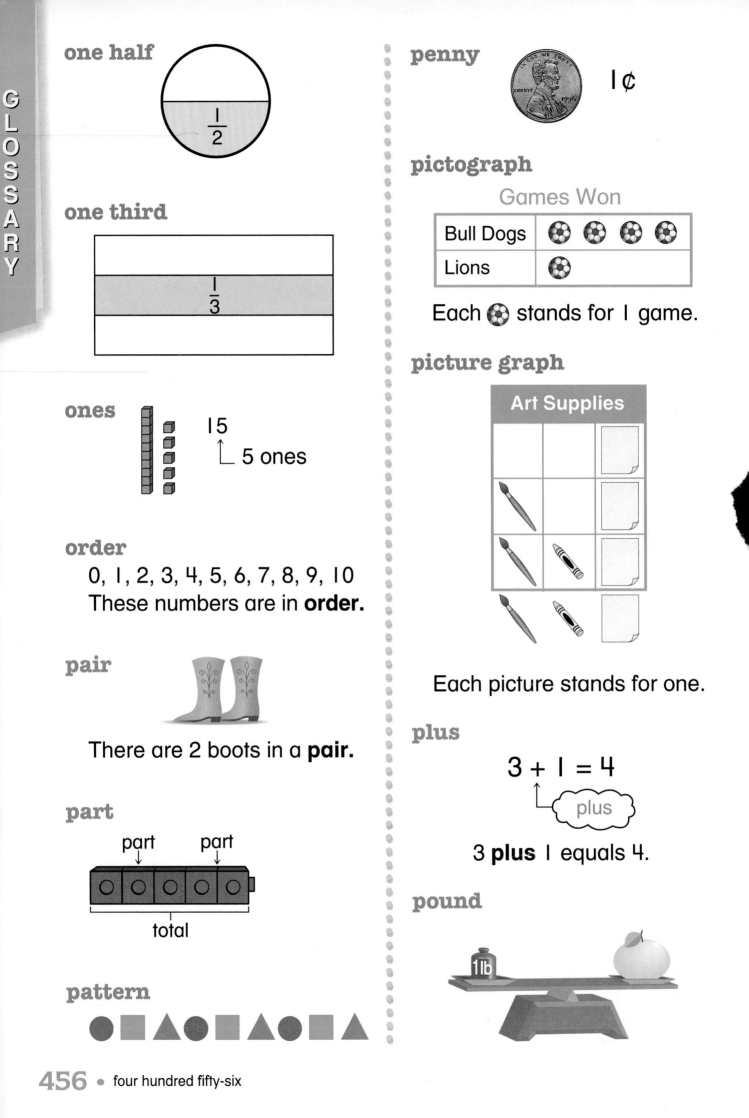

one half

$\frac{1}{2}$

one third

$\frac{1}{3}$

ones

15

↑
└ 5 ones

order

0, 1, 2, 3, 4, 5, 6, 7, 8, 9, 10
These numbers are in **order.**

pair

There are 2 boots in a **pair.**

part

part   part

total

pattern

penny

1¢

pictograph

Games Won

| Bull Dogs | ⚽ ⚽ ⚽ ⚽ |
| Lions | ⚽ |

Each ⚽ stands for 1 game.

picture graph

Art Supplies

Each picture stands for one.

plus

$3 + 1 = 4$

plus

3 **plus** 1 equals 4.

pound

1lb

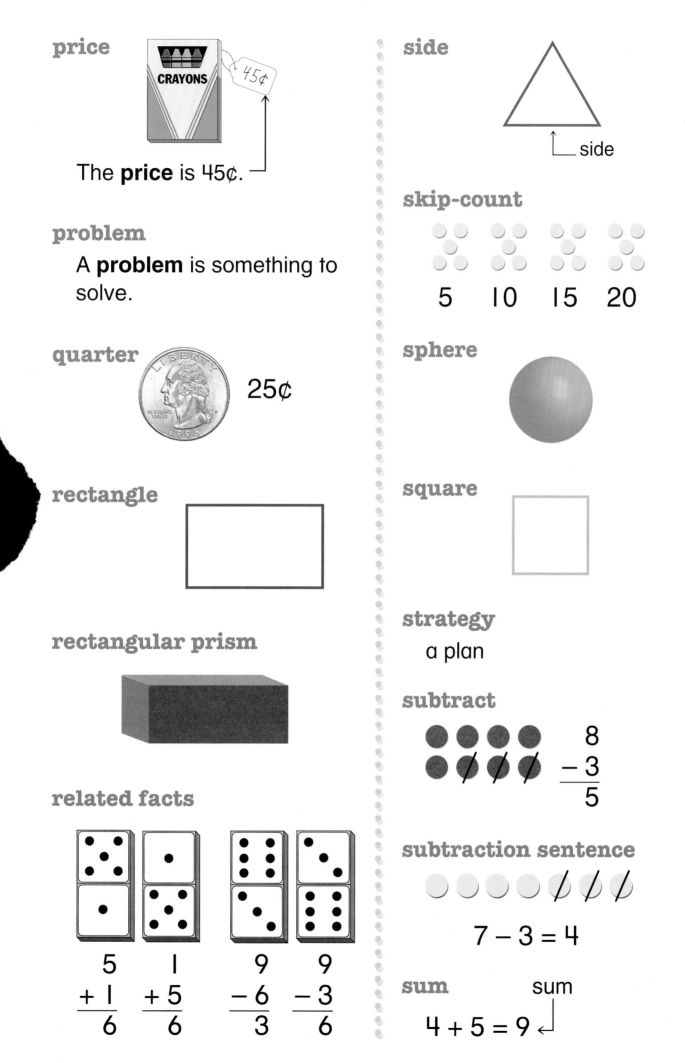

price

The **price** is 45¢.

problem

A **problem** is something to solve.

quarter

25¢

rectangle

rectangular prism

related facts

$$5 + 1 \over 6$$ $$1 + 5 \over 6$$ $$9 - 6 \over 3$$ $$9 - 3 \over 6$$

side

side

skip-count

5   10   15   20

sphere

square

strategy

a plan

subtract

$$8 - 3 \over 5$$

subtraction sentence

$7 - 3 = 4$

sum

sum

$4 + 5 = 9$

PICTURE GLOSSARY

table

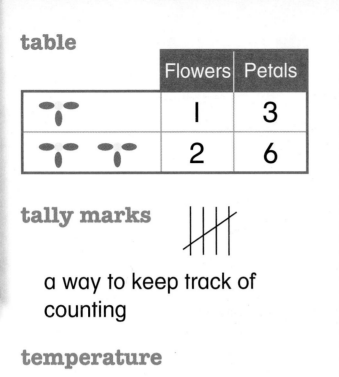

	Flowers	Petals
	1	3
	2	6

tally marks

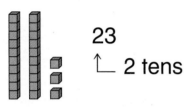

a way to keep track of counting

temperature

how hot or cold something is

tens

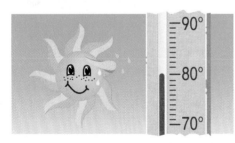

23
⌐ 2 tens

thermometer

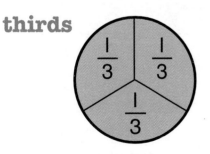

thirds

3 equal parts

today

The day that is now is **today.**

tomorrow

The day after today is **tomorrow.**

total

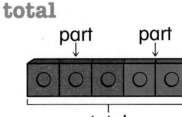

part   part

total

triangle

unlikely

something that does not have a good chance of happening

week

There are 7 days in a **week.**

weigh

You **weigh** something to find out how heavy it is.

GLOSSARY